Celebrate the SEASONS

The Best of
Holidays & Seasonal Celebrations

Issues 9-12

Teaching & Learning Company

1204 Buchanan St., P.O. Box 10
Carthage, IL 62321-0010

This book belongs to

_____

Edited and compiled by Donna Borst

Cover photos by Images and More Photography

Cover designed by Teresa Brierton

Illustrations by

Janet Armbrust	Becky Radtke
Cara Bradshaw	Shelly Rasche
Kevin Butterfield	David Seavey
Gary Hoover	Luda Stekol
Sherry Neidigh	Veronica Terrill
Chris Nye	Gayle Vella
James Potter	

Copyright © 1998, Teaching & Learning Company

ISBN No. 1-57310-110-9

Printing No. 987654321

Teaching & Learning Company
1204 Buchanan St., P.O. Box 10
Carthage, IL 62321-0010

The purchase of this book entitles teachers to make copies for use in their individual classrooms only. This book, or any part of it, may not be reproduced in any form for any other purposes without prior written permission from the Teaching & Learning Company. It is strictly prohibited to reproduce any part of this book for an entire school or school district, or for commercial resale.

All rights reserved. Printed in the United States of America.

At the time of publication every effort was made to insure the accuracy of the information included in this book. However, we cannot guarantee that agencies and organizations mentioned will continue to operate or to maintain these current locations.

Table of Contents

Fall 7

Fall (poem) 7	Cooking with Kids 64
Kid Space: Fall in the Great Outdoors 8	Holiday Wind Sock 66
Awesome Autumn Activities 14	Countdown to Halloween 67
Weather WISE 18	Fall Book Sensations 70
Brighten Your Autumn Classroom 21	Halloween poems 72
All Fall Down 23	A Switch for a Witch 73
Kid Space: Create with Nature 27	Holiday Sing-Alongs: Let's Go to the
Have an Earth-Friendly Fall 29	Pumpkin Patch 74
Fall into Art 31	One Halloween Night (poem and activities) ..75
"Apple"tivities 34	Bath Time for Little Ghosts 78
Welcome the School Year 37	Ready! Set! Go! Read!
September Safety 39	Celebrate National Book Week 79
Holiday Fingerplays 42	The Great Turkey Rumpus 82
Holiday Sing-Alongs: Labor Day 44	Let's Talk Turkey 83
Celebrate Grandparents' Day with	Turkey Time 88
Gifts from the Heart 45	Thanksgiving Book Nook 89
Making Memories: Activities to Celebrate 47	Holiday Sing-Alongs: Ten Little Turkeys 92
The High Holidays: Rosh Hashanah and	Turkey Puppet 93
Yom Kippur 49	Have an Earth-Friendly Thanksgiving 94
Rosh Hashanah: Jewish New Year 51	Molly's Pilgrim 96
Fire Safety at Home & School 52	Fall Newsletter (A Family Take-Home) 99
Columbus Day 56	Clip Art for Fall 102
Holiday Sing-Alongs: Columbus Sailors'	Clip Art for Back to School 104
Song 57	Clip Art for Fire Safety 105
Jewish Thanksgiving: Succoth 58	Clip Art for Halloween 106
Dictionary Day 60	

TLC10110 Copyright © Teaching & Learning Company, Carthage, IL 62321-0010

iii

Winter 107

First Ride (poem) 107	Ta Chui: The Festival of Peace and Renewal 168
Do a Polar Bear's Feet Get Frozen? (poem) 108	Winter Newsletter (A Family Take-Home) 170
Something Missing (poem) 109	Brand New and Still You: A New Year's Story .173
Flakey, the Freezin', Sneezin' Snowman (poem) 110	National Pizza Week Celebrations in January 177
Warm Up for Winter 112	Hat Day 181
Kid Space: Learning Adventures 114	Gung Hay Fat Choy! 183
A Feast for Feathered Friends 117	Let's Talk Teeth .185
Weather WISE 118	Black History Month 188
Touch and Texture Make Your Winter Curriculum Terrific 126	Groundhog Day 192
Skating Through Winter 129	Valentine's Day Book Nook 194
Snowman Buttons 132	Dancing Heart .196
The Silly Snowman 133	Have a Heart on Valentine's Day 197
December–The Giving Month 134	Animal Heart Game 200
In Remembrance of St. Lucia 136	Valentine's Day .201
Safe Holidays Are Happy Holidays 138	Planning Presidents' Day 203
Have a Safe Holiday 139	An American Celebration for February . . .205
Hanukkah 140	Hebrurary Folidays 208
Dodie's Lucky Christmas Eve (poem) 143	Holiday Fingerplays & Sing-Alongs 210
Santa's Book Nook 144	Cooking with Kids 214
Beanbag Toys 146	Clip Art for Winter Holidays 216
Stocking Stuffer Math 150	Clip Art for Thanksgiving 217
Santa's Trail Mix .151	Clip Art for Christmas 218
Holiday Sing-Alongs: He'll Be Coming O're the Rooftops 152	Clip Art for Winter 220
Christmas Ornament Border 153	Bookmarks/Decorative Note/Borders/ Note Pad 222
Tomie dePaola's Christmas Books 154	Clip Art for Hanukkah 224
Christmastime in Poland 158	Clip Art for Kwanzaa 225
Kwanzaa 162	Winter Newsletter (A Family Take-Home) 226
Boxing Day 165	

iv

TLC10110 Copyright © Teaching & Learning Company, Carthage, IL 62321-0010

Spring and Summer 228

Spring Song (poem) 228	Cinco de Mayo 277
Kid Space: Spring 229	Mother's Day Tea 279
Caterpillar Fun 233	Gift Giving 280
Let the Wind Blow 234	Father's Day Book Nook 281
Cory and the Wind (story) 236	Father's Day Punch & Munch 283
Come to the Spring Carnival 238	Holiday Sing-Alongs: Flags 284
Passover 245	Summer Safety Tips 285
First of April (poem) 247	Summer Fun for Little Ones 288
April Showers 248	Holiday Fingerplays 292
Peanut Butter Lovers' Day 251	Summer "Snack"tivities 294
Dr. Seuss Day 253	A Teddy Bear's Picnic 296
Celebrate St. Patrick's Day 254	Watermelon Wishes 299
Pinch, Paula, Pinch: A Do-It-Yourself	July: A Literature Unit Based on
St. Patrick's Day Story 255	the Book July 303
Kid Space: St. Patrick's Day Green Hike .257	National Hot Dog Month 306
The Middle Eastern New Year 258	Sum Weighs Two Knot Forget
Purim 260	Watt Eye Tot U 308
It's Spring; It's Easter 262	Happy Birthday, USA 309
Decorated Eggs 263	Summer Newsletter (A Family Take-Home) ...312
Easter Eggs Are for Hunting 264	Clip Art for Spring & Summer 314
Edible Easter Baskets 266	Clip Art for St. Patrick's Day 317
Be Earth-Friendly Outdoors: Every Day	Clip Art for Earth Day 318
Can Be Earth Day 267	Clip Art for Easter 319
Weather WISE 270	End of School Year:
Holiday Sing-Alongs: Maypole 273	Bookmarks/Note Pad 320
Mother Goose Day 274	

Dear Teacher or Parent,

Here it is! We know you have been anxiously awaiting the third installment of our "Best of" Series and now you have it. Our first two compilations taken from our magazine *Holidays & Seasonal Celebrations* have been so popular we have done it again with *Celebrate the Seasons: The Best of Holidays & Seasonal Celebrations—Issues 9-12*. We're positive you will be just as pleased with this book and will use it over and over again as you plan for all those special days in the classroom. We don't just stop with the major holidays like Christmas, Valentine's Day and Thanksgiving, we spark up your days with ideas for Dr. Seuss Day, Mother Goose Day, National Hot Dog Month, Peanut Butter Lovers' Day, Pizza Week Celebrations and much, much more. With this book your students will learn more about the Presidents, dental health, safety for all seasons, and celebrations from around the world. There are so many great ideas in this one book, you'll be able to celebrate every day in the classroom!

Once again we want to thank every artist, author and teacher who have made this book possible. We are so pleased that you allow us to share your work with educators and parents from all over the world. We all want what's best for our children, and hopefully this book will in some small way make a difference.

If you would like to be a part of future issues of *Holidays & Seasonal Celebrations*, please direct your submissions or inquiries to:
    Teaching & Learning Company
    Holidays & Seasonal Celebrations
    1204 Buchanan Street, P.O. Box 10
    Carthage, IL 62321-0010

Sincerely,

Donna

Donna Borst

Fall

My favorite time of year is fall.
I like fall the best of all.
Big orange pumpkins on the ground
Feel so hard and smooth and round.
I love the smell of fresh cool air.
That means warmer clothes to wear.
Leaves to see, floating down—
Red and yellow, green and brown.
Yummy things to taste and try—
Apples, turkey, pumpkin pie.
Hear the geese honk as they go,
The swishing leaves and winds that blow.
I'm very glad when fall is here.
I wish that it would stay all year.

by Mary Ryer

Fall in the Great Outdoors

Kid Space is an ever-changing fascinating place where children can connect with the natural world around them. It is a safe place where kids can explore freely, embark on adventures, and make learning discoveries all on their own. Make the most of the smells, the colors, the textures, the sounds, the excitement, the freedom, and the peace and quiet of the Kid Space available to you.

The Great Back-to-School ABC Hunt

It's autumn and nature is brimming with harvest foods, vibrant colors, earthy scents, and creatures preparing for the winter months ahead. Enjoy the season in the great outdoors with the following activities.

You Need:
- a group of kids
- the great outdoors
- area parameters
- pencil and paper for each participant/group

What to Do:
1. Provide children (or groups) with pencil and paper.
2. Clearly identify the area in which the hunt is to take place.
3. Instruct children to hunt for and record things that they see, hear, or feel.
4. Children must record (in alphabetical order) one sight, sound, or feeling for each letter of the alphabet. You may allow children to pass one, two, or three times on their choice of letters.

by Robynne Eagan

Attention, Nature

Are you concerned about venturing outdoors with a large group of kids? There are no walls to confine the group, no seats to keep them in one place, and many sights and sounds to distract them. Sometimes the surrounding noise can make it difficult for children to hear you and you quickly lose their attention. Your concerns are valid and can be easily addressed. You won't be able to control the wind, the rain, or other elements of nature, but you should be able to control your group of students!

Venturing into the outdoors may require some flexibility, patience, and creativity, all of which are valuable qualities in themselves to model for your students. The natural environment will provide you with exciting, and often spontaneous, learning opportunities that will require particular group dynamics to make the most of.

The particular dynamics of outdoor education require that the leader be able to call on the group for their attention as required. How can you get the attention of your group with all of the natural competition? These following simple tips will help you to make the most of the exciting outdoor learning opportunities on your doorstep.

- If outdoor education is a new concept for your group, be prepared for a little excitement. In time children will come to recognize that the rules of conduct for the outdoor classroom are the same as those for your indoor classroom.

- Develop a visible symbol that can be used indoors and outdoors to attract attention and eliminate talking. A raised hand, a raised peace sign or "bunny ears," a finger to the lips, or a hand on the head can be used to stop chatter and draw the group's attention. In the outdoors this gesture should attract attention, stop chatter, and draw the group into a huddle where you can best communicate.

- Ensure that you have the attention of the entire group before you begin speaking. Students who keep the group waiting too long should be offered a warning and then a consequence for such behavior consistent with your classroom discipline techniques.

- If you find it necessary, you can bring a rope to create a listening space, or line. Students should find a place in the space created by a rope placed on the ground or a spot on an outstretched rope forming a line. Some children will find the structure of this aid helpful.

- Use a whistle to draw attention during lively, noisy activities.

- Before venturing outside, have your group devise rules and safety precautions to keep themselves safe and to protect the natural environment.

- Appreciate the energy and enthusiasm generated by your learning environment and make the most of it!

City-Wide Nature Search

Take students on a hike through an urban environment and help them discover signs of nature. This hike should encourage students to develop observation skills, to recognize the forms of life that can exist in an urban environment, and to develop an understanding of the natural environment.

What to Do

1. Pre-determine the route—marking stop points where signs of nature will be most evident.
2. Make copies of the City-Wide Nature Search sheet and a copy of the information/permission form included below for each child.
3. Provide a pencil, clipboard, and sketch paper for each child to take on the hike.
4. As you hike, encourage children to use all of their senses to search for signs of life around them.
5. Help children recognize the differences that may be observed on the various sides of a building due to wind resistance, varying temperature, and varying degrees of sunlight.
6. Assist children in recognizing signs of bird life on the ground, in the trees, and on buildings.
7. Have children sketch the forms of the trees that they see. You will be able to see the tree forms best at this time of year when they are without foliage. Talk about how the trees look when the spring weather arrives.
8. Talk about the tree's effect on the wind and the sunshine. Does the tree affect nearby homes or streets?

Dear Parents/Guardians:

Our class will be taking an Urban Nature Hike to _____

on _____ .

We will be looking for signs of nature in this area and discussing how these life forms affect and are affected by the surrounding environment. Please ensure that your child is dressed appropriately for the weather on this day.

- -

_____ has my permission to attend the

Urban Nature Hike on _____

_____

Parent's/Guardian's Signature

School Yard Learning Adventures

The Family Discovery Page

Dear Families,

There is a wonderful educational setting right on your doorstep—the great outdoors! You can take advantage of your outdoor environment by sharing these educational activities with your child in autumn.

Seed Investigation

It's that time of year! Seeds are everywhere! Encourage your child to look for them. Flower-producing plants produce seeds over the warmer months to be dropped at this time of year. Many seeds are ready to drop, sail, scatter, or be carried to the Earth where they will stay over the winter as they prepare to sprout in the spring.

Help your child to explore seeds by asking the following questions: Where are the seeds on this plant? How many seeds do you think this plant produces each season? How are the seeds of this plant scattered? Can you find a variety of seeds? How are seeds different from one another? Why do you think seeds need to be different? Compare the shapes, sizes, and types of seeds you find.

The Falling Leaves

Look around at the colorful leaves of autumn. What is happening to the trees around you? Trees that lose their leaves are called deciduous trees. When the weather turns cooler and the hours of sunlight become shorter, these trees no longer produce the chlorophyll that gives their leaves the green color. Without the chlorophyll the green of the leaves fades and the other colors that are present become visible. Talk about the many colors, textures, shapes, and smells of the leaves that you find.

- Watch leaves blowing in the autumn wind and then pretend that you are a leaf blowing in the wind.

- Give your child the important job of raking your leaves or the leaves on a friend's yard. The responsibility will be welcomed and the quantity of leaves will be better understood!

- Play in a pile of leaves just for the fun of it!

Have fun and enjoy the autumn weather.

Sincerely,

11

TLC10110 Copyright © Teaching & Learning Company, Carthage, IL 62321-0010

Seeds, Seeds, Seeds

Do your students know why there are so many seeds around at this time of year? Flowering plants generate new plants through their seeds. The seeds of these plants are usually ripe in the fall and separate from the original, or parent, plant. Plants must produce seeds in order to ensure their survival.

What Happens to the Seeds?
The first thing the ripe seed does is travel! When a seed leaves the parent plant, it may travel a few inches or many miles to a home in the earth where it will wait over the winter. Seeds travel in some interesting ways! Some seeds travel by means of tiny, fluffy parachutes, some in helicopter-like husks, some scatter through a tiny explosion, and others hitch a ride. Talk about these means of travel as you look at the seeds around you.

When we look inside a seed, what we are seeing is actually a baby plant called the plant embryo. If the embryo scatters to a spot where it will receive the right amount of warmth, moisture, and sunlight, it will grow into a new plant in the spring.

What do we use seeds for? Encourage your group to think about how they use seeds in their lives; rice, oats, wheat, mustard, nutmeg, walnuts, and coconut oil for instance.

Gathering Seeds
Plan a seed hunt. Encourage students to search for seeds of all kinds.

- Attach tape with the sticky side out as wristbands for the hike. Children can stick their smaller seeds to this wristband for discussion after the hunt.

- Talk about the various places that the seeds of a plant are found. Many seeds are found inside the fruit of a plant, some wait to attach to a carrier, and some are deep within a hard shell.

- Discuss the methods of travel used by the various seeds.

- Think about whether or not humans, birds, or animals eat a particular seed.

- Talk about the animals that depend on seeds for their survival.

- Compare seeds. Discuss the unique features that ensure the survival of the plant.

- Make graphs and charts to record information about the seeds.

- Return the seeds to their natural environment so they can grow into plants in the spring.

Seed Hunt
Purchase a sack of sunflower seeds or other large seeds for a game of seedy hide-and-seek. Hide the seeds in your designated Kid Space or other area of the school yard.

Kid Space
School Yard Learning Adventures

Allot children a particular amount of time to be birds or chipmunks hunting for seeds. Children try to find as many seeds as they can before the time runs out.

The gathered seeds can then be used for an indoor or outdoor crafty creation. Have children trace or draw Thanksgiving designs such as turkeys or cornucopias. This shape can be cut out and covered with paste. Cover the sticky surface with the collected seeds for a seasonal creation.

Prepare Seeds

An important part of gardening is thinking beyond this year's bounty to next year's harvest! For thousands of years farmers and flower growers have selected seeds from their best plants and saved them for next year's planting, allowing farmers to grow better plants and obtain healthier crops every year.

Instead of purchasing packages of seeds, why not gather and prepare your own seeds and help them to hibernate? If your Kid Space allows for a garden, go on a garden seed hunt. If not, visit student family gardens or local farms.

In the Northern Hemisphere the seeds of most plants dry out and then go through a period of freezing before they will germinate, or start to grow, in the spring. To get your seeds growing you will have to imitate all the seasons including winter.

You Need:
- seeds
- cardboard or baking sheets
- sunny days
- envelopes and writing device
- storage box
- cool, dry place

What to Do:
1. Collect seeds in August or early September from gardens or from the inside of fruits and vegetables.
2. Wash the seeds and dry them in the sun on the cardboard or baking sheets. Keep the seeds in separate drying areas.
3. Label envelopes with information about the kind of seed, where it came from, and when you packed it into the envelope. Place the dried seeds in the sealed envelopes and place the envelopes in a box in a cool, dry place to sit undisturbed until spring.
4. Plant the seeds in your garden in early spring.

Awesome Autumn Activities

Autumn offers a variety of manipulatives sure to spark interest in hands-on learning. You can help your children become more aware of the natural changes taking place all around them and use the "fruits" of these changes to develop motor, math, language, and science skills. If you live in an area where seasonal changes are not as observable, this can be a great time to learn about life-styles in different parts of the country, while making use of leaves, nuts, seeds, and so on indigenous to your area.

Autumn's Door

Open a door to colorful counting by decorating your classroom with a fall number tree. Cover your door with bulletin board paper. Have the children help you paint a tree trunk and branches on the paper. Prepare a variety of colorful leaves and write a different numeral on each leaf. Ask the children to each choose a leaf, and help them name the numerals they have chosen. Provide the children with scissors, then have them fringe their leaves, matching the number of cuts to the numerals (for example, a leaf numbered 3 would have three snips cut into it). After everyone has snipped and counted, help the children tape their leaves to the painted tree.

Woodland Sculptures

One fine fall day, take your class on a nature hike around the neighborhood or playground. Provide each child with a bag, and ask children to collect natural objects they find interesting, such as colorful leaves, unusual rocks, dried flowers, and small twigs with leaves still attached. When you return to the classroom, invite individual children to share one special find with the class. In the science center, provide play dough and encourage the children to use their natural objects and a play dough base to make individual woodland sculptures. When completed, remove the sculptures to a waxed paper-lined tray and allow them to air dry for several days, until the play dough has hardened. Collect and save any leftover leaves, flowers, and twigs for other projects.

by Marie E. Cecchini

Leaf Creature Puppets

What could be more fun than a scary creature you've invented? You can recycle the leaves from your sorting center, or have the children collect more for this project. They will need leaves, paper scraps, scissors, paper lunch bags, markers, and glue. First, let children use the paper scraps to create facial features for their creatures. Next, have them glue the face parts to the flaps of their bags. Finally, let them glue leaves all around the rest of their bags to cover their creatures' bodies. The open bags can be set over cans or bottles to allow the glue to dry.

Dancing Leaves

When autumn winds blow, the fallen leaves actually do seem to dance as they twirl and flip over grassy lawns. Invite the children to make leaf wands using paper towel tubes, ribbons, and paper leaves. First, use a hole punch to make three holes at one end of each tube. Help the children tie a length of ribbon through each hole. Prepare or have each child cut out three paper leaves. Tape or staple one paper leaf to the end of each ribbon length. When the wands are finished, allow the children to experience the movement of autumn leaves to music. Have the children perform leaf dances with their wands as you play musical selections with different tempos. Have children respond to fast, slow, loud, and soft sounds. What will happen to the leaves when there is no music?

Leaf Baskets

Ask the children to collect a few different kinds of leaves from home to bring in and share with the class. Use the children's contributions to compare leaves from different kinds of trees. Invite individual children to match leaf pairs by shape or color. Gather the leaves and a few baskets to prepare a project for sorting. First, fasten a different leaf to the side of each basket. Then encourage individual children to put leaves from the collection into the appropriate baskets. Be sure to have them match either color or shape.

Color-Magic Leaves

Making these leaves will almost seem like a magic trick. Provide the children with white paper and markers. Tell them to make use of several colors (one at a time) to scribble all over the front sides of their papers. When they have finished adding colors, have them flip their papers over and ask them to draw a large, simple leaf on this side. Supply scissors to cut out these white leaves. When they turn the white leaves over—abracadabra—they have colorful autumn leaves.

Harvest Basket Game

Fall is harvesttime in many parts of the world. Help your children harvest some fun and practice motor coordination with a colorful autumn beanbag game. Use felt and dried beans to prepare beanbags in fall colors. Let the children take turns tossing the set of beanbags, one at a time, into a "harvest" basket a short distance away. Keep track of how many bags in red, yellow, orange, and brown go into the basket. Afterward, with the children's help, tally your results on a bar graph to discover which colors were tossed into the basket the least and most often.

Pumpkin Pockets

Square pumpkins are unusual to say the least, but fun to fill none the less. Provide the children with 6" x 12" orange rectangles, 1" x 3" green rectangles, and glue. Show them how to fold their orange papers in half, matching corners, to make a 6" x 6" square. Have them re-open to the rectangle shape and glue the green rectangle stem to the top in the center of one half of the orange rectangle. When the glue is dry, let them refold their orange rectangles, and help them staple their pumpkins closed across the bottom and up one side. The top will open, forming a "Pumpkin Pocket." Have the children think about the kinds of things they may decide to keep in these pockets. Invite them to share their ideas with the class.

Maple Fizzy Punch

A natural resource we can eat is maple syrup. Your children are probably most familiar with maple syrup as a tasty treat to add to pancakes or waffles. Invite them to experience this flavor in a new way. Combine 1/4 cup of maple syrup with 1 quart of milk. Mix thoroughly or use a blender. Pour this mixture to fill several glasses halfway. Fill the rest of each glass with ginger ale; stir and drink. A cinnamon stick makes a tasty stir stick.

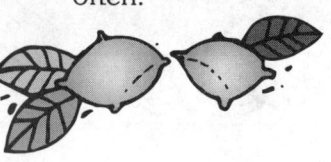

TLC10110 Copyright © Teaching & Learning Company, Carthage, IL 62321-0010

Nut Roll

Let the children experience the difference between chutes and tunnels using whole nuts for manipulatives. You will need several cardboard paper towel tubes and whole nuts. Have an adult cut a few paper towel tubes in half lengthwise, each tube forming two chutes. Leave a few tubes intact as tunnels. Invite the children to hold and tilt the chutes and tunnels (over a table or on the floor) as they place nuts, one by one, at the top and watch them roll out the opposite end. Ask children to describe the difference between a chute and a tunnel.

 ← Remember, a peanut is NOT a nut!

Missing Nuts

Make use of the whole nuts from the previous exploration to play a math game. Display several nuts on a tray. Have the children look closely at the nuts and count them. Ask the children to hide their eyes, and remove the tray. Pick up a few of the nuts. Replace the tray, have the children uncover their eyes, and ask them to figure out how many nuts are missing.

Nut Knowledge

Squirrels may be the most famous nut eaters, but people eat nuts, too. Purchase a bag of whole nuts to share with the class. Name the different nuts and talk about the characteristics of each. Sort them into matching piles. Many children can have an allergic reaction to eating nuts. Tasting is *not* recommended.

Rhyming Acorns

Encourage the children to work independently to matching rhyming sounds at this acorn activity center. Cut out several acorn shapes. Have the children help you search magazines for rhyming pictures. Glue each pair of rhyming pictures to a different acorn, one picture at the top, the other at the bottom. Label each picture. Now, use scissors to separate the top from the bottom of each acorn. Mix the pieces together and challenge the children to match the rhymes.

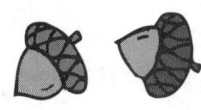

17

Weather WISE

Fall Weather Watching

Weather is a constant source of fascination for inquisitive kids. This ever-changing medium provides kids with a hands-on science lab right on the school doorstep! "Weather WISE" activities are designed to help kids learn about weather through active investigation involving that natural environment and kids' natural curiosity. Simple procedures and the use of everyday materials make the projects easy for children and educators. Encourage children to formulate questions, investigate, make discoveries, and become weather wise!

Fall Weather Walk

From blustery, leaf-tossing, cool days to the last sun-kissed remnants of summer, fall is an exciting season for exploring weather. What better way to understand fall weather than to take a walk in it? Use these questions and activities on your walk to open children's eyes to the wonders of nature and to help children understand the changes in the world around them. Encourage children to observe and discuss the weather they experience as they go.

1. What season is this? Which season comes before this season? What season comes after this one?
2. Is this a usual fall day? What other kinds of weather can we expect at this time of year?
3. How does the sky look? What do the clouds look like to you? Do you know the scientific names for any of the clouds you see? (You can introduce the cloud names or allow children to follow up by researching back in the classroom.)
4. What kinds of precipitation can we expect in the fall?
5. How does this weather affect the plants and animals? Do you notice any changes around you?
6. Estimate the temperature. You can follow up with a scientific study to find the temperature. A simple thermometer will do the trick.
7. Do you smell anything or hear any sounds that you only hear in the fall?
8. Do you feel any wind? Which direction do you think it is going? You can use a compass to help children become familiar with north, south, east, and west.
9. How does the changing weather affect humans?
10. Can you think of any people who are affected by weather changes more than others?
11. How does this weather make you feel?

by Robynne Eagan

You'll Fall for Fall

Who wouldn't fall for this wonderful season of bright colors, changing temperatures, and harvest? In the Northern Hemisphere, fall officially begins on or around September 22, when the autumn equinox begins. On this special day there are 12 hours each of daylight and darkness. As we near the date of the autumn equinox, you can help your students discover that the sun seems to wane, the temperature drops, precipitation patterns (and type!) change, and daylight hours become fewer. This decrease in daylight hours and the drop in temperature triggers many changes in plant and animal life, especially in temperate regions where the four seasons are most predominate.

Challenge Question

What would happen if . . . the weather didn't change this fall? You can follow this discussion with a reading of Chris Van Allsburg's book *The Stranger*, Houghton Mifflin Co., 1986.

Moving Air

Wind is air that is moving around the Earth. Every puff of wind that breezes by is caused by temperature differences. These differences occur in the atmosphere for various reasons. When one part of the Earth is facing the sun, the air is warmed. When that part of the Earth turns away from the sun, the air cools. The continents and the oceans heat up and cool down at different rates causing further temperature differences. This warming and cooling of the Earth's air causes the air to move and become the wind that blows. Our weather is greatly affected by this wind that blows.

You Need
- ice cubes
- bowl
- timer

What to Do
1. Fill the bowl with ice cubes. Feel the air next to the bottom of the bowl and feel the air above the bowl.
2. Let the bowl of ice sit in this location for five minutes.
3. Feel the air at the bottom and above the bowl again. Do you notice any differences?

What Happened?
You probably noticed that the air around the bottom of the bowl was cooler than the warm air above the ice. The cold air is heavier and pushed the warm air (which is lighter) to the top of the bowl. The bowl of ice caused air to move and create wind!

Windy Weather Walkabouts

Enjoy the wind and have some fun. On an especially windy day, bundle up your children for some windy weather fun.

1. Collect some maple seeds, leaves, pinwheels, mini parachutes, or kites for just such a day. Have children find their own spots and watch these items take flight in the wind.
2. Have children find their own spots to observe, listen to, and feel the wind. Come together as a group to discuss their observations about the wind.
3. Have children come up with as many adjectives as they can to describe the wind.
4. Have children pretend to be a tree, a cloud, a bird, or a leaf blowing in the wind.
5. Have children complete these sentences, "The wind whistled past like a . . ." or "If I could ride the wind . . . ."
6. Challenge children to answer the age-old query, "Can you see the wind?" Help children to understand that different people see things differently!

Make a Wind Chime

Take advantage of the windy fall weather to create a musical masterpiece!

You Need
- a few balls of yarn or lengths of ribbon
- four to eight metal objects per child
- 12" length (30 cm) of light-gauge wire per child
- one 8" (20 cm) long, 1/4" (5 mm) round dowel for each child

What to Do
1. Begin a collection of light metal objects that produce a chiming sound when they clink together. Consider large washers, pieces of copper tube, discarded keys, discarded jewelry, or hardware.
2. Have children wrap each end of the wire around the dowels to form hangers for their objects.
3. Tie a string from the center of each wire for hanging.
4. Have children tie at least four strings in a balanced fashion to each dowel.
5. Have children select and hang chiming objects from their strings. It may be necessary for children to adjust the positions and lengths of the objects to have them clang together.

An old saying tells us a dark blue sky means wind is on its way. Have your group discover whether or not this is true. What methods can they come up with to determine the validity of this saying?

Brighten Your Autumn Classroom

Techniques for Using Color to Enhance Learning

by Dr. Linda Karges-Bone

I was sweeping the steps of my front porch on a crisp November afternoon and was startled by the intense beauty of a crimson-colored leaf. Bending down to pick it up, I realized that the sense of color is the ideal pathway to autumnal curriculum and instruction in primary and elementary classrooms.

Before we look at some specific activities, let's examine the reasons for drawing on a color-rich curriculum.

Color can raise or lower blood pressure. Color can be used to manipulate behavior. Color can create moods and memories. Color can become part of the curriculum or overlay or enhance the delivery of content. During the season of autumn in particular, specific colors which have a potentially powerful impact on learning are available to use in abundance. Let's consider three autumnal colors and possible curricular roles.

This rich language fluency activity lends itself to autumn in the classroom. Create a gold-bordered bulletin board (use wrapping paper for a border), and showcase unusual color words. Divide your board into sections using broad gold ribbon, and lump the words into color families.

Red Words	Yellow Words	Brown Words
cerise	orange	tan
crimson	golden	creme
cherry	pumpkin	beige
blush	maize	copper
brick	bronze	chocolate

This can become a productive thinking activity for groups of students. They can use library resources or conduct interviews with interior designers or even a cosmetologist to discover new words for autumn colors.

Color in the autumn classroom is more than 64 crayons in a box. Bring the richness of natural color into your classroom. Set up a display board of autumn treasures. Invite the children to bring in the most colorful leaf, gourd, nut, flower, or fruit. Discuss the differences between autumn colors and summer colors—what a marvelous way to teach the skills of observation. Color marks the change of seasons in a powerful way. Teachers can use the power of autumnal colors—red, orange, and gold—to enhance curriculum in the areas of science, mathematics, language, and the arts.

In my book, *Beyond Hands-On: Techniques for Using Color, Scent, Taste, Touch and Sound to Enhance Learning,* I share background information, research, ideas, and reproducibles for bringing sensory-rich learning into the classroom. During the season of autumn, color begs to decorate your curriculum with stimulating, exciting opportunities for learning.

Orange... for science and the senses

Orange is a phenomenal autumn color. Bring this color into your classroom with a unit of study focusing on pumpkins and gourds. With young children, simply sort and examine the fruits and vegetables of the harvest. Dip the gourds in orange paint and create vegetable prints on paper or shirts.

Pumpkins, with their memorable orange hue, draw older children's attention to mathematical concepts such as shape, weight, and volume. Create a unit of study on "pumpkin math" covering key concepts such as estimation, weight, prediction, and measurement.

Excite the children's and your own spirit of scientific and mathematical curiosity by pairing the color orange with your curriculum.

Gold... a rich color for cognition

Teachers can hit the cognition jackpot using the color gold. Gold appears everywhere in autumn, from the brief early sunsets to the gilding on pinecones to the blazing leaves. I like gold for a language enhancer with the creative arts in the autumn curriculum.

Use glitter for autumn art projects. Teachers tend to hoard their glitter supplies for the holiday season, but bring the glitter out early this year to create autumn greeting cards. Let the children complete this verse inside their cards, and decorate the outside with glitter.

> Celebrate the autumn
> Colored red and gold.
> I'm celebrating autumn by
> _____
> And now my story is told.

Red... for recognition, remembering, and reviving interest

Red is a power color, no doubt about it. However, that power in the classroom must be carefully controlled. Use red as an attention-getter, as a highlighting tool. For example, select red construction paper to print out vocabulary cards. You could even make the cards leaf-shaped. Print in bold, black ink.

Also, try plain white index cards for the vocabulary or spelling words, but let the children print their own words using a red scented marker.

In a unit of study on the seasons and climate changes, use red yarn to outline lines of latitude and longitude on a map, or select red pushpins to mark the continents or regions that are under study.

Of course, units on apples are popular during autumn. However, go beyond the traditional activities this year and focus on the sense of color as you design the unit. Use it to teach skills such as observation. The scent of apple is also a valuable tool for increasing creativity and memory.

Remember, red is the color for memory. Think *red* to focus attention on specific words, dates, and places in your autumn curriculum.

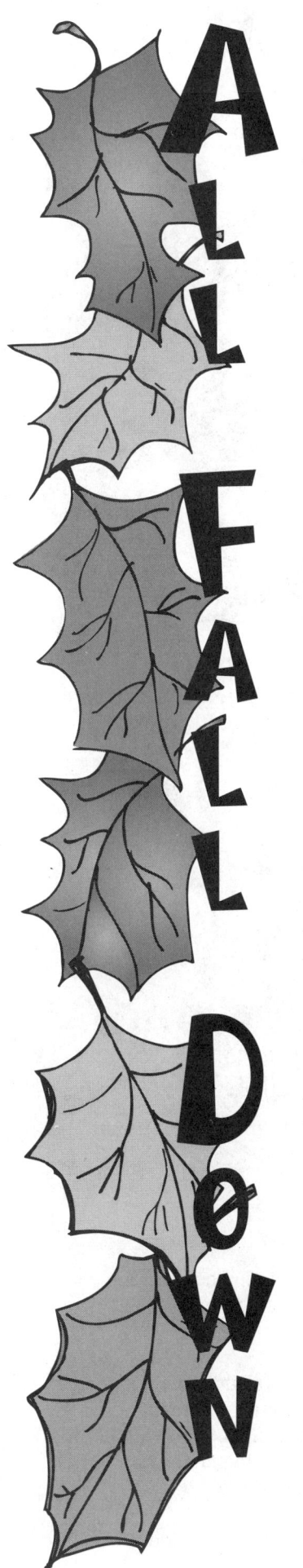

Celebrate nature's wonders with these colorful student activities. They integrate music, art, language, math, and science lessons around the theme of fall. The following activities will involve students in greeting the season by singing, moving to music, playacting, calculating, coloring pictures, and collecting leaves.

Falling for Fall

To the tune of "London Bridge Is Falling Down"

Linden leaves are falling down,
Falling down, falling down.
Linden leaves are falling down.
It is autumn.

Poplar leaves are falling down,
Falling down, falling down.
Poplar leaves are falling down.
It is autumn.

Birch and ash leaves are falling down,
Falling down, falling down.
Birch and ash leaves are falling down.
It is autumn.

Maple leaves are falling down,
Falling down, falling down.
Maple leaves are falling down.
It is autumn.

Brown oak leaves are falling down,
Falling down, falling down.
Red oak leaves are falling down.
It is autumn.

Lovely leaves are falling down,
Falling down, falling down.
Colored leaves are falling down.
It is autumn!

by Jacqueline Schiff

I've Been Raking for My Neighbors

To the tune of "I've Been Working on the Railroad"

I've been raking for my neighbors
All the livelong day.
(Pretend to rake.)
I've been raking for my neighbors
Just to sweep the leaves away.
Can't you see the fallen colors
Piled high so early in the morn?
(Raise one arm high)
Can't you hear my feet jump in them?
(Pretend to jump in leaf pile.)
This month fall was born.

Chorus:
This month fall was born.
This month fall was born.
This month fall was born
So blow your horn.
(Pretend to blow birthday horn.)
This month fall was born.
This month fall was born.
So blow your horn and rake all morn.
(Blow horn, then rake.)

Picture Autumn

Ask children to listen while you sing the song "Falling for Fall." (page 23) Tell them to wiggle their fingers in the air like falling leaves whenever they hear you sing the words *falling down*. (You may substitute a tape made by a talented vocalist friend or family member.)

Divide the class into five groups. Group one will sing the linden leaves stanza. Group two will sing the poplar leaves stanza, group three will sing the birch and ash stanza, group four will sing the maple leaves stanza, and group five will sing the oak stanza. Then the whole class will join together and sing the last stanza. When the song is over, choose children to act out the song while the whole class sings it. Two children will act together when the song calls for two kinds of leaves or two colors of leaves.

The children playing the leaves will stand tall with arms raised over their heads. They will fall slowly by lowering their arms and heads. On the last line, the actors will bend their knees and touch their toes.

Outdoor Leaf Hunt

To the tune of "We're Going on a Bear Hunt"

We're going on a leaf hunt
To find some autumn colors.
  (Walk in place.)
What a crisp, fall day!
We can't wait.

Oh look, trees!
  (Look up.)
Big autumn trees.
We can't climb up them.
We can't climb down them.
  (Climb in place.)
Oh, wait!
We've got to crouch under them!
  (Bend down.)

Oh, wow! Colors!
Under our feet.
  (Point to feet.)
We can't jump over them.
  (Jump in place.)
We can't jump under them.
  (Jump in place.)
Oh, yes!
We've got to stop and look.
  (Touch eyes.)

Wow Whee! Whee!
Wow Whee! Whee!
Wow Whee! Whee!

One long stem!
  (Raise one finger.)
One thin blade!
  (Raise one finger again.)
Lots of veins!
It's a leaf!

Quick! Pick it up!
Pick up the others!
  (Stoop down to pick.)
Hurry! Hurry! Hurry!
  (Pick them up faster.)

Back to our classroom!
  (Walk in place.)
Yippee! Yippee!
Go to our seats.
  (Sit down.)
Pull out the leaves.
  (Pretend to pull out the bag.)

We can look over them.
  (Pretend to look at leaves.)
We can't look inside them.
  (Shake head no.)
Oh, no!
We can't uncurl them!
  (Curl up fingers.)
Curl, curl,
Curl, curl.

Quick! Bring the old phone books!
Press! Press! Press!
  (Palms down in flattening motion.)
Flatten our collection.

We went on a leaf hunt
To find some autumn colors.
  (Walk in place.)
What a beautiful collection!
  (Sit down and look.)
We can't wait to name them.

Outdoor Leaf Hunt Bulletin Board

Before leaving on your outdoor leaf hunt, show children pictures of the different shapes leaves have (fan-shaped, diamond-shaped, triangle-shaped, star-shaped, and oval-shaped). Challenge children to find different-shaped leaves as well as leaves of different colors.

Back in the classroom, collect samples of different kinds of leaves. Display them on your bulletin board titled "We're Going on a Leaf Hunt." Ask questions like: What color is the maple leaf? What color is the ash leaf? Who can come up and show me the fan-shaped leaf? Children may write a short story about the leaf they found. Display on leaf-shaped paper on your bulletin board.

Autumn Math

Explain to the children that leaves fall by floating down or spinning. Tell children to listen to each leaf arithmetic problem. When you repeat it, have them draw the number of leaves in the problem. Then ask them to add or cross out the number of leaves as the problem indicates.

Read each problem. Slowly repeat each problem. Watch the children draw. Read each problem a third time and ask for the answer.

1. 5 autumn leaves fell down from a tree.
   2 blew away and then there were ___.

2. 4 maple leaves up in the air.
   6 lindens joined in.
   How many were there?

3. 4 poplar leaves were spinning from the trees.
   2 joined their spin in the autumn breeze.
   How many leaves were spinning?

4. 7 oak leaves were floating in the breeze.
   4 friends joined them and everyone was pleased.
   How many leaves were floating?

5. 6 linden leaves were spinning from the trees.
   3 ash floated in their path in the autumn breeze.
   How many leaves were there altogether?

6. 10 autumn leaves were left on the trees.
   10 fell down.
   How many were left?

7. 9 maple leaves were found on the ground.
   A boy picked up 4.
   How many were left?

8. 11 hickory leaves were raked in a pile.
   A girl bagged 9.
   How many were left?

9. 9 autumn leaves were covered in a book.
   5 fell out.
   How many were pressed?

10. The dog played with 12 sycamore leaves.
    He took 4 home.
    How many were left?

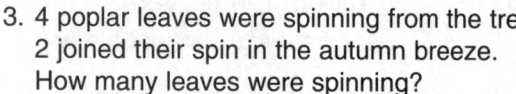

Autumn-Time Rhyme

Read the children the poem "Autumn Leaves" by Leland B. Jacobs (from the book *Just Around the Corner*). Then ask the children: What are the colors of the leaves in the poem? (green, yellow, red, brown)

- What kind of leaves are falling? (oak, maple, apple, pear)

- What are the two sizes of the leaves in the poem? (big, little) What are the shapes of the leaves? (pointed, round)

- Tell the children you will read the poem again but you will stop somewhere. When you stop, you want them to call out the missing word or words.

Teacher reads: Green leaves . . . blanketing ___ ___.
(Children answer *the town*.)

Teacher reads: Oak leaves . . . whispering ___ ___ ___!" (Children answer *Autumn's in the air!*)

Teacher reads: Big leaves . . . carpeting ___ ___.
(Children answer *the ground*.)

Create with Nature

Use nature's bounty to help you create playthings in the great outdoors. Children of long ago from all cultures often turned to nature or their gardens for materials for their playthings. Try these nature-inspired traditional crafts to make a plaything of your own!

Corn Husk Creatures

If you grew corn in your Kid Space this year, you have a mouth-watering treat and the supplies for an exciting outdoor craft. If you weren't able to grow any corn, you can always visit the vegetable stand for a few fresh cobs!

You Need:
- corn husks
- scissors
- towel
- yarn or string
- spray bottle full of water

What to Do:
1. Strip the husks from corn and let them dry in the sun.
2. Spray the husks with water and pat dry with a towel.
3. Fold the corn husk in half.
4. Tie the string about 1" (2.5 cm) below the fold to form the head.
5. Fold another husk sideways with the ends tucked in and tie either end closed at the edges for arms.
6. Tuck the arms into the first husk and slide up to the neck tie.
7. Tie a string below the arms.
8. Decorate and finish creatively in a way geared to the age group.

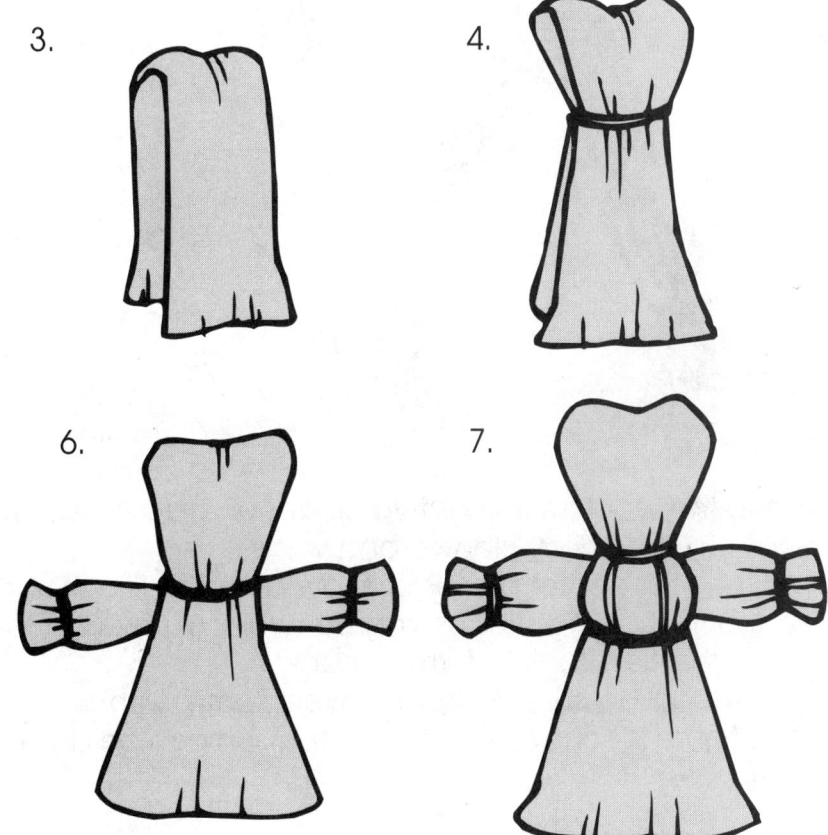

Try This:
1. Cut the dress vertically up the center and tie the bottom of each piece to form two legs.
2. Glue thin strips of husk, a hat made from a husk, corn silk hair, a fabric handkerchief, yarn, or braids of any materials to the head.
3. Draw a face with marker if desired.
4. Tie a string around the neck to make a loop for hanging the figure.

by Robynne Eagan

Straw Figures

The Iroquois of North America have been making straw figures for centuries. Let students try their hand at this traditional craft—it's not difficult and the end result is terrific! These creations can be incorporated into a harvest wreath, garland, or centerpiece or hung up all on their own. If your Kid Space isn't laden with straw, you can take a trip into a local farm field and round up the straw for yourself, or have a bale or two delivered to your classroom.

You Need:
- 12 strands of straw for each figure
- bucket or basin of warm water
- few balls of yellow or cream yarn
- scissors
- ruler

What to Do:
1. Soak your straw in the warm water for about one hour. It can be forced underwater by placing a heavy object on top.
2. Remove the straw and place it on pads of cloth or plain newsprint. Let it dry for about 10 minutes.
3. Have each child collect 12 tubes of straw and cut them into 12" (30 cm) lengths.
4. Gather eight tubes together and tie with one piece of yarn just above the center of the bundle to form the waist of the figure.
5. Below the waist, separate the straw into bundles of four, which will become the legs.
6. Tie strands of yarn around the knee and at the ankle.
7. Above the waist, separate two pieces of straw on either side of the figure to become the arms. Tie at the shoulders, elbows, and wrists.
8. Fold the four center pieces of straw down to the shoulder and tie to form the head.
9. The four remaining strands can be wrapped around the top of the shoulders and tucked into one of the tie wraps to form a neck.
10. Figures can be sprinkled or sprayed lightly with water if they become too brittle. When the basic figure is complete, the straw person can be dampened and positioned in a chosen pose to dry.

Try This:
1. Children may work in pairs to help shape and tie off the figures.
2. Finished figures can be decorated with natural objects such as seeds, dried grasses, berries, leaves, and flowers.
3. Encourage children to be creative with their figures. Suggest animal, bird, or tree figures.
4. Create a backdrop and pose figures in front for a seasonal display.

Have an Earth-Friendly Fall

Beginning in Your Classroom
You can help save Earth's trees by
- taking care of your books. (They're made from trees.)
- not breaking or over-sharpening pencils.
- using both sides of a sheet of paper.
- having a recycling box for paper that still has one good, unused side.
- saving pieces of construction paper in a scrap box.
- not damaging wooden chairs and desks.
- putting away math manipulatives, all puzzle pieces, and game pieces. They can be used over and over. (Making new ones means using more materials and more energy. That's wasteful!)
- turning off lights when leaving the room. (That saves energy.)

When You Are in the Restroom
You can help conserve resources by
- saving water. Run the faucet only long enough to wash your hands.
- turning the faucet off tightly so no water will drip away.
- using only enough paper towels to dry your hands.
- running an electric hand dryer only long enough to dry hands.

When Eating in the Cafeteria
You can help by
- not wasting food. If you pack your lunch, bring only what you will eat. If you buy lunch, ask for portion sizes you know you will eat.
- taking only one straw.
- taking only one paper napkin. Better still, bring a reusable cloth napkin or washcloth from home.
- not littering. Throw garbage in the trash can.
- putting plastic or metal containers in the recycling container. If your cafeteria doesn't have one, ask your teacher to help you get one placed there.

Some Other Ways to Be Earth-Friendly This Fall
- Take care of your school clothes by changing into play clothes when you get home. (Laundering uses water and energy; detergents can cause water pollution. Ironing uses energy, too. Try to reduce the amount of laundering your clothes need.)
- Reuse school clothes by passing good clothes that no longer fit you on to others. Recycle old play clothes (T-shirts and sweats).
- If you get to school by car, carpool with other children in your neighborhood. (Be sure to buckle up!)
- Whenever possible, carpool for after-school or weekend activities.

Activities
- Have children make posters for the positive practices listed on this page. Put these posters into the appropriate places around the school (classroom, bathroom, cafeteria).
- Make a bulletin board collage of recycling symbols or messages from paper or plastic products (cereal and cracker boxes, loose-leaf packaging, toilet tissue wrapping, paper towel labels, plastic products).
- Reuse shirt-size cardboard gift boxes as containers for sheets of paper that have one unused side to draw on or use as scrap paper. Ask to put a box in each classroom.

by Elaine Hansen Cleary

Name _____

Fill the Lunch Box

Directions:
Discuss which lunch box items help our Earth. Then find pictures of these items and glue them in the lunch box.

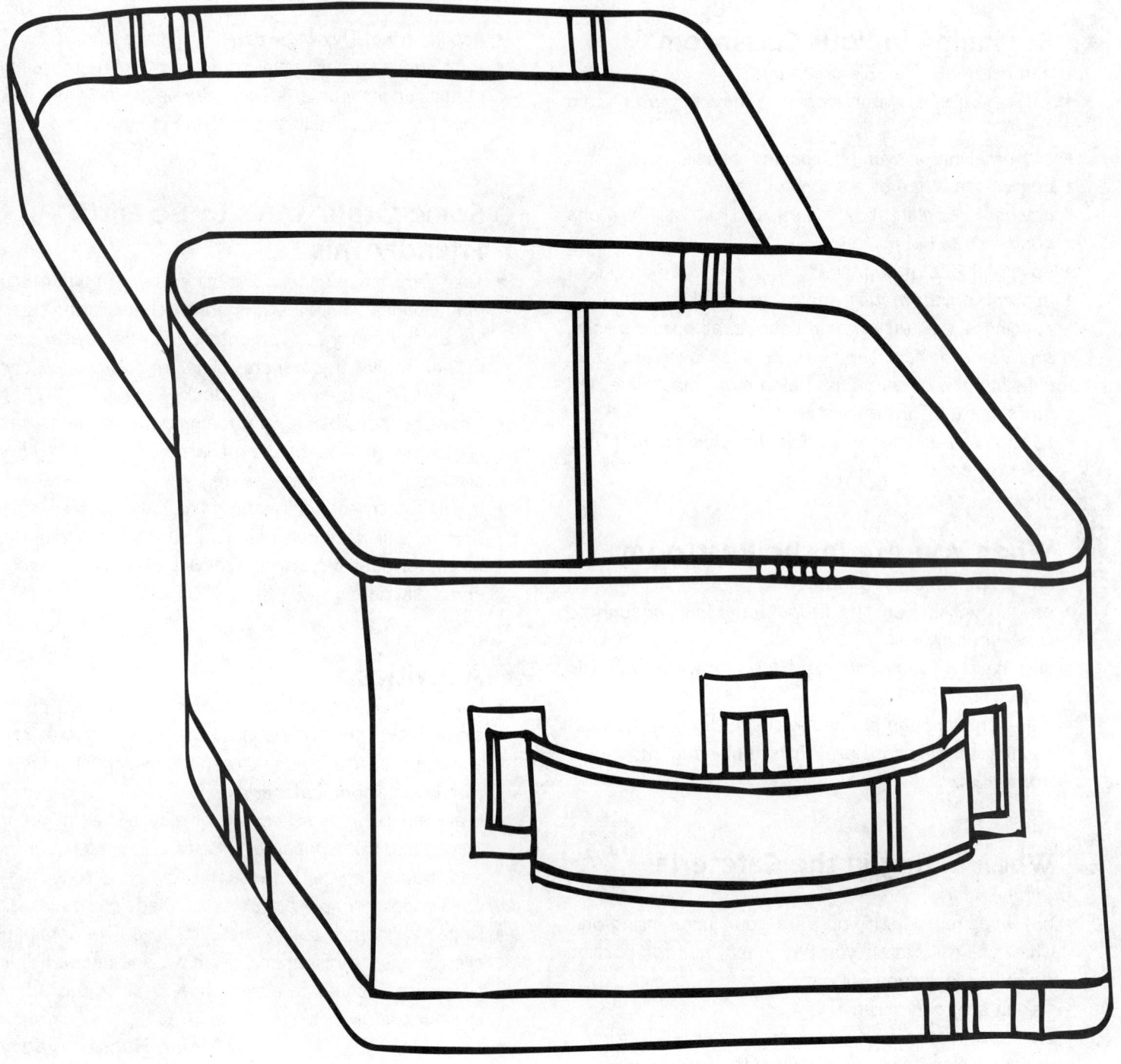

30

TLC10110 Copyright © Teaching & Learning Company, Carthage, IL 62321-0010

Fall into Art

Winnie Witch

coat hanger
panty hose
construction paper
felt
scissors
glue

Bend hanger into a diamond shape; bend hook in slightly to meet hanger. (An adult may need to assist younger children here.) Pull panty hose over hanger and tie tightly at end where hook is.

Cut out a witch's hat from felt or construction paper, and glue onto top of diamond—about 1/3 of the way down (opposite end from hook).

Cut out facial features (eyes/ears/nose/mouth) from construction paper or felt and glue on. Add strips of construction paper for hair; curl with scissors, if desired.

Fraidy Cat

paper lunch bags
black pipe cleaners
newspaper
markers/crayons
construction paper
glue
black tempera paint
scissors
small rubber bands

Paint lunch bag black. Allow to dry thoroughly. Stuff bag three-fourths full of crumpled newspaper. Braid two or three black pipe cleaners together. Tie off bag using pipe cleaners; twist around bag end once or twice, then leave rest of pipe cleaner hanging lose for your cat's tail. Using markers, crayons, or construction paper, make a face and ears for your cat. Cut long, skinny strips of paper to glue on for whiskers; curl with scissors.

Leaf People

fresh leaves (any kind)
white bond paper (copy paper)
maple seeds/acorns/pine needles
markers/crayons/colored pencils
glue

Place one leaf, vein-side up, under paper. Gently rub over the leaf using a lead pencil to get the imprint. Use as many leaves as you wish to make your leaf person. Using markers, crayons, or colored pencils, draw the face, legs, arms, and whatever features you need to complete your person. Imprints of smaller leaves may be used as arms and legs.

You may wish to glue on maple seeds, acorns, pine needles, or pinecones for facial features or limbs, or use them to add scenic features to your picture. Be creative!

by Teresa E. Culpeper

Veggie Prints Lunch Bag

potatoes
celery
carrots
peppers
zucchini
onions
paint
brown paper bags

Have students cut vegetables into various-sized chunks. Dip into paint and press onto paper lunch bag. Allow to dry.

Fall is a great time for this activity because it is harvesttime. There is an abundance of food. My students enjoyed using their autumn lunch bags for several lunches afterwards.

If you are fortunate enough to have a laminating machine, you can laminate the bags. It really brings out the colors and they last about a month. Just slit open the top of the bag after laminating it. The students had a blast with these.

Pumpkin Pal

orange, green, and brown felt
tongue depressor sticks
foam chips/tissue paper or newspaper
construction paper
glue
scissors
markers

On two 12" x 12" pieces of orange felt, draw the outline of a pumpkin. (Younger children may need a bit of help.) Cut out both outlines. Glue around the edges of one of the felt pieces, leaving about 3" free of glue on top.

Lay the second felt pumpkin on top and press securely around the glued edges. Dry thoroughly. Stuff with foam chips, crumpled newspaper, or tissue paper. Put a couple of foam chips on a piece of brown felt, about 3" x 5", and make into a roll. Glue both ends. This is your pumpkin's stem. Glue about one-third of the stem into the opening of the pumpkin. Close up the pumpkin with glue. Dry thoroughly. Using markers or bits of felt, make a face for your pumpkin.

Some students may wish to make a body for their pumpkin pal, using bits of felt or construction paper. They can add tongue depressor sticks behind the body parts for added strength and support.

32

TLC10110 Copyright © Teaching & Learning Company, Carthage, IL 62321-0010

Scrappy Scarecrow

- assorted scraps of fabric
- stiff cardboard
- assorted buttons and sequins
- assorted pasta
- scissors
- glue
- markers

Trace the scarecrow outline on cardboard and cut out. Cover with pasta. Using scraps of fabric, cut out clothes for your scarecrow (pants, shirt, vest, hat and so on). Glue on top of pasta. Glue some spaghetti or fettuccini under the brim of the scarecrow's hat and at the end of his pant legs and shirt. Make scarecrow's face using markers, buttons, or sequins.

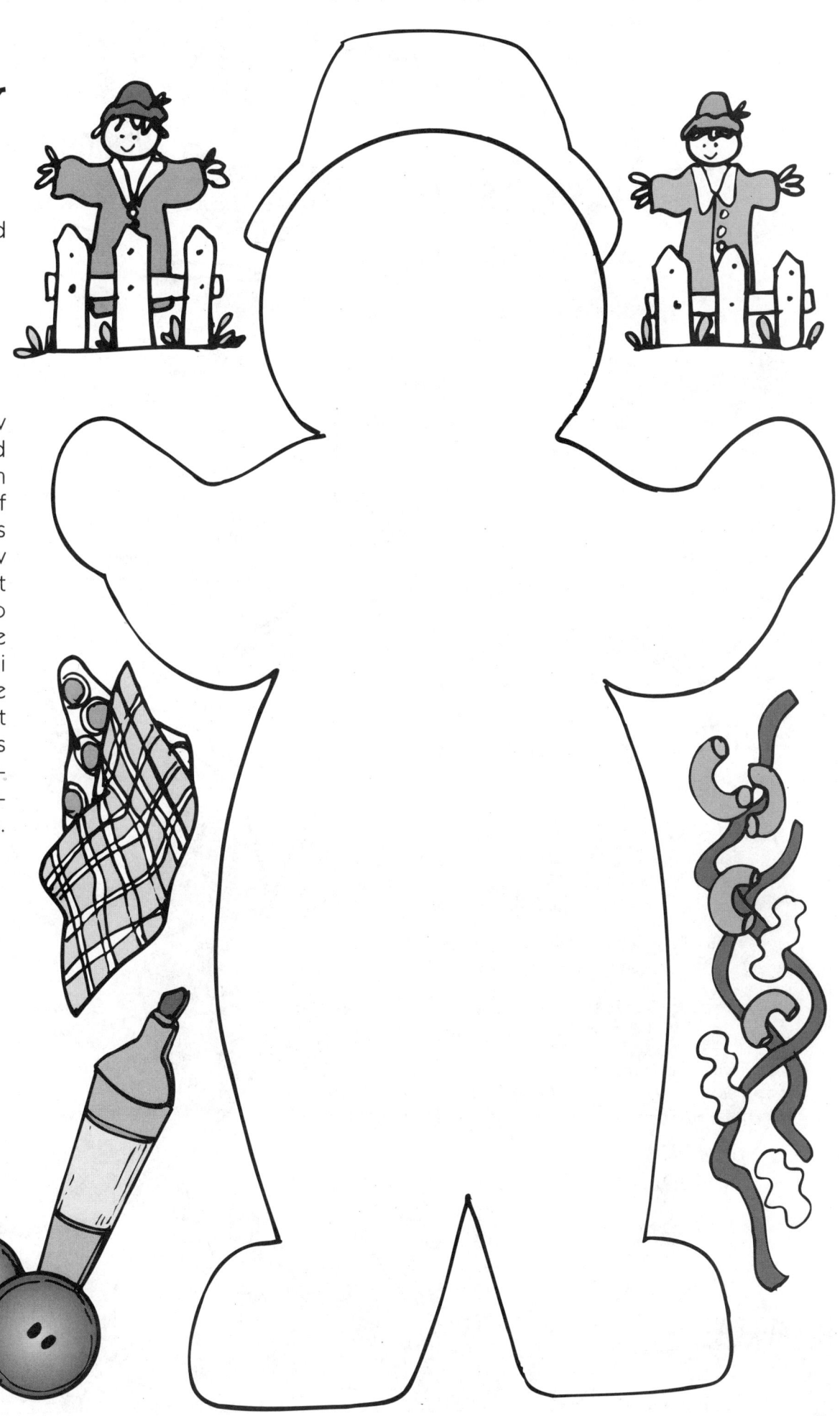

"Apple"tivities

Social Studies

- Have students research and record information for their family tree.
- Discuss the phrase "One bad apple can spoil the whole bunch" and how it relates to honoring the family name.
- Discuss the phrase "You can count the seeds in an apple, but you can't count the apples in a seed" and how it relates to good citizenship, education, developing talents, and so on.
- Mark a map of the world or the United States showing where apples are grown.
- Make graphs showing which locations grow the most apples.

Writing and Reading

- Alphabetize a list of the most common types of apples.
- Read about Johnny Appleseed and William Tell.
- Discuss Greek myths that include apples: the golden apple the goddess Eris delivered to the banquet she wasn't invited to attend, the golden apples that Hercules was to obtain from the Hesperides, or the golden apples Hippomenes used to win the race against Atalanta.

Science

- Dry apples.
- Research the most common types of apples. Bring a variety of types to class for the students to sample. Hold a contest to determine which type is the favorite.
- Discuss whether all apples have the same number of seeds. Cut up apples to find out.
- Make an apple pie, applesauce, apple crisp, or apple cake. Work on fractions while measuring.
- Discuss the nutritional value of apples. Does it change as apples are dried, made into pie, applesauce, etc.? Does the phrase "An apple a day keeps the doctor away" have any truth to it? Why?
- Study how an apple grows, the parts of an apple blossom, and the function of bees.
- Discuss the procedure for grafting trees.

Math

- After determining the favorite type of apple among students, have them count votes, discuss *greater than* and *less than*, graph the results, and write story problems.
- Practice division, multiplication, and fractions by determining how many apples are needed to feed the class if the apples are divided in halves, thirds, fourths, and so on.
- Work with money, subtraction, and addition in relation to the cost of various types of apples.

by Lisa H. Fernelius

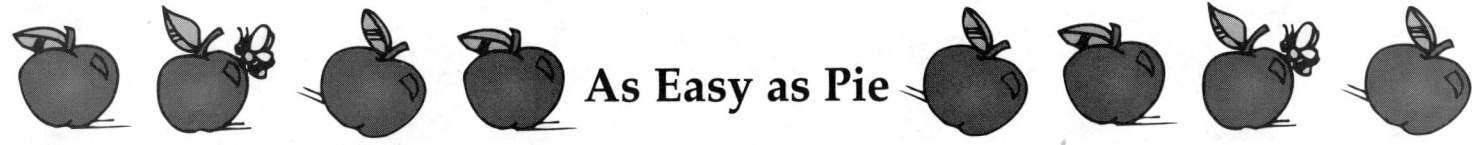

As Easy as Pie

Provide each child with six circles of the same size but of six different colors. The circles could be copied on different colored paper, or the students could color them. The circles should be divided and labeled as shown below. Ask the students to cut out the circles along the lines. The teacher's set should be made out of felt and used on a flannel board or out of cardstock and laminated.

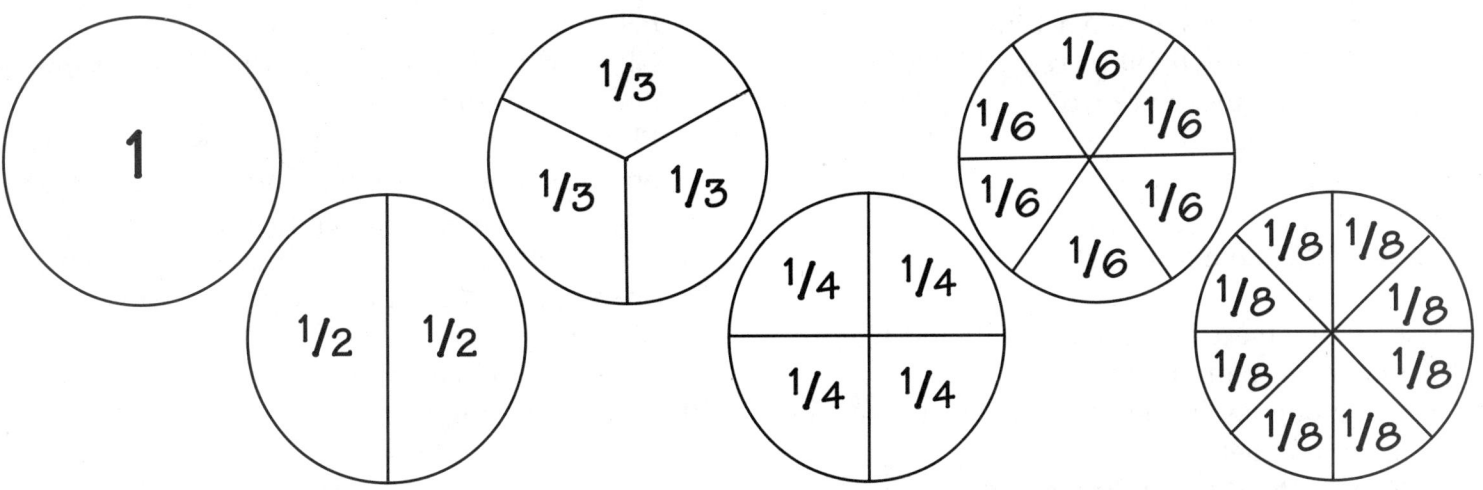

Using the various pie sections, the children are to answer problems such as the following:

1. Which is greater: 2/3 or 3/4?
2. Is 1/2 equal to 2/4?
3. How many eighths are in 1/4? What does 3/8 plus 1/4 equal?
4. If a pie were divided into six parts and three pieces were eaten, how much pie would be left? What is another way of writing that fraction?
5. How many sixths are in 1/3? What is 5/6 minus 1/3?

Apple Magnets

1. Pin leaf pattern to two pieces of green felt. Cut out.
2. Pin stem pattern to two pieces of brown felt. Cut out.
3. Pin apple pattern to two pieces of red felt. Cut out or use the leftover red felt circles from the Apple Potpourri Bags activity on page 36.
4. Glue a stem and a leaf to the back of one felt apple.
5. Glue two 1/2" magnet strips to the back of the apple.
6. Repeat steps 3 and 4 with other stem, leaf, apple, and magnet strips.

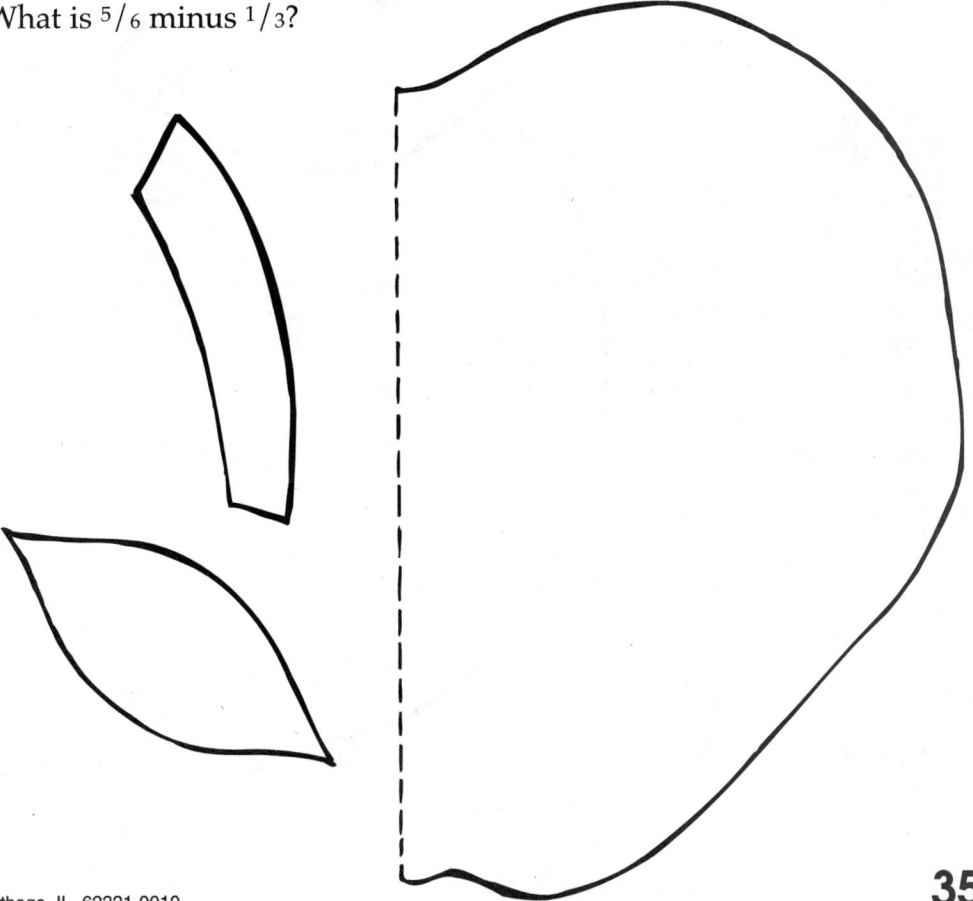

TLC10110 Copyright © Teaching & Learning Company, Carthage, IL 62321-0010

35

Apple Potpourri Bags

Materials
- two 5" x 6" red felt pieces
- two 5" x 6" pieces of fine netting
- four 1" x 2" brown felt pieces
- four 1" x 2" green felt pieces
- 1/4 cup potpourri
- tacky craft glue
- straight pins
- four 1/2" magnetic strips

1. Fold one piece of red felt in half and pin dotted line of pattern on fold.
2. Cut along solid lines. Save the inside for the apple magnet.
3. Repeat steps 1 and 2 with the other piece of red felt.
4. Pin leaf pattern on two pieces of green felt. Cut out. Glue together.
5. Pin stem pattern on two pieces of brown felt. Cut out. Glue together with leaves placed between stems.
6. Glue stems and leaves to top center of one open apple ring.
7. Place open apple ring with stems and leaves on flat surface. Put glue around inside edge, leaving 3" open at the top to add potpourri.
8. Place both pieces of netting and the other open apple ring on top of glue to form bag. Let dry.
9. Trim off excess netting.
10. Gently add potpourri to bag.
11. Glue top of sack closed.

Apple Cards

1. Copy the front of the apple card.
2. Color the apple, leaf, and stem.
3. Fold the paper in half near the leaf and stem.
4. If you want the card to be in the shape of an apple, cut out the apple, leaving the portion between the stem and leaf uncut to keep the front and back of the card attached at the fold.
5. Write a message on the inside of the card.

Welcome the School Year

School bells ring. Students arrive with new fall clothes. Lunch boxes and backpacks sport the latest logos. Teachers work on lesson plans that support the curriculum. School has started, again.

Within the next few weeks, most schools invite parents to an open house. If you're trying to come up with innovative ideas that reinforce learning or give visitors a glimpse of your program, try some of these ideas.

Hands United in Learning

Make a doorway banner that welcomes parents and visitors to your room. Use a 3' x 3' piece of brightly colored paper. Write the slogan "Hands United in Learning" in the center. Ask students to trace around their hands using contrasting colored paper. Cut out the paper hands and paste to the larger sheet. Position each hand where it will touch another. Display on your door or in a corridor leading to your classroom.

Footprints Lead to Learning

Choose one color of paper and trace around students' feet. Have children personalize their paper feet with their names and drawings. Cut out and laminate. With your principal's approval, tape footprints from the front entrance leading to your room. Post a sign nearby asking parents to follow the footprints.

Set the Stage

Select quiet classical music to play on a recorder or the CD ROM drive of your computer during open house. Soft background music provides a calming effect, yet does not interfere with conversation.

Clean Up, Brighten Up

Welcome guests with a clean, fresh room. Schedule a time for students to help clean chalkboards, dust furniture, and straighten bookshelves. Do away with clutter. Bring in a few green plants left from your summer garden. Small animals, such as fish or a hamster, add to the setting. This tells parents the classroom environment is important to these children.

by Carolyn Ross Tomlin

Our Summer Vacation

Before open house, ask students to bring photos of an activity they enjoyed during the summer. Some of the children may have traveled, taken swimming lessons, gone to a camp, or learned a new skill or sport. Display these on a bulletin board for visitor viewing. A photo display provides a good place for guests to meet one another.

Ask Guests to Sign In

Have parents sign in on a sheet of paper. This provides a list of those present. Materials can be sent home to those who do not attend.

Offer Light Refreshments

Coffee, tea, soft drinks, and small cookies add to the friendly, pleasant atmosphere.

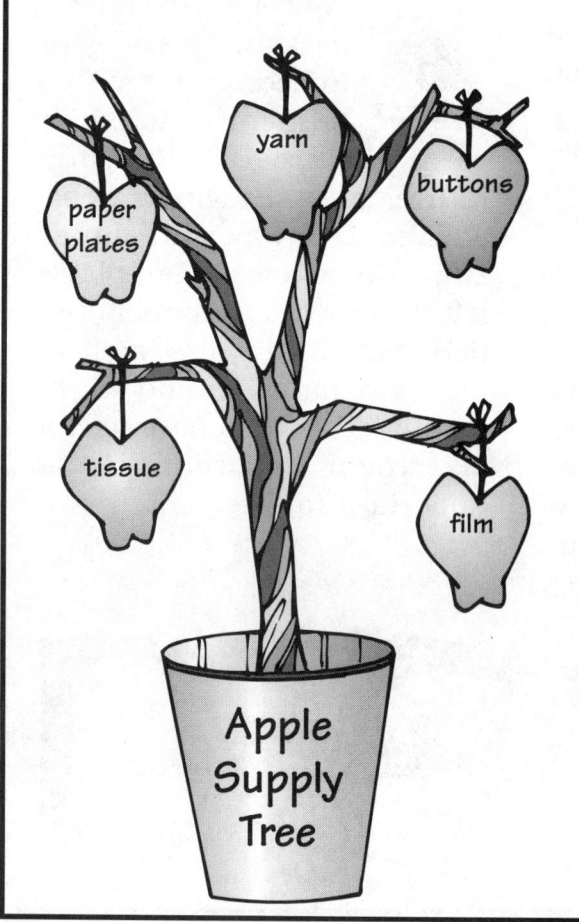

Just Like Me

Display your students' artwork. Older students may help one another outline a body form on butcher paper. (One student lies down while another draws around the body with a black marker.) Teachers can assist younger students.

Students color their skin tones, hair, eyes, and clothing. Cut out on the black lines. Fold the figures and place in the assigned seat. Children and parents will delight in seeing these "students" in their chairs.

Provide a Map

Provide a map of the school for new parents. This information gives directions to the gym, cafeteria, library, office, computer lab, and other areas.

Apple Supply Tree

All classrooms need supplies the school may not furnish. Allow families to help with art projects and classroom materials. Cut out 4" red paper apples and tie on a bare twig inserted in a can filled with sand. List one supply on each apple. You may have several apples with the same supply. Fold a piece of poster board that says: "Supplies You Can Provide. Please pick an apple and help our class."

tissues	paper plates
shaving cream (for writing on tables or desks)	liquid soap
drinking straws	yarn
small paper bags (for puppets)	buttons
plastic self-closing bags (pint and quart size)	stickers
small mints or candies	film

September Safety

It's school time again, and that means it's time to review the rules for staying safe and well both IN and OUT of school.

School bus stops are **not** play stops. Be sure to wait, away from the road, and when the bus arrives, get in an orderly line.

Eyesight is precious. If you need glasses, be sure to wear or take them to school. Never "try on" anyone else's glasses nor let them try yours.

Pointed objects can cause puncture wounds. Keep pencils, scissors, and other sharp objects in pencil cases when not using them.

Tell your family or a teacher if a stranger hangs around your bus stop or tries to talk with you or give you a ride.

Every time you cough or sneeze, be sure to cover your mouth with a tissue to prevent germs from spreading.

Make sure you scrub your hands with soap and warm water before eating and after going to the bathroom.

Backpacks leave your hands free yet carry all your supplies, but overloading them can hurt your back or cause you to lose your balance.

Exercise is important to both your mind and body. Ask your physical education instructor for some good exercises to do at home.

Running on rough or slippery walks is dangerous, often causing bad falls and injuries. Walk instead.

Stay seated and don't wiggle around or be too noisy while riding to school, whether you are on a school bus or in a car.

Ask for your secret family code word if anyone else says your parents told them to pick you up. If this person doesn't know the word, don't go with them!

Fall leaves are fun to jump in, but never hide in a pile of them because you could suffocate or get run over.

Eat three well-balanced meals a day to give your body the energy and the building materials it needs to grow and ward off illness.

Taking summer plants indoors is fine, but many are poisonous if eaten by an animal or small child. (Ask an adult to check with your local poison control center to see which ones are unsafe.)

Your body needs rest if it is to function properly. Be sure to get nine to ten hours of sleep each night.

by Elaine Hansen Cleary

Review Activity

Have students review the safety rules for each of the letters in SEPTEMBER SAFETY.

In a class discussion, make up your own set of rules. (Use positive wording whenever possible.) Make a set of posters in the shape of a child. Have each child choose a different rule and print it on the front of the poster.

I keep sharp objects in a pencil case.

Remember the Most Important Rule!

Using the words in the box, fill in the correct word to complete each rule.

| before | bus | day | leaves | mouth | play |

Never hide in piles of ___ ___ ___ ___ ___ ___.

Wash your hands ___ ___ ___ ___ ___ ___ you eat.

Stay seated while riding on the school ___ ___ ___.

Never ___ ___ ___ ___ in the road.

Cover your ___ ___ ___ ___ ___ when you cough or sneeze.

Eat three good meals every ___ ___ ___.

Now, copy the letters that appear in the shapes and you will complete a very important rule:

Always remember ___ ___ ___ ___ ___ ___ first!

40

School Safety

Directions: Cut out each square. Paste the six rules that list good safety practices on the bus windows.

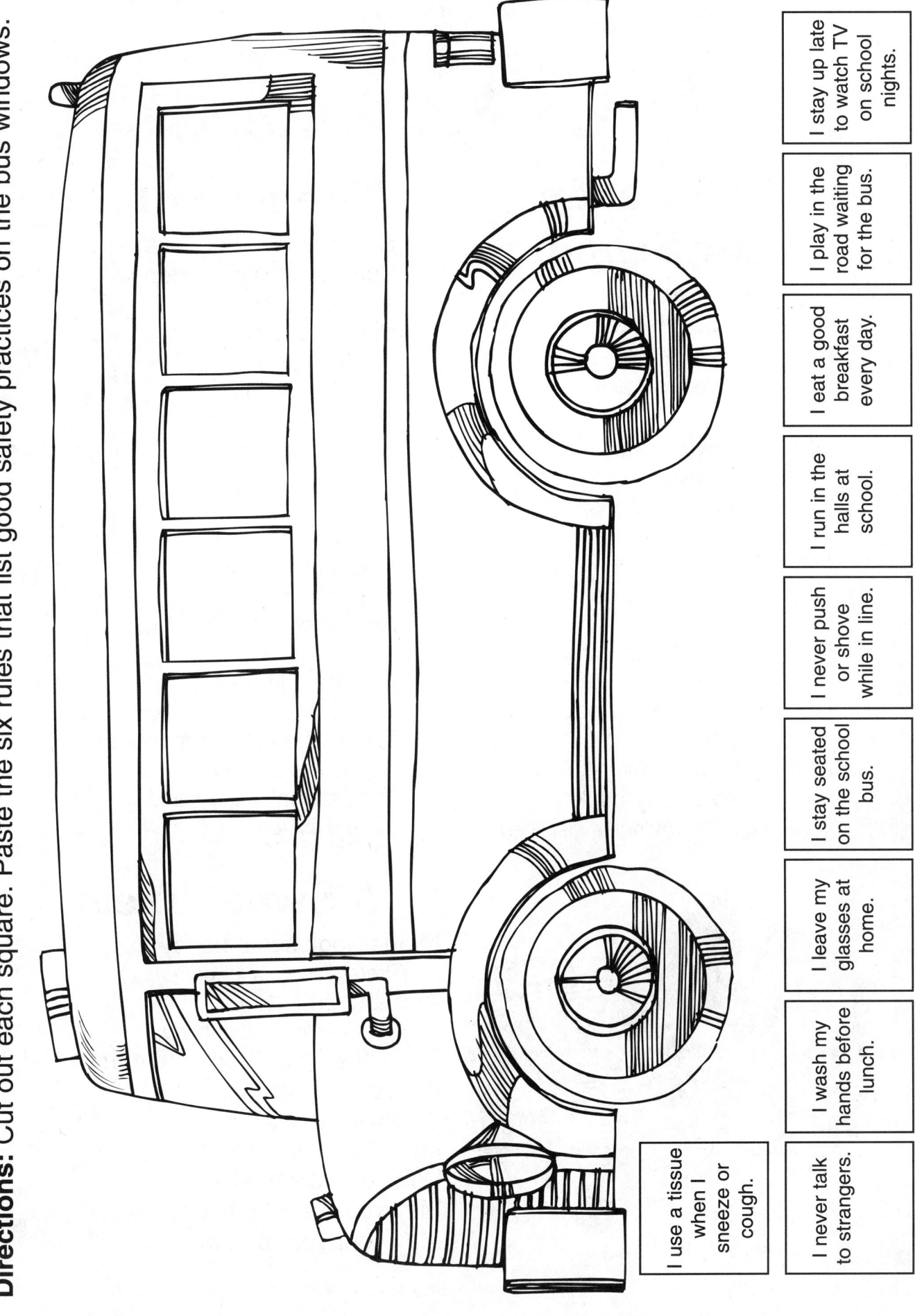

| I use a tissue when I sneeze or cough. |
| I never talk to strangers. |
| I wash my hands before lunch. |
| I leave my glasses at home. |
| I stay seated on the school bus. |
| I never push or shove while in line. |
| I run in the halls at school. |
| I eat a good breakfast every day. |
| I play in the road waiting for the bus. |
| I stay up late to watch TV on school nights. |

Holiday

All Ready for School

Summer is over!
But I'm nobody's fool!
I really like summer—
And I also like school!

I bought new clothes
   (Model clothes.)
And brand-new shoes.
   (Show shoes.)
I saw so many pretty things
It was hard to choose.

I have a box for my lunch
   (Show lunch box.)
And for my books, a pack.
   (Show pack.)
I'll have to carry everything
Right there on my back!
   (Pat back in rhythm to last line.)

by Judy Wolfman

The End of Summer

Summer is almost over—
Summer is almost done.
   (Look sad.)
But this past summer
I had a lot of fun!
   (Brighten up.)
I went fishing
   (Pretend to fish.)
And rode my bike.
   (Pretend to ride.)
I went camping
And took a hike.
   (Walk around.)
And when it got too hot
   (Wipe brow.)
I'd take a little rest.
   (Put both hands to cheek and "rest.")
Then I'd go and play some more—
   (Do lots of things!)
That's what I like best!
   (Big smile.)

A Sweet Treat

Mother took some honey
   (Pretend to hold jar of honey.)
And an apple, too.
   (Hold apple in other hand.)
Then she said, "Come here, my child,
I have a gift for you.
   (Walk around.)
Let's begin the New Year
With this little treat.
May your year be happy!
May your year be sweet!"

Fingerplays

Firefighters

This is a fire truck.
 (Show fist.)
This is the hose.
 (Pretend to hold hose.)
Firefighters work fast
When the siren blows.
 (Quickly "dress"—hat, boots, jacket.)
Climb up the ladder.
 (Pretend to climb up.)
Turn on the hose.
 (Hold hose and aim.)
Out comes the water
 (Continue to "squirt" the water.)
While the siren blows.

First Day of School

Hey! Hey! Look at me!
 (Point to self.)
I'm ready to go to school
To learn to read and write and spell
And learn all the rules.
 (Count off on fingers as each is said.)
I'm going to be very smart—
 (Point to self and nod head up and down.)
You just wait and see—
 (Point to each other on "you.")
And when I become the President
 (Place both hands on chest.)
You'll know it's really me!
 (Tuck thumbs under armpits and be proud.)

Five Little Shofars

Five little shofars in a row
 (Show five fingers.)
The first one said, "I'm hard to blow."
The second one said, "My sound is low."
The third one said, "My sound is slow."
The fourth one said, "I'm best, you know."
The fifth one said, "It's time to go."
 (Show a different finger on each line.)
Five little shofars in a row.
Five little shofars who like to blow.
 (Show five fingers.)

Holiday Sing-Alongs
by Mabel Duch

Labor Day

Did You Ever See a Worker?

This song is sung to the tune of "Did You Ever See a Lassie?"

Did you ever see a builder,
A builder, a builder,
Did you ever see a builder
Saw this way and that?
Saw this way and that way,
Saw this way and that way,
Did you ever see a builder
Saw this way and that?

Did you ever see a painter,
A painter, a painter,
Did you ever see painter
Brush this way and that?
Brush this way and that way,
Brush this way and that way,
Did you ever see a painter
Brush this way and that?

Did you ever see a farmer,
A farmer, a farmer,
Did you ever see a farmer
Plow this way and that?
Plow this way and that way,
Plow this way and that way,
Did you ever see a farmer
Plow this way and that?

Did you ever see a miner,
A miner, a miner,
Did you ever see a miner
Dig this way and that?
Dig this way and that way,
Dig this way and that way,
Did you ever see a miner
Dig this way and that?

Did you ever see a teacher,
A teacher, a teacher,
Did you ever see a teacher
Write this way and that?
Write up here and down there,
Write up here and down there,
Did you ever see a teacher
Write this way and that?

Did you ever see a baker,
A baker, a baker,
Did you ever see a baker
Toss pizza like that?
Toss this way and that way,
Toss this way and that way,
Did you ever see a baker
Toss pizza like that?

Background

Labor Day is more than a hundred years old. In 1894, Congress passed a bill making Labor Day, the first Monday in September, a national holiday. Canada made it a national holiday the same year.

Although we think of Labor Day as a time for fun and play, it is a holiday in honor of workers. We should think of all the people who work to make our lives more pleasant.

Activity

Encourage children to draw pictures of themselves engaged in careers of their choice. Tell them to leave their pictures unlabeled so their classmates can try to guess what occupations they are portraying.

Celebrate Grandparents' Day
with Gifts from the Heart

The first Sunday after Labor Day is Grandparents' Day. Use this opportunity to help your students make a special gift that says, "I made it myself!" Provide wrapping paper and bows, or festive containers. Learning to give as well as receive is an important value worth teaching.

Paper Plate Handprints

Supplies
- paper plate (not Styrofoam™)
- saucer
- washable finger paint
- 1/2 yard ribbon for hanging

Directions
Cover the work area with newspapers for easy clean up. Pour paint into a saucer large enough for a hand. Dip palm of hand into the paint. Position and press the hand on the paper plate. Allow to dry.

Punch a hole in the top center. Thread ribbon through hole for a hanger. Write the child's name and date. Include this thought: "I Love You, Grandma or Grandpa!"

Macaroni Picture Frame

Directions
Remove glass. Place glue along one edge of frame. Cover with macaroni. Continue until all edges are covered. Replace glass. Place child's photo inside the glass frame.

Supplies
- 5" x 7" wooden picture frame with glass
- noodles or macaroni
- white school glue
- 5" x 7" child's photo (school picture)

by Carolyn Ross Tomlin

Pressed Flower Print

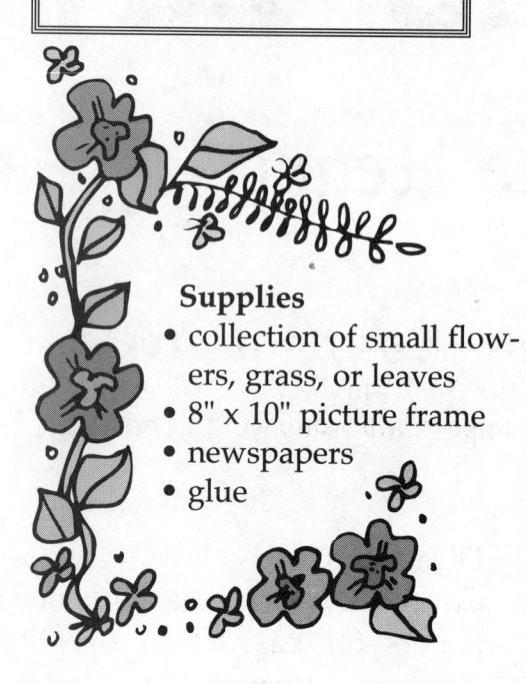

Supplies
- collection of small flowers, grass, or leaves
- 8" x 10" picture frame
- newspapers
- glue

Directions
Gather the flowers after the dew has dried. Press between several layers of newspaper. Weight the paper with heavy books or bricks. Moisture will evaporate and plants will be ready to use in about two weeks.

Remove the glass from the frame. Cut a background for the arrangement from wallpaper, construction or gift paper and tape to the cardboard backing. Decide on the placement of the plants. Hold in place with a small amount of glue. When dry, carefully assemble the frame. This makes a lasting gift for students to give a grandparent.

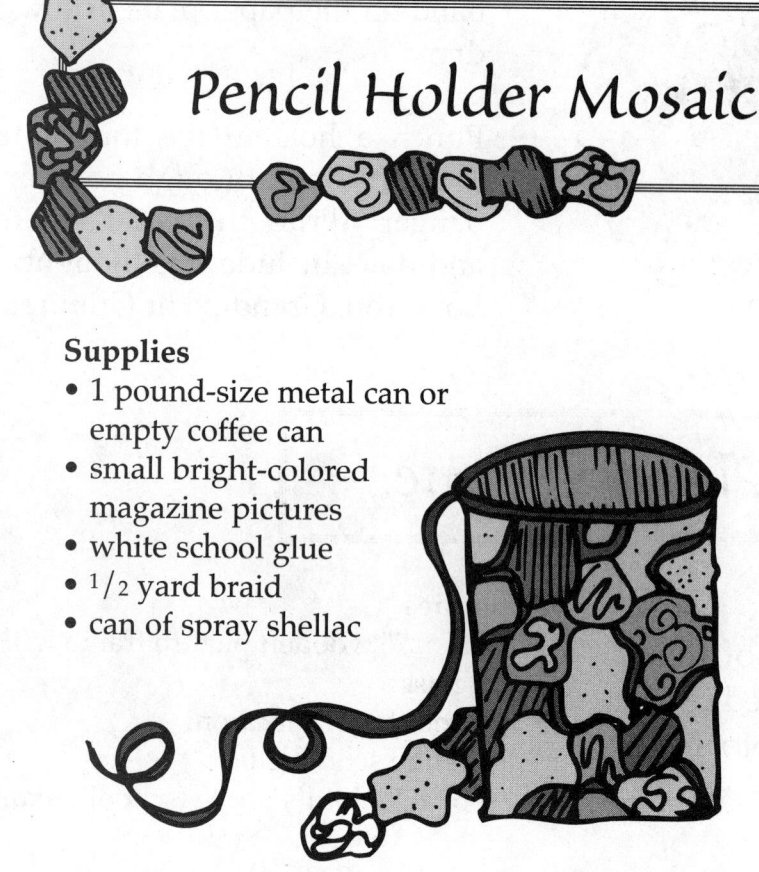

Pencil Holder Mosaic

Supplies
- 1 pound-size metal can or empty coffee can
- small bright-colored magazine pictures
- white school glue
- 1/2 yard braid
- can of spray shellac

Directions
Tear pictures from magazines. Dip in glue. Cover the can with overlapping pictures. Avoid a one-picture design, and work from a random pattern of color. When dry, glue braid around the top and bottom of can. Spray with shellac (adult only).

There is a special time of the year when we recognize the elderly in our community. Children acknowledge their grandparents or elderly friends and listen to and appreciate their wisdom.

In 1973, Marian McQuade wrote to the governor of West Virginia and asked him to proclaim a special day for grandparents and their grandchildren. In 1978, Senator Jennings Randolph of West Virginia introduced a bill to Congress which claimed the first Sunday after Labor Day as National Grandparents' Day.

Strengthening the bond between grandparents and grandchildren enriches both generations. This special day can be extended to become a celebration of all people.

Here are a few activities for discussion, enrichment and creating tokens to help honor Grandparents' Day.

Making MEMORIES
Activities to Celebrate

Start early making a personal scrapbook for each child to present to his or her grandparents on this special day. Collect each child's artwork, creative writing papers, pressed flowers from a nature walk, and photographs brought in from home. Make some "I remember" pages using either real photos or magazine pictures. Topics to write about include: **remember our vacation together, remember when we baked cookies together, remember when you helped pull my loose tooth**, *and so on. Bind this book together with a decorative cover. It makes a cherished and memorable gift.*

Visiting Grandparents

Invite your students' grandparents to the classroom. Adopt people in the community to be foster grandparents, too! Prepare a short program, sing-along, and snack time to share together. Enriching relationships result from the young and the old sharing the day together.

A "Bag Full of Greetings"

Take a paper lunch bag and decorate it with drawings, pictures, and numerous kinds of collage materials. On 3" x 5" index cards print greetings such as "You're the best grandparents," "I love you," "Have a great day," "I can't wait to see you," and so on. Give each child several cards to make, and enclose these in their "greeting bag." The child can now give this bag to his or her grandparents or fold it to send in the mail.

by Tania K. Cowling

Finding Our Grandparents' Homes

Copy or print out a map for each child. Have the children color each state with different color crayons. Help each child locate his or her grandparent's state and/or city. Place a shiny star sticker on the location.

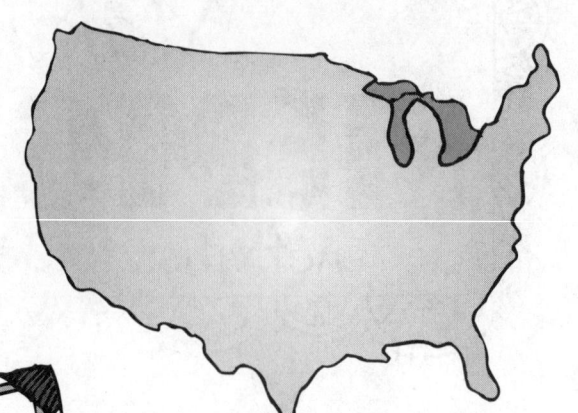

Bulletin Board

Collect pictures of the children and their grandparents. Post these on a bulletin board, and during circle time introduce each child and their family.

Visiting Grandparents

Play this fun game with the class. Start off by saying "I'm going to Grandma's (Grandpa's) house and I am going to take _____." The child beginning the game thinks of an object that begins with the letter A. The next player thinks of an object that begins with B, then C and so on until you reach Z.

Interviewing Grandparents

It's informative to interview a grandparent, and what better fun than to do it on a tape recorder? Use the school recorder on the day grandparents are visiting, or ask if the children can record an interview at home using their own machines. The students should make a list of questions to ask. Here are some examples:

1. Did you have a big family? How many brothers and sisters?
2. Where did you go to school? What was your favorite class?
3. What kinds of games did you play? Did you like books? Which ones?
4. What is your favorite holiday? How did you celebrate it when you were very young?
5. Did you have a best friend? What did you do together?
6. What is your favorite food? Do you have recipes to share?
7. Did you have a pet?

There are so many questions to ask; the list is endless!

A "Hand of Thanks"

Have the children trace both their hands on construction paper. Write *Grandma* on one and *Grandpa* on the other. Fill each finger with a thought or activity that the child remembers doing with their grandparents. For example, baking cookies together, going on a fishing trip, spending the night, telling stories, and so on. Cut out these hands and glue them onto a contrasting sheet of colored paper. Decorate the borders of the page using crayons, markers, stickers, lace, or other collage material.

Make a Cookbook

Ask the children to bring in one of Grandma's or Grandpa's favorite recipes. Have the kids neatly write it on a sheet of paper and then artistically decorate the page. Copy each sheet to make a booklet for each child. What a nice way to share one another's heritage.

The High Holidays
Rosh Hashanah and Yom Kippur

Rosh Hashanah and Yom Kippur

Rosh Hashanah means "head of the year" in Hebrew, and it is the Jewish New Year. It is considered the birthday of the world and is also the beginning of a 10-day period of repentance known as the Days of Awe. This 10-day period ends at Yom Kippur, the Day of Atonement, which is the holiest day of the Jewish year.

All Jewish holidays begin at sundown of the day before the holiday. On the evening of Rosh Hashanah, Jews celebrate at home with a holiday meal. They eat a special bread called challah. The round shape of the challah is symbolic of the round Earth and the cycle of life. Apples are dipped in honey as a way to wish each other a sweet and happy new year. Jews go to synagogue on the evening of Rosh Hashanah and the next morning. In the afternoon, some Jews participate in a ceremony known as tashlich. They go to a stream or river and toss in bread crumbs, to represent throwing away their sins. Many Jews send Jewish New Year cards to friends and relatives.

In the period between Rosh Hashanah and Yom Kippur, Jews are supposed to personally ask forgiveness from any person against whom they have sinned during the year. Then on Yom Kippur, Jews age 13 and over fast for a full day. They spend the entire day in the synagogue praying and asking for forgiveness for their sins against God. After sundown, they have a "Break Fast" at which it is customary to eat bagels, fish, and other light foods.

On Rosh Hashanah, and again at the end of Yom Kippur, it is a custom to hear the sound of a ram's horn, called a shofar. The shofar is a symbol of the holidays. Its sound is familiar and meaningful to Jews around the world.

by Katy Z. Allen and Gabi Mezger

New Year's Cards

Have students make New Year's cards. Provide them with colored paper, scissors, glue, crayons, and/or markers. Encourage children to write *Shana Tova* or *Happy New Year* on the cards. For a more interesting card, have older students draw New Year designs on squares of thin cardboard or poster board. Instruct them to write their names in the corner. Have them color the pictures and the whole cardboard. Then have them draw lines to create puzzle pieces. Have them cut carefully along the lines and then put the pieces for each puzzle into an envelope.

Throw Away Your Bad Habits

Ask students what kinds of bad habits a person might want to throw away. Discuss these ideas with the class. Then provide quiet time for older students to write a journal entry about the things they do that they'd like to throw away. Ask younger students to draw pictures.

Measuring Up

As a follow-up to the previous activity, provide students with the opportunity to discuss their good habits. Attach a large-size measuring tape to the wall. Ask the students how they "measure up." Discuss ways in which they are helpful or kind to each other. Have students write about or draw pictures of their good behaviors. Attach the writings or drawings to the wall alongside the measuring tape.

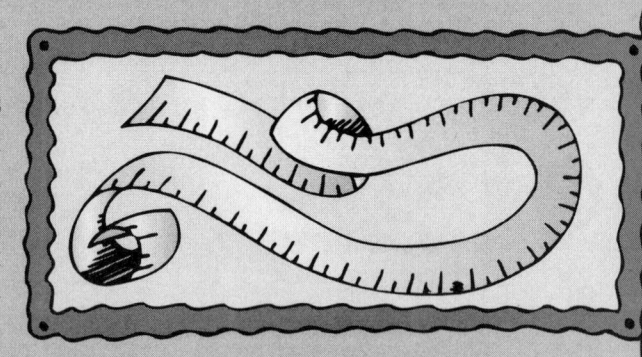

A Sweet New Year

Serve apple slices and provide honey for dipping. Ask students what it means to have a sweet new year. Since Rosh Hashanah falls near the beginning of the school year, many students will feel that a new year is a beginning for them. They may wish to think about what a sweet year in school will mean. Have small groups of older students work cooperatively to make lists. Then ask them to share their ideas while you write them on the board. Have younger students simply suggest ideas. Afterward, have each student draw a picture to illustrate one or more ways to have a sweet year. Create a bulletin board with the title "Have a Sweet Year!" Put a large construction paper apple and a pot of honey in the center of the board.

Rosh Hashanah
Jewish New Year

Jewish Egg Bread – Challah

A special round-shaped bread is served on Rosh Hashanah. The round shape symbolizes the circle of life. Here is an easy, fast version of the traditional bread recipe.

Utensils
- 1 large bowl
- measuring cups and spoons
- large wooden spoons
- baking trays

Ingredients
- 2 cups warm water
- 4 tablespoons sugar
- 2 teaspoons salt
- 2 eggs
- 4 tablespoons shortening
- 2 packages or 2 tablespoons of fast-rising active dry yeast
- 4 1/2 cups all-purpose flour
- 1 beaten egg or mayonnaise

Mix together water, sugar, salt, eggs, and shortening. Add dry yeast. While stirring, pour in four cups of flour, a cup at a time.

Vigorously knead dough on floured board for at least five minutes. Dough should be smooth. Cover the dough with a wet towel or large garbage bag. Let it rise in a high place or in an unheated oven away from drafts until doubled, for about 30 or 40 minutes.

Divide dough. Give each child a portion. Have the children roll out the dough into a long "snake." Then coil the snake into a bun. (See diagram.) Spread beaten egg or mayonnaise on bun. Let rise for a half an hour and put in 400°F oven. Or let the children take the dough home and bake it there. Refrigeration retards the rising process.

by Devorah Stone

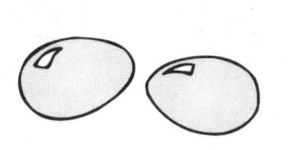

Helpful Hints
- Check the date on the fast-rising dry yeast.
- Quarter cups are easier than whole cups for small hands.
- Knead the dough to lively music.
- Dough can be put in a refrigerator overnight and then used the next morning.
- You can freeze it after the first rising and thaw it out to use the next day.
- How fast dough rises depends on your altitude and the moisture and temperature of the air as well as the type of yeast used.
- Optional: Add 1 cup raisins when kneading the dough. Sprinkle poppy seeds on top after shaping the dough.

FIRE Safety at Home & School

Stop, Drop, and Roll!

Be safe, be smart,
Don't dash and dart.
If ever your clothes should flame,
Stop, drop, and roll!
Don't run away!
Just smother out that flame.

Stop, drop, and roll!
Stop, drop, and roll!
Don't let the flames remain.
Stop, drop, and roll!
Stop, drop, and roll!
Be safe, be smart, be sane.

by Jeanene Engelhardt

Information for Teachers

Each October schools and communities observe Fire Prevention Week with its attendant lessons, fire drills, demonstrations, and field trips to local fire stations. The stress is rightly on PREVENTING fires, yet knowing the causes of fires must be an integral part of practicing ways to prevent them.

As adults we must recognize that children can and do start fires, accidentally as young as two years old, intentionally beginning at age three. Young children, more often than not, are victims of their own curiosity. Two- to seven-year-olds are especially vulnerable. They have a normal curiosity about fire but do not comprehend fire's destructive nature. They light small fires by playing with matches, lighters, and candles. This age group needs to have formal lessons about fire so that they will not have to learn by experimenting themselves.

Because more fires start in the home than any other place, it is vital to get parents and caregivers involved in lessons about fire prevention. Sharing the following information may help motivate their interest.

- Most fires start in the home—50% between 11 p.m. and 6 a.m.
- Eight out of every 10 deaths from fire are in homes or apartments.
- The kitchen is the #1 room for house fires to start.
- Cigarettes and smoking materials cause most home fire fatalities.
- The #2 cause of home fires is faulty electrical systems.
- Preschoolers and seniors are most at risk in home fires.
- Smoke inhalation claims more victims than flames do.

Some of the following fire prevention lessons involve parents, but even for those that do not, please keep parents informed about what is being taught and ask for reinforcement at home.

by Elaine Hansen Cleary

FIRE Safety

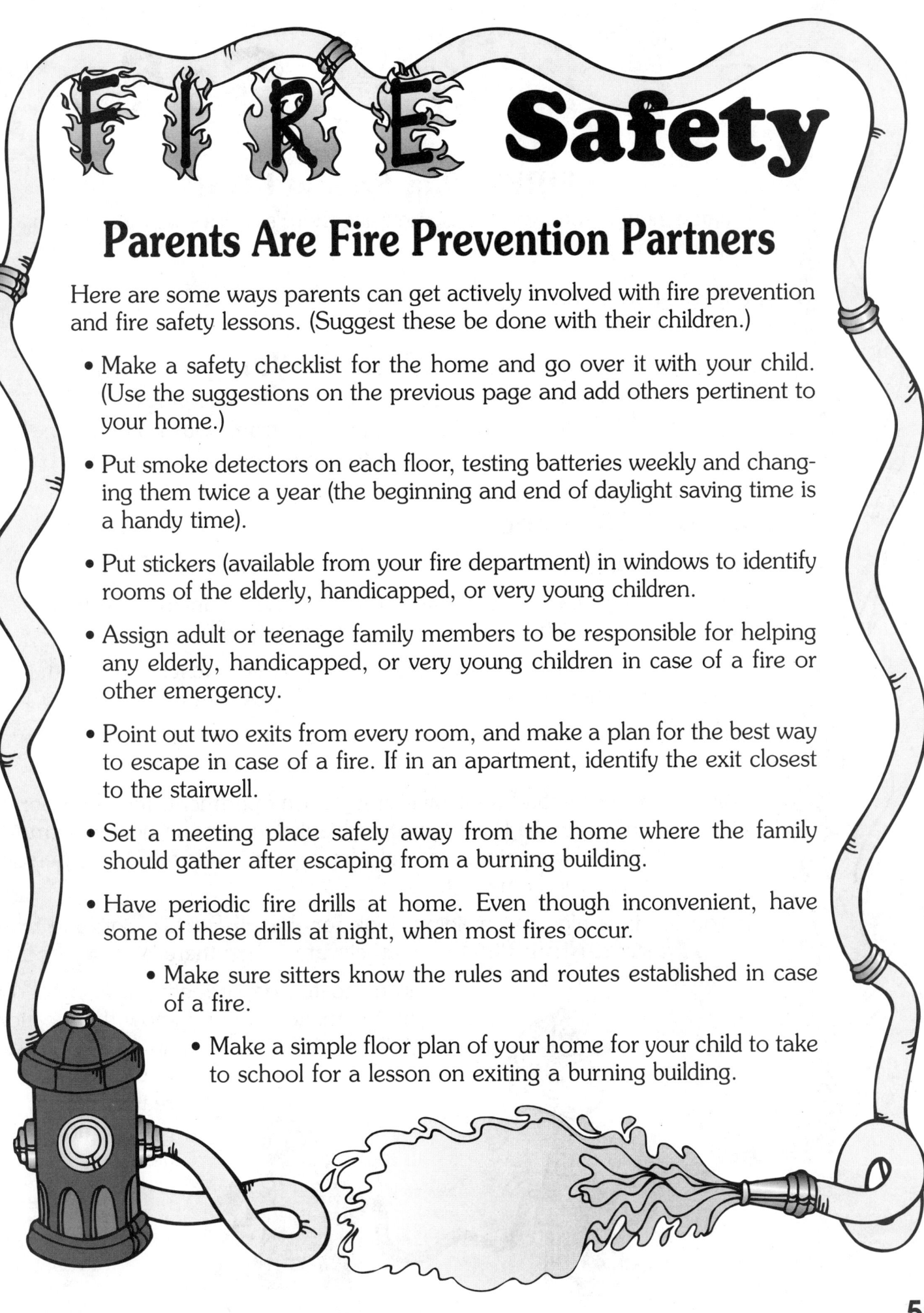

Parents Are Fire Prevention Partners

Here are some ways parents can get actively involved with fire prevention and fire safety lessons. (Suggest these be done with their children.)

- Make a safety checklist for the home and go over it with your child. (Use the suggestions on the previous page and add others pertinent to your home.)

- Put smoke detectors on each floor, testing batteries weekly and changing them twice a year (the beginning and end of daylight saving time is a handy time).

- Put stickers (available from your fire department) in windows to identify rooms of the elderly, handicapped, or very young children.

- Assign adult or teenage family members to be responsible for helping any elderly, handicapped, or very young children in case of a fire or other emergency.

- Point out two exits from every room, and make a plan for the best way to escape in case of a fire. If in an apartment, identify the exit closest to the stairwell.

- Set a meeting place safely away from the home where the family should gather after escaping from a burning building.

- Have periodic fire drills at home. Even though inconvenient, have some of these drills at night, when most fires occur.

  - Make sure sitters know the rules and routes established in case of a fire.

    - Make a simple floor plan of your home for your child to take to school for a lesson on exiting a burning building.

FIRE Safety

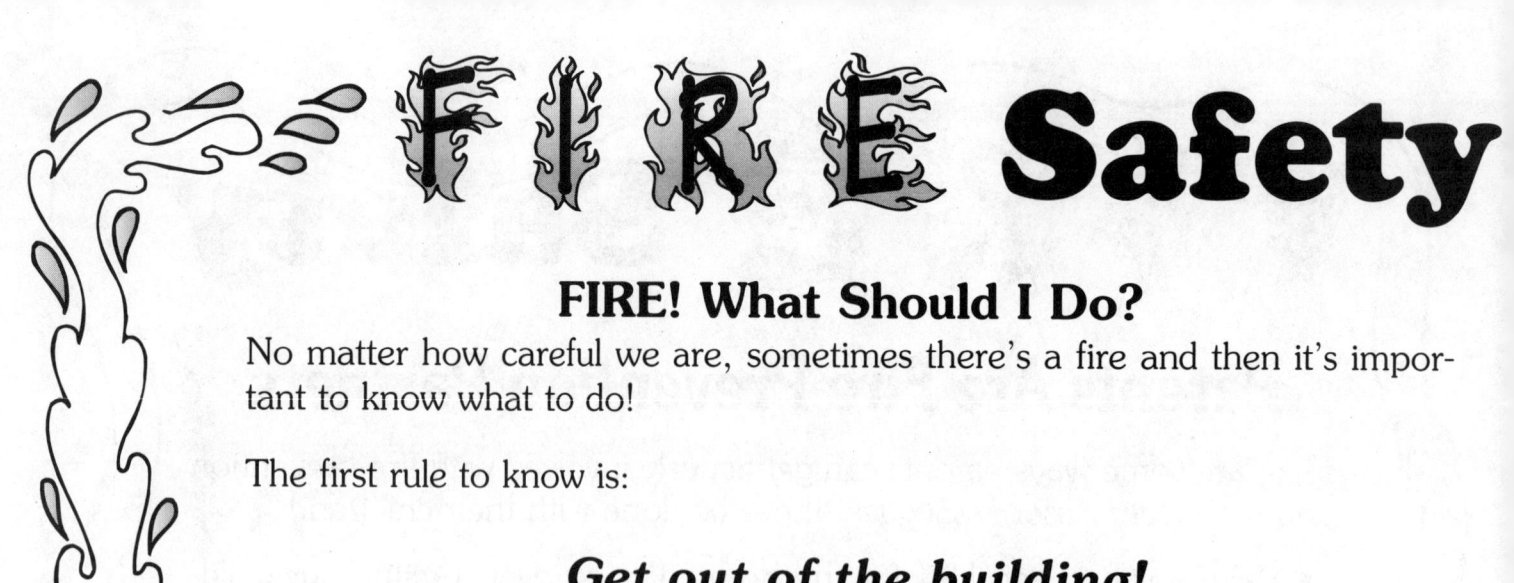

FIRE! What Should I Do?

No matter how careful we are, sometimes there's a fire and then it's important to know what to do!

The first rule to know is:

Get out of the building!
*Don't stop to get dressed or to grab belongings.
And DON'T try to call the fire department from your home phone!
After you are safely out, go to a neighbor's to phone.*

Things to Remember

- Once outside, go immediately to the spot your family has decided upon.

- Never try to go back in the building for anyone or anything. If there is a person or animal left inside, tell a firefighter instead.

- Don't try to put out the fire yourself. If it's a small kitchen fire and there's a fire extinguisher nearby, let an adult use it! YOU get out!

- If there's smoke, crawl low near the floor. If possible, put a wet cloth over your mouth.

- If you're on the second floor or in a high-rise apartment, feel the door. If it's hot, don't open it. Put a towel or blanket under the door (so smoke won't get in) and then signal for help from your window. Rescue personnel will see you and come to help.

- If you are in a high-rise building, look for the FIRE EXIT sign and walk down the stairs. NEVER try to use an elevator when there is smoke or fire!

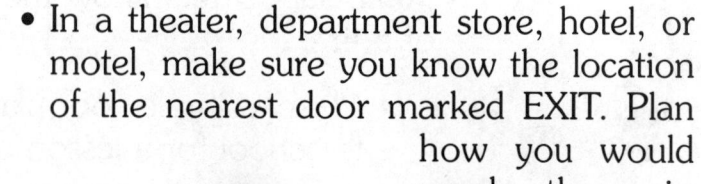

- In a theater, department store, hotel, or motel, make sure you know the location of the nearest door marked EXIT. Plan how you would reach there in case of an emergency.

FIRE Safety

Dial 9-1-1

- Trace over large 9-1-1 numerals at the board and on paper. Using flash cards with numbers 0-9, have children find 9-1-1 cards and put them in the correct order. Using play phones, have children take turns calling 9-1-1 or the appropriate emergency number. Once they are familiar with the numbers, teach them how to report a fire. With a teacher on another phone to "answer," let each child practice making the call.
- Divide the class into groups of two. Take turns being "caller" and "listener" when dialing 9-1-1 to report a fire. Be sure to include the kind of fire and the location of the house (or building), and stay on the line until told to hang up. The person who answers the call might have other questions to ask.

Where's the Exit?

- Have children learn to read the word EXIT. Discuss what it means and why it is usually printed in red. Outline the letters on paper, and have children trace over them with red crayon or marker. Take a "field trip" around the school looking for EXIT signs.
- Have a student pretend he or she is a firefighter talking to the class. Tell very clearly how to EXIT the classroom and what to do if the nearest EXIT is blocked. If possible, visit all rooms the class might be in (gym, cafeteria, library, art or music room, etc.) and go through the same process, taking turns until each student has had a chance to speak.

Safe Homes

- Find pictures or describe fire safety features that should be in every home. Discuss why these things are important. Then ask children to decide where in the home these features should be placed. (Pictures could be taped in the correct places.)
- On 3" x 5" cards write (or have students write) descriptions of fire safety features for homes. Write the name of the features on other cards. Take turns reading the clues (descriptions) and guessing which item it is and where it should be.

Suggestions for Features
Smoke detector, fire extinguisher, electrical outlets with one cord plugged in, container for matches, ashtray, fireplace screen, uncluttered stairs, windows away from stoves.

Escape!

- Using a dollhouse and play figures, have children take turns showing ways to get out of the house from various rooms.
- Using floor plans drawn by parents (or the teacher), draw pencil lines showing escape routes from various rooms.

Columbus Day

Ask if students know how they get to school. Do they know their home addresses? The distance from their house to school? How long it takes them to get to school? Explain that in the time Columbus lived, people really didn't know too much about distances across the ocean or what was on the other side of the ocean! Provide students with information about their addresses if they do not know them, and make learning their addresses a homework assignment. This would be a good time to see if the students all know their phone numbers as well.

Take students outside the classroom. Have them describe their location in reference to the main office, cafeteria, library, and gym. Is there more than one way to arrive at these destinations? About how long would it take? Where are the closest restrooms? How long would it take to get there?

Using a world map, show students the location of the United States and the distance Columbus had to sail from Spain to reach San Salvador, his first stop. Ask if they can figure out the distance between where they live and San Salvador.

Columbus' three ships were the *Niña,* the *Pinta* and the *Santa Maria.* Show pictures of sailing vessels of the period. Ask students to pretend that they are sailors on one of the ships. Discuss what it might have been like to spend a day aboard. Remember, there were no TVs, radios, or other conveniences. Brainstorm a list of daily chores such as "swabbing" the decks, mending sails, steering and navigation, and meal preparation. What did sailors do at night for entertainment? How long was the average voyage?

Students can write a diary page as part of a class ship's log.

What if Columbus could visit the classroom? What questions would students ask? Have students role-play parts as interviewer and Columbus.

In 1492 Columbus sailed the ocean blue. How many different ways can students rewrite the four-digit number? (Examples: 1429, 1249, 1294, 1924, 1942.)

Ask students to pretend that they will be going on a three-month ocean voyage. Tell them that the cabins they will have to sleep in will be very small, and they can only bring 10 items other than clothing. Ask what items these would be. Students can work in small groups to write lists. After these have been compiled, tell them to rank the most important item as 1, the next most important as 2, and so on until all 10 have been ranked. Discuss what the top three items were. What reasons can students give for making these selections? Compare responses and reach a class consensus of the top three.

by Teddy Meister

Columbus Sailors' Song

This song is sung to the tune of "Three Blind Mice."

Three small ships,
Three small ships,
See how we sail,
See how we sail.
Tossed about by the ocean waves,
Columbus said, "We must be brave.
So crew and captains, please behave
On three small ships."

Nine long weeks,
Nine long weeks,
See how we sail,
See how we sail.
Columbus said, "We can't turn 'round
'Til the Indies we have found.
Then we'll stand on solid ground,
Not three small ships."

Three more days,
There more days,
See how we sail,
See how we sail.
Columbus said, "Let's all agree
To spend just three more days at sea
Before we turn. Do this for me.
Just three more days."

I see land!
I see land!
Come and look!
Come and look!
Columbus said, "Some land I see.
This must the famous Indies be.
You all can come ashore with me.
I thank you, friends."

Holiday Sing-Alongs

Background

The *Niña,* the *Pinta,* and the *Santa Maria* took 10 weeks to reach an island (San Salvador) in the West Indies, which Columbus believed to be an island in the eastern "Indies" (southeast Asia).

After three weeks, the crews became restless and wanted to turn back. Although persuaded to sail on, the restlessness continued.

Finally, on October 10, 1492, Columbus promised that if they did not sight land within three days, they would turn back.

Two days later, October 12, 1492, land was sighted, and they landed.

We celebrate Columbus Day on the second Monday in October, in remembrance of that day.

Activity

This could be an opportunity for role playing.

The sailors try to convince Columbus to turn back. What will they say to persuade him? How will he answer? How is an agreement reached?

When land is sighted, what do the sailors say and do? What does Columbus say and do?

by Mabel Duch

Jewish Thanksgiving

Succoth

Around the world many people celebrate Thanksgiving. Jewish people celebrate by building and decorating *succahs*, or outdoor booths. A succah is an outdoor structure—either free-standing or attached to a house with wooden beams and tree branches for a roof. People eat in these temporary buildings for eight days of the Succoth festival. It is reminiscent of both the temporary buildings the Jewish people lived in during their wanderings in the desert and the dwellings farmers built during the harvest season in ancient Israel. Succoth is both an historic religious celebration as well as an agricultural festival. People rejoice in the fall harvest and thank God for their bounty.

Shoe Box Succah

Materials
- shoe boxes (no lids)
- twigs, small branches, greenery, or green construction paper
- pipe cleaners (brown, green)
- paste

Teacher Preparation
Ask students to bring in small branches or greenery. Cut twigs and branches to fit over the tops of shoe boxes or use green construction paper. Cut out a large hole or door on one side.

Student Activity
Bring twigs and small branches to school. Make a roof with the twigs, laying them horizontally and vertically. Connect them with pipe cleaners. Or you could do a loose weave with the paper strips and paste them to the box. Draw where the hole or door should be.

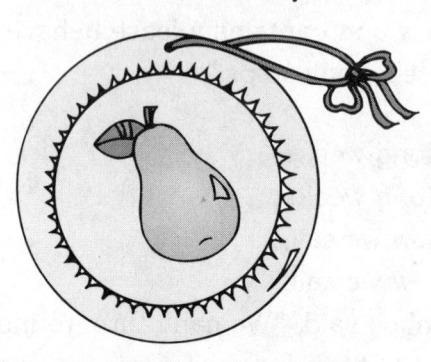

Succah Decorations

Succahs are often decorated with fruit, vegetables, ornamental gourds, and children's artwork.

Materials
- paper plates
- pipe cleaners or string
- pictures of fruit and vegetables
- crayons
- paste
- scissors

Teacher Preparation
Poke a hole at the top of the paper plate. Hang finished product.

Student Activity
Draw or cut and paste pictures of fruits and vegetables on both sides of the paper plate. Fasten a pipe cleaner in the hole.

Helpful Hints
- Try to find a real succah (call a Jewish temple or community center), or decorate some outdoor structure (gazebo, overhang, playground equipment, and so on).

by Devorah Stone

Honey Apple

This dish symbolizes the sweetness of the new year.

Utensils
- microwave-safe plates
- small spoons

Ingredients
- small apples, one for each child
- liquid honey or sugar and cinnamon
- yogurt, finely ground nuts (optional)

Prick small apple. Place apple, stem-side down on a plate. Put in microwave for 1 1/2 minutes and let cool. Let the children spoon out the core. Pour liquid honey or sprinkle a mixture of cinnamon and sugar on top.

Let the children scoop out the soft sweet apple with a small spoon.

Helpful Hints
- Put out a tub of water and towel so children do not crowd the bathroom with sticky fingers.
- Use oven mitts when taking apples out of the microwave.
- Use honey swizzle sticks.

Honey Applesauce Mixture

Ingredients
- applesauce
- honey or sugar and cinnamon
- maple syrup, finely ground nuts, yogurt, raisins (optional)
- bread or crackers

Put out bowls with different ingredients. Let the children mix applesauce with the honey, sugar and cinnamon, and so on. Then let children spread the mixture on bread or crackers.

Fish Stream Craft Project

Fish symbolize prosperity because of their numbers and rapid reproduction.

Materials
- 1 long wide piece of blue crepe paper or two strips
- large white paper
- construction paper
- crayons
- glue or staples

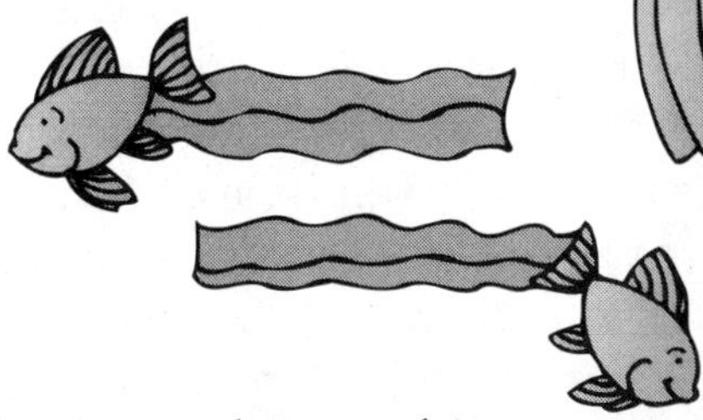

Teacher Preparation
Paste or staple blue crepe paper to a large white paper or surface. Optional: Cut out fish shapes.

Student Activity
Draw, color in, and cut out fish. Glue or staple fish to crepe paper.

Helpful Hints
- Let children trace a fish shape.
- This art project could be used for any undersea life project or for other festivals involving fish.

Dic•tio•nary Day
\\'dik-sh -,ner-ē\\ \\'dā\\

October 16 is Dictionary Day. It's also the birthday of Noah Webster, the American teacher and lexicographer, who gave American English a life of its own. Since 1783, his famous Blue-Backed Speller has never been out of print and is estimated to have sold over 100 million copies. In 1828, at the age of 70, he published An American Dictionary of the English Language. It wasn't nearly as successful as his spelling book, yet when most people think of dictionaries, they think of Webster.

Enjoy these word activities with your students and be sure to plan a special celebration of words for Dictionary Day on October 16.

Many Kinds of Dictionaries

Create a display of dictionaries, including children's, regular, special interest, and foreign language. Encourage younger students to browse through the dictionaries. Prepare study sheets for older students to do in their spare time. Questions would depend upon the dictionaries in your display and on the students' abilities, but might include questions such as: What's the last *z* word in *Webster's College Dictionary*? What's the French word for *tree*? Which of these might frizzle: a caterpillar, a stone, or bacon? Which dinosaur was longer: a brachiosaur or a triceratops? Where does a riparian animal live? Once the students have completed several study sheets, invite them to make up their own for other students to do. Make sure they give you an answer key!

Word of the Day

Introduce a new word each day. Have the students look each up in the dictionary to find out what it means. Invite the students to listen for you to say that word or watch for you to write the word. Anytime students hear you say or see you write the word, have them signal you. (Ideas: stand up, put their hands on their ears, raise their hand, etc.) Give those students a small treat. If someone uses the word of the day correctly, give them a treat. Invite the students to make suggestions for the word of the day.

Dictionary Scavenger Hunt

Divide the class into small groups. Give each group a list of items to find in a dictionary. The first group to finish with all the correct items is the winner, or the group that finds the most correct items within a specified amount of time is the winner. Here are some examples of items that could be included on a list: 1. Find the name of an animal that begins with the letters *guin-*. (Possible answers: guinea pig, guinea fowl, guinea hen.) 2. Find the name of something that you might put on top of a pie that starts with the letters *meri-*. (Answer: meringue.) 3. Find the word that means the highest part of a hill and begins with the letters *sum-*. (Answer: summit.) 4. Find the name of a game that starts with the letters *bow-*. (Answer: bowling.) 5. Find the name of a member of the Royal Canadian Mounted Police that begins with the letters *Mou-*. (Answer: Mountie or Mounty.) 6. Find the name of a food that starts with the letters *tof-*. (Answers: toffee or tofu.)

by Carolyn Short

Alphabet Line-Up

Preparation: Make a set of cards, each card having a different letter of the alphabet written on it. Bring a stopwatch or a watch with a second hand. Hand each student one of the cards. Explain that on the signal from you, students are to line up in alphabetical order, beginning with A and ending with Z. Show them where A should stand and approximately where Z will be standing. If your class has fewer than 26 students, leave out some of the letters between A and Z, but be sure to include those two. If your class has more than 26 students, invite the extra students to do these tasks: time, give the signal, check the order of the letters. Inform the class that you will be keeping track of how long it takes for them to line up in alphabetical order.

To Play: Give the signal and start the timer. Stop the timer when students appear to be lined up. Invite everyone to say the alphabet together to check if they're in the right order. If they are, write down their time. If they aren't, have them rearrange themselves to get in the right order. Then collect the cards, shuffle them, hand everyone a different card, and let them try again. Each time students play, challenge them to try to beat their previous time or their best time.

Variation: Once the students are easily able to line up in alphabetical order, write words on cards. At first all the words should begin with a different letter. Once the students have figured out how to alphabetize by first letter, include words where they will need to look at a second or third letter of the word in order to line up in the correct order. Some word lists to use for this variation: students' first or last names, their spelling list, science or social studies vocabulary list, and so on.

Before and After: Which Letter Am I?

Preparation: Use the letter cards made for "Alphabet Line-Up" or make a set for this game. Tape is needed.

To Play: Invite the students to stand in a circle. Stand in the middle of the circle and ask students to turn halfway around so that their backs are facing you. Tape a letter onto each person's back. While you're taping, explain the game and answer any questions. Tell students that when you give the signal, they are to start asking one another "before-and-after" questions to figure out which letters of the alphabet they have on their backs. They are not allowed to ask, "Am I *D*?" Instead, they are to ask questions such as "Do I come before the letter *H*? Do I come after the letter *D*?" Once students think they know who they are, they should come to you and tell you which letters they think they are. If they're right, remove their letters and have them return to the group to help answer others' questions. If they're wrong, send them back to ask more questions. The game ends when everyone has figured out their letters.

Variation

Spelling Word: Which Letter Am I? Instead of asking before-and-after questions to figure out their letters, students ask questions such as: Am I in the word *dog*? Am I in the word *house*?

Other Ideas for Celebrating Dictionary Day

1. Make alphabet pretzels by shaping letters of the alphabet from bread dough. Brush egg white on them and sprinkle with salt before baking.
2. Bring in commercial word games to play.
3. Have a spelling bee.
4. Encourage students to share new words they've learned and to teach them to their classmates during show-and-tell time. (Request that students show you their words before they introduce them to the class.)
5. Have your students collect new words. They can write each word on a 3" x 5" index card along with a short definition, illustration, or sentence containing the word. Make containers for these cards from herbal tea boxes or other containers of the right size. The outside of the box or container can be decorated with a collage of words and/or letters cut from old magazines and newspapers.

Alphabet Bingo

Teacher Preparation: Make copies of this Bingo board. Make a copy of the clues, cut apart, fold, and place in a container. A bag, bowl, or small box works well. Bring small objects to use as markers, such as beans, corn kernels, small blocks, paper clips, and so on.

Class Preparation: Give everyone a Bingo board. Invite students to write a different letter of the alphabet in each blank space. Two letters of the alphabet will need to be left out. Tell students to write the letters randomly, not in alphabetical order. Mention that each person's Bingo board should look different from everyone else's board. Give each person or small group a container of markers.

To Play: Explain that you will read a clue and students are to figure out which letter the clue is referring to. (When first beginning the game, have the students figure out each clue aloud as a class.) If that letter appears on a Bingo board, the student should cover that square with one of the markers. Everyone can begin by covering the "Free Space" with a marker. When there are five markers in a row, either horizontally, vertically, or diagonally, the student should call out "Bingo!" The first student to get a Bingo is the winner.

Alphabet Bingo Clues

What is the first letter of the alphabet?	Which letter comes after K and L?
What is the last letter of the alphabet?	Which letter comes between M and O?
Which letter comes between A and C?	Which letter comes after N?
Which letter comes before D?	Which letter comes before Q?
Which letter comes after B and C?	Which letter comes between P and R?
Which letter comes between D and F?	Which letter comes after O, P, and Q?
Which letter comes before G?	Which letter comes before T?
Which letter comes after D, E, F?	Which letter comes between S and U?
Which letter comes between G and I?	Which letter comes before V, W, X, Y, and Z?
Which letter comes before J and K?	Which letter comes after T and U?
Which letter comes after I?	Which letter comes between V and X?
Which letter comes between J and L?	Which letter comes before Y and Z?
Which letter comes before M, N, and O?	Which letter comes after U, V, W, and X?

A B C D E F G H I J K L M

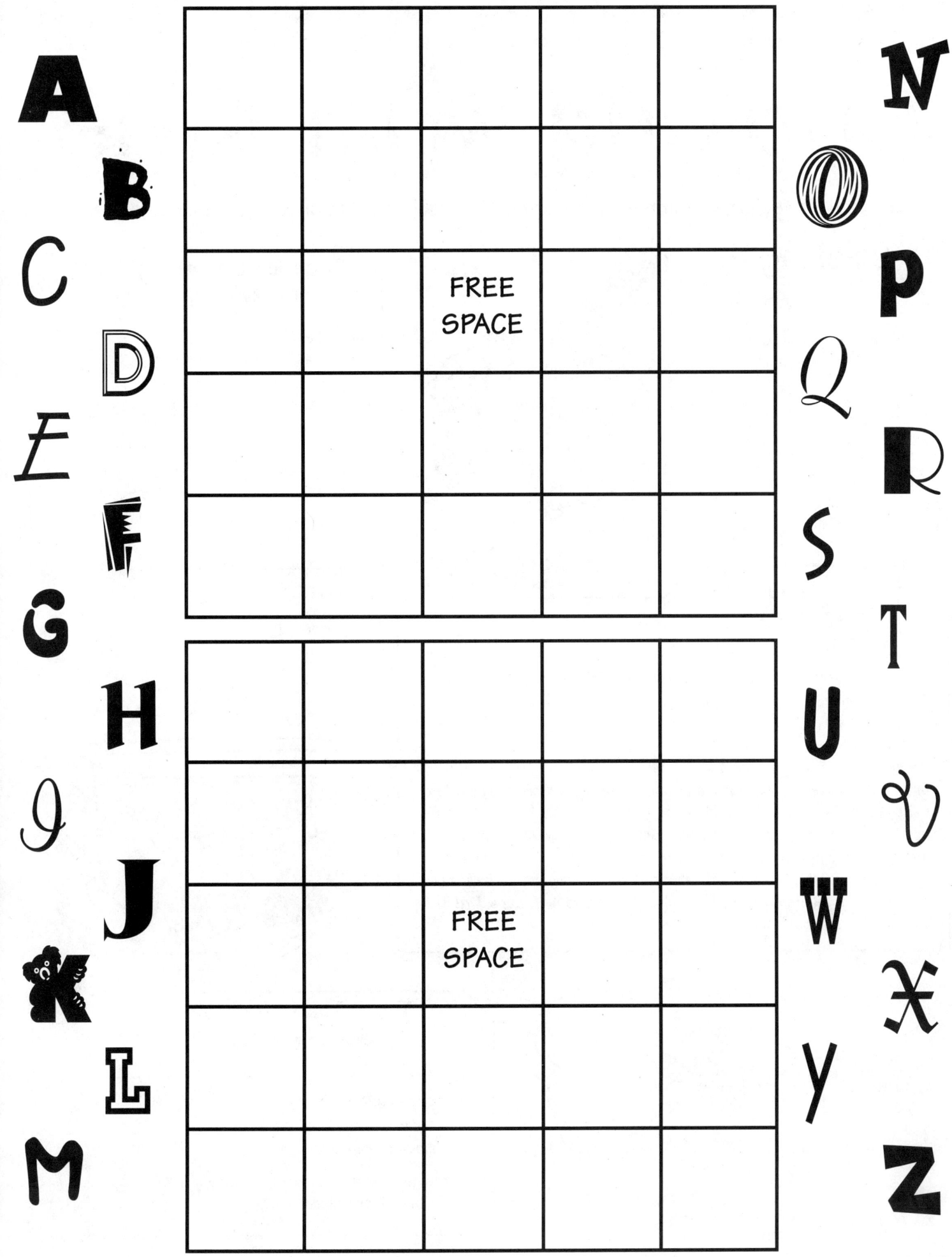

N O P Q R S T U V W X Y Z

		FREE SPACE		

		FREE SPACE		

Cooking with Kids

Celebrate the end of summer and beginning of fall with super recipes for special days.

Cooking to Learn

Mix a quarter cup of science
With a half a cup of math,
Add a quarter cup of language
And then color, just a dash.

Stir it up, and pour it out,
Then bake until it's done.
Hands-on learning
Is our recipe for fun.

Friendship Pudding
Friendship Day

Ingredients
- 2 soft, ripe bananas
- 1/2 cup applesauce
- 2 tablespoons peanut butter
- 2 tablespoons honey

Cut and mash the bananas until smooth. Stir in the applesauce, peanut butter, and honey. Beat with a wire whisk until smooth. Chill and enjoy.

Minty Orange Tea
Grandparents' Day

Ingredients
- 6 oranges
- 1 lemon
- 1 1/2 quarts water
- 1/2 cup dried mint leaves
- orange and lemon rind
- gauze and string

Squeeze the juice from the oranges and lemon. Place the juice in a large pot. Add the water. Grate the citrus peels and crush the dried mint leaves. Place the citrus rind and the mint leaves into a piece of gauze, form a sack, and secure the sack with string. Drop the sack into the liquid in the pot. Stir the liquid and heat to boiling. Reduce the heat and simmer about 15 minutes. Cool slightly before serving. Add honey, if desired. Note: This recipe makes about 12 cups. Dried mint leaves can be found at a health food store.

Tasty Toast Topping
Grandparents' Day

Ingredients
- 1 cup sugar
- 1 tablespoon grated orange rind
- 1/2 cup orange juice

Thoroughly mix all of the ingredients together. Spread on toast, bread, or crackers.

by Marie E. Cecchini

Candied Nuts
Sweetest Day is in October

Ingredients
- 1 cup shelled nuts (your choice)
- 4 tablespoons sugar
- 4 tablespoons honey

Mix all of the ingredients together. Stir well to completely coat the nuts with the sugar/honey mixture. Spread the mixture out on a cookie sheet. Bake at 350° for about 10 minutes. Carefully transfer the hot, candied nuts to waxed paper and cool. Eat them warm, or refrigerate them to eat chilled.

Festive Autumn Rice
First day of autumn is in September

Ingredients
- 1 1/2 cup quick-cook rice
- 1 1/2 cup water
- 1 box frozen, mixed vegetables

Prepare the rice and vegetables as per package directions. Add the cooked vegetables to the prepared rice and stir. Mix in butter or margarine, if desired. Sprinkle with paprika and curry powder for added color. Serve warm.

Orange Yogurt Pops
Halloween Fun

Ingredients
- 1 quart vanilla yogurt
- 1 large can frozen orange juice
- 1 tablespoon vanilla
- 1/4 cup honey

Mix the yogurt with the orange juice. Add the vanilla and honey. Mix well and pour into small paper cups. Add a craft stick to each cup. Freeze. To serve, run the pops under hot tap water until they loosen from the cups.

Mini Cereal Cakes
Halloween Fun

Ingredients
- 2/3 cup butter or margarine
- 1/3 cup golden corn syrup
- 1 cup sunflower seeds or chopped nuts
- 2/3 cup raisin bran cereal, slightly crushed
- orange food coloring

Melt the butter and corn syrup in a saucepan over low heat. Add several drops of food coloring. Remove the pan from the heat. Stir in the cereal and the seeds or nuts. Mix well. Spoon out onto waxed paper, cool, and serve.

Holiday Wind Sock

1. Measure and cut 1/2" x 6" strips from different colors of construction paper or fabric. Cut three 1 1/2" x 6" strips from three different colors of paper or fabric.

2. Staple, glue, or tape the narrow strips to the bottom of a 4" x 1/2" toilet tissue tube so that they hang down, alternating colors about 1/2" apart.

3. Glue or tape the 1 1/2" x 6" strips around the tube.

4. Using a hole punch, make three holes at top of tube, spaced evenly apart.

5. Cut three 12" pieces of yarn, ribbon, or string and tie one to each hole.

6. Join strings at top in knot.

7. Hang where the breeze blows.

8. Decorate with stickers or cut-outs for the holidays.

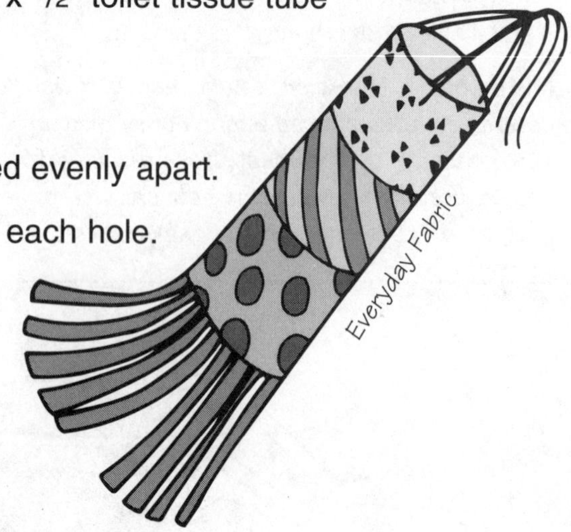

(Put gummed stars on a red, white, and blue mini wind sock for the Fourth of July; pumpkins on a yellow, orange, and black one for Halloween; hearts on a pink, white, and red one for Valentine's Day; shamrocks on a green and white one for St. Patrick's and so on.)

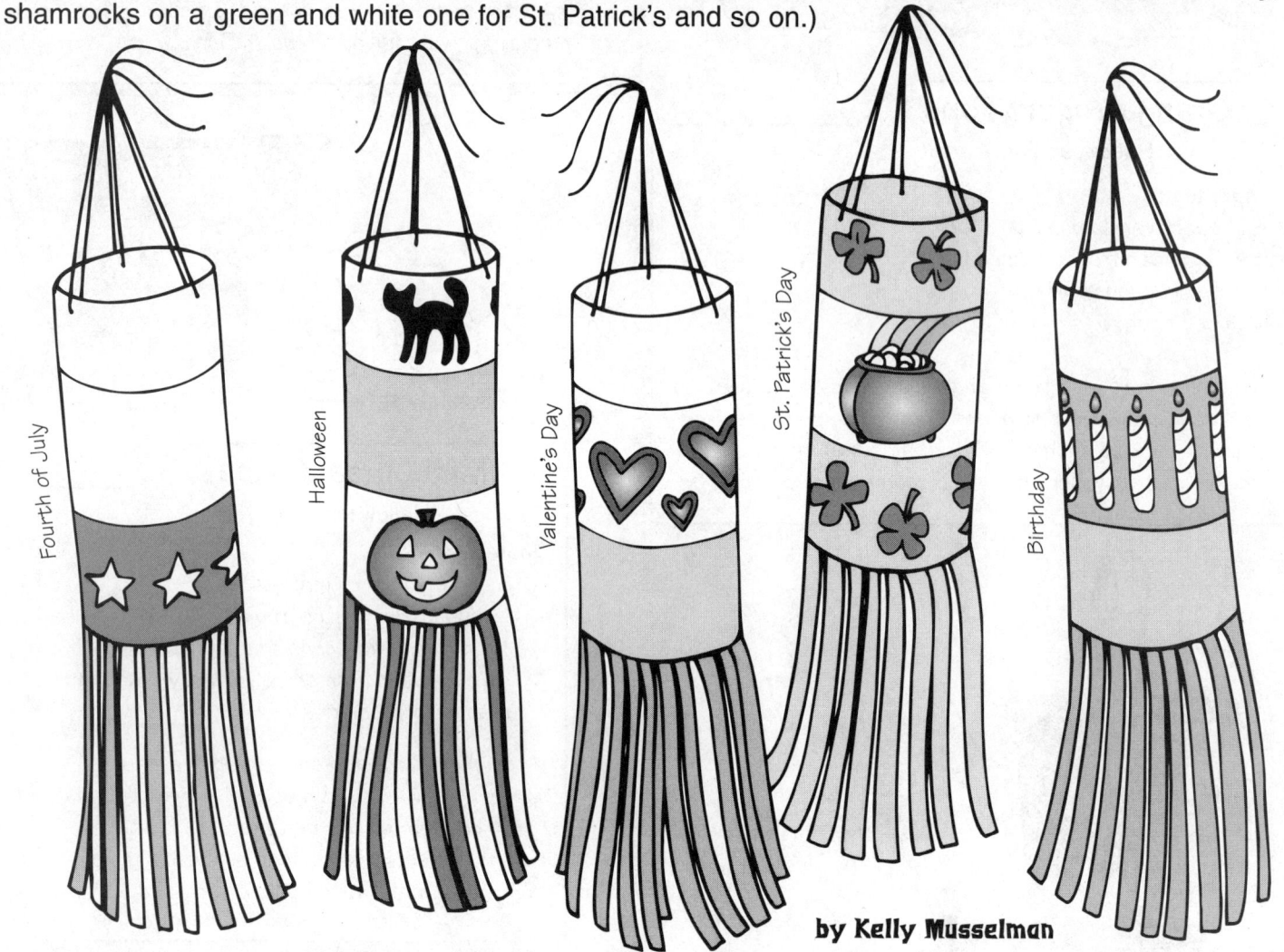

by Kelly Musselman

Countdown to Halloween

Here are lots of ways to keep your monsters at bay, as they wait so impatiently for Halloween day.

Abracadabra

Provide the children with white paper and white crayons. Have them draw several ghosts. Next, supply them with dark watercolor paints, and tell them to paint over the entire page. Talk about why the paint does not adhere to the crayon.
Note: Pictures can also be painted over with a diluted tempera paint wash.

Molded Pumpkin Snack

For this activity, you will need to cube or slice 8 ounces of cream cheese and 16 ounces of American cheese. Let the cheeses stand at room temperature until softened, then blend them together. Let the children shape them into small balls, then add a green pepper to the top for a stem.

No Bones About It

Display a jointed skeleton decoration. Have the children find the main body parts (arms, legs, chest, and so on). Invite individual students to count the number of bones in the leg, rib cage, hand and so on. Have them feel their own hands and legs for their bones. Can they find their rib cages?

Stand-Up Jack-O'-Lantern

Help the children fold a 9" x 12" sheet of orange paper into three equal sections. Show them how to hold the folded paper together as they use scissors to round off each of the four corners. Have them unfold their papers and help them tape the 9" ends of these papers together. Show them how to sit one flat side of their three-fold papers on the table to form a stand-up pumpkin. Provide them with glue, scrap paper, and scissors for adding the facial features.

Bobbing Bands Hats

Cut a poster board strip for each child. The strips should be about 2" wide. Punch three vertical pairs of holes around each band. Provide the children with paper, scissors, and markers, and allow them to create three Halloween cut-outs, no taller than 4". They may choose to make monsters, ghosts, jack-o'-lanterns, and so on. Let them tape each of their cut-outs to a pipe cleaner. Help them thread each pipe cleaner through one vertical pair of holes in their bands. Reinforce the pipe cleaners with tape. Fit and staple each child's band. Provide a mirror so children can watch their Halloween critters bob as they move their heads.

by Marie E. Cecchini

Bat Puppets

Ask each child to bring in an old, dark-colored sock. Let the children glue on button eyes, white paper-snip fangs, and black triangle ears. Sticking a piece of waxed paper in the sock before gluing will help avoid the glue soaking through. Allow to dry. Then let children design and cut bat wings from black paper to glue to the backs of their bats. Allow to dry completely, then remove the waxed paper so the children can slide their hands in and let their bats take flight.

Pumpkin Seed Math

Prepare 6" x 12" strips of paper equipped with several pumpkin shapes. Write a different numeral on the stem of each pumpkin. Provide each child with a strip of pumpkins, glue, and a container of pumpkin seeds. Have children read the numeral on each stem, then glue the corresponding number of seeds onto each pumpkin shape.

Halloween Reading Fun

By the Light of the Halloween Moon by Caroline Stutson, Lothrop, Lee, and Shepard.

Go Away, Big Green Monster by Ed Emberley, Little Brown.

Humbug Witch by Lorna Balian, Abingdon Press.

Making Friends with Frankenstein: A Book of Monstrous Poems and Pictures. Candlewick Press.

Proud Pumpkin by Nora S. Unwin, E.P. Dutton and Co.

The Witch's Hat by Tony Johnson, G.P. Putnam and Sons.

Trick or Treat?

Fill a bag or basket with pretend Halloween treats, such as trinkets, sweets, and fruit. Prepare a bar graph that labels these categories. Invite individual students to remove one item from the bag, name the object, then place a Halloween sticker in the corresponding column of the bar graph. Tabulate and compare the results. This would be a good time to discuss Halloween snacking safety.

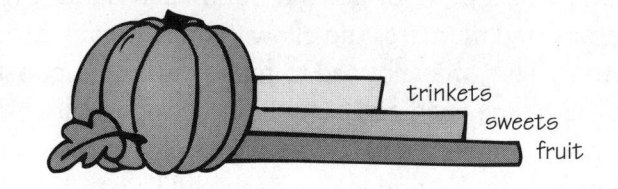

68

TLC10110 Copyright © Teaching & Learning Company, Carthage, IL 62321-0010

Guess Who?

Provide each child with a 12" x 18" sheet of paper, markers, and scissors. Fold the paper in half, to open like a book, then draw a picture of a door on the front. Cut along three lines of the doors so it will open. Have children think of characters they might see when they open the door on Halloween night. Let them unfold their papers and draw these characters inside. When the drawings are complete, have them refold their papers. Knock, knock. Who's there?

Invisible Ghosts

Have each child bend a 6" piece of pipe cleaner into a ghost shape. Tie a strand of yarn, string, or dental floss to the top of each ghost shape for hanging. Lay the ghost shapes flat on waxed paper and help the children fill the center of their shapes with glue. Let them drop hole-punch eyes and a mouth into the wet glue. Allow to dry thoroughly, then carefully peel them off of the waxed paper to make invisible, hanging ghosts.

Pumpkin Toss

This game can be played independently or by dividing the class into teams. You will need a large plastic jack-o'-lantern and several beanbags. Have the children take turns tossing the beanbags into the jack-o'-lantern from an established standing line.

Body Masks

Provide the children with large sheets of tagboard, scissors, markers, glue, and assorted "cast-offs," such as cardboard tubes, scrap paper, bits of fabric and foil, yarn pieces, odd buttons, and so on. Have them cut large shapes from the tagboard, then use their markers, glue, and other materials to create giant masks. These masks can be used for dramatic play or hung on a wall as Halloween posters.

Midnight Paintings

Provide the children with white paper, black tempera, paintbrushes, plastic forks, and combs. Have them brush a thick coat of black paint over the white paper, then show them how to pull the fork and comb through the paint to form spooky Halloween squiggle pictures.

FALL BOOK Sensations

Celebrate the fall season with *The Pumpkin Patch*, story and photographs by Elizabeth King (Dutton Children's Books, 1990). The appealing color photographs and interesting text will give your students a firsthand look at the growth and development of pumpkins.

Delight your class with the seasonal poems in *Who Said Boo? Halloween Poems for the Very Young* by Nancy White Carlstrom (Simon & Schuster Books for Young Readers, 1995). The colorful watercolor illustrations and the lively verse add up to a real holiday kid-pleaser! After sharing the poems with your students, have them create their own Halloween poems.

by Mary Ellen Switzer

The Best Halloween of All

by Susan Wojciechowski
New York: Crown Publishers, 1992

Ben recalls all of the past Halloween costumes that his parents made him wear, especially the embarrassing year he appeared as a bunch of grapes. When he decides to make his own costume this Halloween, he ends up with the best costume of all!

- Draw a picture of your favorite Halloween costume. Write two sentences describing it.

- Wow, what a costume! Ben made an intergalactic robotron costume for Halloween. Draw a picture of what his costume may have looked like.

- Blast-off! Write a story about the space adventure of an intergalactic robotron.

The Hallo-Wiener

by Dav Pilkey
New York: The Blue Sky Press, 1995

Everyone makes fun of Oscar the dachshund, especially when his mother dresses him up as a hot dog for Halloween. Oscar becomes a brave "hero sandwich" when he rescues some dogs from a monster on the loose!

- Pretend that Oscar was your pet. How would you dress him for Halloween? Draw a picture of the costume.

- Create a trophy to honor the Hallo-Wiener "hero."

- Be an author! Write a story about another Halloween hero. Use these words to help you in your story: *Halloween*, *haunted house*, *children*, *scared*, and *rescue*.

The Great Leaf Blast-Off

by John Himmelman
New Jersey: Silver Press, 1990

Ever wonder what to do with all those fall leaves scattered in your yard? Meet the "Fix-it Family"—Orville and Willa Wright and their children Alexander, Graham, and Belle. These bright inventors are determined to create new leaf-raking machines to make their lives easier. Will their machines work?

- Do you think the Wright family members were good inventors? Tell why.

- Be an inventor! Create a robot that can rake leaves in just minutes. Draw a picture of your amazing invention. Label the parts.

- Hear all about it! Think of a catchy name for your new robot. Write a radio commercial about this useful invention.

A Halloween Happening

by Adrienne Adams
New York: Charles Scribner's Sons, 1981

You are cordially invited to a very special Halloween party given by a group of friendly witches. Join a group of happy children as they attend an unforgettable holiday event, including a ride in a bat-wing glider.

- The children enjoyed flying high in the bat-wing gliders at the Halloween happening. Draw a picture of what the bat gliders looked like.

- Go batty over bats! Did you know that there are around 1,000 different kinds of bats in the world? Read *Bats, Creatures of the Night* by Joyce Milton (Grosset & Dunlap, 1993) to find out more about bats. Create a poster report with pictures and facts about this remarkable animal.

The Real-Skin Rubber Monster Mask

by Miriam Cohen, illustrated by Lillian Hoban
New York: Greenwillow Books, 1990

While trick-or-treating, Jim decides that his monster mask is just a little too scary after he sees his reflection in some big glass doors. A friend comes to his rescue with the perfect plan—he shares part of his Halloween costume with Jim.

- Draw a large picture of a trick-or-treat bag. On the inside of the bag write at least four tips for having a safe Halloween. Decorate the rest of the bag with Halloween designs.

- Congratulations! You have just won first prize for the scariest Halloween costume. Draw a picture of what your costume looks like.

- Write a story telling how you won this award.

Henry and Mudge Under the Yellow Moon

by Cynthia Rylant
New York: Bradbury Press, 1987

Hooray for autumn! Henry and his big dog Mudge enjoy the fall season together, especially playing in the colorful leaves. When Halloween arrives, Henry discovers that listening to spooky noises seems better with his friend Mudge beside him!

- Draw a picture of one of the things Henry and his dog Mudge enjoyed doing in autumn.

- Write three doggone good tips you would give to a dog owner on caring for a pet.

- Extra! Extra! Read all about it! Pretend you have the biggest pet in the world. Write a news story telling all about this amazing pet. Include a "news photo" picture.

Jeffrey's Halloween Costume

It was time for Halloween.
Now what should Jeffrey be?
Costumes hung around the store
As far as he could see.

Pirates, pilots, goblins, ghosts,
Astronauts, and kings,
Monkeys, mice, and elephants,
And lots of other things!

"No, I want a costume
There's just one of," Jeffrey said.
"And so I think that I will go
Dressed up as ME instead!"

by Bonnie Compton Hanson

My Pumpkin-Headed Pal

My jack-o'-lantern has no hands.
He has no legs or feet.
He sits there on our windowsill
And smiles at all the street.
He's just a pumpkin-head, I know,
With quite a silly name.
But trick-or-treaters smile right back,
And love him just the same.

by Bonnie Compton Hanson

Halloween Is Coming

(Tune: "Skip to My Lou")

Halloween is coming.
The family's having fun
Carving up the pumpkins.
There's one for everyone.
Children in their costumes,
Marching down the streets,
Ringing all the doorbells,
And doing tricks for treats.

by Sylvia Watson

A Switch for a Witch

Winnie the Witch was sorry and blue;
Her magical broomstick was broken in two.
Halloween is coming—what'll she do?
The kiddies would miss hearing her "Boo!"

She went to the doctor who lived down the lane.
"I cannot cure it!" he was quick to explain.
Next Winnie asked a plumber named Crane,
But he was an expert at fixing a drain!

"A carpenter might be the one I should see."
So Winnie the Witch asked two or three,
But they all shook their heads, sad as can be;
Fixing up houses was their specialty!

To the garage Winnie next went.
She wouldn't give up—she was intent!
The friendly mechanics knew what she meant,
But all they could fix was a bad fender dent!

"The time's running out!" poor Winnie did cry.
"Just how can I go on my Halloween fly?"
Then all at once she said, "My, oh, my!"
"I just now remembered someone I could try!"

Winnie the Witch picked up her phone,
Called Santa Claus, a fellow she'd known.
"Please, could I use the sleigh that you own?"
Kind Santa agreed; it was ready to loan!

'Til Halloween night Winnie hardly could wait.
She climbed in the sleigh along about eight.
Her broomstick, forgotten, was left by the gate.
Said Winnie the Witch, "A sleigh ride is great!"

So off she sped 'neath the stars all so bright.
To the people below she gave quite a fright.
She cackled and crowed as she rode out of sight
"To one and all . . . Happy Halloween night!"

by Norma T. Balding

Holiday Sing-Alongs

by Mabel Duch

Let's Go to the Pumpkin Patch

This song is sung to the tune of "London Bridge Is Falling Down."

Let's go to the pumpkin patch,
Pumpkin patch, pumpkin patch.
Let's go to the pumpkin patch.
It's October!

We need a pumpkin, big and round,
Big and round, big and round.
We need a pumpkin, big and round.
It's October!

A jack-o'-lantern we will make,
We will make, we will make.
A jack-o'-lantern we will make.
It's October!

Let's give him a great big grin,
Great big grin, great big grin.
Let's give him a great big grin.
It's October!

We'll set him on our windowsill,
Windowsill, windowsill.
We'll set him on our windowsill.
It's October!

When you come to "Trick or Treat,"
"Trick or Treat," "Trick or Treat."
When you come to "Trick or Treat,"
He will smile at you.

His smile will say, "You're welcome here,
Welcome here, welcome here."
His smile will say, "You're welcome here.
Happy Halloween!"

Note

You may change *windowsill* in the song to wherever you will place your classroom jack-o'-lantern.

Discussion

When picking out a pumpkin for a jack-o'-lantern, what should we consider?
1. Color—a uniform bright orange.
2. Size—large, but not too large for the area where you will place it and not too heavy to carry easily.
3. Shape—nicely rounded, but one side can be slightly flattened for a face.

Activities

Take a field trip to a pumpkin farm. Arrange ahead of time for the proprietor to talk to the children about how pumpkins are raised, and let them see the pumpkins growing on the vines.

With the children's input, choose a pumpkin for your classroom jack-o'-lantern.

When back in the classroom, let each child draw a picture of what he or she thinks the jack-o'-lantern should look like. Suggest a happy jack-o'-lantern to go with the song.

Number the pictures. Write corresponding numbers on slips of paper. Fold them and place in a sack. Ask another adult to shake them up and pull one out. Use the picture with that number as your guide when carving the jack-o'-lantern.

After you remove the jack-o'-lantern's lid, let the children help scoop out the pulp.

The children can make their own small jack-o'-lanterns using orange gourds and orange and black adhesive-backed plastic tape.

Cut triangles, squares, circles, ovals, and rectangles from the tape. Place them on sheets of waxed paper for the children to peel off and use as facial features on their miniature jack-o'-lanterns.

Serve roasted pumpkin seeds and an orange drink as a Happy Halloween treat.

What a surprise!
Oh, what a fright!
And it all happened

One Halloween Night

The wicked witch
Hopped on her broom.
She cackled aloud
Then flew from the room.

The old black cat
Gave one big yawn.
He opened his eyes
And sang until dawn.

The blinking owl
Didn't stop to stare.
He gave a great hoot
And flew through the air.

The very black bat
Drank bright green brew.
He flew from the cave
And shouted, "Yahoo!"

The scary ghost
Began to mew.
Then he remembered
He better say, "Boo!"

Jack-o'-lantern
Just winked and smiled.
"How GREAT to be out
On a night so wild!"

What a surprise!
Oh, what a fright!
And it all happened
One Halloween Night.

by Patricia O'Brien

One Halloween Night

The verse introduces a large cast of Halloween characters. Seasonal activities are suggested to augment the theme. Opportunities are presented to practice listening and speaking skills. Art activities are designed to extend the theme and provide creative experiences. Write the verse on chart paper. Read the poem aloud, pointing out the words while the children follow.

Stick Puppet

Materials: templates, tagboard, craft sticks, glue, crayons, felt-tipped pens

Procedure
1. Select one character to copy.
2. Trace and color the figure.
3. Glue to a piece of tagboard and cut out.
4. Attach a craft stick to the base of the figure.

The puppets may be used
- to enhance a choral reading presentation.
- to focus a creative dramatics activity.
- to promote oral language as students create dialogue between two puppets.
- to present an original puppet play.

Mobile

Materials: templates, heavy paper, 1" x 18" construction paper, yarn, glue, scissors, stapler

Procedure
1. Trace the figures on heavy paper or tagboard.
2. Draw in the features and color the figures.
3. Cut out.
4. Staple or glue a length of yarn to the top of each shape. Attach the other ends along the 18" x 1" strip of construction paper.
5. Staple the ends of the strip together to form a ring. Staple four lengths of yarn evenly spaced along the band. Tie the ends together and hang the mobile.

Additional Activities

1. Plan a class shape book featuring pumpkins, owls, bats, or cats.
   a. Enlarge the Halloween figures on a copy machine or use an overhead projector.
   b. Share information about the subject using books, pictures, and film.
   c. Listen to student ideas about the subject and revise any discrepancies.
   d. Each student may then complete one page, contributing what he or she thinks is important to include regarding the theme.

Bulletin Board

1. Trace the figures on black construction paper using a white crayon. Cut eyes from brightly colored construction paper. Arrange the figures on a bulletin board in and around a large haunted house to create a seasonal mural.

2. The mural may be used for counting activities. How many pumpkins do you see? Are there more owls or bats? Have the students think of additional questions to ask their classmates.

Something to Talk About

1. After the children have listened to the verse, discuss what happened one Halloween night.
   a. What did the characters do on a night so wild?
   b. To what places might the witch, owl, and bat fly?
   c. What do you think they could have seen along the way?
2. Describe one of the Halloween characters. How did it look and sound?
3. Take turns relating adventures they could have had.

Something to Do

1. Chant the poem chorally with the children.
2. Find the pair of words that rhyme in each stanza. Work together to think of additional rhyming words. Using the list, write more lines to add to the verse.
3. Divide the class into groups to prepare for a choral-speaking presentation. Have each group memorize the refrain and one other stanza. Emphasize speaking in unison and oral expression. Recite the poem together with everyone joining in the chorus.
4. Direct the students to select one of the following activities to complete.
   a. Fold a sheet of paper into four parts. Choose one Halloween character to draw in each section.
   b. Select one stanza to copy and illustrate.
   c. Draw a picture to show what happened on Halloween night.

Patterns for One Halloween Night

77

BATHTIME
for Little Ghosts

There were three little ghosts
Sitting on posts,
Eating cinnamon toast
'Cause they like it the most.

Crunch, crunch, crunch.
They eat a whole bunch,
Especially at lunch
With lemon-lime punch.

Oh, but what's this?

You can't trick-or-treat
With cinnamon on your sheet!
So "into the washer" said I
"and out on the clothesline
to dry!"

This is a cute poem that beginners will have fun learning to read. It is especially enjoyable when presented with little ghosts who can stand up on posts and then be shaken out to dry. Here's how to do it. Cut three small squares out of an old white T-shirt (100% cotton works well). Using thumb and index finger, pinch one up in the middle to form a ghost. He should stand by himself unless the square is too big. You'll be able to see where the face should be, so go ahead and give him one.

The other necessary props, fence post and a clothesline, can be one piece. Find a small box like a cereal or shoe box. Lay it flat and decorate one edge like a fence. A piece of wire or perhaps a wire hanger can be used for the clothesline. Bend it to fit the size of your box and tape it at the ends. The ghosts can then sit on the fence posts and later be hung over the clothesline like sheets. (If desired, cinnamon toast could be cut from a sheet of sandpaper or brown paper with cinnamon and sugar glued on it. Use tape to let your ghosts hold it.)

by Sheila M. Hausbeck

Ready! Set! Go! Read!

CELEBRATE National Book Week

Literature and good books are part of every school day. However during National Book Week, add special interest areas to encourage reading and listening. Use these activities to help students make reading a lifelong adventure.

Student/Teacher Activities

1. Teach young children the correct way to handle a book. As you turn pages carefully, talk about books being our "friends." Treated with care, books will last a long time. Then others will enjoy them, too. Point out the following:
   - front cover
   - pages
   - author's name and illustrator's name
   - back cover

   Riddles help teach and make learning fun. Use these or make up some of your own:
   a. I'm strong and protect the pages. What am I? (the cover)
   b. My name is on the front cover. I wrote the book. (author)
   c. I'm important, too. I drew the pictures. (illustrator)
   d. If you count me, you know how long the book is. (pages)

2. Bulletin Board — "Books Open the Door to Learning"
   Cover a bulletin board with newspapers. Check with your local library or area bookstores for a variety of newspapers from major cities, or ask parents to contribute newspapers. Overlap and place the front page with the paper's name at various angles to cover the board. Cut out the caption in large red letters. Pin book jackets to the board to complete the theme. Choose selections that represent various cultures. Place a globe on a table in front of the board. Emphasize that books open the door to learning about the world.

by Carolyn Ross Tomlin

3. Use book jackets with bright colors to highlight the hall leading to your room. Place them at eye level for young children.

4. Follow the Footprints Using bright-colored construction paper, trace around children's feet and cut out footprints. Students can write titles and authors of favorite books they have read on the footprints. Laminate for durability. Tape these from the front door of your school to your room. Tape additional footprints on the floor of your classroom.

5. Meet the Author Check with a large bookstore in your area for dates that an author will be present for a book signing. Invite the author to visit your classroom or school. Hopefully, a children's author or illustrator will be available.

6. Classroom Author and Illustrator Day Children's favorite books are often the ones they write themselves. Give each child two pages of typing paper. Cut them in half, then fold them to make a book of eight pages. Staple together. Print on the board *My First Book* for students to copy. Point out the spot for them to write their names as authors. Suggest the following pictures and words:

    page 1: personal portrait
    page 2: my house
    page 3: my family
    page 4: my friends
    page 5: my pet
    page 6: my toys
    page 7: foods I like
    page 8: what I do best

Make copies for each student. Let each student autograph his or her own creation. Serve cookies and punch for a special party.

7. My Favorite Character Day Read aloud to students throughout the day. Encourage students to dress the part of a favorite character. Send a note home for parents. Even a hat, scarf, walking cane, or other object will give a clue to their selection.

8. **Caldecott and Newbery Awards** Designate a special table or shelf to recognize winners of the Caldecott Medal and Newbery Medal. Include some older books as well as newer selections.

9. Encourage parents to sign up their youngster for a library card. This teaches children responsibility and introduces them to the wonderful world found in the library.

10. **Celebrate National Book Week** Focus on a different author and book each day. Set the stage by dressing in costume or bringing in props to go along with the daily selection. The following books are among the top 20 all-time-best-selling hardcover children's books. You may use these selections or choose other favorites.

The Pokey Little Puppy by Janette Sebring Lowrey (Golden, 1942); 14,000,000 copies. Supply chenille stems to create "puppies." Talk about other words that mean the same as *pokey*. Ask children to walk in a pokey way; then to skip, to run and to crawl.

The Tale of Peter Rabbit by Beatrix Potter (Frederick Warne, 1902); 9,331,266. Display several books written by Beatrix Potter. Point out the beautiful watercolor drawings in her original works. Ask students to bring a toy rabbit or other animal for show and tell.

Green Eggs and Ham by Dr. Seuss (Random House, 1957); 6,065,197. Collect several Dr. Seuss books to share with children. Plan to cook scrambled eggs with green food coloring after reading the book.

The Giving Tree by Shel Silverstein (HarperCollins, 1964); 4,075,925. Take an outdoor walk near your school. Point out the different trees. Invite students to share why trees are important in their life.

The Real Mother Goose illustrated by Blanche F. Wright (Rand McNally, 1916); 3,600,000 (as of 1989). Dress in a cape and long dress, and tuck a toy goose under your arm. Read selections throughout the day.

THE GREAT TURKEY RUMPUS

Let your students express themselves through free, creative movement as they act out this turkey dance.

Divide the class into black, white and brown turkeys. Have each student cut out several feathers in the color that matches their group. Make headbands using a piece of tagboard two inches wide, and long enough to fit around the students' heads with some overlap. Staple the overlapped edges so the band fits snugly. Staple the feathers to the back of the headband.

First, read the story to the class one time so the students become familiar with the words and actions. Explain that when you read the story again, they are to follow the directions in the story and be creative in their movements.

The Great Turkey Rumpus

One dark night at the turkey farm, a strange thing happened.

The black turkeys started to move slowly, and to gobble, gobble very softly. Then they stopped!

The white turkeys started to move slowly, and to gobble, gobble very softly. Then they stopped!

The brown turkeys started to move slowly, and to gobble, gobble very softly. Then they stopped!

All was quiet. Then slowly the black turkeys, the white turkeys and the brown turkeys began to move about. Back and forth, side to side, around and around they went. They gobbled and they gobbled.

Then the great turkey rumpus began! Faster and faster the turkeys moved. They gobbled and they gobbled as they moved this way and that way, this way and that way.

"Stop!" yelled the farmer from the upstairs window. "Stop that rumpus!"

The turkeys froze! The farmer went back to bed. The turkeys quietly tiptoed into the turkey barn. They shook their feathers, settled down and went to sleep with big smiles on their happy turkey faces.

by Jean Stangl

The turkey is a large fowl (bird) belonging to the Meleagrididae family. Distinct features are the turkey's large, bright tail of feathers and the folds of skin along the sides of the head and neck known as the wattles. The wattles range from a pink color to a full red when the turkey is excited. The male turkey is called a tom or gobbler, and the female is called a hen.

There are two living species of turkey. Both are native to North and Central America. The common turkey (meleagris gallopavo) is the source of all domesticated turkeys. It is one of the largest American birds, reaching a length of about four feet. Wild turkeys live in open forests. They feed on seeds, nuts and berries and roost up in the trees at night. They live together in flocks and do not migrate. They can fly but only for short distances. The female hens build nests on the ground and lay anywhere from 8 to 15 spotted eggs. These hatch in one month's time. The young are called poults.

The turkey is a symbolic part of Thanksgiving. On the following pages, you will find turkey activities that go across the curriculum. Try these in your classroom.

Let's Talk Turkey

TURKEY MASK

Bend a wire clothes hanger into a circle, leaving the hook at the bottom for a handle. Cover the entire circle with a sheer nylon stocking. Cut out eyes, beak, wattles, feet and feathers from felt or construction paper. Glue these onto the stocking mask. The feathers stand better if they are made from construction paper. This is a great mask for small children because they are able to see through the nylon stocking.

THE TRADITIONAL HAND TURKEY

There are two traditional forms of hand-turkey art: the crayon drawing and the painted hand. Lay the child's hand on paper. Spread the fingers and trace around the hand with a crayon. Brightly color the outlined fingers for tail feathers, color the thumb for the head. Draw legs below the outline of the palm. Don't forget eyes, beak and wattles.

Have the children paint their fingers and palm brown and their thumb red using tempera paints. Press the hand down onto paper to make a "turkey print." After the paint dries, add the facial features and legs with markers or crayons.

by Tania K. Cowling

TURKEY BULLETIN BOARD

In preparation for this board, take the children on a nature walk around the school to collect colorful fall leaves. Draw and cut out a large turkey shape to be placed on the bulletin board. Glue or staple the autumn leaves onto the board to form the turkey's tail feathers.

Variation: Trace the students' hands, color and cut them out. Attach them to the bulletin board to form the tail.

TURKEY FIELD TRIP

This would be a good time to visit a turkey farm, if possible. The children can observe the behavior of turkeys and the foods they consume. If a farm is not close by, try visiting the library for an informative film on the fowl.

MATCHING FEATHERS

Make a large turkey shape and attach it to the wall or a bulletin board. Make tail feathers from wallpaper scraps. Cut two feathers from each wallpaper pattern. Place one onto the turkey shape and another into a box for a matching activity. Invite children to pick a feather from the box and then match it to the corresponding tail feather on the turkey shape.

TURKEY KEEPER (GAME)

You will need a small plastic turkey or one cut from cardboard. Instruct one child to cover his or her eyes. The teacher quietly hides the turkey in the classroom. Tell the child to open his eyes and search for the turkey. The rest of the class can help with clues. As the child gets closer to where the turkey is hidden, the class says, "gobble, gobble" faster and faster. If the child is far away from the turkey, make the gobble sounds very slowly. Once the turkey is found, another child becomes the turkey keeper.

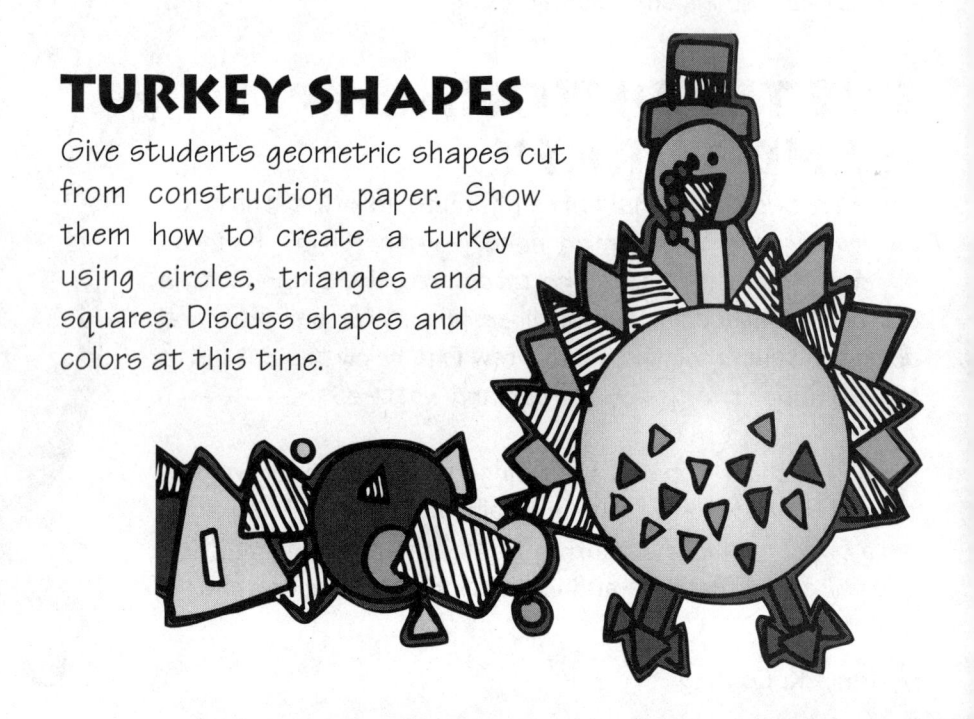

TURKEY SHAPES

Give students geometric shapes cut from construction paper. Show them how to create a turkey using circles, triangles and squares. Discuss shapes and colors at this time.

DROP THE WISHBONE

Have the children sit in a circle. Choose one child to walk around the outside of the circle, carrying a wishbone (either a real one or one cut from cardboard). The walker is instructed to drop the wishbone behind one of the other children. The child who has the wishbone dropped behind him must pick it up and chase the first child until the first child finds the empty spot in the circle formation. If he is tagged by the runner before he sits, he is "it" again. If not, the second child becomes "it" and starts the game again. This is a variation of the traditional game Duck, Duck, Goose.

TURKEY BASTER FUN

Place two bowls on a table. Fill one with water and use the turkey baster to transfer water from one bowl to the other. Add a few drops of food coloring and fill one bowl halfway with red water and the other bowl with yellow water. As you keep transferring the water, eventually it will turn orange, a harvest color of Thanksgiving.

TURKEY TEACHER

Take a paper plate and divide the circle into pie sections. Write a color word in each slice. Use spring-type clothespins as your game pieces. Color one clothespin to match each color word. Cut a small turkey face from construction paper and glue this in the center of the plate. Have the children match the color and its word by attaching the clothespins to the plate. **Note:** You could also make plates teaching skills like uppercase/lowercase letters, numerals/dots/number words and so on.

FEATHER PAINTING

Draw a turkey shape on construction paper. Dip a real feather into tempera paint and press down to make feather prints. Arrange these prints to create a turkey tail fan.

TURKEY TROT

Place a trail of turkey footprints around the classroom, using pieces of masking tape. Have the students follow the trail around the classroom, stepping onto the footprints. Add music for fun and do the "turkey trot."

EDIBLE APPLE TURKEY

Insert toothpicks into an apple to create tail feathers. Have the children fill the toothpicks with goodies such as raisins, colored miniature marshmallows, chunks of cheese and so on. Draw a turkey head and cut it from cardboard. Have children color the facial features; then have the teacher make a small slit in the apple with a knife to insert the head inside.

MOVE LIKE A TURKEY

Show the children how to bend down and waddle like a turkey. As you sing the song below, give directions for the children to dramatize.

Act like a: fast turkey, slow turkey, happy turkey, proud turkey, sad turkey.

To the tune of: "Here We Go 'Round the Mulberry Bush"

Here we go 'round the turkey trail,
Turkey trail, turkey trail.
Here we go 'round the turkey trail,
To celebrate Thanksgiving Day!

Turkey Salad

Ingredients
- 2 cups chopped cooked turkey
- 2 T. mayonnaise
- 1 T. pickle relish
- 1/8 cup finely chopped celery

Mix ingredients together and serve on toast or crackers. Note: You will need to adjust the recipe according to the size of the class.

TURKEY Patterns

87

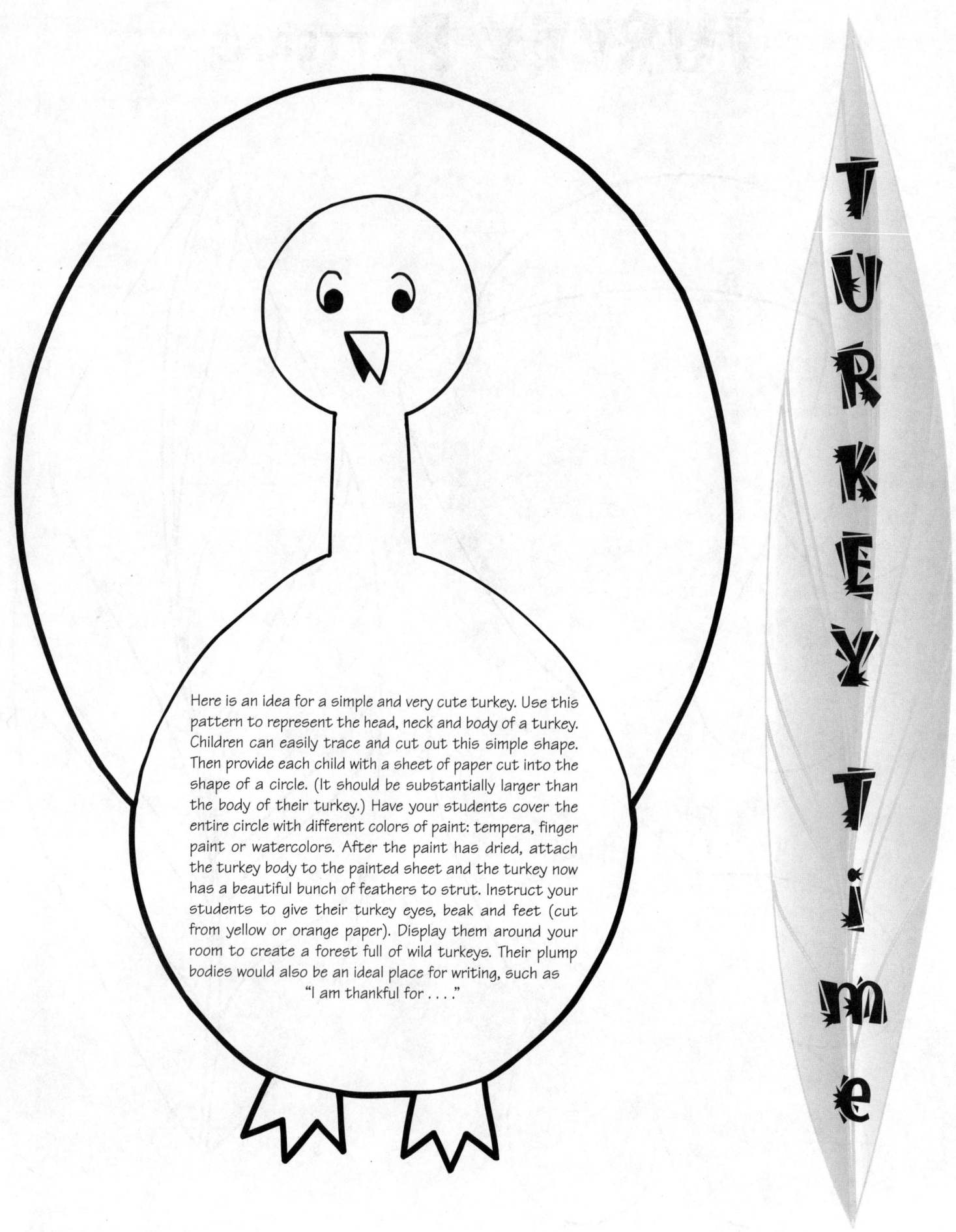

Turkey Time

Here is an idea for a simple and very cute turkey. Use this pattern to represent the head, neck and body of a turkey. Children can easily trace and cut out this simple shape. Then provide each child with a sheet of paper cut into the shape of a circle. (It should be substantially larger than the body of their turkey.) Have your students cover the entire circle with different colors of paint: tempera, finger paint or watercolors. After the paint has dried, attach the turkey body to the painted sheet and the turkey now has a beautiful bunch of feathers to strut. Instruct your students to give their turkey eyes, beak and feet (cut from yellow or orange paper). Display them around your room to create a forest full of wild turkeys. Their plump bodies would also be an ideal place for writing, such as "I am thankful for . . . ."

by Sheila Hausbeck

Thanksgiving Book Nook

Celebrate Thanksgiving with our exciting collection of seasonal books.

Share *Circle of Seasons* by Gerda Muller (Dutton Children's Books, 1995) with your students. This beautifully illustrated book highlights fall and the other seasons of the year.

Get your class in the holiday mood with the wonderful craft and decorating ideas in *Happy Thanksgiving! Things to Make and Do* by Judith Conaway (Troll Associates, 1986). Treat your youngsters to a real Thanksgiving feast of Old English "Sallet," Maple-Nut-Berry Popcorn Balls and Indian Cornbread. Challenge your class to a game of pilgrim spoonball or play the stone toss game.

Delight your class with *Thanksgiving, Stories and Poems* edited by Caroline Feller Bauer (HarperCollins Publishers, 1994). This gem of a collection includes work by popular children's authors, such as Eve Merriam, Jack Prelutsky, Aileen Fisher and Eloise Greenfield. Your students are sure to enjoy such favorites as "Supermarket Thanksgiving," "The Thanksgiving Day Parade" and "The Thankful Mouse."

Gobble, Gobble, Giggle by Katy Hall and Lisa Eisenberg (HarperFestival, 1996) is sure to tickle everyone's funny bone! This lift-the-flap riddle book features a collection of turkey-time riddles. After sharing the book with your class, have your students compose their own Thanksgiving riddles.

Daisy's Crazy Thanksgiving

by Margery Cuyler, illustrated by Robin Kramer, Henry Holt and Company, 1990

Daisy gets more than she bargains for when she decides to spend a more "quiet" Thanksgiving with her grandparents. In the company of her lively cousins, two Great Danes, three cats, a pet monkey and a box full of lizards, Daisy spends the wackiest Thanksgiving ever.

- Draw a picture of your favorite part of the story.
- Design a place mat that Daisy's family could have used for their Thanksgiving dinner.
- Be an author! Write a story called "Thanksgiving at My House."

How Spider Saved Thanksgiving

by Robert Kraus, Scholastic, 1991

That amazing arachnid is at it again! Thanksgiving is here and Miss Quito's class is putting on a play to celebrate. There's just one problem—Miss Quito forgot to bring the turkey for the play. Spider comes to the rescue by using some colorful balloons to create the perfect turkey.

- Draw a picture of what Spider's balloon turkey looked like.
- Arachnid Playhouse! Make stick puppets of the characters in this book and create a puppet skit of the story.
- Be a spider detective! There are two kinds of spiders—wandering spiders and web-building spiders. Use an encyclopedia or reference book to find out how they are different. Write an "Amazing Spiders" report on your favorite kind of spider.

Turkey on the Loose!

by Sylvie Wickstorm, Dial Books for Young Readers, 1990

Watch out! The chase is on as a little boy tries to catch a runaway turkey. Join the merry romp through an apartment house as everyone gets in on the turkey chase. Can they capture the flighty bird?

- Think of a name for the run-away turkey in the book. Tell why you chose that name.

- Extra! Extra! Read all about it! Write a news story about a runaway turkey who visits your school. Remember to include the five Ws: *Who? What? Where? When?* and *Why?*

- Create a comic strip about a run-away turkey.

Dinosaurs' Thanksgiving

by Liza Donnelly, Scholastic, 1995

Come along with Rex and his dog Bones for a very extraordinary Thanksgiving celebration—a holiday dinner with a group of friendly dinosaurs. Join the happy gathering as they feast on salad, ferns, potatoes and for dessert—berries, of course.

- Dig that dinosaur! What is your favorite dinosaur? Create a book with pictures and facts about the dinosaur.

- Draw a picture of the dinosaurs Thanksgiving Day Parade.

- Let's pretend! Wanted: A story about the day you celebrated Thanksgiving with some friendly dinosaurs.

Albert's Thanksgiving

by Leslie Tryon, Atheneum, 1994

Hip! Hip! Hooray for Albert! That diligent duck is busy helping the students prepare for the PTA Thanksgiving feast. Despite the frequent messages from PTA President Patsy Pig adding more tasks to his list, Albert manages to create a perfect holiday feast for all!

- As an extra surprise, there is a recipe for Albert's Pumpkin Pizza Pie on the back cover of this book. Think of a new pumpkin dessert of your very own that everyone would rave about. Draw a picture of your tasty dessert and write directions for making it.

- Create a thank-you card that Patsy Pig could have written to Albert, thanking him for all his help with the Thanksgiving feast.

- Congratulations! You were asked to be in charge of a school Thanksgiving feast. What food would be on the menu? What activities would you plan? Design a sign to advertise your special feast.

A Turkey for Thanksgiving

by Eve Bunting, illustrated by Diane de Groat, Clarion Books, 1991

When Mrs. Moose mentions to her husband that she would like a turkey for Thanksgiving dinner, he decides to find one for her. Mr. Moose enlists the help of his animal friends, and they manage to find a reluctant turkey. The poor turkey, expecting to be the "cooked" centerpiece for Thanksgiving dinner, is happy to learn that he is the guest of honor at the holiday meal!

- Draw a picture of the food Mrs. Moose served for Thanksgiving dinner.

- Do Not Disturb! Turkey made signs around his nest to discourage visitors. Design a sign that he could have used.

- Be an artist! Design a new book jacket for *A Turkey for Thanksgiving*.

Clifford's Thanksgiving Visit

by Norman Bridwell, Scholastic, 1993

Clifford soon becomes a seasoned traveler when he sets out to visit his mother for Thanksgiving. This determined dog overcomes many obstacles along the way, from traffic jams to a crowded Thanksgiving parade. Will he arrive in time for Thanksgiving dinner?

- Write a make-believe interview with Clifford's owner, Emily Elizabeth. What questions would you ask her about Clifford?

- Be an architect! Design a giant-sized doghouse, just for Clifford.

- Describe your favorite pet and tell why you think it's so special.

by Mary Ellen Switzer

Holiday Sing-Alongs

by Mabel Duch

Ten Little Turkeys

This song is sung to the tune of "Ten Little Indians."

One little, two little,
Three happy little turkeys.
Four little, five little,
Six happy little turkeys.
Seven little, eight little,
Nine happy little turkeys.
Ten happy little turkeys
On Thanksgiving Day.

Uh, ohhh! Uh, ohh!
Here comes the farmer!
Uh, ohhh! Uh, ohh!
Here comes the farmer!
Uh, ohhh! Uh, ohh!
Here comes the farmer
On Thanksgiving Day.

Ten little turkeys,
See them all scatter.
Ten little turkeys,
See them all scatter.
Ten little turkeys,
See them all scatter
On Thanksgiving
    Day.

Directions

1. Why are the turkeys happy? (They think they have escaped being someone's Thanksgiving dinner.)
2. Why are they afraid of the farmer? (He might be looking for one more Thanksgiving turkey.)
3. Why is turkey a traditional part of our Thanksgiving dinners? (Because wild turkeys were served at the first Thanksgiving.)

Performing the Song

Have 10 children stand at the front of the room, each with a turkey puppet behind his or her back.

As the song is sung, the turkeys appear one at a time. (Example: "One little" one turkey pops out and stays. On "two little" another appears and so on.)

Have the children hold their turkeys to one side and turn slightly so the turkeys' face can be seen.

On, "Uh, ohhh! Uh, ohh! Here comes the farmer!" have a child wearing a straw hat appear. Turkeys and children look at the farmer. The turkeys shake.

On "See them all scatter," children with their turkeys move off quickly in different directions.

Turkey Puppet

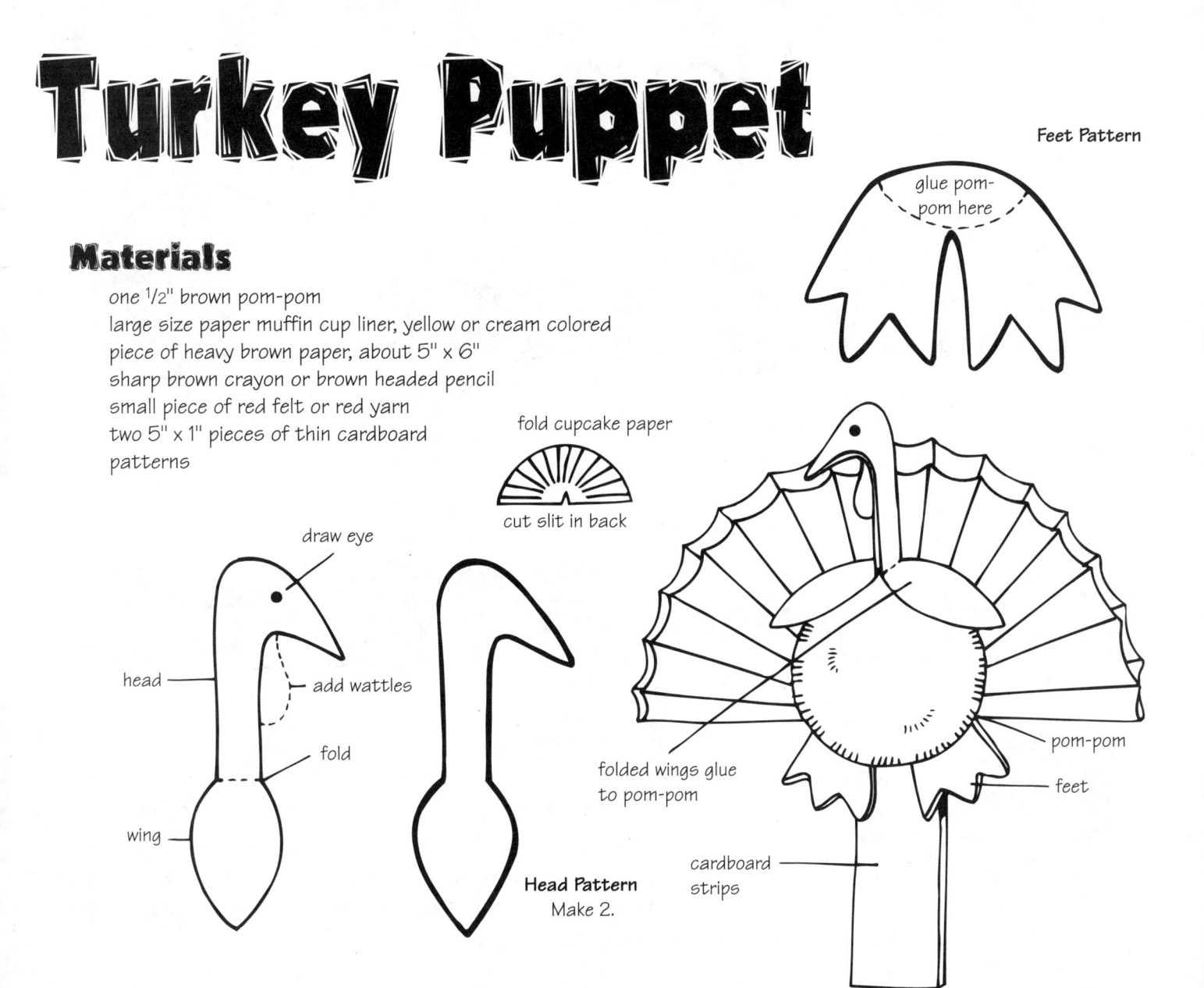

Feet Pattern

glue pom-pom here

Materials

one 1/2" brown pom-pom
large size paper muffin cup liner, yellow or cream colored
piece of heavy brown paper, about 5" x 6"
sharp brown crayon or brown headed pencil
small piece of red felt or red yarn
two 5" x 1" pieces of thin cardboard
patterns

fold cupcake paper
cut slit in back

draw eye
head
add wattles
fold
wing

Head Pattern
Make 2.

folded wings glue to pom-pom
pom-pom
feet
cardboard strips

Directions

Color the outside of the muffin cup liner, between the raised "ribs." Fold in two with one edge not quite meeting the other. Color the inside part which shows on the longer side.

Make a cut in the middle of the plain semicircle three-fourths of the way to the ribbed portion. Gently pull the sides of the semicircle so the cut opens and the folded muffin cup liner is flatter. (Optional: Solidly color the plain semicircle on the longer side of the folded muffin cup liner. This will be the back of your turkey.)

If necessary, push the plain semicircle on the shorter side so it is slightly convex. Keep the sides of the cup separated. Glue the pom-pom to this semicircle below the ribbed area. Using the patterns, cut the feet, two head, neck and wing pieces.

Glue the head and neck pieces together down to the rounded area at the bottom. Do not glue these together; they will be the turkey's wings. With a pencil, draw eyes on the turkey's face.

Fold back the wings below the neck and spread out. Glue to top of pom-pom, so wing tips stick out. Cut a narrow, slightly rounded piece of red felt (or red yarn), about 1" long, and glue the end to the turkey's chin. Glue the feet to the bottom of the pom-pom.

Tape the two cardboard strips together at the top, bottom and one place on each side. Fold down 1" at the top. Use tape to fasten the turkey to the cardboard holder with the folded edge at the back.

Shake the stick or push on it to see what you can do. (Using two thin strips of cardboard allows more movement than one heavy strip.)

by Mabel Duch

Have an Earth-Friendly Thanksgiving

Along with having a feast and giving thanks, we might stop and think of the first Thanksgiving when the Pilgrims thanked the Indians for their help. The Pilgrims learned valuable lessons from the Indians, and we can, too, for those Native Americans had been taking good care of the Earth for thousands of years. They knew how to treat the Earth gently and use its resources wisely. Here are some of their Earth-friendly practices. Read them and discuss how we can adapt some of these methods to save Earth's treasures today.

- When clearing land, they left fruit and nut trees standing.
- They never cleared more land than was absolutely necessary.
- They never killed animals, birds or fish just for fun or sport.
- They killed only as many animals as they could use and used all their parts.
- When planting, they put dead fish, ashes or crushed shells into the ground.
- They took only as much food as they could eat, and never threw any away.
- They stored meat and vegetables by smoking or drying them.
- They were careful with fires, always clearing the land around them.
- They cleared dead brush from the forests and weeded their gardens.
- They never threw refuse into lakes or streams.
- They used and reused materials until they were completely worn out.
- They shared food and resources with each other.
- They helped each other care for young children and old people in their tribe.
- They respected all life—animals and plants alike.
- They taught their children how to use Earth's treasures wisely.

by Elaine Hansen Cleary

Name _____

Thanksgiving Poem

Use the words below to fill in the last word in each line of this poem. Then make a Thanksgiving card using the poem for your verse. (Hint: This poem is in couplet form where two successive lines rhyme.)

air   eat   feet   found   give

ground   live   pleasure   wear

Thank you, Earth, for all your treasures—

Sandy beaches that give us ___ ___ ___ ___ ___ ___ ___ ___,

Soft grass that grows beneath our ___ ___ ___ ___,

Rich soil to grow the food we ___ ___ ___,

Plants to make the clothes we ___ ___ ___ ___,

Trees that purify the ___ ___ ___,

Coal and gas and oil in the ___ ___ ___ ___ ___ ___,

Lakes and streams where fish are ___ ___ ___ ___ ___.

Thank you, Earth, for these treasures you ___ ___ ___ ___.

I will use them wisely as long as I ___ ___ ___ ___.

by Elaine Hansen Cleary

Molly's Pilgrim

A Literature Unit Based on the Book by Barbara Cohen

Introduction

The celebration at the first Thanksgiving feast was organized by a grateful group of pilgrims who had found a home in a new land. They had come seeking freedom to worship. They had found the freedom they longed for and friends who helped them get started in an unknown land.

The story *Molly's Pilgrim* is a reminder that pilgrims are still arriving in America. They come from many countries seeking opportunities and bringing with them their culture, customs, language and hopes for the future.

Procedure

The story is divided into three parts. Each section may be read and discussed separately. The students are invited to answer questions about ideas and issues that are presented in the book. They are also encouraged to ask questions and bring their own backgrounds to the reading. Activities are designed to enrich and extend the reading experience.

Story Summary

Molly, a Jewish immigrant from Russia, is unhappy at her new school. The other children laugh at her because she speaks and acts differently. Molly learns about the pilgrims of Plymouth Colony and the first Thanksgiving. Her classmates learn about modern-day pilgrims and the Jewish celebration that may have inspired the first Thanksgiving feast.

About the Author

While growing up, Barbara Cohen listened to her relatives tell tales of their childhoods. In the story *Molly's Pilgrim,* she combined these memories with her own experiences. She wrote a story that inspires and teaches a lesson about our attitudes toward people who seem different than we are. As a storyteller, she has woven together the real and the imaginary to create a Thanksgiving story that is repeated as modern pilgrims continue to come to America.

by Patricia O'Brien

Day One

Molly came with her parents from Russia. After living in New York for a while, they now live in Winter Hill. Molly is teased by classmates because she is not like them. Mama tries to comfort her but is unable to solve the problem.

Before reading the first pages of the story, ask the following questions.

Prequestions

1. Do you know anyone who has moved here from another country? What do you think is hardest for them?
2. How are new students welcomed into your classroom?

Begin reading the first part of the story.

Questions to Discuss

1. What made Molly most unhappy at the Winter Hill school?
2. Why did she wish to return to New York City? Why would this be a bad move for the family?
3. Why was it impossible for the family to return to Goraduk, in Russia?
4. Why do you think the other children teased Molly?
5. Why didn't Molly want her mother to go to school to talk to the teacher?
6. How could the teacher help Molly to fit in better?

Activities

1. Discuss additional ways to make newcomers feel they belong in your classroom.
2. Role-play ways to make a new student feel welcome in your class. What could you say and do? Take turns acting out the situations.

Day Two

In early November, Molly learned about the first Thanksgiving and the pilgrims who came to America. When Molly's mother heard about the assignment to make a pilgrim doll, she offered to do it. She understood what it meant to be a pilgrim.

Read the opening pages of **The Pilgrims of Plimoth** or another account of the pilgrim's search for religious freedom. Discuss the reasons the pilgrims of Plymouth Colony left their home in England to come to a new land. Read the middle section of **Molly's Pilgrim**. Stop just before she brings her doll to school.

Questions to Discuss

1. How would you explain what a pilgrim is?
2. Are there still pilgrims around today? Do you know any pilgrims?
3. Why did Molly and her family come to America?
4. What were Molly's thoughts when she first saw the doll Mama had made?
5. Why did Molly view the doll with mixed feelings?
6. How would you feel if you thought you were bringing in the wrong assignment?

Activities

1. Pretend you are a student who is new to the school and the neighborhood. Write a letter to a friend telling about your experiences in this unfamiliar place.
2. List all the ways you can think of to celebrate Thanksgiving.
3. Make a list of the things for which you are thankful.

Day Three

Through Molly's explanation, everyone learns there is more than one kind of pilgrim. She helped her classmates to understand that while everyone is different, they are also the same. Read to the end of the story.

Note: Sukkot, the Jewish holiday of Thanksgiving, commemorates their trip out of Egypt through the desert to freedom in a new land. It is also a harvest celebration, a time to give thanks for the food that has grown all summer.

Questions to Discuss

1. How did the other children react when they first saw Molly's pilgrim? Why did they respond as they did?
2. If you were there, how would you have acted?
3. Because of the assignment to make a pilgrim doll, what did Molly discover? What did her classmates learn?
4. Do you think the children will be more understanding now?
5. In what ways is Molly different from her classmates? In what ways is she the same?

Activities

1. Write a letter from Molly's point of view to a friend in New York or Russia. Tell your friend what it is like in your new home and school.
2. Write an episode relating what happened next in the story.
3. Make a list of things you think Molly and her family are thankful for.

Enrichment Activities

Molly's Pilgrim: The Video

If possible, view the video of *Molly's Pilgrim*. It is the same story with enough differences to make for interesting discussion.

Note: The crossing guard is played by the author, Barbara Cohen.

1. Compare the book with the film version. How are they alike? In what ways are they different?
2. Which characters appear in the film but not in the book? Make a chart to show the main characters in the book and video.
3. Why do you think more characters were added?
4. Do both versions take place during the same time period? How can you tell?
5. How do the plots differ? What happened in the film that is different from the book?
6. Which version did you prefer? What is the reason for your decision?

The First Thanksgiving

Depending on the age and interests of the students, relate the story of the pilgrim's voyage and their first year in the New World. *The Pilgrims of Plimoth* by Marcia N. Sewall or *N.C. Wyeth's Pilgrims* by Robert San Souci may be read in whole or in part.

1. Younger children may benefit from a brief discussion as the pictures are shown. Encourage them to ask questions about the events depicted.
2. Older students may use the illustrations as story starters. Have them select pictures from the books to use in first-person narratives. As they imagine themselves being there, they should describe where the action takes place, what is happening, what they are doing and how they feel about it.

Related Materials

The following two picture books portray the arrival of newcomers to America. Readers get a feeling for hardships the travelers endured on their way to a new country.

1. In *Watch the Stars Come Out* by Riki Levinson, two young children travel by ship across the Atlantic Ocean to join their parents and older sister who are already in New York City waiting for them. The story is presented on a *Reading Rainbow* program that includes immigrants' first impressions of the United States. They gather at an ethnic festival where the food, music and dance of many countries are enjoyed.
2. In *How Many Days to America?* by Eve Bunting, a family knows it is time to leave their home in the Caribbean when soldiers come in the night. The trip on a small boat is difficult. After spending several days at sea and overcoming many obstacles, they are welcomed to America on Thanksgiving Day.

References
Bunting, Eve. *How Many Days to America?* New York: Clarion Books, 1988.
Cohen, Barbara. *Molly's Pilgrim.* New York: Lothrop, Lee & Shepard Books, 1983.
Levinson, Riki. *Watch the Stars Come Out.* New York: Dutton Children's Books, 1985.
San Souci, Robert. *N.C. Wyeth's Pilgrims.* San Francisco: Chronicle Books, 1991.
Sewall, Marcia. *The Pilgrims of Plimoth.* New York: Atheneum, 1986.

Videos
Molly's Pilgrim. 24 min. Phoenix Films, Inc., 468 Park Avenue South, New York, 10016, 1985.
Watch the Stars Come Out. 30 min. *Reading Rainbow.* Great Plains National, P.O. Box 80669, Lincoln, NE 68501, 1985.

Fall newsletter

A Family Take-Home

How to Use These Pages

Making the home-school connection is not often easy. Use these take-home ideas to bridge the gap between home and school. You will love the fact that you can incorporate some of these ideas into everyday life.

Because Learning Never Stops

As parents, you are the most important adults in the lives of your children. By becoming involved in their education and demonstrating a personal interest in and love of learning, you can encourage your youngsters to be enthusiastic about learning, too. Spend a few minutes each day working together on simple, enjoyable tasks. Inspire your child to learn.

Simple Science

The yearly ritual of cleaning out a pumpkin and creating a jack-o'-lantern offers several opportunities for scientific discovery. As you help your child remove the top, take a peek inside and talk about what you see. Can your child identify the pulp, seeds, pumpkin meat, and outer skin? Talk about what would happen if you dried and saved some of the seeds to plant in the spring; then choose some seeds to save. Before you carve the face, try an easy candle experiment to demonstrate that fire needs air, just as people and plants do. Place a votive candle in the hollowed-out pumpkin. Light the candle, observe the flame, then replace the top. Wait a few minutes, then lift the lid off and peek inside the pumpkin. What has happened to the candle? Remove the candle, then carve out the facial features. Replace and relight the candle. Set the top on the jack-o'-lantern and observe the flame. What happens this time? Help your child determine that air can now enter the pumpkin shell through the carved-out face.

On the Move

Physical exercise is an important part of growing up healthy. Even simple games can improve coordination and develop muscle tone. Autumn is the perfect time of year to catch things that are falling down. First, you will need to remove the bottom half of a clean, plastic gallon container. An empty milk or bleach bottle works well. The top part with the handle is now the scoop or cup you need for the game. You will also need either a beanbag or a rolled sock. The object of the game is to toss the beanbag or sock into the air, hold the cup by the handle, and use it to catch the bag or sock. Older children will be able to toss the bag into the air with one hand and catch it with the cup using the opposite hand. For younger children, you may want to toss the beanbag in their direction so they can simply concentrate on catching it in the cup.

by Marie E. Cecchini

Creative Kitchen

Cooking is both an art and a science. Cooking with your children can also enhance their math and language skills, as well as improve their manual dexterity. Invite your child to join you in creating an especially delicious orange autumn treat.

Orange Juice Cupcakes

1 c. orange juice
1 egg
2 c. flour, divided
1/3 c. salad oil
1 pkg. yeast
1/2 tsp. salt
2/3 c. plus 1 T. honey
1 tsp. vanilla

Heat the orange juice in a saucepan until warm. Remove from heat and stir in the yeast, 1 tablespoon of honey, and 1 cup of flour. Set aside until mixture is warm and bubbly, about 10-15 minutes. Meanwhile, place the egg in a bowl and beat until foamy. Stir in the salad oil, 2/3 cup of honey, 1 cup of flour, salt, and vanilla. Add the bubbly yeast mixture to the bowl. Place the batter in muffin papers or greased muffin cups and allow to rise 40 minutes in a 150°F oven. Then increase the oven temperature to 350°F and bake the cupcakes for 20 minutes.

Frosting and Decorating

Mix confectioners' sugar with a small amount of milk until you reach a spreadable consistency. Stir in a few drops of orange food coloring and a few drops of orange extract. Frost cooled cupcakes. Turn each cupcake into a jack-o'-lantern by adding candy corn facial features and a green jelly-candy stem.

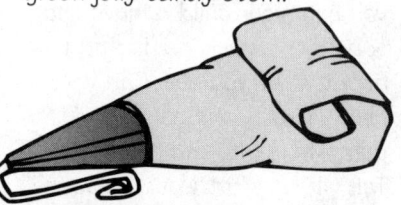

Communication Station

Language is communication. When children can express themselves clearly, they can communicate more effectively. Writing out party invitations is one way to practice language skills, and it won't even seem like "work." Since National Popcorn Week falls in October, why not consider having a popcorn party? Provide your child with paper and markers for invitations, and together you can design and write your own. Let your child help write the guest list and add the date, time, and place to the invitation. Visit the library or video store and have your child choose one or two favorite videos for the party. On the planned day, prepare the popcorn, provide a beverage, and welcome your young guests. One roomful of children, two action-packed videos, and several large bowls of popcorn is the perfect recipe for communication—just listen.

From the Art Cart

Enjoy these magically colorful art ideas with your child; then frame a few of the finished pieces to give as gifts for Grandparents' Day.

Paper Towel Prints: Fill two small bowls about half full of water. Add food coloring to the water to make it red in one bowl and yellow in the other. Now fold a paper towel (coffee filters work, too) several times. Dip it in the red water first and the yellow water second. Carefully open the paper towel and allow it to dry. Your child will be delighted with the red, yellow, and orange designs that have appeared. I wonder where the orange came from?

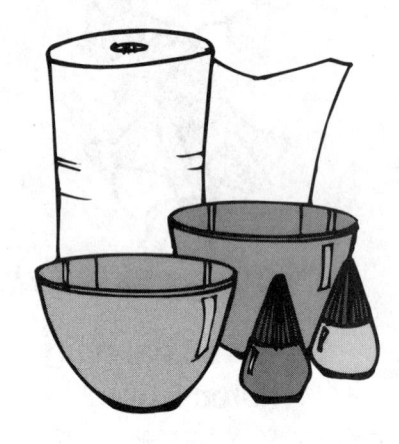

Bleach Art: Pour a small amount of bleach into a container. Provide your child with dark-colored construction paper (blue, red, and green work well) and cotton swabs. Show your child how to dip the cotton swab into the bleach and use it to draw a design on the colored paper. This activity requires direct supervision.

The Reading Room

Wonderful words and delightful illustrations make these books fabulous fall finds. Spend 10 minutes a day reading to your child. It may be the best investment you'll ever make.

Grandmother Bryant's Pocket by Jacqueline Briggs Martin, Houghton Mifflin, K-3.

Heckedy Peg by Audrey Wood, Harcourt Brace, PK-1.

The Monsters' Test by Brian J. Heinz, The Millbrook Press, PreK-3.

Possum's Harvest Moon by Anne Hunter, Houghton Mifflin, PreK-2.

Pumpkin Pumpkin by Jeanne Titherington, Greenwillow, PreK-3.

Sing a Song of Popcorn, a book of poems selected by Beatrice Schenk de Regniers, Eva Moore, Mary Michaels White and Jan Carr, Scholastic, PreK-3.

Stellaluna by Janell Cannon, Harcourt Brace, PreK-3.

Poetry in Motion

Children enjoy the rhythm, imagery, whimsy, and word play brought to life in poems and songs. Encourage your child to think creatively as you take turns using words and actions to invent simple rhyming stories. Ideas should be abundant with Halloween fast approaching. For example, you might begin with,

I am a cat
   (Make finger whiskers)
Who wears a hat.
   (Shape hands into hat over head)
I am a cat
   (Make finger whiskers)
Who is quite fat.
   (Circle arms in front of stomach)
I am a cat
   (Make finger whiskers on face)
Who caught a rat.
   (Pretend to catch something with hands)
Meow, meow, meow.

I am a frog
   (Squat in frog-like stance)
Who sneaks through fog.
   (Tiptoe around)
I am a frog
   (Squat in frog-like stance)
Who rides a dog.
   (Pretend to be riding something)
I am a frog
   (Squat in frog-like stance)
Who hops on logs.
   (Hop around)
Ribbit, ribbit, ribbit.

Use your imagination and be silly together. Older children may want to write their rhyming stories in a book. Why not visit a copy machine and turn this one book into several, enough to share with some special friends?

Mathworks

Math is such a big part of day-to-day living. If we just take a minute to think about it, we can find many ways to reinforce math skills in all areas. With the new school year just beginning, why not let younger children count out and package their own snacks; older children their lunch money? How about writing down special times of the day we need to remember: when the school bus arrives, dinner, and bed times? Then have your child check the clock to follow the schedule. Why not hang a blank monthly calendar in your child's room and have him or her fill in the numbers, weekdays, and months? You can also have your child set the dinner table, one place setting per person, or count the stairs on the way up to bed. Enlist your child's help in sorting the laundry into appropriate piles, matching pairs of socks. Does your child know your home telephone number and how to dial it? Does he or she know the house or apartment number? Math is so available that you can't help but practice these skills daily.

Clip Art for **Fall**

Clip Art for **Fall**

103

Clip Art for Back to School

Welcome Back

104

Clip Art for Fire Safety

Clip Art for Halloween

First Ride

Yowie! Yikes!
I didn't know
Just how fast
This sled could go!

I'm whizzing down
In such a whir,
All the trees
Seem one big blur.

The snow is flying
In my face.
Eee! My stomach's
Lost in space.

My hands and feet
Are getting numb.
Hey, where did
That bush come from?

Phew, I missed it.
Oh, no, what now?
A giant bump.
Ka-thump, yee-ow!

Whoa, I almost
Missed that bend.
When's this ride
Going to end?

At last I'm stopping . . .
But wait, hey!
I made it, look!
All the way!

That was easy;
That was fun!
I'm going for
Another run!

by Paige Taylor

Do a Polar Bear's Feet Get Frozen?

Do a polar bear's feet get frozen
   when they walk upon the ice?
Do their noses get so cold
   that some cocoa would be nice?
Do a penguin's little toes
   turn blue and make them shiver?
Do their feathers catch the cold wind
   and make their big beaks quiver?
Does a seal ever catch cold
   and sneeze right at a whale?
Does an otter ever catch the flu
   or get a tickle in his tail?
Maybe when I grow up,
   all these answers I will know.
Till then I'll just ask questions,
   and keep playing in the snow.

by Terry Lynn Pellegrini

Something Missing

One day I saw a snowman
Appearing rather sad,
As if there might be something,
That he wished he had.

He seemed well-dressed enough,
Clad in a Scotsman's kilt,
Vest with bright red buttons,
And tam placed at a tilt.

He had two eyes of plums,
A nose of crooked-neck squash,
His ears were carrot curls,
His mouth was . . . oh my gosh!

Ah-ha! That's what was missing.
I stood there for awhile,
Then gave him my red licorice,
And he gave me a smile.

by Paige Taylor

Flakey, the Freezin', Sneezin' Snowman

Flakey the Snowman
Was cranky as *heck*.
His friends, they all called him
A PAIN IN THE NECK!

The kids who had built him
Had made him a frown.
His eyes, they looked mad,
And his mouth, it turned *down*.

Now Flake had a problem.
The truth must be told:
Unlike *other* snowmen,
He always felt COLD!

He *shivered* and *shuddered*
And sneezed in the snow.
His nose was a carrot,
That just wouldn't *blow!*

"OH YOWCH!" blubbered Flakey.
"It's COLD! I'M LIKE ICE!
I'll go to Snowlene
And I'll ask her advice."

Of course, it's no secret,
When nobody's there,
All snowmen and women,
They walk EVERYWHERE!

A cold moon was shining
When Flake started off.
Snowlene was so kind,
She would help with his cough.

He saw her, at last,
In her usual place.
She gazed at the moon
With a smile on her face.

"SNOWLENE, HEY, SNOWLENE!
You're my snowwoman friend!"
He liked her so much
That he needn't pretend.

"Snowlene, you must *help* me.
Why DO I feel cold?
You always feel *fine!*
You're so brave and so bold."

"Well, thank you," said she,
"But I found something out.
Whenever I'm crabby,
Or wanting to pout,

I think something funny,
And slowly I start
To smile a BIG SMILE
And it warms up my heart."

"The trouble with *you* is
You don't have a smile!
It makes your heart cold.
It's been cold for a *while*."

"OH WOW!" hollered Flakey.
"I'VE HAD A BRAINSTORM!
A SMILE WARMS MY HEART
AND MY WHOLE SELF GETS WARM!"

"But look at these stones,
The mouth on my face.
They seem to be frozen
And *stuck* there in place."

"The sun," said Snowlene,
"I often have proved,
Will soften your face
And the stones can be *moved*!"

"And then I could MOVE them
And make you a SMILE!
But still we'd be taking
A chance for a while."

"If someone should see,
With the sun shining bright,
We'd have no more freedom
Or fun every night."

"LET'S DO IT!" said Flakey.
"We'll wait for the sun.
You'll make me a smile
And I'll thank you and run!"

They hid by the fence
Till the morning was light.
The sun, it looked down
On a *wonderful* sight:

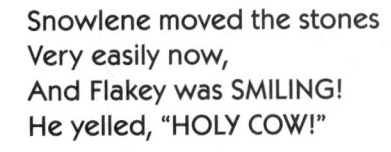

Snowlene moved the stones
Very easily now,
And Flakey was SMILING!
He yelled, "HOLY COW!"

"My heart, it feels WARMER!
MY BODY'S WARM, TOO!"
He kissed Snowlene's cheek,
Then he practically FLEW!

"I'll see you tonight!"
It was getting too LATE!
The door opened up
As he tore through the gate.

He stood in the yard,
In his usual place.
He felt warm inside,
With a smile on his face.

The family came out,
But they passed right on by.
They *thought* he was different,
BUT DIDN'T KNOW WHY!

Now Flake and Snowlene,
They have fun every night.
They play in the snow
Till it ALMOST gets light!

by Irene Livingston

Warm Up for Winter

New Year's Hats

Cut a 3" wide paper band that fits around the child's head. Use tape to attach both ends of six 1" wide paper strips to the headband in a crisscross pattern, creating a top for the hat which will set on the crown of the head. Decorate the New Year Hat with an assortment of items: paper spirals, chenille stems wound in a spring shape, glitter, foil stars, clumps of holiday icicles, buttons, scraps of colorful gift wrap, ribbons, or bows.

A Very Special Classroom Calendar

Divide the bottom half of a 22" x 28" piece of poster board into a calendar grid, seven squares wide and five squares long. Cover the poster board with clear adhesive paper. On separate paper, write the months of the year, the days of the week, and the numbers 1 to 31. Use rolled tape to attach these to the calendar. Prepare paper stars or other shapes to mark holidays and other special classroom events. Write the name of the special day or event on the star. Use the top half of the poster board to display photographs of children and classroom experiences, project samples, artwork, and children's quotes that occur throughout the month. Don't be concerned with filling the space as soon as the month begins; add to the display throughout the month. This is a calendar that grows and changes as the month progresses, presenting a visual record of the classroom experiences. When the month concludes, take a photo of the calendar before removing the upper half and changing the numbers. Place the photos on a second chart, titled 1998. Label the month under the photo and hang the chart next to the calendar as a cumulative record of the school year.

Clock Making

Take advantage of the changing year to discuss the passage of time. Children can make paper plate clocks with clock hands attached with a brass fastener so that they can be moved. Read *Time To* by Bruce McMillan and invite children to make the hands on their clock match those in the book. Write a classroom version of the book, highlighting the daily routine hour by hour. Share this idea with parents so that they may extend the book-writing activity at home, if they wish.

by Carol Ann Bloom

Resolution Paper Chain

Discuss resolutions for the new year with the children in the classroom. Choose goals that are easily attainable and beneficial to the classroom or community as a whole.

- Use a new word today.
- Be more courteous or cooperative.
- Read a new book.
- Try something new today.
- Write a thoughtful note to parents.
- Clean up litter around the school or neighborhood.
- Share something with others today.

Write each resolution on a strip of paper and interlock the strips to form a chain. Tear off one strip each day and try to accomplish it.

"Feed the Birds" Garlands

Be kind to our feathered friends in the cold weather. String cranberries and round cereal on yarn. Tie the ends to a branch and loop the garland from branch to branch.

Bird Feeders

Remove the bottom half of a gallon plastic water or milk jug. Place two holes on opposite sides of the jug, about an inch from the rim. Decorate it with markers or paint. Tie a heavy cord through the holes to make a hanger for the bird feeder. Fill the feeder three-fourths full with birdseed and hang it from a tree branch. Try to choose a tree that is close to a classroom window so that the birds can be observed from inside.

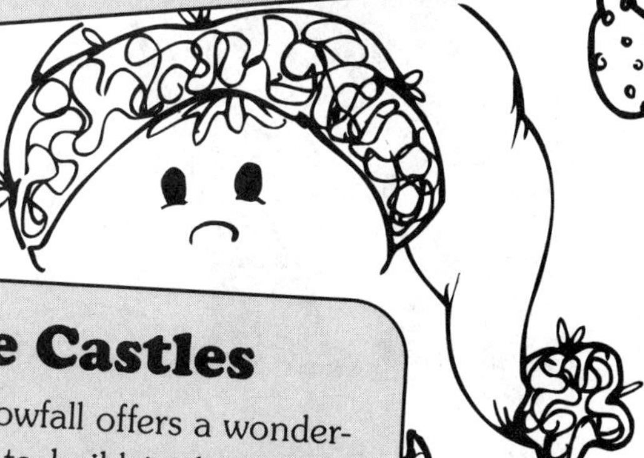

Icicle Castles

The next big snowfall offers a wonderful opportunity to build icicle castles. Take children on an icicle hunt and collect as many icicles as possible. Provide buckets, molds, plastic cups, and shovels for children to build snow castles, much the same way as sand castles are built. Finish the snow castles by placing the icicles on and around the structures like shiny, shimmering ice towers and spires.

Make Giant Icicles

Fill two- or three-liter bottles or gallon plastic jugs halfway with water and freeze. Use a hammer and nail and place several holes in the bottom of the frozen bottles. Hang the bottles of frozen water outdoors from a sturdy tree branch or a piece of playground equipment. As the temperature outside fluctuates, the water will begin to drip and freeze, resulting in a long, giant icicle. Add more water to the bottle by removing the cap and pouring water into the bottle while it hangs.

Kid Space
School Yard Learning Adventures

Winter Learning Adventures

Kid Space is a place of school yard beginnings. It is an ever-changing, fascinating place where children can connect with the natural world and learn all kinds of things. Kid Space is a safe place where kids can explore freely, embark on adventures and make learning discoveries all on their own. Make the most of the smells, the colors, the textures, the sounds, the excitement, the freedom and the peace and quiet.

Winter Greenery

Get whisked away in winter's wonderland of educational adventures. Use the crisp white landscape as a springboard for activities to warm young minds.

Hunt for Green on the Winter Scene
Turn a winter hike into a quest for green. Encourage students to search for color amidst the grays and whites of winter. What other colors do they see? How do the colors in the winter environment make them feel? Sketch the trees and shrubs from afar and up close. Study the greenery and try to identify the particular trees and shrubs.

Look at the "Big Picture"
Do you want to look at the world in a whole new way? You may get more out of a winter hike by learning to use "scanning vision." This is a method of viewing an area with a slow, sweeping glance from one side of the horizon to the other. Do not let yourself focus on any one particular object that comes into view. Scanning in this way will allow you to better observe your entire surroundings.

Why Do Some Trees Lose Their Greenery?
Are the trees without leaves dead? They sure appear that way but take a closer look. Upon close investigation you will be able to see very tiny buds on the tips of the branches of the trees. Some buds are coated with a sticky, waterproof substance that helps to keep the bud warm and dry. Take one bud back to the classroom and let it thaw. Cut the bud open and examine it under a microscope or with a magnifying glass.

The trees that lose their leaves during the winter months are called deciduous trees. They go into a dormancy or resting period during the winter. This period is similar to a drought because the trees are surrounded by water but have no access to it because it is frozen! Deciduous trees must retain as much water and nutrients as they can during this dormancy phase so the supply of water to the leaves is cut off before the coldest weather arrives. The food-producing leaves are not needed when the tree is in its dormancy phase. During this cycle, the leaves eventually die and fall to the ground.

by Robynne Eagan

The Gifts of the Evergreens

Evergreens have long provided useful resources for human beings and living creatures. Coniferous forests supply the majority of softwood timber used throughout the world.

- Can you think of things in your life that may have come from an evergreen tree?
- Can you think of animals that rely on these trees? Birds, squirrels, lynx, caribou and reindeer make coniferous forests their home.

The Symbolism and Beauty of the Evergreen

The evergreen provides us with year-round beauty and symbolism. Ancient people who survived without the amenities of modern life respected the strength and symbolism of the plant that could withstand the snow and cold, while plants around it died.

Evergreens like the pine, mistletoe and holly became very important in ancient winter solstice celebrations. These plants became symbols of everlasting life and the renewal of life that was to come. Many of these early symbols were adopted by new religions and became a part of modern traditions.

The Magic of the Mistletoe

Since ancient times, mistletoe has been viewed as a magical evergreen. The Celts and the Greeks believed that this plant held special powers. The plant seemed to grow in the air between the Earth and the sky on its host tree. That made it a mystery to early people. Mistletoe is a parasitic plant. It grows on another plant called the host plant. This hardy plant can live up to 50 years.

The Celtic druids (or priests) cut the plant in a sacred ritual and then used the cuttings in their ceremonies. Although this plant is toxic, scientists are discovering something that the ancient people long believed—in small quantities, mistletoe possesses healing properties for various illnesses.

Mistletoe represented rebirth during the darkest time of the year, and to this day many people, especially those of British heritage, hang mistletoe over a doorway during the Christmas season.

Holly

The shrub with prickly leaves and red berries is the only broad-leaved tree that is an evergreen. Holly took on special significance because it produced its red berries in the heart of the winter. This tree, with its bright green shiny leaves, has come to be a part of many seasonal decorations.

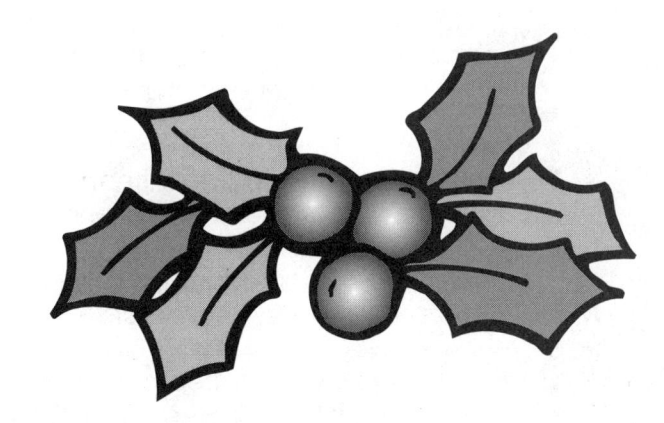

The Decorated Evergreen

The custom of decorating evergreen trees at Christmas comes from Germany, where this tradition was recorded in 1605. The tradition of decorating an indoor evergreen seems to have reached North America by the late 1700s.

Kid Space
School Yard Learning Adventures

Family Discovery Page

Dear Parents/Guardians and Students,

Why not take advantage of the season by taking a trek to a Christmas tree lot to cut your own tree? Children will learn many things by experiencing the cutting of a tree firsthand, and you will be able to celebrate the season with an evergreen. The tree can be adapted to suit your customs and beliefs. Enjoy the winter weather, the scents, the decision-making process and the hot chocolate!

Most tree farms are making good use of land that could not be successfully used for other farm crops. Help children understand that the tree you are cutting may have been growing for close to 10 years. This year's harvest of trees will be replaced by a new crop, which will take that same amount of time to reach maturity. For the sake of the environment, try to find a tree farm that does not use pesticides.

Talk about the ways that your tree has been a home for birds and insects. It may have acted as a windbreak for surrounding roads or plants. It has helped to make the air we breathe a little cleaner by absorbing carbon dioxide and producing oxygen.

Encourage the democratic process as your group attempts to agree on just the right tree!

Try This
Discuss the alternatives to cutting down a Christmas tree. How do they affect the environment?

- The artificial tree can be used over and over again, but does harm the environment when it is produced, packaged and eventually disposed of.

- A live, potted Christmas tree can be purchased at a nursery and added to your landscaping when the weather permits. The tree must be handled with care. A hole should be prepared for it in the fall, it should be brought inside for short periods of time at first and then kept inside for less than 14 days. The tree must then be slowly hardened to survive the cold. Discuss this with a professional at the nursery.

Decorate a living outdoor tree. It will look great and the tree can continue to grow and be part of your celebrations season after season.

Decorate an indoor plant for a twist on tradition. What it lacks in pine scent, it will make up for in quirky character!

Discuss ways that your tree can be recycled. How about standing it in a snowbank and covering it with bird feeders until the harsh winter passes? The birds will thank you! You can put the tree through a chipper and turn it into mulch; the branches may be used for crafts, or to cover walkways or gardens; or the tree may be used for firewood.

Sincerely,

A Feast for Feathered Friends

In the winter months, birds may have a difficult time finding food beneath the snow. A tradition popular at Mexican celebrations, the piñata, can be made to give food to our feathered friends. Piñatas are usually made from papier-mâché. They can be formed into any shape and decorated with brightly colored paints and paper. Traditionally, once a piñata is made or purchased, children take turns trying to break it with a stick while blindfolded. When the piñata breaks open, small gifts and candy scatter to the ground for the children to gather. To make a piñata for our feathered friends, simply fill it with birdseed instead of toys and candy.

Materials

- birdseed
- flour
- string
- water
- bowl
- knife
- tempera paint
- wire
- brush
- newspaper
- tissue paper

Directions

1. Blow up a balloon and tie a knot to keep the air inside.

2. To make the paste, combine 1/2 cup flour with 2 cups cold water. Heat 2 cups water to a boiling on stove. Add the flour mixture. Return to a boil. Remove the pan from the heat. Add 2 tablespoons sugar and cool.

3. Tear strips of newspaper.

4. Dip the newspaper strips one at a time into the paste and wrap around the balloon.

5. Cover the balloon with several layers of newspaper. Set it aside to dry. This usually takes a few days.

6. Paint over the newspaper. Let dry.

7. To decorate, cut small pieces of tissue paper and glue onto the piñata.

8. To hang the piñata, poke two holes near the top. Push a wire through the holes and twist it together. Tie a string through the wire loop.

9. Have an adult cut a small round hole in the piñata.

10. Fill the piñata with birdseed.

Hang the piñata from a tree. Invite children to take turns wearing a blindfold and swinging a stick at the piñata until it breaks open. Instruct children that only the person with the stick stands near the piñata; others must watch from a safe distance and cheer. When the piñata breaks open, the birdseed will scatter. Go inside and watch the birds come for a feast. Viva la fiesta! Hooray for the feast!

by Monica B. Hay-Cook

Weather WISE

Wintertime provides a fascinating, ever-changing backdrop for the study of weather. Make the most of the frosty temperatures to warm young minds with stimulating activities and interesting information.

Winter Arrives

In some places, winter arrives long before its official date of December 21. Encourage your students to notice the changes that winter brings. What happens to the temperature, wind, plants, trees, wildlife and hours of sunshine?

The Touch of Winter

During the winter months, the Northern Hemisphere of the Earth is tilted away from the sun—which means that this part of the Earth receives less sunshine and the temperature is cooler during this time. During these winter months, the days are short, the nights are long, and in many places the ground is covered with snow. Spring officially arrives on March 21, but we often do not experience its touch until sometime later.

Feel the Weather

How does the weather look and feel to you? Describe the weather using as many adjectives as you can think of. How does the weather at this time of the year affect your life? How does the weather make you feel?

by Robynne Eagan

Report the Weather

At this time of year we can experience some unusual weather. We may find ourselves in the grips of winter, or we may bask in the rays of some early spring sunshine that turns the snow into puddles and streams of water. This is an exciting time to have students take notice of the characteristics that make up the weather around them. To enhance your language arts program, have students research and observe the weather and then present written or oral weather reports.

Be a Snowflake Chaser

You can't take a trip to the storm clouds, but you can catch a few snowflakes as they make their way down to you!

Materials
- glass microscope slide
- clear plastic lacquer spray
- tight-fitting gloves
- magnifying lens

Process
1. The night before the big chase, put your glass slides and lacquer spray in a freezer or the very cold outdoors so they can chill thoroughly.
2. Take children outdoors on a snowy day. Bring the slides and spray from the freezer or your outdoor storage area. Hold the edges of each slide in a gloved hand so your body heat doesn't warm the slide.
3. Coat each slide with a layer of lacquer spray, then hand it to a child.
4. Each child will then "chase" the snowflakes. Children will hold their slide up so a snowflake will land on it.
5. When a snowflake is caught, it is taken to a sheltered outdoor area where no more snowflakes will land on the slide.
6. Leave your snowflakes on the slide outside for at least one hour and then bring the slides inside. These snowflakes will be preserved in the lacquer and can be carefully observed.
7. Discuss your observations. What do you see? Compare the various flakes found by classmates.

Try This
Make drawings to record your snowflakes.

Predict the Weather

For centuries people have watched the sky, the plants and trees, the sea, and even animals for signs of changes in the weather. People passed on to one another wisdom that would help them recognize signs that might indicate changes in the weather.

Discussion
Why is it helpful to know what the weather will be? It is very important for some people to know what the weather will be? Can you think of any people who need to know an accurate weather report?

Snowflake Weather Reports

Snowflakes can tell us something about the weather. Some meteorologists turn to them for information about the weather—not the weather that is on its way, but the kind of weather that existed when the snowflakes were formed. Some of these snowflake-chasing weather watchers fly up into a snowstorm to catch the snowflakes before they are altered by the trip to the ground. Subtle changes in weather can cause snowflakes to develop very differently.

Although snowflake catchers can't tell us too much about the coming weather, their research will lead us to a better understanding of the winter weather that affects our lives.

The Wonders of Water in Winter

Quick, what is the most important resource on the face of the Earth? If you said *water* you are correct. Water is beautiful, powerful, and essential to our everyday lives. This necessary resource is often taken for granted. Help your students recognize and understand the wonders of water. Beyond the life-giving properties of water, it offers a dazzling display in many forms when the thermometer dips.

The tail end of winter and the beginning of spring offer the most exciting opportunities to enjoy the wonders of water in its various states. Venture into a snowstorm to explore the wonders of water crystals. Observe a sparkling icicle from many different angles. Watch the melting snow when the sun shines warmly. Get soaked in a rainstorm and talk about how the water feels. There's no doubt about it—water is awesome.

Talk about all the things water is used for in your life. What other things rely on water? Could we survive without it?

Expanding Water

What happens to water when the temperature is freezing?

Materials
- 2 plastic juice containers with lids
- water
- cold temperatures

Process
1. Ask children the question: "Does water take up more, less or the same amount of space when it becomes a solid?" Talk about how you can find out whether water expands or contracts.
2. Fill a plastic juice container with water and seal the lid tightly.
3. Place the container outside or in a freezer to freeze.
4. Observe the container when the water has frozen. Ask children: "What happened to the shape of this container? What does that tell you about frozen water?"

Turn a Liquid to a Solid

Something amazing happens to water when the temperature reaches a particular point on the thermometer. Try to determine the magic temperature.

Materials
- containers
- water
- pencil
- thermometer
- paper

Process
1. Record the outdoor temperature each day and place two containers outside for three hours.
2. Check and record the temperature each hour.
3. At the end of the three-hour period, describe the contents of your container.
4. Continue the study for about 10 days with varying temperatures ranging above and below 32°F (0°C).
5. Study your findings. Can you determine the magical temperature that turns water to ice?

Try This
Discuss methods that could have (and have) been used to determine the exact temperatures at which changes of state occur.

Falling Ice

Sometimes ice falls from the sky! When the weather turns cold, the water in a cloud freezes and forms ice crystals. The crystals bind together and fall as snowflakes. Sometimes the snow melts slightly as it falls, turning into small, transparent ice particles called sleet. When the temperature of the moisture in a cloud is just below the freezing point, tiny snowflakes combine with cold water droplets and freeze into spherical balls of ice about 1/8" to 1/4" (3 to 6 mm). These white opaque balls are called ice pellets, and when they fall to the ground they seem to bounce in an icy dance. Larger pellets resembling spherical chunks of ice are called hailstones. Hailstones are usually about the size of marbles but have been known to be the size of golf balls and larger!

Hot on the Trail of a Raindrop or Snowflake

Take to the great outdoors to follow the secret trail of the snowflake or raindrop. Where does it come from and where does it go? Follow a raindrop from a dark cloud through the sky and into a puddle from where it runs into a larger body of water or evaporates to join the water cycle once again.

Explore Water

There's no better way to understand the dynamics of anything than to dig right in and get your hands wet. Try to borrow a water table if you do not have one and allow children to freely explore the wonders of water. Add ice cubes or snow to the mix to inspire discussion and analysis.

The Leaning Tower of Water

Can you stack water on top of water? Of course you can—when it is in its frozen state! Have students try to stack ice cubes on top of ice cubes. Can they think of ways to get these ice cubes to stack? Does warming them help? How about snow-glue? What happens to ice when you add a little salt? If you add a little salt between the ice cubes, the ice will melt just enough to allow the cubes to stick together. Salt causes ice to melt—that is why we use it on our walkways and roads in the winter months. Try adding a little salt between your layers of ice and your sculpture just might stick!

Icy Friends

Freeze up an icy character to go along with the weather.

Materials
- paper cups, yogurt cups or other small containers
- craft sticks
- icing sugar
- small candies (jelly beans, cake decorations and so on)
- napkins

Process
1. Mix 1 tsp. (30 ml) icing sugar with cold water until it is the consistency of paste.
2. Paint this paste on the inside of your container to form a face.
3. Quickly press your decorations onto your painted face.
4. Put a large dab of the paste on the bottom of the cup and push a craft stick into it.
5. Place the cups in freezing temperatures until thoroughly frozen—at least a half hour.
6. While the pasty face is freezing, mix up some juice and chill it to almost freezing along with the cups.
7. Pour the slushy juice into the cups and leave to freeze again—about two hours.
8. Run warm water over the cups to loosen the icy characters.
9. Let your characters meet one another. Then enjoy your icy treats!

Ice: A Winter Wonder!

Water is a compound made up of hydrogen and oxygen. In each water molecule there are two hydrogen atoms and one oxygen atom; scientists show this by writing H_2O. Water is best recognized in its liquid state, but water can also be found in a solid or gas state. If you leave water for a long time, it will slowly evaporate and become water vapor, an invisible gas. When water is cooled to the freezing point of 32°F or 0°C, something amazing happens—it becomes a solid. We call this solid water *ice*.

Icy Words

Observe water that has turned to ice. Does it all look the same? Make up some icy words of your own to describe this frozen water! In the language of the Inuit people, there are over 90 words to describe the different kinds of ice.

Icicle Watch

How do icicles form? Observe some icicles on a warm day and find out!

Ice Sculptures

Do something creative with that solid water.

Materials
- containers in various, interesting shapes: funnel, balloons, rubber gloves, juice containers, margarine and yogurt containers, bundt-cake pan, muffin pan
- food coloring
- beads, charms, glitter

Process
1. Add food coloring, glitter or interesting objects to the water before you begin.
2. Pour water into your various-sized containers. The frozen ice shape will need to slide out of the container, or the container can be cut away from the ice form. For balloons, fill them with tap water by pulling the balloon neck over the faucet.
3. Leave the water-filled objects outside to freeze.
4. When completely frozen (the time will vary depending upon the size of the object and the outside temperature), run the form under very warm water until the shape slides from the mold. In the case of the balloons or cartons, tear them away from the molded ice sculpture.
5. Display your objects or combine them to create interesting structures. You can use an icy cement of snow, slush or even water to hold them together.

Crystal Clear, Starry Nights

Who wants to go out on an icy cold night? You do! There's no better time to study the night sky. The crisp, clear air of winter contains few of the particles that are often in the summer air. These crystal clear evenings make star-watching a dazzling experience.

Assign a winter stargazing homework assignment. Have children look for the Big Dipper and the North Star. The two stars that make up the side of the dipper, opposite the handle, point to the North Star. Have students draw an imaginary trail about three hand widths above the top of the pointing stars. The brightest star in view in this position is Polaris, the North Star. The North Star lies almost directly above the North Pole—the sky region known as celestial North. The North Star does not move in the sky, but all of the other stars revolve around it.

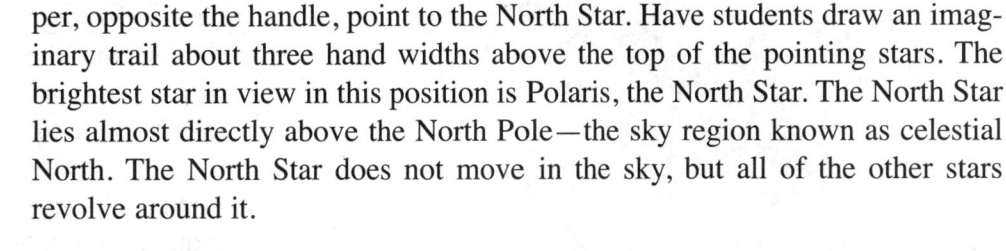

Follow Up
Discuss the stargazing activity the next day in class. What did the children see? What adjectives would best describe their spectacular view? How did sky-watching make the children feel? Did they recognize any stars or constellations? Did anyone see a satellite?

Icy Habitat

You won't want to go anywhere near icy cold water in the winter, but believe it or not, that's just the place that some aquatic insects call home! Water boatmen and backswimmers hang around in the air pockets under the ice or cling to underwater vegetation. Research to find out what happens to other water-dwelling creatures when winter comes.

The Case of the Frozen Trees

The average tree consists of 80% to 90% water, so what happens to the trees when the thermometer dips below freezing? Nature amazes us with its wonders! When the weather turns cold, the sugar content of the tree's cells increase, keeping the tree from freezing completely. The trees do freeze during the coldest snaps of the winter, but usually not long enough to do any damage to the tree. When spring arrives, the high sugar concentration in the sap causes the sap to freeze at night, but it thaws and flows by day.

Did you know that most ocean waters, including the Atlantic and the Pacific oceans, do not freeze with the exception of some shoreline areas? Why do you think that is? The constant motion, the size of the body of water and the salt content help these bodies of water to remain liquids. Occasionally ocean shorelines may freeze.

Snowy Silence

Go outside during or immediately after a big snowfall to experience the hush of the snow. Everything looks different and sounds different. If you have ever thought that the snow seems to absorb sound, you were right! Everything seems quieter after a fresh snowfall because tiny air spaces in the newly fallen snow trap sound waves and absorb the sounds.

Windchill

How cold it feels outside has a lot to do with something called the windchill. The wind can make it feel a lot colder than it really is. Most weather forecasts provide the windchill so you will know how cold it is going to feel outside. The windchill is a combination of the temperature and the wind speed.

Take students outside on a windy, wintry day. How does the temperature feel in an open, windswept area? How does it feel when you move into a sheltered area?

Snow Insulation

Could you ever imagine something icy cold like snow keeping something warm? Believe it or not, it's true! Snow can trap heat. Snowflakes are really frozen, lacy crystals with spaces that contain air and act as insulation. A blanket of snow can insulate the Earth, plants, insects and small animals from the freezing cold of winter.

Insulation from the Cold

Cold things gain heat when they melt and warm things can lose heat. Challenge children to slow down these processes by using different materials as insulators. Trapped air slows down the flow of heat from something warm to something cold, so anything with trapped air in it will work as an insulator reducing the amount of heat that can escape from a warm place to a cold place.

Can you think of any insulators that you use in your life?

Forecasts from the Groundhog and Friends

Have you ever heard about that weather-predicting groundhog? On February 2, many North Americans take part in the tradition of turning to the groundhog for a weather report. Statistics show that this weather forecaster is not really very accurate, but people like to take part in the late winter fun anyway. It seems to remind people that spring is on its way—sooner or later!

If the groundhog emerges from his burrow on this day and the sun is shining, a shadow will be cast and is believed to predict six more weeks of winter. If the skies are overcast and no shadow is cast, it is believed that spring is just around the corner.

It is thought that the tradition of Groundhog Day may have arisen from a medieval saying regarding Candlemas Day.

If Candlemas is bright, winter will have another fight.

If the Candlemas brings rain, winter won't come again.

Have fun making up some animal weather predictions of your own.

If _____, then we will have six more weeks of winter but if _____ then spring is just around the corner.

Bulletin Board Activity

Have some fun! Invite students to draw and cut out the shape of an animal weather forecaster of their choice. Have children print a brief explantation of how this particular animal predicts the weather. Place all the animal shapes on the bulletin board for display. How accurate are these weather forecasters?

Touch and Texture Make Your Winter Curriculum Terrific

How can you help your students feel good about learning during the long winter season? That is kind of a trick question. The answer is: use touch and texture to literally *feel* the content that you are presenting. In my book, *Beyond Hands-On: Techniques for Using Color, Scent, Taste, Touch and Sound to Enhance Learning*, I share an entire chapter on the use of touch and texture in teaching. We will touch on some key ideas in this study of wintertime themes.

Warm Up in the Block Center

A few years ago, I published an article in the early childhood journal, *Dimensions*, that got a lot of attention. Titled "Ten Myths About Block Play," I examined some widely held views about the use and misuse of blocks. One key point: blocks are underused as a curriculum resource, especially in the upper elementary grades. If you are teaching second, third, fourth, or even fifth grade, not to mention the primary grades, you need a block center in your classroom. Blocks help to develop fine motor skills in younger children and more abstract reasoning and observational skills such as prediction, estimation, weight, size, strength, volume, mass, and aesthetics. What budding architect or engineer might you be mentoring with a block center! The winter season keeps many youngsters indoors during recess time, so seize this learning opportunity to warm up minds and hands in your block center.

by Dr. Linda Karges-Bone

Wrapping Paper Writers

Ask parents to donate leftover holiday wrapping paper to be used in a variety of writing projects.

- Give each child a section and ask him or her to list all the adjectives that describe that particular piece. Here is an example: gold, crinkly, stars, cool to touch, raised pattern.

- Give each child a section and invite him or her to describe the gift that this paper might have covered.

- Use the wrapping paper to make covers for individual books in which students describe their winter holiday experiences. Title the booklets "Wrapping Up My Winter Holiday."

Warm Up the Learning

During wintertime, take advantage of natural seasonal changes (in many parts of the country) to observe physical science changes involving heat and cold. Experiments that lend themselves nicely to this season include:

- measuring the boiling point of water and then making red and green "Holiday Jell-O®" jigglers.

- observing the process of a liquid (water) turning into steam (a gas) and then using the hot water to make cups of hot cocoa.

- estimating how long it will take your marshmallow to melt into the hot cocoa and then comparing your estimate to the actual time result.

- comparing the differences between four cups of tap water and those same four cups of water frozen in an ice tray. Does it appear to be more or less? Why?

WINTERTIME

Wintertime curriculum is filled with high-touch opportunities. Here is a final, quick look at 10 simple lessons or transition time activities that involve the season of winter and the sense of touch. Have fun with winter. It isn't just about holidays. It is a season that deserves attention for its diversity and beauty.

Wiggle your fingers to get warm after being outside. Can you name the body part that allows you to wiggle your fingers? (joints)

Itchy is how your skin feels when it is cold outside. Can you explain why your skin feels itchy? (dryness, lack of moisture) Rub a soothing lotion into your hands to make your skin feel better.

Notice the colors in your mittens and caps. Can you graph the most popular colors for winter garb?

Tear into texture by making wintertime pictures. Use cotton balls and white chalk to contrast with a dark blue or black construction paper background. Create winter scenes.

Eating winter treats can help you feel better. What are your favorite winter foods? Do you eat the same kinds of foods all during the year?

Read a poem such as Robert Frost's "Stopping by Woods on a Snowy Evening" and then do the art activity mentioned above.

Take time to notice the scents and colors of winter. Make a list of scents and colors that make you feel like wintertime. Save the list and compare it to one you might make in the spring.

Introduce the concept of the Earth's revolution around the sun every 365 days. Use a flashlight and globe to illustrate the concept.

Make a list of what you might be doing today if you lived in Australia. Why could you do those things?

Examine the trees outside. How does winter affect them? Draw a sketch of wintertime trees and date it. Put it in your science journal or portfolio. Plan to do another sketch in May. What might you see?

Skating Through Winter

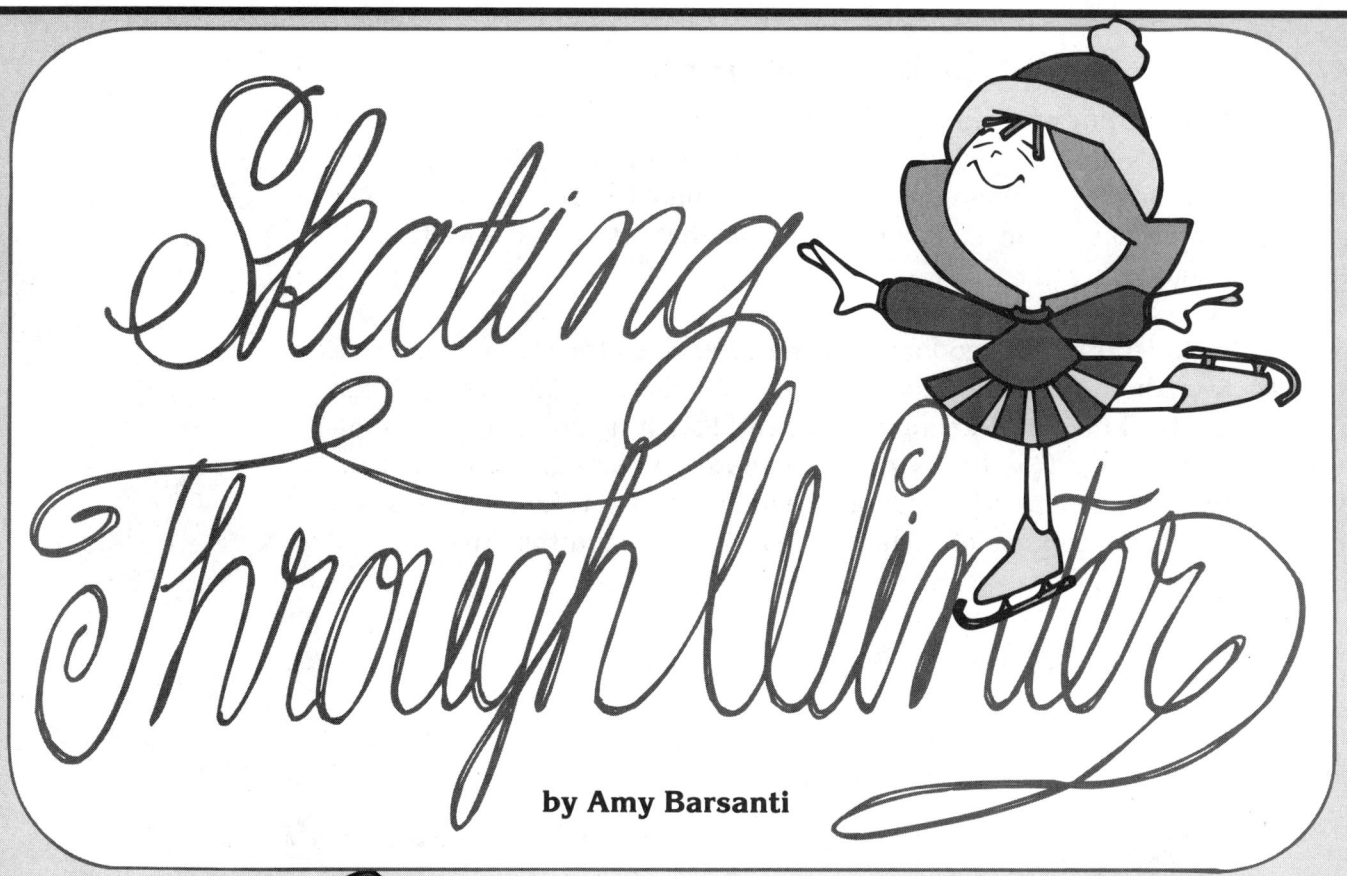

by Amy Barsanti

Invasion of the Snowpeople

Students "snow off" their cooperative learning skills and creativity by making these life-size snowfolk. When completed, they serve as terrific starters for creative writing projects, too. Have groups of students stuff large, white, kitchen garbage bags with newspaper to make giant snowballs. Then have them stack the snowballs and attach them with packing tape. Finally, let students decorate them using construction paper, permanent markers, and even scarves and hats from the lost and found. It's abominably good fun!

Winter Everywhere!

Increase your students' appreciation of different cultures, hone their research skills, and chase away those winter "blahs"—all at the same time! Assign a country or region to each child. Provide resources for your budding researchers to find out what winter is like in the places they are studying. As a culminating activity, have a Winter Festival, with an offering of fun facts, treats, demonstrations, customs, winter celebrations, traditional winter costumes, or folktales from each student.

Skater's Waltz

The word *skate* comes from the Dutch *schaats,* which means "leg or shank bone." It is likely that the earliest skates were boots with pieces of bone attached for easier traveling on the ice. It was not until hundreds of years later that Jackson Haines, a dancer, used movements that resembled a waltz in his skating technique.

Teach your students rhythm counting skills as you enjoy the music of the season. Play a recording of "The Skater's Waltz," encouraging students to listen first, then pretend they are skating to the beat. Play it again, this time pointing out the "1-2-3, 1-2-3" waltz rhythm. Encourage students to follow the beat by snapping fingers, clapping, or tapping feet. Play a variety of selections and see if your students can identify other pieces with three-fourths time.

Snowpeople Printing

This craft activity is a great way to make sure that this month's calendar of classroom events will make it onto the refrigerator instead of into a snowdrift! Have students glue duplicated calendar pages on the bottom half of a 12" x 18" piece of dark blue construction paper. Use two different-sized potatoes for the snowpeople's bodies. Have students dip each in white tempera paint, scrape the excess paint on the side of the container, and print them one above the other. Have them repeat the procedure using a cotton swab to make falling sow. After the paint dries, cut out a hat shape from a sponge and use a pencil eraser dipped in black tempera for facial features.

Bulletin Bored?

Not for long, with this eye-catching, interactive display! Cover your bulletin board with blue paper. Cut huge letters from white paper to spell *WINTER* and arrange them so that they spread across the entire board. Challenge your students, their schoolmates, faculty, staff, and parents to think of winter words and phrases beginning with each letter. Attach a plastic bag with assorted blue markers under a posted explanation. Allow your students to write their words inside the appropriate letter first and encourage them to check for new offerings each day. Everyone's winter vocabulary will improve!

Downhill Racing

Students will love this active science project! They build their own "ski slopes" as they learn about inclined planes, surfaces, and speed. Provide a variety of materials including corrugated and other cardboard, aluminum foil, wood, paper bags, and small, empty milk cartons to act as "skiers." Explain that they have been commissioned by a famous skier who wants to break all existing speed records. Demonstrate the idea by propping any of the materials against a stack of five textbooks, the seat of a chair, and a desktop. Challenge them to discover and report which slopes and surfaces allow the milk cartons to go fastest. Encourage them to devise a system for recording their results. Have students share their results and discuss other factors for skiers, such as weather and safety. After all, the slope that seems fastest isn't as valuable if no milk carton can make it all the way down!

Winter Webbing

To really get your students interested in your winter unit, try this twist on a typical brainstorming session. Before you begin, devise a color code like the one below.

    Animals—yellow
    Activities—blue
    Adjectives—red
    Places—purple
    People—orange
    Sports—green

Ask your students to volunteer winter words for your web, chart, or list. As you record the responses, refer to your color code and write each idea in colored marker according to your code. When your class starts to run out of ideas, ask them if they can figure out the categories that go with each color. Divide the class into small groups and assign a category to each. Have them research to add to their lists. Compile finished lists, illustrated by students if you like, into a book for your classroom library.

Snowman Buttons

Duplicate several of the snowman on the right for this math center focusing on fact families. Program each snowman's hat with a numeral between 1 and 10 and laminate if desired. Provide chocolate and butterscotch chips, or two colors of buttons or other round manipulatives. Explain and demonstrate the following steps:

1. Choose a snowman.
2. Look at the number on the snowman's hat and put that number of buttons on him.
3. How many red (or chocolate) buttons do you have? How many are blue (or butterscotch)? How many do you have all together? Use these numbers to make a fact family with two addition problems and two subtraction problems. Write the equations on a piece of paper. Use the buttons to help you.
4. Now try again with a different snowman.

by Amy Barsanti

Name _____

To complete the story, make new words from the letters in the words *The Silly Snowman*.

The Silly Snowman

Winter was not Joshua's favorite __ __ __ __ __ __.

He thought about summer when he __ __ __ __ in the pool every day with his best friend, and how their swim __ __ __ __ had __ __ __ the relay race at camp. As Joshua rolled the __ __ __ __ into balls and stacked them, he had an idea. Instead of putting a winter __ __ __ on his snowman, he put on __ __ __ __ goggles.

Solutions: season, swam, team, won, snow, hat, swim.

by Martha J. Morrison

133

December —The

Add a *P* to the 3 Rs–Precycle!

When you buy gifts to give to friends and relatives for Hanukkah, Christmas or Kwanzaa, you have a great chance to give Earth a gift, too. How? PREcycle! *Pre* means "before," so you precycle by thinking and looking BEFORE you buy anything. Here are some things to think about and look for.

It takes the same amount of Earth's treasures to make a toy that lasts a long time as it does to make one that will not last very long. Don't choose cheap plastic toys that turn into junk within a few days. They waste both materials and energy, and build up garbage dumps and landfills. Ask a parent or clerk to help you tell the difference.

Look at packaging, too. A lot of expensive packaging not only wastes materials, it may be used to hide a cheap toy.

Avoid buying toys that require batteries. Batteries are made from valuable resources and get used up quickly. For toys that do need batteries, ask to get rechargeable ones that can be used over and over again. (Remember, old batteries should never be thrown into the garbage, but taken to a garage or disposal center that will dispose of them safely.)

Do you have any old toys that are still in good shape? Stop to think about WHY they lasted. What are they made from? How did you take care of them?

Do you have any toys you've outgrown? Clean them up and REUSE them by giving them to a younger child.

If you receive toys as gifts, TAKE CARE OF THEM! When you outgrow them, if they can't be given away, see if they can be recycled.

Hand lotions and liquid soaps come in plastic bottles. Make sure to buy the type that can be recycled. Look for the triangle symbol with a number inside it on the bottom of the container. Find out what numbers your community recycles. Numbers 1 and 2 inside the triangle are recycled the most.

Look for the "made from recycled materials" symbol on any paper products that you buy, such as stationery, cards, gift boxes and wrapping paper. Later, be sure these things are reused and/or recycled, too!

Parent Take-Home for the Holidays

Giving Month

Earth-Friendly Gift Ideas

Save money and help the Earth at the same time. Instead of buying new gifts, make them by reusing materials you can find at home, such as aluminum cans, plastic bottles, glass jars, cardboard boxes, craft sticks, bottle caps, magazines, calendars, egg cartons, old socks, mittens and t-shirts. Collect buttons, beads, ribbons, yarn, plastic flowers and crayons to use for decorating your creations.

The following is a list of materials and a suggested gift you can make by reusing the items.

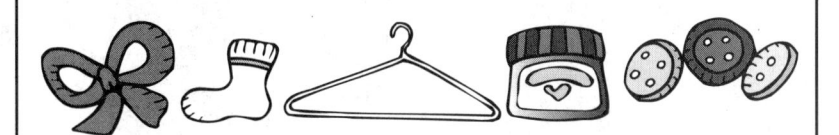

Material	Gift
aluminum cans	paperweights
baby food jars	pencil holders
bottle caps	board game pieces
cereal boxes	file boxes
coffee cans	dolls
detergent bottles	vases
Styrofoam™ egg cartons	seed starters
margarine tubs	candy dishes
mittens	banks
nylon stockings	door draft dodgers
calendars or magazines	picture books
peanut butter jars	litter bags
catalogs	ABC books
plastic milk jugs	bird feeders
craft sticks	picture frames
old socks	dust mittens
empty spray bottles	plant sprayers
t-shirts	"designer" shirts
grocery bags	puppets

by Elaine Hansen Cleary

In Remembrance of St. Lucia

The feast of Saint Lucia (Saint Lucy) Day is celebrated December 13th in Sweden, Norway, and parts of the midwestern United States.

Information about Saint Lucy comes from legend. This young girl was born to wealthy Christians about 283 in Sicily. At this time, Roman rulers forbade anyone to worship Christ. Therefore, her family worshiped in secret. Lucy was engaged to marry a pagan, but he became upset with her—perhaps because she gave money to the poor. Their engagement was cancelled. The young man reported her to the Roman authorities, and she was sentenced to die by fire. However, the blaze did not harm her. Finally, the Romans killed her with a sword.

By the sixth century, Lucy became a popular saint. Bonfires and torchlight processions honored her on December 13th. This date also begins the winter solstice—the shortest day and darkest night of the year.

To celebrate St. Lucia Day, girls may wear a crown of greenery supporting lighted candles. In Sweden, the oldest daughter in each family plays the part of the *Lussibrud* (Lucia bride). She rises early and dresses in a long white dress, red sash and crown. She wakes her family by singing and serves them hot coffee and a special holiday treat called *lussekatter* (Lucia cats).

Show the class a picture of girls wearing Saint Lucia crowns. Use a children's book about Christmas and holiday celebrations in other countries as a source.

Because wearing lighted candles is dangerous, adapt the following paper craft to this age-old custom from Sweden. However, you may want to make a crown with real candles for a display. Light the candles when you talk about this Swedish holiday.

by Carolyn Ross Tomlin

Materials
white poster board or very stiff paper
rope of artificial holiday greenery or garland
yellow felt-tip markers
stapler or hot glue gun

Directions
1. Cut a strip of poster board, 2" wide and long enough to go around each student's head. (Use a tape measure for size.)
2. Cut a length of greenery the same size.
3. Staple ends of poster board together, making a band to fit the child's head. Using school glue, fasten garland to the headband. (Adults may prefer a hot glue gun.)
4. Cut out seven candles from poster board (see patterns below). Use felt-tip markers to color the flame yellow. Position each candle an equal distance apart and staple to a poster board headband.

Invite children to form a line and parade around the school grounds or corridors wearing the crowns. Return to the room for Lucia cats and warm apple juice.

Lucia Cats Recipe
Ingredients
package of refrigerated biscuits
powdered sugar glaze
raisins

Give each student one biscuit. Roll the biscuit into a rope about 8" long. Form the dough into an X. Decorate with raisins. Bake according to package directions. Brush with a glaze made from the powdered sugar and water. Serve warm.

Safe Holidays Are Happy Holidays

December brings Hanukkah, Christmas and Kwanzaa, all special holidays, each with its own customs and festivities. There's one thing they all have in common, though, and that's the use of lights. Whether candles or electric bulbs, used indoors or outdoors, for services or as decorations — lights require special safety precautions.

Candles

A candle's open flame can burn you or anything else near it. Keep younger children away, and make sure things like curtains, decorations or pageant costumes aren't close enough to be ignited.

Play it safe by letting adults light the candles. Matches and lighters are both safety hazards, so never play with them, and make sure they are not left lying around where young children can reach them.

If you must hold a lighted candle, make sure you have a protective shield on the bottom so hot wax won't drip onto hands or clothing. (A small paper plate covered with aluminum foil works well.)

In school, it is safer to tape paper flames to real candles. For a pageant or procession, make a "lighted" candle by putting a tissue paper or crepe paper flame over the lens of a flashlight. (Cover the rest of the flashlight with paper the color you want your candle to be.)

Electric Lights

Electric lights are pretty to look at, but they, too, can cause injuries or fires if safety rules are not followed.

Most important—every string of lights should have a label that says, *UL Approved* to show they are safe.

Don't overload sockets by plugging in too many cords.

Make sure extension cords are neither in the way where they could be tripped over, nor hidden under a rug where wires could become frayed and cause a fire.

Bulbs get hot. Don't touch them or let them touch curtains or decorations where their heat could ignite a fire.

And *never,* never leave decorative lights on when no one is in the room! (Fires start *so* easily.)

Let adults put up lights and other decorations. Make sure that a safe ladder is used, rather than a box or chair. (No one needs a bad fall!)

Decorations

Real Christmas trees can be a fire hazard if they are not kept in a bucket of water and brought outside as soon as the needles start to get dry. (Artificial trees are a good substitute.)

Ornaments and decorations should be safe with no sharp edges. If an ornament gets broken accidentally, be sure to clean up the pieces quickly and carefully so no one gets cut.

If plastic or foil "icicles" are used, place them high up out of reach, so small children can't put them in their mouths. (They could choke!)

Holiday plants such as poinsettias, holly and mistletoe are beautiful, but they are poisonous if eaten. Plastic or silk plants look just as nice and are much safer.

Gift Giving

When buying toys for small children, make sure there are no small parts they can put in their mouths or sharp edges that could cut them.

Stay away from any toys that shoot or whiz through the air; someone could accidentally get hit. Many eyes have been injured this way.

Remind children to always stay with an adult when shopping. Don't run ahead or linger to look at something. For safety's sake, children should have an identification card with their name, address and phone number fastened *inside* their coat (where strangers can't see it). And, of course, children should never talk to strangers.

by Elaine Hansen Cleary

Name _____

Have a Safe Holiday

Circle all of the unsafe things you see happening in this holiday picture. Color the picture.

TLC10110 Copyright © Teaching & Learning Company, Carthage, IL 62321-0010

139

HANUKKAH

Hanukkah Candles

We'll light one candle for each night,
For seven nights plus one,
Until eight candles shine out bright
When Festival time is done.

Eight candles Hanukkah's story tell,
While one to light them makes nine.
We'll spin our dreidels and sing, as well,
While our Hanukkah candles shine!

by Bonnie Compton Hanson

Hanukkah *is the festival of freedom and miracles. When the Greeks ransacked the temple in Jerusalem (165 BC) and put up idols, the Jewish people rebelled. The Jews under Judah Maccabee gathered an army of farmers and shepherds. They fought back Antiochus the Greek leader. When the Jews regained the temple, they found only one small container of oil. There was only enough oil to light the menorah for one day, but the oil miraculously lasted for eight days and nights.*

Hanukkah is an eight-day festival, with each day starting at sunset. Every night, Jews light a candle on a nine-branched menorah. People light one candle on the first night and an additional candle each following night. Every night people light the middle candle called the shamash or helper candle. Jews celebrate the festival with fried foods like potato pancakes and doughnuts to remember the oil in the temple. Children play the dreidel game with Hebrew letters that commemorate the miracle. Parents give presents or traditionally coins and nuts to children.

Oven Potato Balls

Ingredients
- 4 medium potatoes
- 3 T. vegetable shortening
- 2 T. minced onions or onion salt
- 1/2 tsp. salt
- 1 1/2 cups dry bread crumbs
- 1 T. mayonnaise

Utensils
large pot, large bowl, measuring cups and spoons, oven tray, potato masher

Boil potatoes till just tender. Set aside till room temperature. Mash the potatoes till an even consistency then add softened vegetable shortening, onions, salt and bread crumbs. Stir or mush up with clean hands.

Every child can then roll their own ball about half the size of a large egg. Then smooth mayonnaise over each ball. Bake in a preheated oven at 425°F for 20 minutes or until brown.

Traditionally, Jews eat shredded potato pancakes called latkes on Hanukkah. Fried foods like potato pancakes and doughnuts are symbolic of the miracle of the oil in the menorah. This recipe is an oven-baked adaptation, and it still has oil in it. It's easier to prepare in a classroom situation than the traditional recipe.

Helpful Hints
- Boil all the potatoes before class or have every student bring one small boiled potato.
- Scrubbed potatoes, are less work and more nutritious than peeled ones.
- You can microwave the potatoes, but they do not have the same texture as boiled ones.

by Devorah Stone

Menorah

Materials
- 19 empty wooden spools of thread (preferably the same size) or 9 empty wooden spools and 10 old toy wooden building blocks
- all-purpose white glue or paste
- long wooden base
- aluminum foil
- poster paint
- candles

Teacher Preparation
- Draw nine evenly spaced circles.
- Take all paper off of spools and toy wooden blocks.

Student Activities
- Each child is responsible for one wooden block or spool.
- Have each child paint a wooden block or spool, but leave the top and bottoms clean.
- Wait till dry.
- Paste a spool or block to each circle.
- Then stick a spool on the top of the first block or spool.
- Place another layer on the middle candlestick.
- Carefully glue aluminum foil on top of each candlestick.
- When finished, place candles in spool candle holders.

Helpful Hints
- If you light the candles, do not let them burn down—the spools may not be fire retardant, even with aluminum foil.
- Have the children make pretend flames for the candles with red transparent or crepe paper.
- If you want an even larger menorah, work together with other classrooms.
- This could be a school-wide project.
- A variation on this could be used for Kwanzaa.

Individual Menorahs

Materials
- 9 bottle caps
- 1 piece of wood
- paint

Paste bottle caps to wood. Paint wood.

Helpful Hints
- Paste a wooden block in the middle of the wood for the middle candle.

Traditional Children's Song

I made a little dreidel;
I made it out of clay.
And when it's dry and ready,
Oh, with it I shall play.
Dreidel, dreidel, dreidel,
I made you out of clay,
And when you're dry and ready,
Oh, with you I will play.

Helpful Hints
- Children like to spin around while singing this song.

141

TLC10110 Copyright © Teaching & Learning Company, Carthage, IL 62321-0010

Dreidel

The dreidel game goes back to the 9th century in Germany. It is a game of chance. The Hebrew letters on the dreidel stand for "A great miracle happened there." The game reminds children of the miracle of the lights in the temple.

Sort-of-Dreidel

Materials
- sharpened pencil
- thread spool

Stick the pencil through the spool just above sharpened part. If the hole is too big, wrap an elastic band around the pencil at the bottom. Draw the Hebrew letters on it. Spin the dreidel on the sharpened end.

Dreidel Game

Materials
- 1 dreidel per four children (Contact the local Jewish Community Center or temple to find out where to buy dreidels or make the sort-of-dreidel.)
- lots of pennies, plastic chips, jelly beans, nuts, buttons or bottle caps

Divide children into groups of four. Have each group sit in a different area. Provide each group with one dreidel. Give each child four pennies. Place a larger, but even, amount of pennies in the middle of the table (eight, ten, twelve, fourteen, and so on). The teacher needs extra pennies to refill the pot as necessary. To play, one child spins the dreidel. When the dreidel stops spinning, the child looks at the symbol it has landed on and follows the directions that go along with that symbol.

Dreidel Symbols

If it lands on:

Nun stands for "Nes" (miracle) then the child does not do anything.

Gimmel stands for "Godol" (great) then the child gets whatever is in the pot.

Hay stand for "Hayay" (happened) then the child gets half of what is in the pot.

Shin for "Shom" (there) the child gives everything he or she has to the pot.

Every child gets a turn. Every time the pot is empty the teacher fills it back up. Game ends when there are no pennies left.

Dodie's Lucky Christmas Eve

"My friends are away until Christmas,"
Said Dodie the duck with a groan.
"I'd like to trim trees and sing carols.
But what can I do all alone?"

"I'll look in the halls of my building
And see if I have any luck
In finding, among all my neighbors,
Just one little, nice little duck!"

She knocked on the doors so politely,
Explaining it down to the end,
"I'm looking for somebody little
And yellow like me, for a friend."

"I'm sure there is somebody somewhere."
And while she was wondering who,
Along came a green alligator.
"I'm Ava," she said, "How are you?"

"It's Christmas tomorrow," said Dodie,
"And no other ducks do I see
To celebrate just for the evening."
And Ava said, "What about ME?"

"You're BIG!" stuttered Dodie, astonished.
"I'm sure you don't quack, and you're green!
We'd look very funny together.
I'm sure you can see what I mean."

Then Dodie looked right at her neighbor,
And Ava looked back for a while.
"Well, green's a nice color," said Dodie.
"You do have a beautiful smile."

Now that is how Dodie met Ava,
And wonderful friends they became.
So people who seem very different
Can turn into friends just the same.

by Irene Livingston

Santa's

Ho! Ho! Ho! Santa's back to get the winter season off to a merry start with some seasonal reading treats just for you!

Christmas Around the World by Emily Kelley (Carolrhoda Books, 1986) will introduce your class to Christmas customs in other countries. A colorful world map is included, as well as a recipe for some tasty Christmas cookies.

Give your students a firsthand look at an old-fashioned holiday season by sharing *A Little House Christmas, Holiday Stories from the Little House Books* by Laura Ingalls Wilder (Scholastic, 1995). This wonderful collection of stories features the Christmas celebrations of a frontier girl and her family.

Have a "Pooh"rific Christmas with the fun-filled collection of short stories in *Winnie the Pooh's Stories for Christmas* by Bruce Talkington (Disney Press, 1996). The five short stories about that lovable Pooh and his friends are sure to be holiday reading favorites—from "The Bite Before Christmas" to "Snow Time Like Christmas."

How the Reindeer Saved Santa
by Carolyn Haywood
illustrated by Victor Ambrus
Mulberry Books, 1986

Santa thinks his sleigh is getting too old and decides to use a helicopter this year to deliver presents. When Santa loses his helicopter key in the snow, his faithful reindeer quickly come to his rescue. He soon realizes nothing can replace his sturdy sleigh and devoted reindeer.

- Design a helicopter that Santa could use to deliver his presents. Draw a picture of your helicopter and label the parts.

- Write a pretend conversation on Christmas Eve between two of Santa's reindeer.

- All aboard! Write a story about the year Santa used a train to deliver his presents.

- Want to find out more about helicopters? Be sure to read *Helicopters (A New True Book)* by David Petersen (Childrens Press, 1983) and become a whirlybird expert.

Merry Christmas, Old Armadillo
by Larry Dane Brimner
illustrated by Dominic Catalano
Boyds Mill Press, 1995

It's Christmas Eve, and a lonely armadillo thinks that his old friends have forgotten him. When he falls asleep, his friends plan a wonderful holiday surprise—they decorate his house and trim a special Christmas tree for him.

- Be an armadillo expert! Find out more about this amazing animal. Use an encyclopedia or reference book to help you. Create a picture book featuring facts and pictures about armadillos.

- Challenge yourself! Make a list of all the words you can think of using the letters in *armadillo*.

- The holidays are a great time to do something special for your friends. You could make a greeting card or perhaps a homemade gift. Make a list of things you would enjoy doing for a friend.

by Mary Ellen Switzer

Book Nook

Aunt Eater's Mystery Christmas
by Doug Cushman
HarperCollins Publishers, 1995

That super sleuth is back! Even though it's a busy Christmas Eve, Aunt Eater simply can't resist an opportunity to solve another mystery. She soon puts her detective skills to work trying to foil a jewelry store robbery, investigating a mysterious stranger and helping a neighbor find some missing clothes.

- Pretend you are a detective. Make a list of things you would use to help solve the case. Don't forget a magnifying glass!
- Calling all detectives! Write a crime report about "The Case of the Missing Santa."
- Draw a "missing" poster showing what Santa looks like. Write Santa's description at the bottom of the poster.

Merry Christmas, Dear Dragon
by Margaret Hillert
illustrated by Carl Kock
Modern Curriculum Press, 1981

Come along and join the fun as a boy and his pet dragon get ready for the holidays. There are so many things to do—build the perfect snow dragon, cut down just the right Christmas tree and of course, create some tasty cookies.

- Would you like to have a dragon for a pet? Why or why not?
- Pretend you had a pet dragon. What would you name this unusual pet? Tell how you would care for it.
- Be an architect! Design a special home for your pet dragon. Draw a picture of your design.

The Forgetful Bears Help Santa
by Larry Weinberg
illustrated by Bruce Degen
Scholastic Hardcover, 1988

It's Christmas Eve and Santa seems to be stuck in the Forgetful Bears' chimney. Mr. Forgetful thinks he's Santa and decides to deliver the Christmas presents. This magical, merry mix-up is sure to tickle everyone's funny bone!

- Do you think Mr. Forgetful made a good Santa? Explain your answer.
- Draw a picture of your favorite part of the story.
- Write a funny story about how you helped Santa deliver Christmas presents.

The Christmas Party
by Adrienne Adams
Charles Scribner's Sons, 1978

Meet the famous Easter egg artists—Orson Abbott and his parents. Even though it's the Christmas season, these talented rabbits are busy painting eggs for Easter. When Orson is asked to help plan a surprise Christmas party, he decorates the prettiest tree ever—with Easter eggs, of course!

- Write a "Dear Diary" entry that one of the rabbits might have written telling about the Christmas party.
- The rabbits decorated the Christmas tree for the party with strings of popcorn and Easter eggs. Draw a picture of what the tree might have looked like.

Beanbag Toys

As the holidays approach, and kids are having trouble concentrating, it is often a good idea to focus on a topic of real interest to them. What better time to incorporate the current beanbag toy craze into your curriculum? Children will be so involved with their favorite pets, they will forget about the approaching festivities and settle in for some real fun (and learning). Here is a complete unit on beanbag toys, integrating them into all subject areas. Worksheets, organizers, activities, poetry and touches of science are included. Let the learning fun begin!

Begin discussion by asking children to bring their beanbag toys to class. Be certain they are marked with students' names so they do not get lost or mixed up. Introduce the toys to the class and talk about their significance in your daily routine. Most children develop a friendship with their beanbag toys and enjoy talking about them.

by Jo Jo Cavalline and Jo Anne O'Donnell

Display Units for the Beanbag Toys

Children will want to show their collections in the classroom. Here are some ideas for different ways they can display their collections.

- Collect cardboard drink holders from fast food restaurants and put a toy in each holder. These holders can be stacked up for easy storage, too.

- Fill a box with lids from large bottles of liquid detergent. Put one toy in each lid.

- Display the collections on windowsills.

- Use index cards to divide a shoe box. Each little section can become an individual space for a beanbag toy.

Categorizing—In display units, categorize the toys according to species, color, friendly/nonfriendly or size. Make a list of all the different ways they can be grouped. Sort the toys in different ways and let the other students guess how they are categorized.

Habitats for Beanbag Toys

- Supermarket delis package food in reusable plastic containers with clear plastic domes. These throwaways make great habitats for beanbag toys. For sea creatures, make blue "water" on the bottom of the container. Decorate the inside lid with cotton balls for the sky and clouds. For land animals, make an outdoor scene. Use twigs, stones and moss you gather outdoors.

- Boxes of all sizes can easily be divided into rooms to make houses for the toys.

- Florists have boxes that vases and other tall breakables come in. These boxes have strong cardboard dividers. Make a house for the toys by laying the box on its side. The dividers make separate rooms.

Beanbag Toy Geography

Help the students become aware of the various habitats for animals and people around the world. Place a world map in the classroom that can easily be seen by all. A globe will work for small group instruction. Have the students decide where each of their toys would live if they were in their natural habitat. Discuss how animals and people adapt to their environment.

For a fun assessment, place the names of several toys on small pieces of paper. Fold the papers and place in a container. During the assessment, the student selects a folded paper from the container, reads the name and locates its natural habitat on the world map. For a more formal assessment, give children an individual map at their desks. Hold up a toy and have the students write its name and correct habitat.

More Fun with Beanbag Toys

1. Use beanbag toy names for your spelling list.
2. Beanbag toy names make great words to decode using phonics rules.
3. Brainstorm all the names of beans. Keep adding to your list.
4. Have a beanbag toy party. Have parents bring in their child's favorite bean recipe. Beans may not be a favorite with some kids, so make sure you have jelly beans on hand.
5. Use your beanbag toy to learn about measuring. Line up the toys in the hall. How long is the line? How much do 10 toys weigh?

Make Your Own Beanbag Toy
Materials
- old sock (any color)
- blunt needle
- thread
- bag of small beans
- felt scraps
- buttons
- magic markers
- fabric glue

Use the materials above to create your very own beanbag toy. Don't forget to name it and give it a birthday.

Beanbag Toy Home
Materials
- shoe box
- construction paper (variety of colors)
- magic markers
- tape
- glue
- odds and ends

Using a shoe box, create a home suitable for your beanbag toy. Make sure your new home meets all of the needs for its natural habitat.

Beanbag Toy Garden
Materials
- 15-20 bean seeds
- string
- potting soil
- 4-5 empty bean cans (with the labels)
- tape

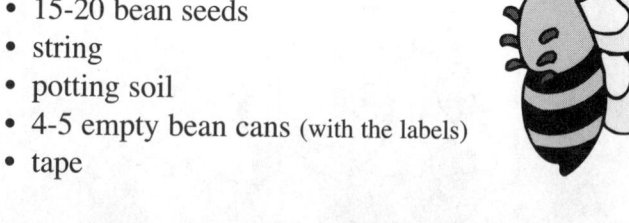

Create your own classroom beanbag toy garden. Purchase inexpensive bean seeds and plant several in each empty can.

Place the cans on the windowsill. Tape three lengths of string to the back of each can. Extend the string to the top of the window and secure with tape. The students will be delighted to see their bean garden climb up the string.

Beanbag Toy Games
Beanbag Toy Drop
This game is played much like Drop the Handkerchief or Duck, Duck, Goose. The children form a large circle facing the center of the circle. One child is selected to be "it." "It" holds a beanbag toy as he walks around the outside of the circle, with the students chanting, "Beanbag . . . Beanbag . . . Beanbag . . ." "It" then yells, "drop" as he drops the toy behind another child. "It" runs around the circle while the other child chases him. If "it" sits down in the open spot in the circle before getting caught, the other child is "it." If "it" gets tagged, he's "it" again.

Beanbag Toy Toss
Prior to playing this game, a gameboard needs to be created. The gameboard is shown in the diagram and can be made using a variety of materials. If you are playing outside, draw the gameboard on the sidewalk with chalk. For a more permanent board, construct it from sturdy cardboard. Tape it to your classroom floor using brightly colored tape.

The rules are simple: Each child tosses three beanbag toys onto the gameboard. Add up the points and see who wins.

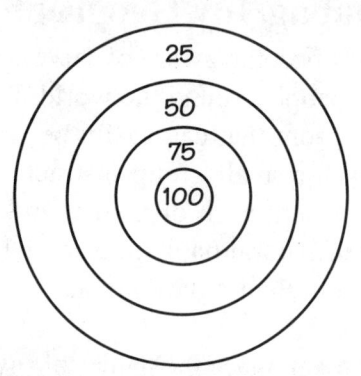

Hide-and-Go-Seek
Hide-and-Go-Seek was never so much fun as when you play it with a beanbag toy. Have the students bring their toys to school for a fun-filled day of learning. Children make up a math problem to hide with their toy. Send the children out of the room, then hide all the toys and problems. As the children find the toys, they must give the answer to the problem. Don't limit the fun just to math class—use scrambled spelling words, social studies facts or vocabulary words.

148

TLC10110 Copyright © Teaching & Learning Company, Carthage, IL 62321-0010

Math Games Beanbag Toys

Put all the toys in a big beach towel. Have students hold the corners and toss the toys into the air. The one that "jumps" the highest wins. Make a chart on the board to record the data. Enter the information in different ways.

- Use the toys as manipulatives for math problems.

- Write story problems for beanbag toys. Example: Binky and Bongo have two new friends. They all went skiing together. They met two more friends there. How many toys went skiing? Which friends do you think they met there? Why?

- If one toy is worth $5.00 today and increases in value by the same amount every year, how much will it be worth in five years?

- Allow your favorite beanbag toy friend to help you with a math test. Put the toy's name on the paper next to yours for credit.

Math Challenges

1. Fred the unicorn was born October 1994. Agnes the cow was born May 1995. How much older is Fred the unicorn?

2. Compare the weight of Tom the cat and Oinker the pig. Who weighs more? "Guesstimate" the difference in weight of a real cat and pig.

3. Kimmy has 17 beanbag toys. Cara has 22 toys and Niki has 15. How many do they have in all?

4. Jill has 25 beanbag toys in her room. Jack came in and hid all of them. How many did Jill have to find?

5. Janet bought 2 toys at the store. Each toy costs $4.99 (including tax). She then bought 3 toys from her friend Buzzy. He charged her $2.00 for one and $2.50 for the other two. How much money did it cost Janet to buy all of the toys?

6. Angelo decided the class should line up all the beanbag toys and measure the length of the line. The line was 100 inches long. If each toy was 5 inches long, how many toys were in the line?

7. Davey thought it would be fun to weigh all the toys in their classroom. He placed 20 toys on the scale and they weighed 10 pounds. What was the average weight of each toy?

8. Caleb the crab lives in Florida, and he wants to visit his friend Wally the worm in Pennsylvania. How far will he have to travel to visit his friend? Give an approximate answer.

9. Teddy the bear wants to have a party and invite some of his beanbag toy friends. He decides to invite 10 friends. Teddy wrote out the invitations and needs to know how much money to take to the post office to buy stamps. Each stamp costs 32¢. How much money will Teddy need for the stamps?

10. The beanbag toys decided to have a party at the beach. There were 150 toys invited. Only half of the toys went to the party. How many were at the beach party?

Stocking Stuffer Math

by Rusty Fischer

As a class, brainstorm 20 or 30 items that might fit in a holiday stocking. List them on the chalkboard. Next to each item, write a realistic price for it. Then have each student take out a sheet of paper and pick eight items from the board. Next, pass around a jar full of pieces of paper with dollar amounts written on them. The amount each student chooses is the amount they are allowed to spend on their "stocking stuffers." Have them total their eight items. If their chosen dollar amount is less than their total, they must review the list and choose the eight items from the board that come as close to their total as possible. If their chosen dollar amount is more than the total for their items, they get to choose more items from the list until they reach their dollar amount!

I usually just get candy,
and so does my brother Randy.
But this year will be dandy,
since we borrowed some stockings from our sister Mandy!

Though they're not quite as strong,
and it might be quite wrong,
to hang them up, since to us they don't really belong,
they are very, very, very long!

150

TLC10110 Copyright © Teaching & Learning Company, Carthage, IL 62321-0010

Santa's Trail Mix

Package three to four cups of Santa's Trail Mix in brown lunch bags. Fold the top down twice. Punch two holes in the center of the folds. Slip a length of twine through the holes and tie in a bow. Attach the poem and you have great gifts straight from the kitchen of Mrs. Claus! This recipe makes about 10 to 12 bags.

Santa's Trail Mix is lots of fun to make and even more fun to give. Have students give Santa's Trail Mix as a special holiday treat to school secretaries, principal, nurse, janitors and other school friends.

Santa's Trail Mix also makes a fun, inexpensive gift for your students. Just follow the simple recipe Mrs. Claus has passed down from generation to generation. Allow the students' imaginations to fly by having them make up and share stories about how the trail mix saved Santa, the elves and the reindeer from various dangers during their Christmas Eve ride.

by Jo Jo Cavalline and Jo Anne O'Donnell

Santa's Trail Mix

Ingredients

- 2 cups salted peanuts
- 5 cups Cheerios® cereal
- 5 cups Wheat Chex®
- 10 oz. mini pretzels
- 2 packages vanilla chips
- 1 lb. M & M's®
- 3 T. cooking oil

- very large bowl or pan
- microwave oven
- microwave-safe bowl
- spoon for stirring
- measuring cups and spoons
- waxed paper

Mix all the ingredients (except the vanilla chips and oil) in the large bowl or pan. Melt the vanilla chips and oil in the microwave until creamy. Pour the creamy vanilla mixture over the dry ingredients. Stir until all of the dry mix is coated. Spread the coated trail mix on waxed paper to dry. (This only takes about 30 minutes.)

Santa's Trail Mix

This special Christmas trail mix is made each year
for Santa, the elves and all the reindeer.
They have a nibble in each hemisphere
On their annual trip to spread Christmas cheer.

Holiday Sing-Alongs

He'll Be Coming O'er the Rooftops

This song is sung to the tune of "She'll Be Coming 'Round the Mountain."

He'll be coming o'er the rooftops
    when he comes.
He'll be coming o'er the rooftops
    when he comes.
He'll be coming o'er the rooftops,
He'll be coming o'er the rooftops,
He'll be coming o'er the rooftops
    when he comes.

He'll be driving eight fleet reindeer
    when he comes.
He'll be driving eight fleet reindeer
    when he comes.
He'll be driving eight fleet reindeer,
He'll be driving eight fleet reindeer,
He'll be driving eight fleet reindeer
    when he comes.

He must be very quiet
    when he comes.
He must be very quiet
    when he comes.
He must be very quiet,
He must be very quiet,
He must be very quiet
    when he comes.

He'll be bringing Christmas
    presents when he comes.
He'll be bringing Christmas
    presents when he comes.
He'll be bringing Christmas presents,
He'll be bringing Christmas presents,
He'll be bringing Christmas presents
    when he comes.

He'll make all the children happy
    when he comes.
He'll make all the children happy
    when he comes.
He'll make all the children happy,
He'll make all the children happy,
He'll make all the children happy
    when he comes.

Discussion

1. Whom is the song about? (Santa Claus, of course!)
2. Do you know the names of some of Santa's reindeer? (Rudolph, of course. Before Rudolph, there were the eight mentioned in the poem "A Visit from St. Nicholas" by Clement C. Moore.* They are Dasher, Dancer, Prancer, Vixen, Comet, Cupid, Donder and Blitzen.)
3. When Santa needs Rudolph, do you think he uses nine reindeer, or do you think one of the other reindeer takes a rest?
4. Santa will need help to make all the children happy. How do people help him? (By giving to such things as Toys for Tots, the Salvation Army, churches and other religious organizations and other charities.)

Activity

Have children bring in pennies and other small coins for Toys for Tots or a charity of your choice.

If Toys for Tots, buy a toy or toys with the money. See if you can have a marine come in to receive the toy or toys.

by Mabel Duch

For Bulletin Boards

CHRISTMAS ORNAMENT BORDER

Here's an inexpensive bulletin board border you can make yourself or let your students make. Use any colored, silver or gold 8 1/2" x 11" paper. Fold as shown and cut into 3" pieces. Reproduce the patterns below on tagboard, trace onto the paper strips and cut border as you would a paper doll. This makes a great center activity. Place prefolded strips and pattern stencils in the center. Let children spend several days making border pieces and placing them in a box or basket. Then use the borders to decorate your room.

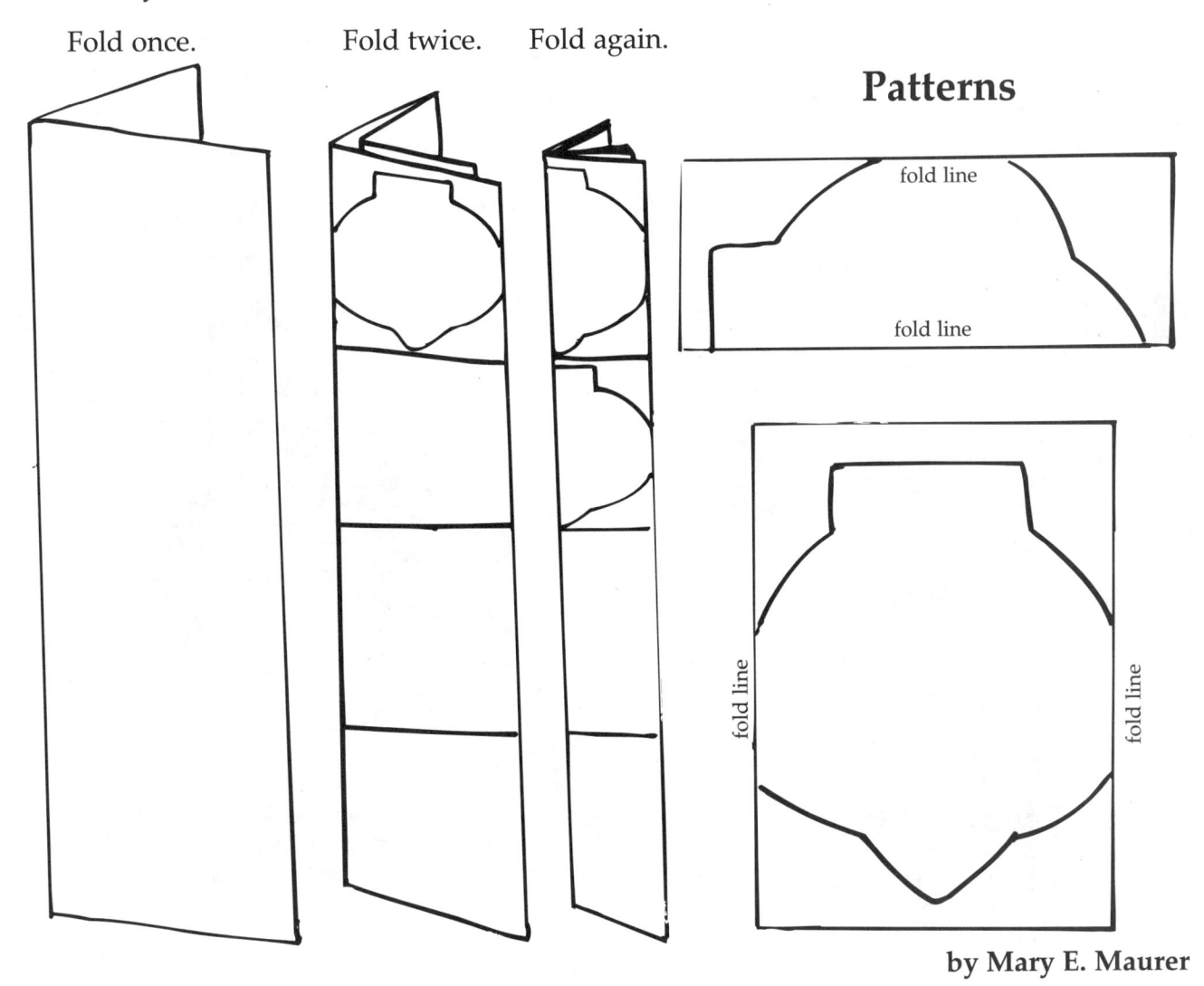

Fold once.   Fold twice.   Fold again.

Patterns

by Mary E. Maurer

Tomie dePaola's Christmas Books

Every year Tomie dePaola writes a Christmas book. These pages mention several of his books and enhancement ideas that correlate with the stories.

Tomie dePaola (de POW la) was born on September 15, 1934, in Meriden, Connecticut. He now lives in New Hampshire and has lived there for quite some time.

After attending Pratt Institute in Brooklyn and earning a Masters of Fine Arts from the California College of Arts and Crafts, his first career was that of an artist. Besides exhibiting his fine works, he also taught college classes in New London, New Hampshire. In this beautiful part of the country, dePaola bought and renovated several homes. At his home studio he writes and illustrates his books. Tomie dePaola has wonderful memories of his childhood and these are the source of many of his stories.

The Christmas holidays are special to Tomie. He loves to decorate and bake. He also has many other book topics to seek and explore.

Robert Hechtel, Tomie dePaola's publicist, produces a newsletter which announces new books, author information and products that can be ordered. Write to:

Redwing Farm Collection
County Road RFD #1, Box 444
New London, NH 03257

Back in the early 1800s in a small New England village, you didn't even know Christmas was near. There were no decorations nor celebrating. Then a family that came from Germany moved into a farmhouse. They were known as "the Christmas family" because of how they joyously celebrated the holiday. They made bayberry candles, paper ornaments, strung popcorn, dried apple rings, baked goodies, decorated trees and lit candles on all the windowsills. The neighbors watched and one by one joined in on all the Christmas celebrations.

An Early American Christmas
by Tomie dePaola, Holiday House, 1987

Candle Holder
Make candle holders to decorate the windowsills or take home as gifts. Use lids from spray cans that have a small circular rim inside. Decorate the lid by gluing rickrack braid or other trimmings to the outside. Place a candle inside the inner rim.

by Tania K. Cowling

The Legend of the Poinsettia
by Tomie dePaola, G.P. Putnam's Sons, 1994

Paper Weaving

Learn the technique of weaving Lucinda learned from her mother but use construction paper instead of yarn. Start with two different colors of the same size paper. Cut one piece into strips. Fold the other sheet in half. Starting at the fold, cut slits across the paper, stopping about one inch from the edge. Weave the strips in and out of the slits you have cut. Start the first one going over one slit then under the next one. The second strip should start under and then over. Tape the paper strips at the ends so they don't slide out.

> This Mexican legend is about a mother and daughter who were weaving a blanket to be placed at a nativity display in their village. After the mother became ill, Lucinda (the daughter) tried to weave the blanket herself. She tangled the yarn and the task became too difficult. Instead she gathered a bunch of tall weeds to take to the procession. To everyone's amazement, the tips of the weeds became a flaming red color. They looked like Christmas stars.
>
> To this day, these plants in Mexico are called "la Flor de Nochebuena" (the flower of the Holy Night). The poinsettia found its way to the United States through Dr. Joel Roberts Poinsett, who served as the United States minister to Mexico from 1825 to 1830. He took cuttings home to South Carolina when he returned from Mexico in 1830. The Christmas plant, the poinsettia, was named after Dr. Poinsett and is one of the holiday symbols today.

The Poinsettia

Copy a picture of the poinsettia flower for each child. Young children can color the picture. A cut-and-paste collage project would be great for creative hands. Supply your children with red construction paper or red tissue paper. Cut out small squares and then glue these inside the border of the poinsettia flower. Finish with some yellow paper dots in the center. See page 219 for poinsettia.

Four Stories for Four Seasons
by Tomie dePaola, Prentice-Hall, 1977

Seasonal Art

Divide a paper into four sections, drawing a cat, dog, pig and frog into one of each section. Show them celebrating one of the four seasonal events told in the story.

An enrichment idea would be to write a short story on how your own family celebrates each season.

> Four friends spend seasonal adventures together. Missy Cat, Master Dog, Mistress Pig and Mister Frog are close friends. They went boating during spring, planted a garden in the summer, planned a dinner party together during autumn and a Christmas celebration in the winter.
>
> Mr. Frog decided to stay awake during the winter instead of hibernating. He was busy planning festivities for the Christmas celebration, however, he became tired and decided to take a short nap. He awoke too late and found all the stores closed on Christmas Eve. Disappointed, he went home. To his surprise, the doorbell rang. One Santa-suited friend after another brought Christmas things to Mr. Frog's house. All of Mr. Frog's friends came to his rescue. The four good friends celebrated a very Merry Christmas together.

This book is made of hard cardboard especially to be handled by babies. It is strictly a picture book with all the sights of Christmas. The pictures include a wreath, candles, holly, manger, candy canes, angel, star, stockings and decorated cookies for Santa to eat.

Baby's First Christmas
by Tomie dePaola, Putnam Publishing Group, 1988

Symbolic Art

Take any of the pictures from the book, copy and cut out a large shape from construction paper. Let the children glue on all kinds of collage trims that you provide. This would be a good project for the younger preschool children.

In a small village in Italy, there was an old woman who spent her days sweeping her little house and walks. She also liked to bake cookies. One day she heard noises and saw a procession of royal-looking men, camels and horses crossing her path. They said they were looking for the way to Bethlehem to find the Child King. Old Befana decided she would bake cookies to take to the child and also try to find Him. She searched and searched, but with no success. The legend says that every year on January 6 (The Feast of the Three Kings), Old Befana visits all the children of Italy and leaves them candies, cookies and gifts. It is said that she is still searching for the Christ Child.

The Legend of Old Befana
by Tomie dePaola, HBJ Publishing, 1980

Sugar Cookies

This is a good story to read and then bake cookies together afterward. There are many recipes for sugar cookies, and even easy refrigerator dough for convenience. Here is a standard sugar cookie recipe.

1 c. softened butter
3/4 c. sugar
1 large egg
1 tsp. vanilla extract
2 3/4 c. flour
1 tsp. baking soda
1 tsp. cream of tartar

Cream the butter and sugar in a large bowl until fluffy. Add the egg and vanilla and beat well. Combine the flour, baking soda and cream of tartar in a container and slowly add it to the butter mixture until thoroughly combined. Refrigerate the dough until cool. Then work it with your hands until pliable. Place it on a floured board and roll out the dough until it is 1/4" thick. Cut the dough with cookie cutters. Bake these cookies in a preheated 350°F oven for 8 to 10 minutes. You can spread sugar on the dough before baking or spread them with frosting and sugar when they are baked and cooled.

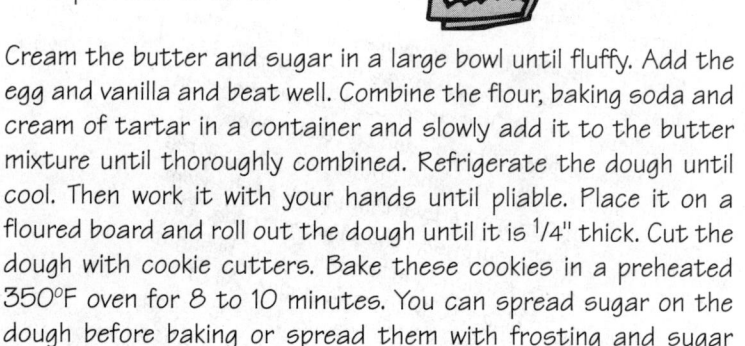

Old Befana

Illustrate the story on paper. Draw and color Old Befana sweeping her house, baking cookies, searching for the Christ Child or visiting the children each year with gifts. Share everyone's pictures with the class or display them on bulletin boards.

This book is about two children and their parents who cut down and decorate their own Christmas tree. The family discusses many fascinating facts about this holiday tree. In the book, you will learn how the tree became part of Christmas in America, how it became decorated, the beginning of tree stands, why electric lights replaced candles on the tree and facts about the first ornaments.

The Family Christmas Tree Book
by Tomie dePaola, Holiday House, 1980

Tree Art

Cut two identical triangles from green construction paper. Slit one triangle up from the bottom to the center and the other from the top point to the center as shown. Glue decorations on the triangles such as gummed stars, sequins, felt pieces, rickrack or small pictures. Slide the two slits together and the tree will stand.

Ornaments

There are so many kinds of tree ornaments to make. There are instructions to make an angel ornament in the back of this storybook. Check craft books on making ornaments in your classroom.

Satellite Ornament

Crush pieces of aluminum foil and mold them into a ball. Pierce colored toothpicks thorough the sphere to make it look like a satellite. Insert a paper clip inside the foil ball and thread yarn through the loop for a hanger.

Merry Christmas Strega Nona
by Tomie dePaola, HBJ Publishing, 1986

Art

Reproduce a picture of Strega Nona for the children to color. The kids can add their own drawings of the friends and the feast.

It was the first Sunday of Advent and everyone was getting ready for Christmas including Strega Nona. She cleaned and decorated the house. She would ask her helper, Big Anthony, to do errands. Go get the baccala (dried codfish for the Christmas stew), soak it in water every day until Christmas Eve. Big Anthony asked her to do magic instead of his errands. Strega Nona said, "No magic at Christmastime—Christmas has magic of its own."

Through the story, Strega Nona was disappointed with her helper, Big Anthony. He forgot to do all the chores. But to Strega Nona's surprise, when she went home after the church mass, she found all her friends gathered around the table where the holiday feast was finished. Big Anthony did it all for Strega Nona because she always worked so hard for everyone else. Christmas did have a magic of its own!

Christmastime in POLAND

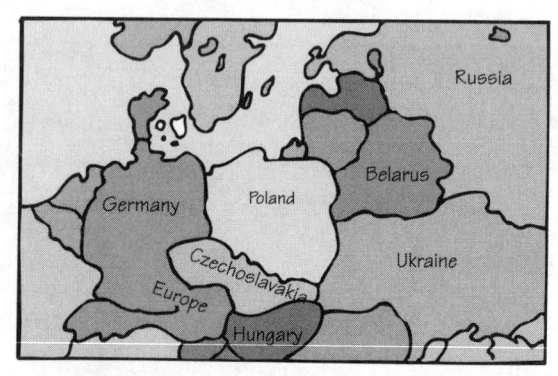

Frosty weather may chill the air at Christmas in Poland, but the season sparkles with warm traditions. Children decorate their homes and Christmas trees with brightly colored paper cut-outs as they prepare for the biggest holiday of the year—Christmas Eve.

Family and friends gather on this day for a special meal of vegetables and fish. They eat nothing the entire day until the first star of the evening shines brightly in the night sky. The star has special meaning and is woven into Christmas customs. The Christmas tree, glowing with colored paper-cut ornaments, is also an important part of the celebration. Children carefully place a beautiful paper-cut star on the top of the tree as a reminder of the evening star. Christmas presents or "star gifts" are placed under the tree. When the gifts are exchanged, everyone attends midnight mass.

The season's celebration continues until January 6th, the day of the Three Kings, who bring more "star gifts." These Three Kings (local people) may even test children on their religious knowledge!

Children busily engage in the centuries-old art of paper-cut decorations during this season. These beautiful paper designs are used to decorate their homes. As new decorations are created, the old ones are taken down and used elsewhere. Some even find their way into the barn for the animals to enjoy. When the Christmas season is over, invite the children to take the decorations that they created in the classroom home to enjoy during the winter.

Children in Poland also perform a szopka play—a Christmas tradition that dates back to the 14th century. Your students will love building their own Szopka Puppet Theater, designing the puppets and performing a Polish folktale play.

Bibliography

Holz, Loretta. *The Christmas Spider*. Philomel Books, The Putnam Publishing Group, New York, NY.

Metcalfe, Edna. *Christmas Around the World*. Ideal Publications, From "The Trees of Christmas," Abingdon Press.

Foley, Daniel J. *Christmas the World Over*. Chilton Book Company, Radnor, Pennsylvania, and Thomas Nelson and Sons, Ltd., Ontario, Canada.

by Barbara Fischer

Cut-Paper

Paper-Cut Flowers

Materials: colored paper, pencils, glue, scissors

Decorate your bulletin boards and rooms with paper cut-outs. Fold a piece of colored construction paper in half. Trace a design on one half as shown. Cut along the drawn design and unfold the shape. Lay it flat on the table. Choose another colored paper to cut out different sized petals, circles and heart shapes. Fringe the edges and glue onto the shaped design to create a flower. Make several layers beginning with the largest and ending with the smallest. Glue a circle to the flower center. Glue hearts on the circle. Add green stems and leaves. The flowers will also make an interesting border around your windows and doors as well as bulletin boards.

Snow-White Snowflakes

Materials: white typing paper, scissors, pencils

Cut a circle 6" in diameter. Fold the circle in half three times. Draw designs on the folded edges only. Open the circle and you'll have a round snowflake to hang from the ceiling. Tape some to your windows for a snowy effect.

Colorful Ornaments

Materials: white paper, pencils, colored construction paper, scissors, glue

Begin by making two identical snowflakes. Choose a piece of brightly colored paper and cut the same 6" circle as the snowflake. Glue one white snowflake to each side of the colored circle, sandwich style. Punch a hole in the top for thread. Hang these traditional Polish paper ornaments on your tree.

The Evening Star

Materials: colored construction paper, pencils, scissors, tape

The star is an important Christmas symbol in Poland. Make these stars by cutting a 6" circle. Fold the circle in half three times. Draw a V. Cut along the V line. Open to find an eight-point star as shown. These can be placed at the top of the Christmas tree; used to decorate Christmas cards, star gifts and the Szopka Puppet Theater.

TLC10110 Copyright © Teaching & Learning Company, Carthage, IL 62321-0010

159

Christmas Szopka
Puppet Theater

Materials: cardboard box about 16" x 30", tagboard or flat cardboard, scissors, pencils, paper-cut decorations, tempera paint, markers

The Szopka Theater and play is a wonderful Polish custom dating back to the 14th century. The portable theater is the stable where the Christ Child was born. It is decorated with paper-cut flowers, snowflakes and stars.

1. Cut an opening in the center front of the box from the bottom about 12" high and at least 18" wide. Cut a hole in each side for the puppets to enter and exit the stage.

2. Use the tagboard or flat cardboard (be sure it is taller than the box) to make two identical towers. Glue these to each side of the box facing the front.

3. Cut one long rectangle and two triangles from the remaining cardboard pieces. Glue or tape the rectangle shape upright to the top middle of the box. Glue one triangle to the top of each tower.

4. Paint the theater with bright colors. When dry, decorate with snowflakes, stars, flowers and other paper cuts that you have learned to make.

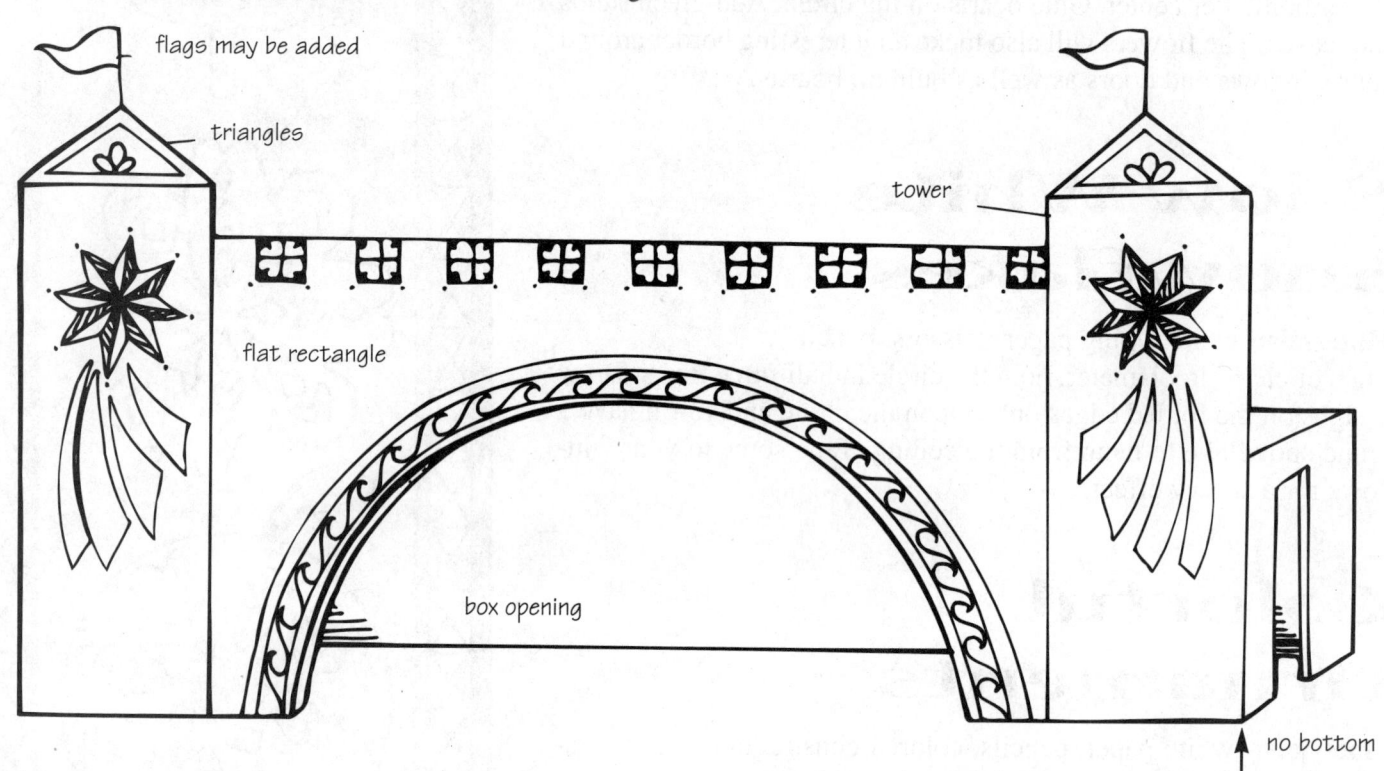

Labels on diagram: flags may be added, triangles, tower, flat rectangle, box opening, no bottom

The Puppet Play

- Read the Polish folktale, "The Christmas Spider." Note: Polish legend tells us that animals talk on Christmas Eve.
- Make puppet characters.
- Write a script.

Puppet Characters

1. Draw a cow, donkey, rooster, Mary, Joseph and the Christ Child (lying in a manger). Tagboard works well.
2. Color and cut out.
3. Glue characters to craft sticks. Be sure to glue the stick to the side of the puppets. The puppets enter and exit from the holes in the side of the box.
4. Spider: Paint a small Styrofoam™ ball black. Add wiggly eyes and pipe cleaner legs. Tie a string to a Christmas ornament hook. Poke the hook into the top of the spider. (Spider needs to dangle in the stable.)
5. Cut a small snowflake from black paper for the web.

Write a Script

- Review the story and discuss what each character might say. Write a few sentences for each.
- You may want to have a narrator open the play with the first paragraph and end with the last paragraph.
- All puppets except Spider enter and exit from the side. Spider drops down from the top.

Find an audience and have fun with your szopka puppet performance.

The Christmas Spider

Long ago, a big, black spider lived in the town of Bethlehem. One day he crawled to the rim of an earthen jug and saw his reflection in the water. How crooked his legs were! How hairy they looked! No wonder people were frightened when they saw him. He was ugly! Spider decided to run away and hide. The stable at the end of the road would be a safe place. Once there, he found a corner near the roof and began to spin his web.

Now Spider was not alone. Rooster, cow and donkey lived in the stable. They welcomed Spider, for they knew he would keep the flies away. One night, Spider was awakened by a bright light. He opened his eyes to see people there. He saw a man and a woman comforting a tiny baby who was lying in the manger. The baby was crying. "Joseph," the woman said. "The night is cold and our baby has no blanket to keep him warm."

"Take my feathers," said Rooster.

"Thank you," said the mother. "But there is a cold wind blowing. You need your feathers to keep warm."

Spider heard all this. He crawled from his web on his crooked legs over to the mother. "You may have my web to keep the baby warm," he told her.

"Thank you, Spider," she said. "That is kind of you. Look! Your web has become soft and warm. How can I repay you?"

"Oh, I wish I were beautiful," Spider said. "Then people would not run away from me."

"Little Spider, I cannot change who you are. Your legs need to be crooked to walk on your web. But I will grant you this: Whenever someone sees a spider after dark, they will think it is good luck," said the mother. "They won't run away from you anymore."

Now Spider was happy. He still walked on crooked legs, but he was pleased that although he was the smallest one, his gift was just right.

KWANZAA

How would you like to start celebrating all over again the day after Christmas? You wouldn't go to church, because the celebration isn't a religious one. Instead, you would spend time with your family every night for a week, lighting candles and eating lots of good food. You might get presents, but they would probably be made by someone you love, not purchased at a store. Each night you would learn a new Swahili word that tells something about the things you are celebrating.

This holiday is called Kwanzaa. Dr. Maulana (Ron) Karenga wanted African Americans to have a holiday that made them feel proud of their heritage and their community, so he started Kwanzaa in 1966.

Each night of Kwanzaa celebrates something different. The seven ideas that are celebrated during the seven nights of Kwanzaa (December 26 to January 1) are umoja (unity), kujichagulia (self-determination), ujima (collective work and responsibility), ujamaa (cooperative economics), nia (purpose), kuumba (creativity) and imani (faith). These are called the "seven principles of Kwanzaa."

Though Kwanzaa is an African American celebration, the ideas that it celebrates are the things that keep communities together and that all people can celebrate, no matter what their skin color.

Kwanzaa Colors

The colors red, green and black are an important part of Kwanzaa.
Red stands for struggle.
Black stands for the African American people.
Green stands for three things: the hills of Africa, the future and hope.
Use these hints to color the flag (bendera) below.

Bendera (ben-DER-ah)

The top stripe stands for the hills of Africa.

Color it _____.
The middle stripe stands for the people.

Color it _____.
The bottom stripe stands for struggle.

Color it _____.

Kinara (kee-NAH-rah)

Use the hints below to color the candles in the candle holder (kinara).
The first three candles stand for struggle.

Color them _____.
The middle candle stands for the people.

Color it _____.
The last three candles stand for the future.

Color them _____.

by Lisa Lawmaster Hess

Preparing the Kwanzaa Table

It's time to prepare the Kwanzaa table!
First, color the items on the table.
There is one ear of corn on the table. Do you need to add any?

(There should be one ear of corn for each child in the family.)

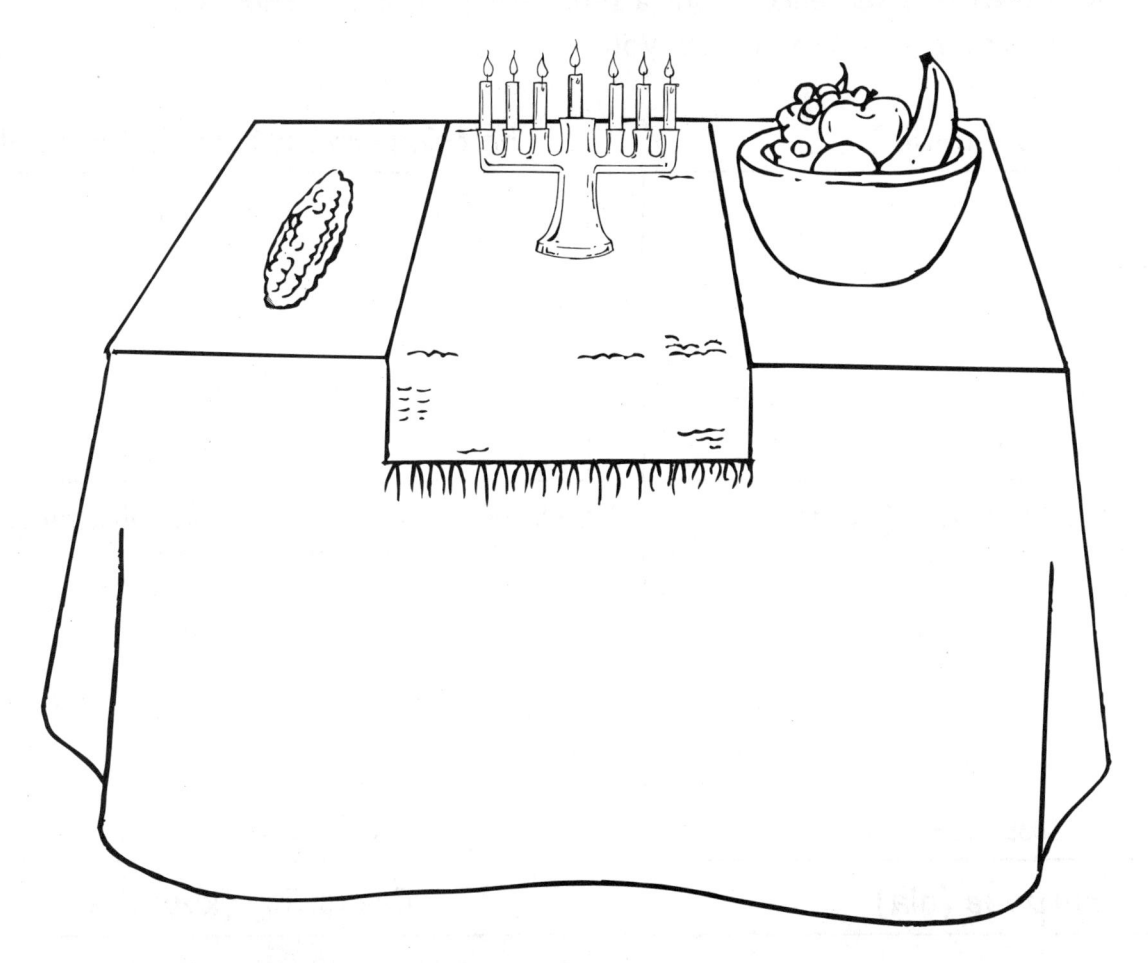

Now, use the Swahili words in the chart below to label the items on the table. Swahili words are used during Kwanzaa because people in many areas of Africa speak Swahili. Using these words helps African Americans to celebrate their culture.

Swahili Word	Pronunciation	Definition
mkeka	(m-KAY-kah)	straw mat
kinara	(kee-NAH-rah)	candle holder
mazao	(mah-ZAH-oh)	crops (fruit)
vibunzi	(vee-BOON-zee)	ears of corn
mishumaa saba	(mee-shoo-MAH-ah SAH-bah)	seven candles

The Seven Principles of Kwanzaa

The number seven is an important part of Kwanzaa. There are seven letters in *Kwanzaa*, seven nights of Kwanzaa and seven candles in the kinara. Most important, though, are the seven principles of Kwanzaa.

Draw a picture or write a sentence about a time that you or a friend used each principle of Kwanzaa. Use the hint in each box to help you.

Unity (umoja)

Sticking together

Self-Determination (kujichagulia)

Standing up for what is right

Working Together (ujima)

Cooperating

Working Together to Make Money (ujamaa)

Working as a group to earn things

Purpose (nia)

Doing your part

Creativity (kuumba)

Making things and making music

Faith (imani)

Believing

Are these things important at other times of the year, too? Why or why not?

BOXING DAY

Boxing Day is a holiday celebrated in the United Kingdom. The December 26th holiday originated with the custom of giving boxes of food, clothing or other items to lamplighters, drivers and others who served the community throughout the year. Boxing Day is now a day to exchange gifts and is an annual banking holiday throughout the United Kingdom. Celebrate this English holiday with your class as part of your "Holidays Around the World."

FAMILY BOX

Families come in all different sizes and shapes. With the help of parents, collect quart-sized milk cartons, cereal boxes and other miscellaneous four-sided boxes. Cover these with white paper, but leave the top open. Instruct each student to label the first side ME, the second side FAMILY, the third side HOME and the fourth side TOGETHER. On the side labeled ME, instruct students to draw pictures of themselves performing a favorite activity.

Direct students to illustrate the remaining sides with pictures of family, home and a favorite family activity. Copy the following poem and put it inside the box.

> This box is me.
> Here's my family.
> This is my home.
> Here's where we like to roam.

WHAT'S IN THE BOX?

Wrap several boxes, each containing a different small toy or classroom item. During discussion time, invite students to shake, weigh and examine the boxes. Encourage them to ask *yes* or *no* questions until someone is ready to guess what is in the box. Take turns guessing until someone correctly identifies the item hidden in the box.

GRAHAM CRACKER BOXES

At snack time, use frosting to make graham cracker boxes. Set a graham cracker on a plate and place four other crackers vertically around the edges. Use frosting as mortar between the crackers. Fill the inside of the cracker box with cereal or other dry snacks.

BOX PICTURES

Set up your art center with different colors of tempera paint and sheets of art paper. Cut sponges into different-sized squares and rectangles. Demonstrate how to dip a sponge into paint and make a print on the paper. Have students make "box pictures" using different-shaped sponges and various paint colors. Allow pictures to dry. After each student has finished a picture, display them around the room.

BY TERRY HEALY

SORTING BOXES

Set up a display of the following empty, labeled boxes and the matching objects. Ask students to sort objects or pictures into the appropriate boxes.

Box Labels	Objects/Pictures
shiny/dull	small holiday ornaments
consonant sounds	magazine pictures that begin with those sounds
living/nonliving	magazine pictures
1-2-3	pictures of objects in groups of 1, 2 or 3
shapes such as circle, square, triangle	common objects or pictures (triangle, square, circle)

BOX TOWN

With help from parents, collect a wide assortment of small boxes. Invite students to build a small town with the boxes, decorating them with construction paper, paints and artificial snow. Use the town as a starting point for discussions about differences between seasons as well as the holiday customs of your country and the United Kingdom. For practice with ordinal numbers, ask students to identify the first, second, third, fourth or fifth house. Use the town to practice giving directions to specific destinations in Box Town.

COMMUNITY BOXES

With permission from the principal, set out large boxes in which to collect food for the local food bank. Have students graph the number and type of food donated. The Boxing Day donations may also include toys, clothing, coats or other times that are needed by community organizations. An alternative suggestion is to make up small boxes of toys, coloring books and activities for children spending Boxing Day in the hospital. Check with local organizations to see what type of boxes and gifts are most needed.

BOXES OF FOOD

Set out several boxes or containers of various foods. Ask students to answer the following questions:
- Which box contains the most food?
- Which box has the most packaging? Is the packaging needed?
- Which box is the best buy?
- Do any of the boxes contain the same amount of food?

NUTRITION IN A BOX

Use the food containers from the "Boxes of Food" activity to study nutrition. Explain to students that important nutrition facts are now found on the outside of each food container. Information on serving size, servings per container, calories per serving, as well as other information is given on a chart. Print the following items on a reproducible for students to complete after examining one of the food containers. Invite students to devise math problems from the information they gather.

Food Name _____

Weight _____ g or _____ lb. _____ oz.

Serving size _____   Servings per container _____

Calories per serving _____   Calories from fat _____

GIVING BOXES

It may be the thrill of opening up and looking inside or the anticipation of what you might put inside—whatever the reason, boxes hold a special fascination for adults and kids alike. These fun-to-make homemade gift boxes can be given as gifts in themselves or filled with seasonal surprises.

Materials
- plastic cup or container
- paintbrush
- white glue
- water
- assortment of cardboard boxes, containers
- magazines and newspapers
- wrapping and tissue paper
- seasonal cards
- construction paper
- fabric and felt
- glitter (optional)

Process
1. Mix an equal amount of glue and water in the container.
2. Cut or tear the paper or fabric into small pieces.
3. Remove the lid from the container to be decorated separately.
4. Paint the glue mixture onto one side of the box.
5. Cover the painted side with the paper or fabric pieces until completely covered.
6. Cover the entire surface with a light coat of the glue mixture. Sprinkle on glitter if desired.
7. Repeat this process until all sides of the box or container are covered.
8. When glue has dried, paint another coat over the entire container.

Try This
1. Make tiny clay mice or other critters to peek out of the tiny boxes, then hang them on the tree.
2. Fill the boxes with homemade candy, jewelry, poetry, stationery, candles or heartfelt messages or poems.
3. Complete the box with a ribbon and homemade card.

CLEVER COOKIE BOX

Make one large box or three small ones.

Materials
- 1 cup (250 ml) brown sugar
- 1/2 cup (125 ml) butter or margarine
- 1 egg
- 1 tsp. (5 ml) vanilla
- 1 1/4 cups (300 ml) flour
- 1/2 tsp. (2 ml) baking powder
- 1/4 tsp. (1 ml) salt
- mixing bowls and spoons
- foil-wrapped cardboard
- scissors
- rolling pin
- spatulas
- oven and oven mitts

Process
1. Preheat the oven to 350°F (175°C).
2. Make or find a small cardboard box. Cut the box into pieces. How many sides are there to a box?
3. Wrap the cardboard pieces in foil.
4. Combine sugar, margarine and vanilla in a large bowl.
5. In a separate bowl, mix the flour, baking powder and salt.
6. Add the flour mixture to the sugary mixture and stir gently until the mixture forms a doughy ball.
7. Turn the ball onto a floured surface and roll it out to about 3/8" (1 cm) thickness.
8. Place the foil-wrapped pieces over the dough and cut the patterns into the dough.
9. Using spatulas, carefully transfer the dough to a cookie sheet.
10. Bake for 10 minutes or until brown.
11. Let the box pieces cool.
12. Place a container of chocolate in a bowl or pan of hot water and melt on the stove or in the microwave. Keep the container in a bowl of warm water while you construct your box.
13. Cement the sides of the box together using the chocolate as "cement." Do not cement the top of your box in place—it will be held in place with a ribbon when the gift box is filled with surprises.

Try This
Fill the boxes with tiny cookies, candies, chocolates, cookie cutters or a touching message.

by Robynne Eagan

Ta Chiu, The Festival of Peace and Renewal, is celebrated in Hong Kong. A list is made naming everyone who lives in the area. The names are read publicly and attached to a paper horse, which is burned so the smoke from the names rises to heaven.

While you may not wish to burn your lists, a little public recognition may help bring renewed peace to your classroom. Provide students with a list of everyone in your classroom. Leave sufficient space for students to write beside or below each name. In addition, each student may wish to add names of parents, siblings, friends, grandparents and pets to their list.

Beside every name, each student will write something they like about that person. They might write something that the person is good at. Lists will be displayed, so writing should be done in complete sentences, with correct spelling and neat handwriting! Be sure students include something positive about themselves!

Have students use the following instructions to construct paper horses. Attach the lists to the completed horses and display them so that everyone can see and read positive affirmations of themselves and others.

For younger students, make a large class list and post it on your wall. Have students dictate something they like about each child as you record it for them. Make paper horses in many bright colors and arrange them around your master list.

by Gloria Trabacca

Ta Chiu
The Festival of Peace and Renewal

Ta Chiu Horse

Provide each student with a copy of the accompanying reproducible. If possible, make the reproducible in a variety of colors, or all in white so that students may decorate them. Read the following instructions to your students, allowing time for completion of each step before moving on.

1. Cut your paper in half lengthwise, along the solid black line.
2. Fold each rectangle in half on the single dotted line.
3. Then fold your papers on the double-dotted line, so that the dots are hidden.
4. Shape #1 is the head and front legs of your horse. Place it on your desk so that the short head is angled pointing to the right, and the long leg section is pointing towards you.
5. Shape #2 is the body and back legs of your horse. Place it on your desk with the short leg section on the left pointing toward you.
6. Place the body section at a right angle behind the front leg section. Make sure the front and back legs are lined up evenly. Glue or staple in place. Glue the remaining folded sections together so the horse lies flat.
7. Using yarn or scraps of paper, make a mane and tail for your horse. Eight-inch lengths of yarn, doubled and attached to the horse using staples or glue, work well for both the mane and tail. Add a face and decorate your horse as desired.

1.

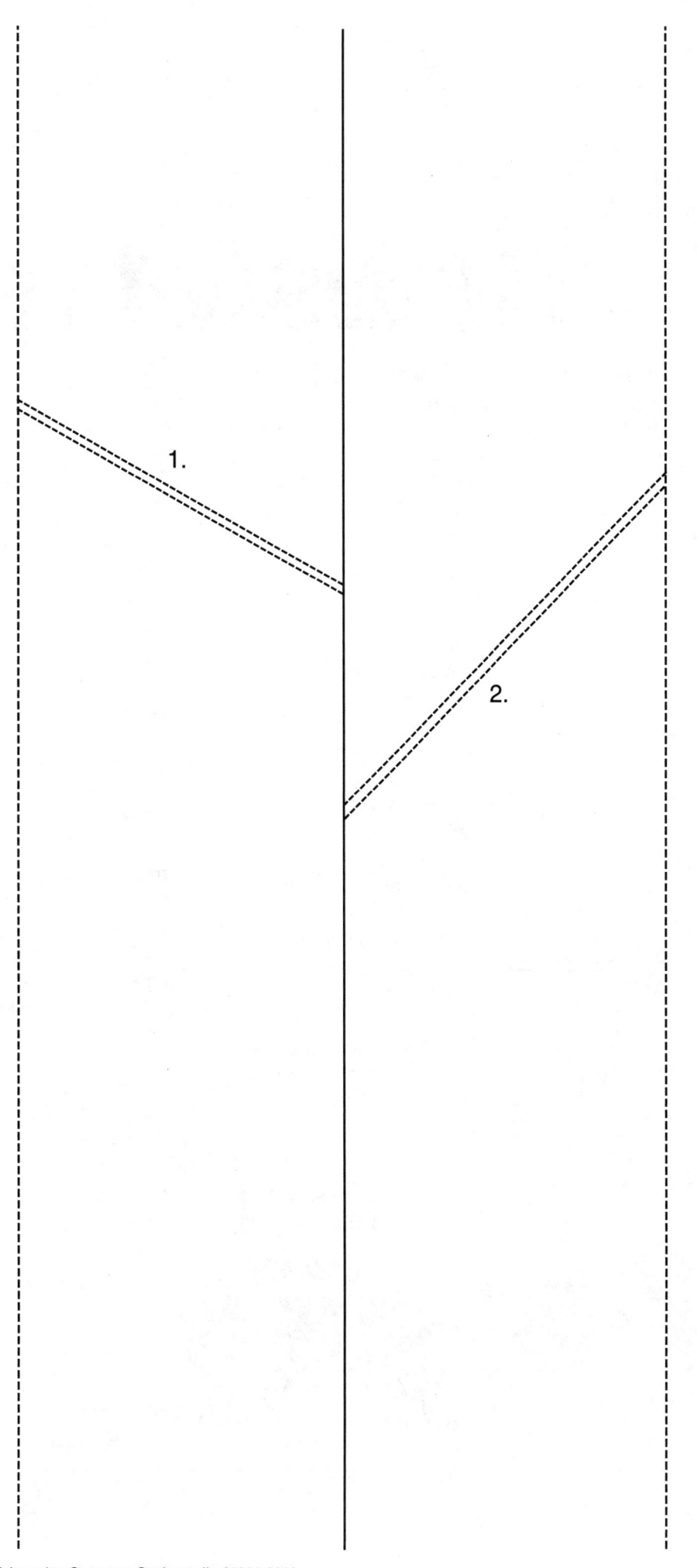

2.

Winter newsletter

A Family Take-Home

A Family Take-Home

Holiday time is family time, whatever your faith or traditions. Enjoy sharing some of the following holiday activities with your child. To do is to learn, and your time is the best gift you can give.

Simple Science

Many families drink more carbonated beverages during the holiday season than at any other time of the year. Children (adults, too!) can be fascinated by the bubbles of gas and fizz that appear upon pouring and continue to rise to the top of the glass. As your child observes the bubbling action, suggest dropping a few raisins into the glass. What happens? The raisins naturally sink to the bottom. Now, wait and watch a little longer. Call attention to the bubbles forming around each raisin. What happens to the raisin when it is surrounded by bubbles? It floats to the surface of the beverage as the gas bubbles have given it buoyancy. When it reaches the surface and the bubbles pop, what happens? It sinks to the bottom to start the same process over again. Your child will enjoy demonstrating the raisin dance to friends and family members.

On the Move

What could be more exhilarating than outdoor play in the crisp air of the holiday season? Small or large group activities definitely have a place during this time of sharing, caring and giving. Together, you and your child can prepare a game flyer to use with the whole family or a group of friends. Have your child decorate the backs of two paper plates with holiday designs. Your children will need scissors, glue, paper and markers or paint to create the designs. Older children may also want to write holiday words or messages on the plates to accompany their designs. When the plates are decorated, have your child place a line of glue around the rim on the front of one plate; then place the second plate over the first, matching the rims. Allow the glue to dry, then take the flyer outdoors to toss and catch. Older children may also enjoy tossing the flyer for distance or height, or you could set up a target area using empty soda bottles.

by Marie E. Cecchini

Creative Kitchen

Invite your child to help you in creating a "sense"ational holiday gift from the kitchen. As you prepare the fudge recipe below, have your child compare the textural differences between the powdered ingredients and the salt. Each of you can wet one of your fingers, and then dab it into the various ingredients to taste them. Ask your child to describe the different tastes. During preparation, note the look and sound of boiling water. Observe how the texture of each ingredient changes as it is heated and/or combined with something. As the fudge chills and hardens, work together to create inventive packaging ideas for sharing your special recipe with friends and family.

Melt-in-Your-Mouth Fudge

1/2 c. butter/margarine
1/3 c. boiling water
4 1/2 c. powdered sugar
1/2 c. nonfat powdered milk
1/2 c. unsweetened cocoa powder
a pinch of salt
1/2 c. chopped nuts (optional)

Stir the butter into the boiling water until melted. Add the powdered sugar, powdered milk, cocoa powder and salt. Mix with a wire whisk or electric mixer until smooth. Stir in the nuts, if desired. Pour the mixture into a buttered 8" x 8" square pan and refrigerate several hours or overnight. Cut into 1" squares.

Communication Station

Every celebration has its own unique vocabulary. The best way for children to become familiar with these words and their meanings is to use them. Encourage your child to make use of some of these new words in the process of constructing a holiday banner or flag. Have your child begin by drawing the banner design and writing a slogan on a piece of paper. Next, cut out a large rectangle of felt for the background. Use smaller felt pieces, markers, scissors and letter stencils to create the shapes for the design and letters for the slogan. Arrange the pieces for proper placement on the large rectangle, then remove and glue one piece at a time until the banner is complete. When the design is dry, spread glue along one edge of the large rectangle. Then roll the glued portion around a dowel or stick. Cover the glued portion with a strip of waxed paper. Use spring-action clothespins to hold the felt in place until the glue dries. Display your banner during the holidays; then roll it up and pack it away to save for next year.

From the Art Cart

Invite your child to join you in creating special holiday magnets to use and save from year to year. They will make a practical addition to your seasonal decor when you use them to hang favorite recipes and important reminders on your refrigerator. This is also a project children can make on their own to give as gifts. To make the magnets, use foam trays or purchase inexpensive craft foam from a local store. Instruct your child to trace festive cookie cutter shapes or shapes of his or her own design onto the foam using a pencil. Next, cut out the shapes with scissors or decorative edging shears. Embellish these shapes with markers, fabric paints, glitter, ribbon, yarn, feathers, buttons and so on. When the decorations have dried, glue a magnetic strip to the back of each shape.

Poetry in Motion

Engage your whole family in the fun of pantomime as you enjoy a game about giving. First, have each person select one item to be used as a pretend gift, then place these items into a box. Any simple household item can be included, such as a pencil, cup, ball, card, comb, silk flower, adhesive badge, toothbrush and so on. The more unusual the "gift," the more humorous the pantomime. Each person takes a turn repeating the following rhyme and performs a pantomime describing the gift. The person who correctly identifies the "gift" will have the next turn. For older children, gift words can be written on cards or paper then placed into a bag. Each person would then draw a word card from the bag, recite the rhyme and perform the pantomime.

I'm hiding a present
I made by myself.
I wrapped it up tight
And it's up on the shelf.

Although I can't tell
What I've made for you,
Maybe you'll guess,
If I give you a clue.

Mathworks

Games are a great way to practice math skills at home. There are many board games available that strengthen counting, adding and subtracting skills. Also, teaching your child a few simple card games can reinforce the idea that math is part of many things we do. For something a little different, try a homemade game even the youngest of players will understand. Provide the players with 20 whole peanuts and one craft stick. Have one of the players color one side of the craft stick with a marker. To play, each player takes a turn holding the stick above the floor or a table, then dropping it onto the surface below. If the stick lands with the colored side showing, the player receives one nut. If the stick lands with the plain side up, they don't get a nut. When all 20 nuts have been distributed, each player totals the number of nuts he or she has collected. Older children may also want to make this into a game of probability by having each player drop the stick 10 times and record the results. After each player has had a turn, they can review the results and draw conclusions as to how many times the colored side will appear in every 10 turns.

Reading Room

Bring the warmth of the season into your home as you share with your child the universal meaning of the holidays, whatever your faith or background, through reading.

Crafts for Kwanzaa by Kathy Ross, The Millbrook Press, Inc., Grades 1-3.
Gracias, The Thanksgiving Turkey by Jay Cowley, Scholastic, PreK-3.
The Magic Dreidels by Eric A. Kimmel, Holiday House, PreK-3.
The Oldest Elf by James Stevenson, Greenwillow, PreK-3.
The Perfect Present by Michael Hague, William Morrow, PreK-1.
The Ugly Menorah by Marissa Moss, Farrar, Straus and Giroux, K-3.

How to Use These Pages

Let our family take-home and clip-art designs take some of the stress out of your holiday season. Use these parent-and-child activities and seasonal drawings to enhance your usual holiday communication.

Brand New and Still You
A New Year's Story
by Dr. Linda Karges-Bone

Starting over, starting new.
Time to make a better you.
New Year's Day, a place to start.
Change your body, change your heart!

Betty Jo Bunny sang her little tune while she jumped rope. Since she was a rabbit, jumping rope seemed like the perfect exercise for the new year. Betty Jo wanted to lose some weight. She thought she was too fat.

"What's that song and what *are* you jumping around like that for?" asked her cousin Harriet Hare as she loped into the clearing.

"It is my New Year's resolution song," replied Betty Jo. She kept on jumping, building up a nice sweat as she huffed and puffed. "I ate too much holiday carrot cake and now my legs are positively plump. I want to improve myself."

"I think you look fine. Why worry so much about how you look? It is the inside that counts," Harriet told her cousin.

"The inside of what?" inquired Peter Possum, who was returning from a night of hunting and scavenging.

"I was telling Betty Jo that you need to like yourself for who you are inside, not to worry so much about the outside," said Harriet.

"Don't you want to be better in the new year, Peter?" asked Betty Jo.

"Sure I do. I could use some change in my life," agreed Peter. "Do I have to jump rope?"

"I wouldn't think so," replied Betty Jo. "You are pretty trim from all that foraging around at night. But wouldn't you like to sleep at night like me? Why, I'll bet you could change your night gathering to daytime gathering, and really make your life better."

"Possums are nocturnal," muttered Harriet.

"Did you say something, dear?" asked Betty Jo.

"I said 'knock yourself out.' Go for it," announced Harriet.

"Sounds great to me," agreed Peter.

Starting over, starting new.
Time to make a better you.
New Year's Day, a place to start.
Change your body, change your heart!

Betty Jo and Peter set off to plan Peter's new schedule, and on their way they met Oscar Otter. He was drying off in the sparse winter sun, taking a break from fishing in the stream.

"Greetings, all," said Oscar. He was a very proper and polite creature. He liked things in order. "Could you please identify that catchy tune that you were singing earlier?"

"It is our New Year's resolution song," Betty Jo and Peter told him. They shared their plans to improve and remake their lives in order to have a better new year.

"You should try it too, Oscar," urged Peter. "All this time you spend, keeping your traps clean and your fur sleek, you are missing out on life, man. You need to let up; relax. Change your ways."

"That's right," said Betty Jo. "I'm changing my ways. Instead of running in the woods, I'm jumping in place to lose weight. Change is good."

"Perhaps I am a bit rigid," admitted Oscar. "A few days of change might do me good, and New Year's is a proper starting point, I would agree."

Starting over, starting new.
Time to make a better you.
New Year's Day, a place to start.
Change your body, change your heart!

Together, the three friends sang their song, and continued through the woods to where they found Bernard Bear, cozy and snug, dozing in the shelter of a small cave. Their loud singing woke Bernard up. He had been *hibernating*, a fancy word for "bears who sleep in the wintertime."

"What's that? Is it springtime? Time to wake up?" called out Bernard. He sounded a little cranky.

"It is the day after New Year's," announced Oscar. "January 2nd, old man. We are bringing news of plans for improvement. Are you interested?"

"I'm interested in sleeping," muttered Bernard. He started to roll back over, but Betty Jo got his attention.

"If you changed your ways, Bernard, it could mean a lot more honey."

"Honey? Why didn't you say so?" Bernard perked up and listened.

"Why sure," said Betty Jo. "I mean, if you didn't spend three or four whole months of the winter asleep, you would have lots more time to find honey."

"And eat honey," nodded Bernard. He rubbed the sleep from his eyes and pulled himself out of the hibernation den. New Year's resolutions sounded like a good idea. Too bad he had missed so many New Year's opportunities by hibernating.

Starting over, starting new.
Time to make a better you.
New Year's Day, a place to start.
Change your body, change your heart!

"I don't like all this," Harriet Hare thought. "Things are the way they are for a reason. Nature makes sense. It follows a plan. I'd better stick around and stay sensible. Somebody has to keep a cool head." She followed the foursome, Betty Jo, Peter, Oscar, and Bernard, as they approached the crossroads.

"Okay, here's our plan," directed Betty Jo. "We'll each work as hard as we can on our New Year's resolutions for one week. Then we'll meet here at noon, one week from today, and share our success stories." Everyone agreed to this plan, and went on their way. Harriet lurked in the shadows, shaking her fuzzy head.

Starting over, starting new.
Time to make a better you.
New Year's Day, a place to start.
Change your body, change your heart!

The next day, Harriet met Peter Possum on his way back from a food-gathering expedition. Peter's fur stood on edge, and he was frantic.

"Are they still behind me? Do you see the people with the rakes and brooms?" yelled Peter as he raced into the clearing.

"Slow down. Nobody is behind you Peter. You're back home. What's going on?" asked Harriet in her sensible, calm voice.

"I was almost done in," Peter told her. "I tried my hand at tipping over trash cans during the daytime, and it was disastrous. The people came running out of the house. They had on shoes and sweaters, not their usual pajamas and bare feet, so they could run almost as fast as me. I didn't get a scrap of food and I almost got the sharp side of a garden rake in my tail."

"Sounds like daytime trash runs aren't a good idea," observed Harriet.

"You're right," agreed Peter. "If you see Betty Jo, tell her that I'm going to bed. My New Year's resolution is to be the best nighttime gatherer I can be."

"I told you possums are nocturnal animals," said Harriet, as her friend dragged his bedraggled tail off to bed.

"What's that?" called Peter.

"Night, night," said Harriet.

The next day, slipping down to the stream to bathe and drink, Harriet met Oscar Otter. His usually sleek fur was rumpled, and he looked decidedly displeased about something.

"Greetings to you," began Harriet. She expected Oscar's usual polite return of the greeting, but got a surprise instead.

"I can't be bothered with a greeting," fussed Oscar. "Things are falling apart around my ears. My home is a mess. My life is a shambles. Just two days of letting loose, and things just fall apart. I don't know why I allowed Betty Jo and Peter to convince me to change my ways. They weren't bad ways. It will take me weeks to repair the damage."

"So the *new you* wasn't necessarily a *better you*," Harriet pointed out.

"No need to rub it in," said Oscar. He was busy picking up sticks. "I cannot afford to waste any more time. Two days was more than enough to figure out that this change was not for the best. If you encounter your dear cousin Betty Jo, tell her that I won't be at the crossroads for the weekly check-in. I resolve not to change."

"I'll give her the message," smiled Harriet.

At the stream, Harriet bumped into Bernard. She was surprised to see him soaking in the frigid winter water. He had to break a hole in the ice to get his entire body submerged, but he was soaking anyway.

"You'll catch a terrible cold," warned Harriet. "Don't you know it is wintertime?"

"I should have listened to my body and stayed in the hibernation cave," Bernard told her. He stood up and Harriet saw the angry red welts on his paws and back.

"Ouch," said Harriet. "What got you?"

"Bees," Bernard told her. "I was so greedy for the honey that I went right out and tried to get some. But I guess my body was not really awake, and I couldn't move fast enough to escape the bees. They were really mad."

"I see that," said Harriet. "Now what?"

"I'm going to chill these welts with a good soak; hope I don't catch my death of cold, and go back to bed until spring. If you see that troublesome cousin of yours, tell her that New Year's is a holiday that brown bears in the woods don't celebrate. We're supposed to be hibernating."

"Happy hibernation," said Harriet, and went off in search of her cousin. She figured that Betty Jo should hear the news from a family member, and not be left waiting at the crossroads.

Skipping along, Harriet sang her version of the song:

*Starting over, starting new
Might not make a better you.*

She almost went right by her cousin Betty Jo, who was curled up, camouflaged, in a pile of pine straw.

"Why are you hiding in that pine straw?" asked Harriet.

Betty Jo gingerly lifted her back left leg. It was swollen and sore-looking. "I fell down jumping rope and hurt my leg. Now I can't look for food or look out for enemies. I'm getting too thin. Help me out, Harriet."

"I thought you were too fat," Harriet said.

"Don't rub it in," moaned Betty Jo. "I'm hurting and hungry."

"All right, already. You lay low and stay covered. I'll see what I can dig up for lunch. Maybe I can find some herbs to rub on that sore leg, too."

"You're a good cousin," said Betty Jo.

"Maybe you've learned a lesson about New Year's resolutions," warned the sensible Harriet.

"I have," said Betty Jo. "I'm going to resolve to be very good at being *me*, not at being somebody new and different.

"Perhaps we need a song to seal the deal?" asked Harriet. So the cousins created an improved New Year's resolution song. Which do you prefer?

*Starting over, starting new
Might not mean a brand-new you.
Stronger, better, those are fine,
But don't leave the real you behind!*

Enrichment Activities

1. Complete the Character Analysis Chart as a group or in pairs. Consider how each character learned a valuable lesson during the story.

Character	New Year's Goal	Lesson Learned
Betty Jo		
Peter		
Oscar		
Bernard		
Harriet		

2. Design a perfect New Year's party invitation for you and your friends. What will you do to celebrate? Be creative and original.

3. In your family, do special foods play a part in your New Year's celebration? For example, in the southeastern United States, collard greens are traditionally eaten to insure a "wealthy" new year. Why would *greens* mean "wealth"? Make a list of New Year's foods and what they symbolize.

4. The Julian calendar has 12 months. Can you name the 12 months of the year? Do all cultures use the same calendar? Form groups to research the following calendars: Julian, Early Egyptian, Early Babylonia, Chinese, Islamic.

5. How do the phases of the moon (lunar cycles) and the seasons of the year affect the design of calendars and the holidays and celebrations that we mark on calendars? Discuss these questions after doing your research on calendars.

6. Make a class calendar using a piece of poster board. Count the days of the month and write the dates in the boxes. Use stickers to mark special dates: school holidays, birthdays of famous people, class birthdays, field trips, test dates, etc.

National Pizza Week Celebrations

in January

by Vicky M. Thornton

Writers' Toppings

Rainy Day Recipes

Show the class various formats of recipes. Discuss what information is included in a recipe, such as a list of ingredients, specific amounts, and directions. Have children write their own recipes for "Rainy Day Fun." Make multiple copies of each recipe and allow children to exchange them to take home. Other recipes to write are "friendship recipes," recipes that describe qualities of an ideal friend, or "recipes for happiness."

Rainy Day Fun — Serving Size 1

- 1/2 sofa
- 2 large pillows, fluffed
- 1 lamp (bright light works best)
- 1 pint milk
- 3 1/2 oatmeal raisin cookies
- 1 book of your choice
- 1 (6-inch) bookmark

Fluff pillows to desired thickness. Place pillows comfortably on 1/2 sofa. Turn on lamp and adjust light accordingly. Pour milk in any size glass and set aside. Next, position self on sofa with selected book. Dip 3 1/2 oatmeal raisin cookies into milk as needed. Read book for 1-2 hours or until done. Garnish with bookmark.

Silly Pizza

Have children come up with their own "silly" pizza creations. Suggestions might include "My Pet's Favorite Pizza," "Monster Pizza," "A Pizza Fit for a Queen," or "Baseball Player's Pizza." Children can dictate or write their recipes to be compiled into a class pizza cookbook. Include ingredients, quantities, directions, and illustrations. Duplicate and send home for parents to enjoy.

Pizza Poetry

Have children write couplets or cinquain poems about pizza. Children can write their finished poetry on pizza-shaped paper and illustrate. Have children decide on a catchy phrase for a bulletin board that can be used to display the poems.

A couplet is a poem made up of two lines that rhyme. Each line is made up of the same number of syllables. Show children unfinished couplets first to practice as a class. For example: Let's run from the _____. It's going to _____.

> Pizza
> Top my pizza with cheese and melt until gooey.
> I like it best when it's hot and extra chewy.

A cinquain poem follows this format: Line 1—one word (the title), Line 2—two words (describe the title), Line 3—three words (express an action pertaining to the title), Line 4—four words (express a feeling about the title), Line 5—one word (another word for the title).

> Mushrooms
> Wild, tasty
> Sliced with care
> Love them on pizza
> Food

Pizza in My Journal

Have children write about these "hot" pizza topics in their journal: Describe pizza as if you were seeing it and smelling it for the first time. Write and illustrate a billboard advertisement for the grand opening of a new pizzeria. As National Pizza Week comes to an end, write a journal entry titled: "What I Know About Pizza."

Health Toppings

Interactive Food Pyramid

Make an outline of the food pyramid on a wall or bulletin board using masking tape. Label each section according to the food group it represents. For older children, leave the sections unlabeled. Have pictures of pizza-related foods pre-cut, laminated, and ready for play. Help children to break down the ingredients in pizza sauce and pizza dough and include pictures of those items. An alternative would be to have children search for the pictures in magazines on their own or draw them. Children will sort each food item into the appropriate food group section. Have children place masking tape on the back of pictures to hang them on the wall. If using a bulletin board, use Velcro™ or pushpins to hold the pictures up.

Make-a-Meal

Have children plan a nutritious pizza dinner that will include food items from every food group. Referring to the food pyramid, discuss which food groups are represented the most in pizza. Which are represented the least or not at all? What food items could you add to the meal to make it more complete? What ways can you reduce fat in the meal? What are some healthy alternatives to a traditional pepperoni and cheese pizza? Children can illustrate their nutritious meal on a paper plate or describe it in a journal entry.

The Name Game

Have one index card for every child playing this game. Write the name of a different pizza ingredient on each index card. For younger children, use pictures. Tape one index card on the back of every child. Children have to guess their word by asking classmates "yes" or "no" questions. Examples of questions are "Am I a vegetable?" "Do I have to be cooked?" "Do I come from an animal?" or "Do I taste salty?" Once children guess their word, they must name the food group to which it belongs.

Science Toppings

Gadget Guess

Collect various kitchen utensils that are used in preparing pizza or other foods. Choose unusual gadgets such as a garlic press, pastry brush, round pizza cutter, and so on. Allow time for children to explore each item, then have them predict the purpose of each utensil. Finally, discuss and demonstrate how each item is used in preparing food. Stretch this into an art activity by using the gadgets for printing, or into sensory play by experimenting with the gadgets in sand or water.

Growing Mold

Sprinkle two leftover pizza crusts with 2 teaspoons of water and seal each separately in a small, plastic bag. Leave air in the bags. Place one sample in the dark and one in the sunlight. Have students predict what will happen to the crusts and estimate how long it will take for change to occur. Observe daily and note changes over time in a class log. Discuss how air, light, warmth, and water can affect the results of the experiment.

Where Does It Come From?

Brainstorm pizza toppings on an experience chart. Determine whether each topping comes from an animal source or plant source. Read *Hold the Anchovies: A Book About Pizza* by Shelley Rotner or *Extra Cheese, Please: Mozzarella's Journey from Cow to Pizza* by Cris Peterson to learn where flour, cheese, and tomatoes come from. Have children draw maps showing the process.

Art Toppings

Create-a-Pizza

Create a paper plate pizza using miscellaneous collage materials, fabric scraps, or construction paper. Search through magazines for words that relate to the theme. Paste the words on the back of the finished pizza. Display the pizzas on a clothesline draped across the room.

Pizza Prints

Make prints from cut vegetables or other pizza toppings. Place an absorbent paper towel in a Styrofoam™ meat tray and saturate with paint. Dip objects into the paint, then press firmly on paper. Have children repeat patterns or overlap designs with different colors of paint. Make a class mural or use individual sheets of paper.

Play Dough Pizza

Have fun creating pizzas with assorted colors of homemade play dough or clay. Cover the table with a plastic tablecloth. Provide plastic knives, cheese graters, spatulas, rolling pins, and other kitchen utensils for the cooks.

Miscellaneous Toppings

Parts-of-Speech Pizza

Draw a large pizza shape on the chalkboard or use an overhead projector. Write *adjectives* across the top. Brainstorm words that describe pizza. Do the same for nouns and verbs.

Classroom Pizzeria

Turn the dramatic play area into a pizzeria by adding aprons, chef hats, pot holders, tablecloths, napkins, dishes, serving trays, silverware, play money, cash registers, and notebooks with pencils for writing orders. Include take-out menus from restaurants or have children make their own. As a class, vote on a name for the pizzeria and create signs to hang in the restaurant.

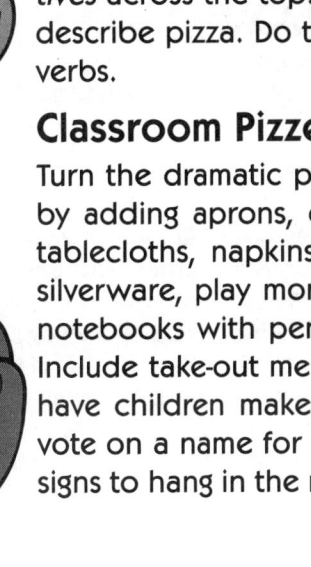

Pizza Party

Have each child bring their favorite pizza topping from home. Make pizza for lunch in the classroom. It may be necessary for children to calculate new measurements when doubling or enlarging the recipes you use.

Makin' Pizza

As a class, sequence the basic steps involved in making pizza using sentence strips.

Pizza Puzzles

Give the children tagboard pizza shapes to color. Have them cut their pizza into 5-10 puzzle pieces. Store the pieces in small baggies. Children can exchange and solve each other's puzzles.

Flannel Board Pizza

Cut out round pizza crusts and various pizza toppings from felt. Allow children to create pizzas on the flannel board.

Pizza Memory

Cut out an even number of pizza shapes using tagboard. Create identical pairs by writing numbers, letters, colors, or names of toppings on one side of each pizza shape. Place the pizza shapes facedown on the playing surface. In small groups or pairs, have the children alternate turning over two pizzas at a time. If the two pizzas match, the player keeps the match and takes another turn. If they do not match, the player returns the pizzas to their original place and passes his or her turn to the next player. Play until all of the pieces have been matched. The player with the most matched pairs wins the game.

Top It!

Encourage the development of creative thinking and listening skills by playing this group game. The first player completes the following sentence: "I'm going to make a pizza and top it with _____." The next player has to think of an original topping to add to the pizza: "I'm going to make a pizza and top it with _____ and _____." Continue the game with each player repeating the correct sequence of toppings that other students have named, and adding a new topping to the list.

Pizza Poll

Take a vote on favorite pizza toppings in the classroom. Make a picture graph on chart or butcher paper to display the results. Ask questions about the graph such as: Which topping is the most and least popular? Are there any toppings that have the same number of votes? How many people were surveyed? How can you tell? How many more people prefer a vegetable topping over a meat topping? Make another graph, such as a bar graph, that will represent the same information or results of the poll.

Book Toppings
Celebrate National Pizza Week in the classroom with the following books:

Extra Cheese, Please: Mozzarella's Journey from Cow to Pizza by Cris Peterson. Honesdale, PA: Boyds Mills Press, 1994.
"Hi, Pizza Man!" by Virginia Walter. New York: Orchard Books, 1996.
Hold the Anchovies: A Book About Pizza by Shelley Rotner & Julia Pemberton Hellums. New York: Orchard Books, 1996.
How Pizza Came to Queens by Dayal Kaur Khalsa. New York: C.N. Potter Publishers, 1989.
Pizza Man by Marjorie Pillar. New York: T.Y. Crowell, 1990.
Rocky Bobocky the Pizza Man by Emily Ellison. Atlanta, GA: Longstreet Press, 1996.
Pizza Party by Grace Maccarone. New York: Scholastic, 1994.
Pizza for Breakfast by Maryann Kovalski. New York: T.Y. Crowell, 1990.

Literature

Incorporate books about hats into the classroom. Add them to the classroom library or reading center and read them aloud for story time. Don't forget other areas of the classroom when introducing books. Place a book about hats in the dramatic play area, the block or construction area, or in the locker or coatrack area. Make a book tray that can be carried anywhere in the classroom. Include a book about hats, a hat of some kind, a photograph of a child or teacher wearing a hat, and a doll or stuffed animal with a hat. Try some of these books about hats:

Caps for Sale by Esphyr Slobodkina
The Cat in the Hat by Dr. Seuss
Jennie's Hat by Ezra Jack Keats

Snack Caps

First have each child draw a face on a paper plate with markers. Then have children use a spoon or plastic knife to spread peanut butter above the face, where a hat might be. Provide a variety of small snacks, such as pretzels, peanuts, dry cereal, raisins, small crackers, diced carrots, and chocolate chips. Children can make a hat on the paper plate face by arranging the edibles on the peanut butter. After the hats are made, eat them for a snack while listening to a hat story.

Beanbag Hat Toss

Place a row of hats on the floor in a line, ranging from close to the tossing area to farther away. Vary the types and sizes of hats. Children stand in the tossing area and throw beanbags into the hats.

Wear-a-Hat Relay

Gather a collection of hats and divide them between two to four boxes. Divide children into teams to match the number of hat boxes. Place the hat boxes on the far side of the room or playground. To begin the relay, place a hat on the first child in each team. Children race to the hat box, take off the hats they are wearing, place another hat on their heads and race back. They put the hat on the next team member and the relay continues until all children have had a turn. Place a mirror next to each hat box for more fun.

Hat Day

January 21

by Carol Ann Bloom

Mexican Hat Dance

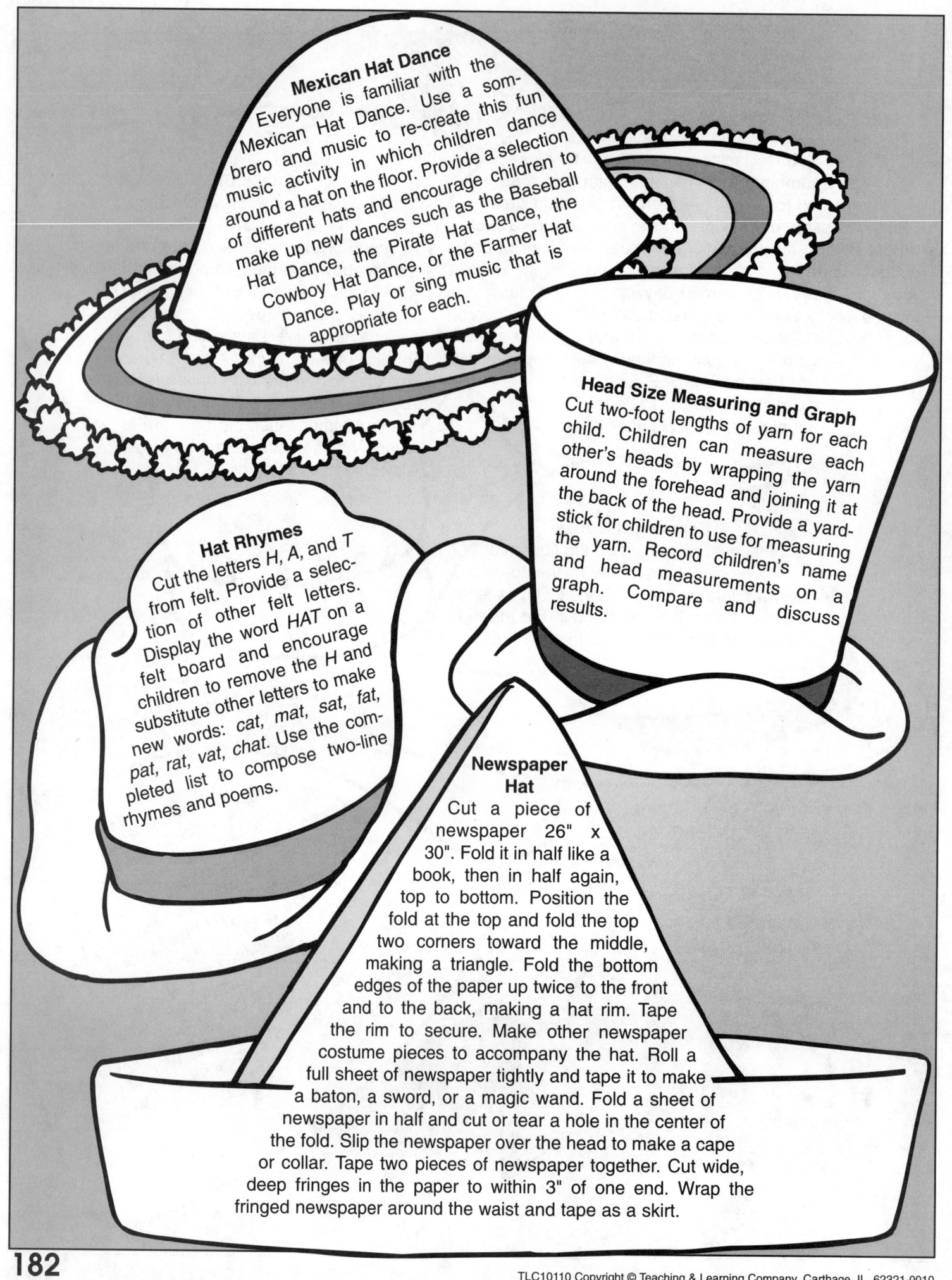

Everyone is familiar with the Mexican Hat Dance. Use a sombrero and music to re-create this fun music activity in which children dance around a hat on the floor. Provide a selection of different hats and encourage children to make up new dances such as the Baseball Hat Dance, the Pirate Hat Dance, the Cowboy Hat Dance, or the Farmer Hat Dance. Play or sing music that is appropriate for each.

Head Size Measuring and Graph

Cut two-foot lengths of yarn for each child. Children can measure each other's heads by wrapping the yarn around the forehead and joining it at the back of the head. Provide a yardstick for children to use for measuring the yarn. Record children's name and head measurements on a graph. Compare and discuss results.

Hat Rhymes

Cut the letters H, A, and T from felt. Provide a selection of other felt letters. Display the word HAT on a felt board and encourage children to remove the H and substitute other letters to make new words: *cat, mat, sat, fat, pat, rat, vat, chat*. Use the completed list to compose two-line rhymes and poems.

Newspaper Hat

Cut a piece of newspaper 26" x 30". Fold it in half like a book, then in half again, top to bottom. Position the fold at the top and fold the top two corners toward the middle, making a triangle. Fold the bottom edges of the paper up twice to the front and to the back, making a hat rim. Tape the rim to secure. Make other newspaper costume pieces to accompany the hat. Roll a full sheet of newspaper tightly and tape it to make a baton, a sword, or a magic wand. Fold a sheet of newspaper in half and cut or tear a hole in the center of the fold. Slip the newspaper over the head to make a cape or collar. Tape two pieces of newspaper together. Cut wide, deep fringes in the paper to within 3" of one end. Wrap the fringed newspaper around the waist and tape as a skirt.

Gung Hay Fat Choy!
Celebrating Chinese New Year

Best wishes and congratulations. Have a prosperous and good year.

The Chinese New Year's celebration is a time of gathering with family and friends. It is a time of festivals and parades. During this period people observe certain customs. Families interpret the traditions in their own way. All prepare for a prosperous new year.

The house is thoroughly cleaned and decorated with flowers, fruits and banners. New clothes are bought. Gifts are purchased to be given to family members and friends. All debts are paid. All arguments are settled. Special food is prepared. This is a time for a new beginning.

The Chinese lunar calendar is based on the cycles of the moon. A new moon signals the beginning of each month. Chinese New Year's Day is the first day of the first month of the lunar calendar. It usually occurs on the Western calendar between the middle of January and the middle of February.

During the celebrations that last for about two weeks, people visit relatives and friends. Small gifts are exchanged. Children are given money wrapped in red and gold paper to spend during the holiday.

The lion dance is preformed in front of shops to scare away evil spirits and bring good luck. Dancers carry the papier-mâché head of a lion and never stop moving as they dance from place to place.

The dragon parade brings the new year celebration to a close. There are marching bands, dancers, drummers and lots of firecrackers to frighten away evil spirits. The multilegged dragon weaves along the route. Many dancers have practiced long hours to be able to participate.

Do you do anything special to celebrate New Year's Day on January 1?

What Chinese customs add to the enjoyment of the celebration of their new year?

ACTIVITIES

1. Traditionally red scrolls are displayed in the home. Couplets are written on the banners, expressing good wishes for the family in the coming year.

    Compose a two-line rhyming verse that sends a message of good luck and happiness for your family's future.

2. Oranges are used to decorate and offer to visitors. As a snack, serve orange sections to the students.

THE CHINESE ZODIAC

Unlike the Western horoscope which is divided into 12 months, the Chinese zodiac is a 12-year cycle. Each year of the Chinese lunar calendar is ruled by one of the 12 animals of the zodiac. The Chinese believe the animal which represents the year of the person's birth becomes his or her sign.

1. Listen to stories or read about the animals of the zodiac. See the resources section for suggestions.
2. Write a story
    a. to show how the tiger was adventuresome.
    b. to tell in what way the monkey was smart.
    c. to explain how the snake acted wisely.
3. Use puppets or live actors to act out the original stories or those found in the suggested readings.

RESOURCES

Bouchard, Dave. *The Great Race.* Brookfield, CT: Millbrook Press, 1997.

Chang, Monica. *Story of the Chinese Zodiac* (in English and Chinese). Taipei, Taiwan: Yuan-Liou Publishing Co., Ltd., 1994.

Demi. *The Dragon Tale and Other Animal Fables of the Chinese Zodiac.* New York: Henry Holt and Company, 1996.

Yen, Clara. *Why Rat Comes First: A Story of the Zodiac.* San Francisco: Children's Press, 1991.

by Patricia O'Brien

The Chinese Zodiac

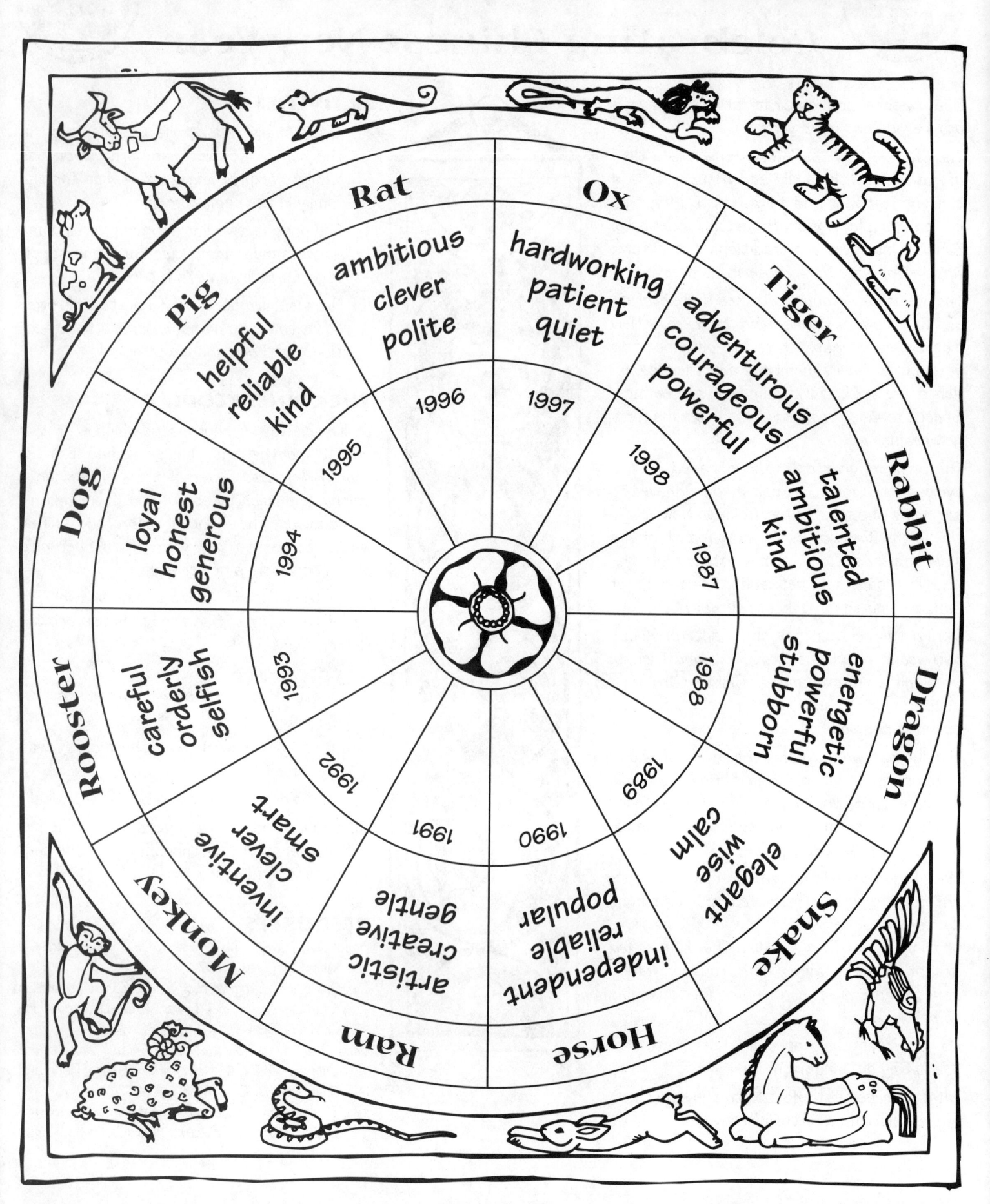

Rat — ambitious, clever, polite — 1996
Ox — hardworking, patient, quiet — 1997
Tiger — adventurous, courageous, powerful — 1998
Rabbit — talented, ambitious, kind — 1987
Dragon — energetic, powerful, stubborn — 1988
Snake — elegant, wise, calm — 1989
Horse — independent, reliable, popular — 1990
Ram — artistic, creative, gentle — 1991
Monkey — inventive, clever, smart — 1992
Rooster — careful, orderly, selfish — 1993
Dog — loyal, honest, generous — 1994
Pig — helpful, reliable, kind — 1995

184

TLC10110 Copyright © Teaching & Learning Company, Carthage, IL 62321-0010

Let's Talk TEETH

February Is Dental Health Month

Keep your students smiling from ear to ear with these fun and creative dental health activities.

Talking Teeth

To tell the "tooth," your students will love learning about good dental health with these three cute characters. Use white felt to cut six large teeth shapes. Make two of the shapes smaller to represent a baby tooth. Sew each set of felt shapes together, leaving a three-inch opening along one side. Then turn each tooth to the "right" side, and stuff with cotton batting. Hand-sew each opening closed with white thread. Make a triangle-shaped diaper for the baby tooth, and pin it closed in the front. Using a permanent marker, draw a happy baby face on the baby tooth, and a happy face on one of the large teeth. Draw a sad face with a cavity on the other large tooth. On the reverse side of the sad tooth, hot-glue a piece of aluminum foil on the top (to represent a filling), and draw a slight smile. Use the tooth characters to teach about good dental health.

So that your information will be accurate and up-to-date, check with your library, ask your local dentist for pamphlets, or write the American Dental Association, Division of Communications, 211 East Chicago Avenue, Chicago, IL 60611.

Tooth Count

This lip-smacking activity will have your students counting, adding, and subtracting with pleasure. Cut out this large lip-shaped pattern for each child. Use miniature marshmallows to represent teeth. Then keeping your students' mathematical skill levels in mind, tell story problems for them to solve. Demonstrate by saying, "Harold had five shiny teeth (count and place five marshmallows on the lip cut-out). Then one tooth got loose and fell out (take one away). Now how many teeth does Harold have left?" Use the students' names to make the story problems more interesting and personalized. Finally, allow the children to eat the marshmallow teeth for a job well done.

by Brenda Hume

Happy Tooth/Sad Tooth

These stick puppets will help the children learn about dental health. Direct the students to cut two teeth from white construction paper (see pattern on page 185). Then allow them to draw a happy face on one tooth, and a sad face with a cavity on the other tooth. Next glue the teeth together with a craft stick sandwiched in the center. Use the toothy puppets during large group time. Ask the students to show the happy tooth when they hear something that's good for their teeth, and show the sad tooth when they hear something bad for their teeth. Then name things such as:

1. Eating lots of candy
2. Using toothpaste
3. Using dental floss
4. Using a worn-out toothbrush
5. Brushing your teeth really fast
6. Eating apples and carrots for snacks

The Dentist's Office

Set up a dentist's office center in your classroom, and fill it with all kinds of dental instruments. Designate a chair for the dental chair, and some others for the waiting room. Supply the waiting room with magazines and books to browse through while waiting for the dentist. Provide lab coats or aprons with large pockets for the dentists and hygienists to wear. An old purse or book bag can serve as a dental bag. Fill the bag with toothbrushes, dental mirrors, dental floss (or white yarn), dental bibs, old dental X rays, cotton balls, face masks, empty medicine bottles, and pads and pencils for writing prescriptions. Some of the items may be donated by a local dentist. Caution the children not to really put any of the items into their mouths, and provide some dolls for the dentists to examine.

My Dentist Kit

Read *My Dentist* by Harlow Rockwell (Greenwillow), and discuss the different instruments a dentist uses. Then make every child in your class a dentist with their own dental bag. Fold a large 11" x 14" sheet of construction paper in half, and cut a handle though the top. Old file folders could also be used. Then write *Dr.* on the front, along with the child's name. On the inside, tape a bandage, a cotton ball, a cotton swab, a piece of dental floss, and a toothbrush (or toothbrush cut-out). The students will feel like real dentists carrying their equipped dental bags.

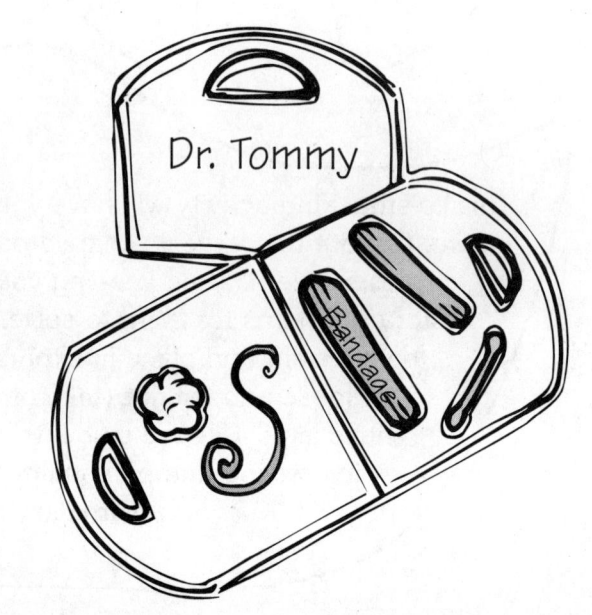

Toothy Tunes

Sing these "toothy tunes" while several students use sand blocks to re-create the toothbrush sound.

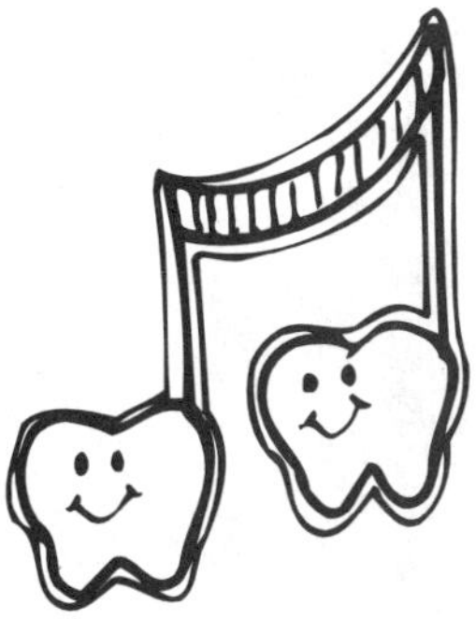

The Brush on Your Teeth
To the tune of "The Wheels on the Bus"

The brush on your teeth goes
brush, brush, brush,
brush, brush, brush,
brush, brush, brush.
The brush on your teeth goes
brush, brush, brush.
Up, down, and around.

Did You Ever See a Toothbrush?
To the tune of "Did You Ever See a Lassie?"

Did you ever see a toothbrush,
    a toothbrush, a toothbrush?
Did you ever see a toothbrush
    when it brushes your teeth?
It brushes, and brushes,
    and brushes, and brushes.
Did you ever see a toothbrush
    when it brushes your teeth?

Arthur's Tooth by Marc Brown (Little, Brown, and Company).
Just Going to the Dentist by Mercer Mayer (Western Publishing Co.).
Little Rabbit's Loose Tooth by Lucy Bate, illustrated by Diane DeGroat (Scholastic Inc.).
My Dentist by Harlow Rockwell (Greenwillow Books).
Pulling My Leg by Jo Carson, illustrated by Julie Downing (Orchard Books).
The Tooth Book by Theo LeSieg, illustrated by Roy McKie (Random House Publishers).
Your Teeth by Joan Iveson-Iveson, illustrated by Bill Donahue (Bookwright Press).

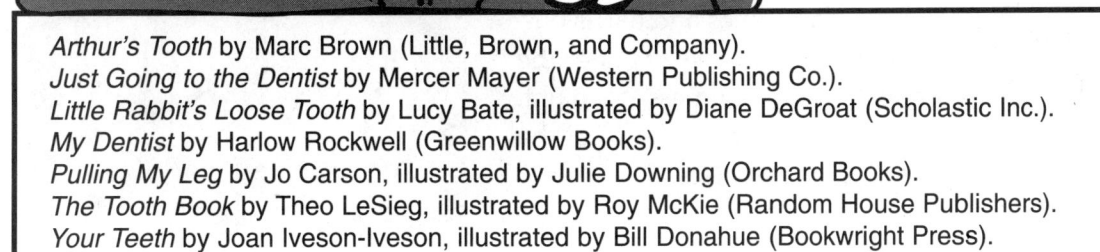

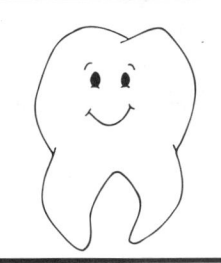

Black History Month

February is Black History Month, a time to look back at the accomplishments of black Americans and celebrate their struggles to rise from slavery to freedom and their continuing struggle against discrimination.

Background Information for Teachers

The first Blacks came to America almost 400 years ago. They were free men and women captured in Africa and brought here on slave boats. Sold to southern plantation owners, they were considered property and did their owners' bidding. They and their descendants never stopped dreaming of being free.

Even though the Declaration of Independence declared liberty as a white man's right, many Blacks joined America's war to win freedom from England, hoping they, too, would be freed. Sixty-thousand of them were as a reward for their services. Most of these lived in the northern states. After the war they helped to get laws passed to abolish slavery to those states. In the South, though, Blacks continued to be slaves. Their ongoing goal was to escape to the North and freedom. Many northerners were glad to help. But in 1850 a law was passed that made it illegal to help or hide runaway slaves; they had to be returned and punished. That meant the escape routes had to be extended to reach the free country of Canada to the north. They crossed Lake Erie on steamboats, and in the winter even on sleds. So strong was the desire for freedom that, despite the danger, escapes continued. Those who succeeded often went back to help others.

The Underground Railroad

The escaped slaves together with the free Blacks and the anti-slavery people in the North together set up a system of escape routes called the *Underground Railway*.

It was not a real railway, but a series of *carefully planned roads, rivers, paths and streams*. It was not underground either. They used that term to mean "hidden" or "secret." Railroad terms were used throughout the system. Leaders were called *conductors*, hiding places *stations*, and station helpers *station masters*. Escapees hid in cellars, attics and barns during the day and traveled under the protection of darkness at night. All who helped them did so at the risk of their own lives.

Make a Slave Quilt

Slaves made quilts designed with the symbols of their faith together with things that represented the Underground Railroad. These quilts were a rare source of beauty in their bleak lives as well as a symbol of their hope for freedom.

Give each student a 6" x 6" square of paper on which to draw and color one symbol. Designs might include a star, the Big Dipper, a candle, a window with a candle in it, a dove, a rainbow, a tree, a heart, a cross or anything else the student believes is symbolic. Glue squares onto a large square or rectangle of craft paper and hang on the wall. Let each student tell about his or her choice of design.

by Elaine Hansen Cleary

Harriet Tubman

One of the greatest Underground Railroad conductors was Harriet Tubman. Born a slave, she grew up working very hard, often being beaten and punished. As a child she heard older slaves talk secretly about the Underground Railroad.

As a young woman, she heard she was going to be sold and decided to risk running away. Using the railroad, she made a successful escape. Later she went back to lead her brothers to freedom, and later still her father and mother. She helped improve the Underground Railroad system, making it larger and more organized. Harriet kept going back to lead others to freedom, making more than 20 trips, helping more than 300 slaves escape. During the Civil War she served as a nurse and spy. Abraham Lincoln freed the slaves during that war. Once freed, they had to learn to take care of themselves. Harriet Tubman spent the rest of her life helping them do that.

Act Out Harriet Tubman's Helping Slaves Escape

Use the following scenario, but let children make up their own words. It will be more natural this way and they won't be as hesitant to take part.

Cast: a man and wife who own the station or safe house, three runaway slaves, two slave hunters, and Harriet Tubman

Put on classroom lights to indicate daytime.

Couple and runaways are seated. Couple reminds them they will have to hid in the cellar and not make a sound.

Slave hunters bang on the door (classroom door) and yell to be let in; they're hunting for escaped slaves to bring them back to their owners to be punished.

Couple motions to slaves to get to their hiding place. Then they open the door and tell the hunters that there's no one else there and they haven't seen any escapees.

After hunters search the house and leave, turn out lights to indicate nighttime.

A signal knock (some sort of rhythm) that couple recognizes. They open the door to Harriet. She comes in; slaves come back into room.

Harriet tells them they will have to hurry in order to get to the next station before dawn. She warns them not to talk or make any noise at all.

Slaves thank the couple and leave cautiously with Harriet.

The Fight Against Discrimination

Many children have no concept of what it is like to be discriminated against. This makes it difficult to teach them about the black people's fight for civil rights. One thing they could identify with might be the feeling when they think a parent has unfairly denied them something or a friend has hurt their feelings. However, to be refused a drink at a fountain, have to go to a separate rest room, not be served at a particular restaurant, or not be allowed to stay at a certain motel just because of skin color is a difficult concept. The following activity may help.

Help Children to Understand "Discrimination" by Experiencing It

Explain to your class that you are going to set up artificial (pretend) situations in which one group is treated unfairly. They are to see how it feels to be in such a group. (Note: Make sure every child has a chance to be in a discriminated group at least once.)

Examples: Children with blue eyes can't sit with others in the cafeteria.

Children with brown hair have to walk last in line.

Blonde haired children may share a locker only with another blonde.

Children with brown eyes can only play with certain toys.

Children with long hair can only play on one section of the playground.

After each experience, discuss how it felt to be in the "special" group. Do the others think it was fair? What might you do to change this? Younger children may want to just talk about it, while older ones could actually act out the scenarios.

Rosa Parks

One day almost 50 years ago Rosa Parks took a bus home from work. In those days black passengers had to sit in a special section of the bus. When the bus became crowded, the driver told the black passengers in the first row of their section to give up their seats to the white people who were standing. They all did except Rosa. She was not only tired from working all day, she was tired of being discriminated against. For doing this, Rosa was arrested and sent to jail.

Her action caught the attention of black leader Dr. Martin Luther King, Jr. He led the black people of that city (Montgomery, Alabama) in a bus boycott. That meant they refused to ride any bus for a whole year, even though it meant long, tiresome walks. Their protest was worth it. It brought about the end of segregation on public transportation in the United States.

Rosa Parks spent the rest of her life working for civil rights.

Act Out Rosa Park's Refusal to Give up Her Seat on the Bus

Cast: bus driver, group of black passengers, group of white passengers, police officer

For easy visualization, "Blacks" could wear dark colored t-shirt or sweat shirts, and "Whites" light colored ones. The bus driver might wear a cap and the police officer a badge.

Setting: Set up student chairs in rows to represent seats on the bus.

Let passengers board the bus a few at a time to be seated. Then a group of "Whites" gets on and there are no more seats left.

From there, let the children act out the story themselves in their own words.

Dr. Martin Luther King, Jr.

Of all the modern-day black leaders, a southern minister, Dr. Martin Luther King, Jr., is perhaps the most famous. He led the black people to fight for equal rights, but not with fists or guns. Dr. King taught them to use words and peaceful actions. They marched with signs that said they should have equal rights. They had "sit-ins," where they refused to leave a place they thought they had a right to be. They staged boycotts, like the one against the buses in Rosa Park's city. Sometimes Dr. King and his followers even got arrested and went to jail rather than give in to unfair laws.

Dr. King gave exciting speeches, too. He helped black people realize their worth. In one of his most famous speeches (given at the Lincoln Memorial in Washington, D.C.) he said, "I have a dream . . ." That dream was of a country where people would "not be judged by the color of their skin but by the content of their character" . . . where "children of all colors could join hands and walk together" . . . where there is "freedom and justice for all."

Dr. Martin Luther King, Jr., was shot and killed in 1968, but the work he started continues. Today black people enjoy the rights he fought for and they work hard against discrimination. As a tribute to his greatness, his birthday has become a national holiday.

Make a Bulletin Board Centered Around Dr. Kings Dream

Talk about Dr. King's dream. Ask each student to think of something good he or she has would dream about. Put these thoughts into a class poem. Write individual sentences about each dream. Draw pictures to illustrate dreams. Display them all on a bulletin board.

Other Outstanding Black People

As a class, in groups or individually, research the contribution of these black people. In groups make up playlets about a main event in each of their lives.

- Garrett A. Morgan (inventor)
- Marian Anderson (singer)
- Jackie Robinson (baseball player)
- Jesse Owens (Olympic medalist)
- Benjamin Banneker (surveyor)
- Maya Angelou (writer)
- Ethel Waters (entertainer)
- Muhammad Ali (boxing)
- Thurgood Marshall (Supreme Court judge)
- Mae C. Jamison (astronaut)
- Bill Cosby (entertainer)
- Booker T. Washington (educator)
- George Washington Carver (educator)
- Harry Belafonte (actor)
- W.H. Handy (composer)

Groundhog Day
Is Spring on the Way?

Background Information

Long ago in Europe, the farmers depended on hibernating animals to signal the arrival of spring so they could plant their crops. If the crops went in too early, a late snowstorm could freeze the young plants. If they waited too long, valuable growing time would be lost.

In Germany, farmers watched for badgers. In England, the hedgehog was used to predict the arrival of spring weather. Around Candlemas Day, February 2, the farmers would watch for these animals to appear after their long winter rest. They believed if the animal came out of its burrow and saw its shadow, it would be frightened and return to its den to sleep. This meant six more weeks of winter. If the day was cloudy, the animal would begin to search for food. The farmers took this as a sign spring was just around the corner, and they would begin to plant their crops. When these people moved to America, there were no badgers or hedgehogs, so they began looking to groundhogs or woodchucks to announce the coming of fair weather.

Groundhogs in Fiction

In two stories about groundhogs, facts and fiction are woven together to tell how each saved the day by predicting the weather.

What Happened Today, Freddy Groundhog?
by Marvin Glass

Freddy learns that although others may call him a low-down groundhog, he is a heads-up groundhog when he predicts an early spring. Read and enjoy the story together.

Questions
1. How did Freddy's digging get him into trouble?
2. If you were Freddy, how would you answer the question asked in the book's title?
3. Which parts of the story could happen? Which parts are pretend?

Geoffrey Groundhog Predicts the Weather
by Bruce Koscielniak

The town eagerly awaits Geoffrey's annual weather prediction. TV reporters crowd around his hole with lights and cameras to record the news. When Geoffrey appears, he is blinded by the lights. The community does not know what to do until Geoffrey figures out a way to give everyone the news. He calls his mother, since she always goes out each February 2 to look for her shadow. Read the story and share the pictures.

Questions
1. Why wasn't Geoffrey able to predict the weather?
2. What major problems were caused because Geoffrey was confused when he came out of his hole?
3. When he finally made his forecast, why was he so sure he was right?
4. What questions would you like to ask Geoffrey Groundhog?

by Patricia O'Brien

Groundhogs

1. Draw pictures to include in a class big book about groundhogs.
2. Dictate a sentence to go with your picture.

Weather

Talk about different types of weather using the words below:

cloudy   foggy   hazy   sunny
rainy   breezy   windy   stormy

a. Can you add more words to the list?
b. Find opposite kinds of weather.
c. Make a two-part drawing showing opposite kinds of weather, such as a sunny day picture and a cloudy day picture.
d. Discuss the difference between breezy and windy, foggy and hazy, and rainy and stormy.
e. Talk about things to do on sunny, breezy, rainy, and cloudy days.
f. Draw a picture that shows yourself doing something you talked about.

Forecasting the Weather

Shortly before Groundhog Day, predict if spring will soon begin or winter will be around for six more weeks. Will the groundhog see his shadow? Make a class graph to show the children's predictions.

At the end of each school day during the month of February, predict what kind of weather you expect for the next day. Keep a record of your predictions. On the following day, make a note of the actual weather and write a new forecast for the next day.

Watch the weather report on TV or check the weather page in the newspaper. Are these predictions correct? Compare them to your own forecast.

Shadows

Take a walk outside on a sunny day. Notice the shadows. Go out again at a different time of day. Are the shadows the same size and in the same places?

Go on a shadow hunt. How many different shadows can you locate?

Measure your shadow at two different times during the day. Make one of the times around noon. The other time may be in the morning or afternoon. Do you know why your shadow is sometimes much taller than you and sometimes you can hardly see it at all?

Make shape pictures to be shown on the overhead projector. Arrange your creation on a sheet of clear acetate film. Cut out simple figures like fish or birds. Use a hole punch to make eyes. Take turns showing your work on the overhead projector.

Listen to and enjoy three poems found in *Read-Aloud Rhymes for the Very Young*—"Hide and Seek Shadow," "Look," and "Poor Shadow."

While working with a partner, take turns mirroring each other's actions like a shadow moves along with you.

Play shadow tag. Whoever is "it" tries to step on another player's shadow. When one's shadow is stepped on, that person is "it."

Resources

Glass, Marvin. *What Happened Today, Freddy Groundhog?* New York: Crown Publishers, 1989.

Koscielniak, Bruce. *Geoffrey Groundhog Predicts the Weather.* Boston: Houghton Mifflin Company, 1995.

Prelutsky, Jack. *Read-Aloud Rhymes for the Very Young.* New York: Alfred A. Knopf, 1986.

Valentine's Day

Celebrate Valentine's Day with this exciting array of holiday books.

Get in the swing of the valentine season with *Happy Valentine's Day!* by Carol Barkin and Elizabeth James, illustrated by Martha Weston (New York: Lothrop, Lee & Shepard Books, 1988). You are sure to find plenty of easy-to-follow holiday ideas, including card-making, recipes, and party suggestions. Surprise your class with treats such as Rosy Applesauce, "Heart"y Pizza, and Valentine Surprise Pudding.

For everything you want to know about Valentine's Day and more, *Valentine's Day* by Cass R. Sandak (New York: Crestwood House, 1990) is the perfect book for you. This interesting book includes the history and customs of this special holiday. It also tells how Valentine's Day is celebrated around the world today.

Delight your budding, young artists with the seasonal arts and crafts projects in *Valentine's Day Things to Make and Do* by Robyn Supraner (Troll Associates, 1981). Some of the kid-pleasing activities include Stained-Glass Hearts, Kooky Clay, Hearty Potato Prints, and Hearts and Flowers Mobile. Need a game for your classroom? There's even directions for a valentine checkers game that your students can make and play!

Winnie the Pooh's Valentine

by Bruce Talkington
illustrated by John Kurtz
New York: Disney Press, 1995

Everyone at Hundred-Acre Wood is excited—Valentine's Day is here. Roo wants to make the perfect valentine for his mother. Winnie the Pooh and friends help him create a special valentine, only to realize it's too big to move. Join the friends as they discover a new valentine "surprise."

- Draw a picture of a big gift box. Inside the box create the perfect Valentine's Day gift for your mother or another special person.

- Be an artist! Design a special valentine for one of the characters in the book.

- Surprise! You have just created the biggest valentine in the world. Draw a picture of what your valentine looks like. Write two sentences to describe it.

The Valentine Bears

by Eve Bunting
illustrated by Jan Brett
New York: Clarion Books, 1983

Mr. and Mrs. Bear never get to celebrate Valentine's Day, because they are hibernating every year when the big holiday arrives. This year, Mrs. Bear decides to give Mr. Bear a valentine "surprise." Share their special Valentine's Day celebration!

- Be an inventor! Design a new alarm clock to wake Mr. and Mrs. Bear on Valentine's Day. Draw a picture of your invention and label the parts.

- Do not disturb! Make a list of other animals that hibernate. Put your list in alphabetical order.

- Choose an animal from your list. Create a book with facts and pictures about the animal.

by Mary Ellen Switzer

Book Nook

Henry's Secret Valentine
by Jeffrey Dinardo
New York: Young Yearling, 1993

Everyone in Ms. Bird's class is excited about Valentine's Day. Even before the big day arrives, Henry is receiving valentines from a secret admirer. Can you guess who it is?

- Frieda was a new student in Ms. Bird's class. How did Henry and his friends make her feel special on Valentine's Day?

- Welcome to our class! Tell how you could help a new student feel special in your class.

- Surprise! Someone is sending you secret valentine messages. Here are some clues: green ink, sports pictures, and a fingerprint. Write a story telling how you solved the mystery.

Clifford, We Love You
by Norman Bridwell
New York: Scholastic Inc., 1991

Clifford, the big, lovable dog, is sad and nobody seems to be able to cheer him up. Emily suddenly has an idea—she'll write a special song telling all the wonderful things about Clifford. Your class can enjoy the song "It's Clifford" too! The words and music are included in this "doggone" good book.

- Just imagine! Pretend you had a giant-sized dog like Clifford. What would you name your pet? Tell how you would take care of it.

- You decide to take your pet to school for "sharing day." Write a "Dear Diary" entry telling what happens.

- Be an artist! Design a special valentine for Clifford.

Nate the Great and the Mushy Valentine
by Marjorie Weinman Sharmat
illustrated by Marc Simont
New York: Delacorte Press, 1994

Everyone loves a mystery, and your students are sure to enjoy this holiday favorite! Super sleuth Nate the Great is back to solve not one, but two baffling cases. First, his dog Sludge receives a secret valentine and then his friend Annie is missing a valentine. Follow along as Nate looks for clues to solve this holiday puzzle!

- Do you think Nate the Great is a good detective? Tell why.

- Design a detective's badge for Nate the Great.

- Be an author! Create your own mystery story called "The Case of the Missing Candy Hearts." Use these words in your story: *Valentine's Day, party, candy hearts, missing, window, fingerprint,* and *muddy tracks.*

One Zillion Valentines
by Frank Modell
New York: Mulberry Books, 1981

Ever wonder what you would do with a zillion valentines? Marvin and his friend Milton had that problem! The boys made "zillions" of valentines to give to their neighbors and still had too many leftovers. Finally, the clever boys came up with a perfect plan—a valentine card sale.

- Just pretend! Imagine that you had a "zillion" valentines. What would you do with them?

- Be a designer! Create a new book jacket for *One Zillion Valentines.*

Dancing Heart

To the tune of "Mary Had a Little Lamb"

See my little dancing heart,
Dancing heart,
Dancing heart.
See my little dancing heart—
It's dancing just for you.

It knows I want to be your friend,
Be your friend,
Be your friend.
It knows I want to be your friend
And hopes you like me, too.

Dancing Heart Puppet

Materials
- piece of 6" x 6" pink or red tagboard or poster board
- pink or white 12" pipe cleaner (chenille stem)
- red and black fine line, water-based markers
- bendable, plastic drinking straw
- pencil
- scissors
- cellophane tape
- construction paper
- patterns

Directions
1. Draw a heart shape on the poster board.
2. Draw a face on the heart shape and cut out.
3. Fold pipe cleaner in the middle and bend into leg shapes, bowing legs and turning feet out slightly.
4. Tape top of legs to the back of the heart, close to the bottom.
5. Place straw, short part down, above the legs. Cut off enough of the short part (about a 1/2") so bendable part does not show above top of heart.
6. Bend straw so long part doesn't show from the front. The long part of the straw will be the handle when you operate the puppet.

Performance
While singing the song, have children dance the puppets by bouncing them up and down. Using the long part of the straw as a handle.

Bounce first on one foot and then the other. Bounce on both feet. Move puppet forward and backward while bouncing.

by Mabel Duch

Have a Heart on Valentine's Day

I'll cut some red paper into a heart,
and paste lace and frills on the front part.
I'll give it to a friend of mine.
Will you be my valentine?

Conversation Hearts

NECCO (The New England Confection Company) first started making candy conversation hearts in 1902. These sweet little heart candies came in six flavors (orange, cherry, lime, grape, wintergreen, and chocolate) and were stamped with cute sayings. In 96 years, they might have new sayings, new colors, and new flavors, however, the tradition of these candies will never fade.

Use construction paper in the flavor colors and cut out heart shapes. Write some of the original sayings or create new phrases. Pass out the hearts to friends or decorate the classroom with "conversation hearts."

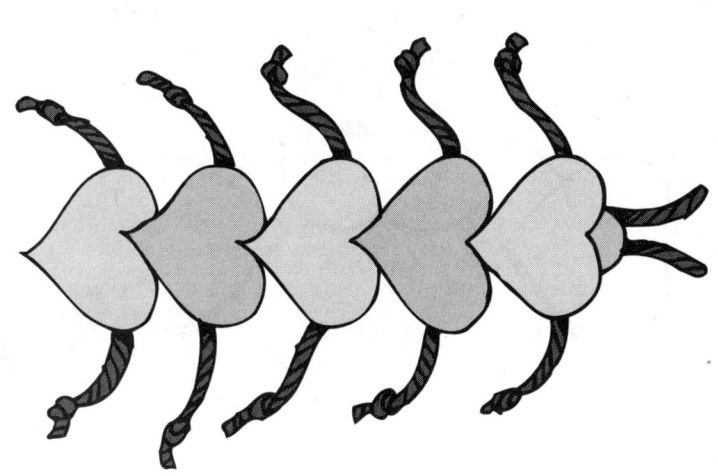

Love Bugs

Butterfly

Use a craft stick for the body and cut two construction paper hearts for the wings. Glue these wings to each side of the stick. Draw facial features on one end of the stick and attach pipe cleaner antennae. Write a cute saying across the wings, like "Valentine, you make my heart flutter."

Centipede

Take a craft stick and cover it with construction paper hearts glued next to each other along the stick. Add antennae at the top and little legs attached to each heart. Use pipe cleaners or small pieces of yarn knotted at the ends for the feet. Add a cute saying, like "I'll walk a mile for my valentine."

by Tania Cowling

Candy Box Math

Cut a large, red heart from poster board. This will be your candy box. Attach rows of paper cupcake liners with glue. With a marker, write an addition or subtraction problem in each liner. From construction paper, cut candy replicas and write the answer to a math problem on each one. Now, match the "candy answer" to the paper liner math problem. Practice filling the candy box with math fun.

Have a Heart Hunt

Before the children arrive, hide several dozen candy conversation hearts in various spots around the classroom. Give the children small paper bags and let them seek and collect as many hearts as they can find. To make the game more interesting, award points in the following manner:

- pink hearts—1 point
- orange hearts—2 points
- yellow hearts—3 points
- purple hearts—4 points
- white hearts—5 points

Award 1 point for every other color you might have. Help the students add up their points; the player with the most points wins the game.

Valentine Angel

This paper angel is made completely of hearts. You will need one large heart and three medium-sized, hearts. Glue these together as shown and add an angelic face. You can tie on a yarn loop or attach a pipe cleaner for hanging.

Rainbow Hearts

Cut out simple heart shapes to use as valentine cards or decorations, using the following method for a rainbow effect. Have the children brush stripes of watercolor paint on a sheet of watercolor paper in this order: red, orange, yellow, green, blue, and violet. When the paper is dry, cut out the hearts (straight or on a diagonal).

Hearts and Frames

Give each child a large sheet of construction paper to use as a background. Then provide the children with several wallpaper samples. Instruct them to start with a square and fold. Then cut out a heart shape from the fold. Then cut out several other heart shapes from the original heart. Have them continue until they have small, solid hearts and several open-heart frames. Instruct children to glue these onto the paper, overlapping some to make a heart collage. Using several different prints will give the collage a modern effect.

Tunnel of Love

Take several large appliance boxes and open all the tops and bottoms. Use heavy tape and attach all the boxes together, making sure the inside flaps are securely taped and smooth. Decorate the outside surfaces with paint. Draw lots of hearts and write *Tunnel of Love* on the outside. Let the children enjoy crawling through the tunnel over and over again.

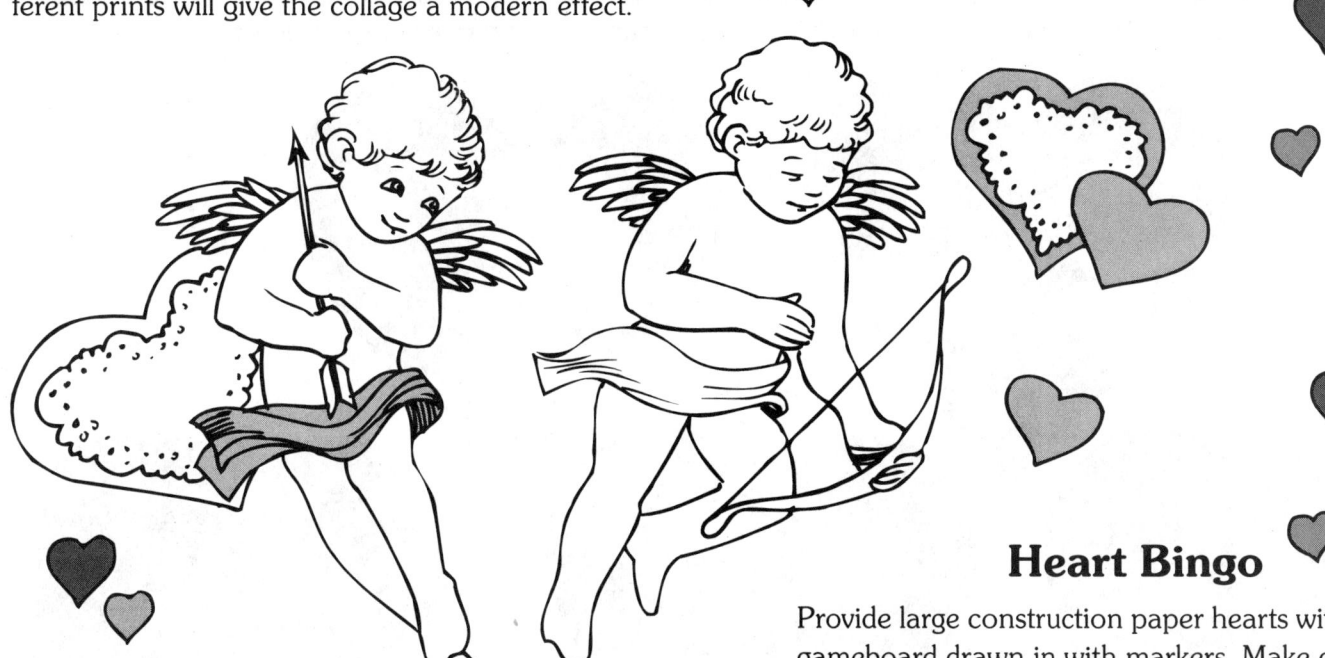

Enhancing Paper Doilies

Glue a white paper doily onto construction paper. Using fabric paints and puffy paints, embellish the flowers and heart designs that are already stamped into the doily. This type of paint takes the same time to dry, but the beauty is worth the wait. (These paints are readily available in most craft stores.)

Heart Bingo

Provide large construction paper hearts with the bingo gameboard drawn in with markers. Make game-calling cards with the bingo numbers and letters written on them. Ask an adult to be the caller as the children play. Use candy conversation hearts as markers. At the end of the game, the kids can keep or eat their candies.

Learning Time

"It's time to be a valentine" and a great opportunity to learn to tell time. Make a cardboard poster that resembles a clock face. Place a small red heart at every hour, marked with the corresponding numeral. Cut out clock hands from cardboard and attach these in the center with a metal fastener. Practice telling time by moving the hands around the clock and asking, "What time is it, my valentine?"

dog bee kitten lamb rooster duck bird lion cow horse

Animal Heart Game

Make 10 red hearts and 10 pink hearts from construction paper. On the red hearts write the animal phrases listed below. On the pink hearts, write these animal names: dog, bee, kitten, lamb, rooster, duck, bird, lion, cow, horse. Have the children match each red heart with the correct pink heart!

- Have a "Buzzy" Valentine's Day
- Don't Say, "Neigh!" Say You'll Be My Valentine
- You're "Purr"fect
- You Put the "Wow" in "Bow-wow"
- We'll Have a "Roarin'" Time, Valentine
- I "Crow" About You
- You are "Tweet"!
- Valentine, Sometimes You "Quack" Me Up
- Get "Baa-ck" Here and Be My Friend
- Picking You for a Friend Was a "Moo"ve in the Right Direction

Valentine's Day

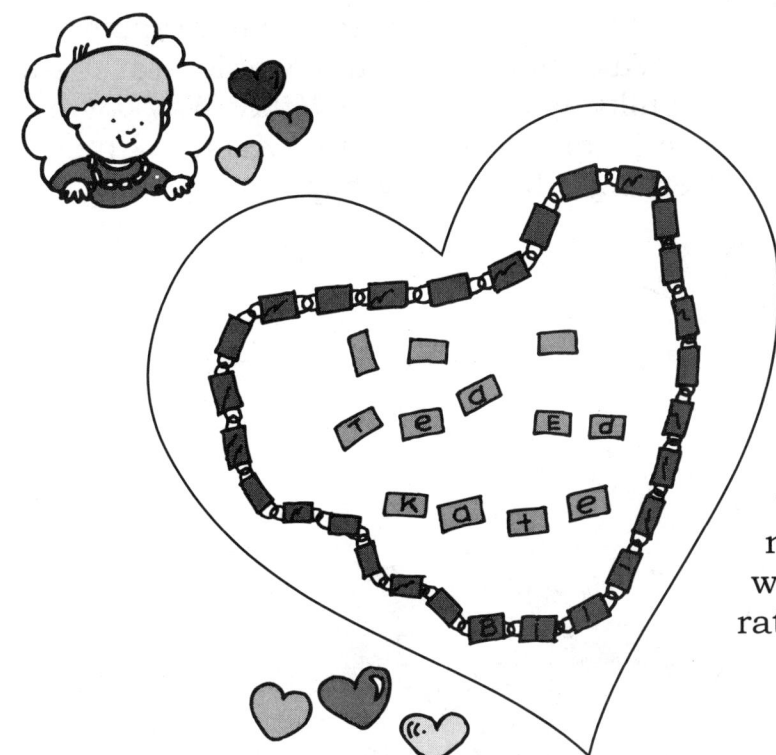

Paper Clip Friendship Necklaces

Linked paper clips form the base for this necklace. Cut small paper rectangles from colorful gift wrap or shiny mylar paper. Paper from glossy magazine pictures works equally well. Glue the rectangles around the paper clips so that only the joined ends are visible. The child's name or a friend's name can be placed on the necklace by writing one letter of the name on a decorated paper clip.

Half Heart Sharing Necklaces

Mix a batch of homemade play dough or clay, either an air-hardening clay or an oven-baked mixture. Tint the clay or dough red or pink. Provide children with rolling pins and heart-shaped cookie cutters. Instruct children to cut a heart shape from their rolled out dough and use a plastic knife or similar tool to cut the heart in half lengthwise. Place a hole in the top of each half. When the heart halves are hard, dab each with glue and add a sprinkle of glitter. Place a ribbon or piece of yarn through the hole in both halves, making two necklaces. Children wear one half and give the other half to a friend or family member.

by Carol Ann Bloom

Candy Bar Wrapper Valentines

Save candy bar wrappers for this project. Children cut large paper hearts and combine a few written words with words cut from the candy bar wrappers to create a valentine message. For example, "Valentine, you send me to Mars" (using a Mars® bar wrapper), or "Valentine, for you I would travel the Milky Way" (using a Milky Way® wrapper) or "Hugs and Kisses" (using Hershey's Kisses® wrappers).

Valentine Heart Animals

Children trace hearts of all sizes and colors, not just the traditional red, pink, and white hearts. The hearts are cut out and put together to create animals. Use the scraps to make ears, faces, and tails. Children write valentine messages on the animals and present them to friends and family.

Jelly Heart Sandwiches

Make sandwiches with strawberry jelly. Place a heart-shaped cookie cutter in the center of the sandwich and press firmly to make heart-shaped sandwiches. Munch on the scraps and set the sandwiches aside until everyone has had a turn. Serve the jelly heart sandwiches with pink strawberry-flavored milk or red fruit punch.

Planning Presidents' Day

They were so good;

They were so true;

They both protected

the red, white, and blue.

Two Presidents in history,

A holiday for all to see.

Presidents' Day honors the contributions of two of the United States' greatest Presidents, George Washington (February 22, 1732) and Abraham Lincoln (February 12, 1809). The holiday is celebrated the third Monday in February.

Patriotic Activities for the Classroom

Presidential Silhouettes
Use a sheet of blue construction paper as your background and border. Paste stripes of red and white construction paper vertically on the blue sheet leaving a border all around the page. Cut a silhouette of Lincoln or Washington out of black paper. Make cardboard stencils from the patterns on this page. Glue this portrait in the center of the striped paper. Decorate randomly with gold and silver star stickers.

Presidential Puppets
Have each child bring a penny and a quarter to school. Glue each coin (face side up) to the ends of two craft sticks. Manipulate the sticks and have George Washington move about and chat with Abraham Lincoln.

The Cherry Tree Game
All the children are directed to sit in a circle with one child standing in the center of the circle. He or she is the "cherry tree." The "cherry tree" closes his eyes or is blindfolded. Quietly the teacher chooses a child and this student touches the "cherry tree" and shouts, "Chop, chop." The "cherry tree" squats down and the player quickly returns to his place in the circle. All the children in the circle say, "Who chopped down the cherry tree?" The "cherry tree" now opens his eyes and tries to guess who touched him. When the person is guessed, he becomes the "cherry tree" and the game is repeated.

by Tania K. Cowling

Patriotic Color Day

Designate a Red, White, and Blue Day. Have everyone dress in the appropriate colors. Plan activities that include patriotic art (only red, white, and blue paint and crayons); color games; and even red, white, and blue snacks. Make a color collage including red, white, and blue paper (tissue, crepe, wrapping); star stickers; and purchased flag stickers. Glue all these collage items on a sheet of construction paper. Every child's collage will be slightly different, so display and praise these works of art.

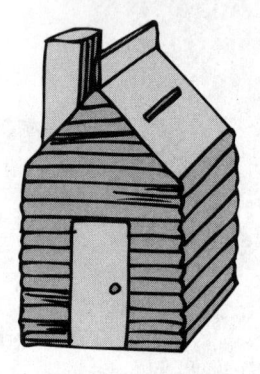

Log Cabin Bank

Collect half-pint milk cartons from the school lunchroom. Make miniature log cabins by covering the sides with corrugated cardboard to resemble logs. Glue the cardboard in place with craft glue. Using construction paper, cut out a door, windows, and a chimney to glue onto each cabin. Cut a slit in the top to drop in your Lincoln pennies.

Coin Play

The penny has Lincoln on it and the quarter has Washington. Set up a table with several of these coins. The children can do money rubbings with paper and crayons. Provide a magnifying glass for observing the coins. Include several containers for the students to sort and count the money.

Here is a quick way to shine those dirty coins. Add a tablespoon of salt to a cup of white vinegar. Stir until dissolved. Drop in the coins, let them soak for at least 10 minutes, and then rinse with water. Dry the coins with a cloth and admire the brilliant shine.

Treat Holder

Teachers, make this George Washington treat holder for your classroom. Take an empty salt box or oatmeal box and cut a section from the top. Glue brown paper around the outside to resemble a log. Make a hatchet from a 1" x 3" strip of heavy red paper. Fold it in half and glue it around a straw. Cut a slit on top of the log and slip the hatchet edge inside. Fill the log with wrapped treats for your students.

Patriotic Wreath

From cardboard or poster board, cut out a circular wreath shape. Cut lots of stars from red, white, and blue construction paper (cookie cutters or a stencil will make the tracing easy). Tape curling ribbon (a scissors edge will curl the ribbon) to the back of each star. Decorate each star with puffy paint, glitter paint, or ordinary glitter and glue.

Paste all the stars to the wreath (ribbon side down), covering the entire circle. Allow this project to dry. Hang these patriotic wreaths around the classroom.

An Americana Celebration for February

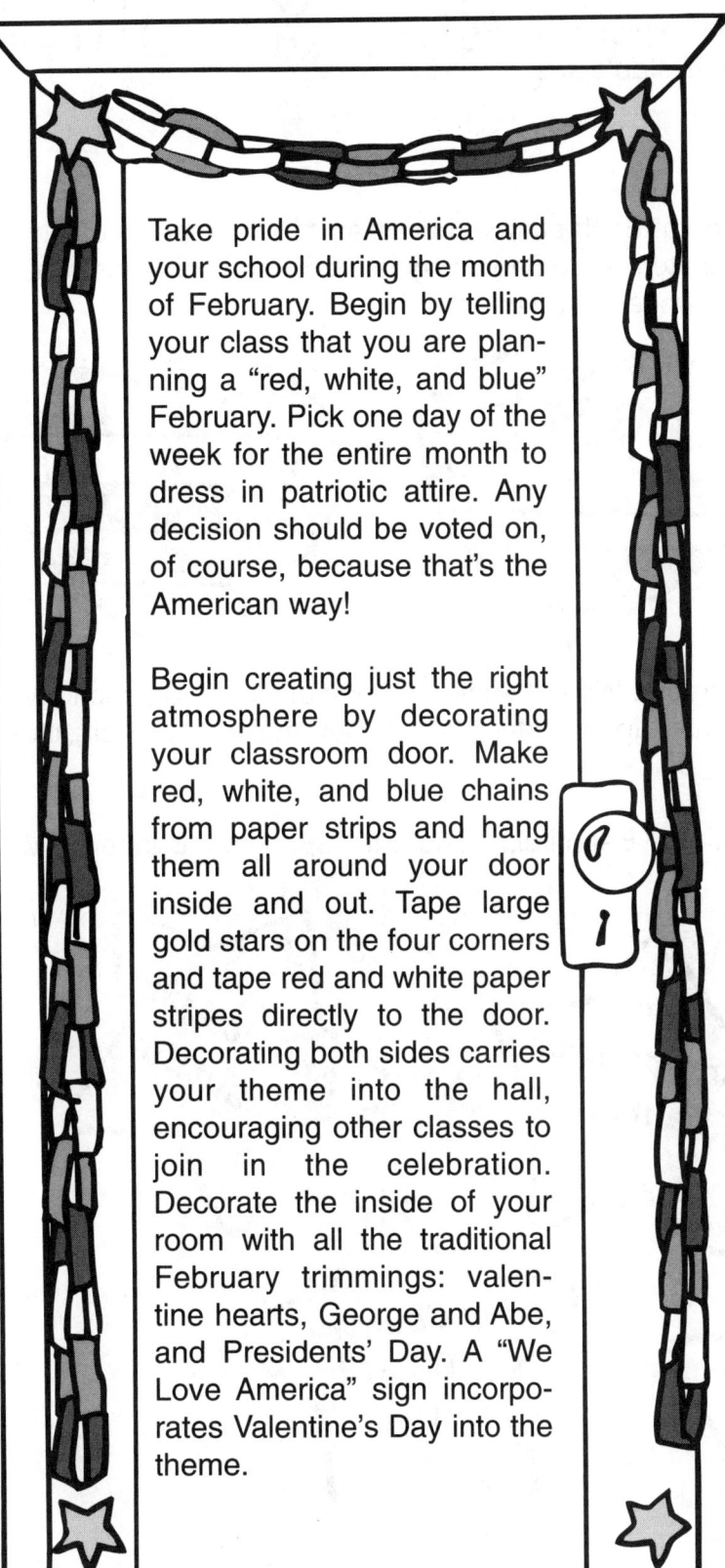

Take pride in America and your school during the month of February. Begin by telling your class that you are planning a "red, white, and blue" February. Pick one day of the week for the entire month to dress in patriotic attire. Any decision should be voted on, of course, because that's the American way!

Begin creating just the right atmosphere by decorating your classroom door. Make red, white, and blue chains from paper strips and hang them all around your door inside and out. Tape large gold stars on the four corners and tape red and white paper stripes directly to the door. Decorating both sides carries your theme into the hall, encouraging other classes to join in the celebration. Decorate the inside of your room with all the traditional February trimmings: valentine hearts, George and Abe, and Presidents' Day. A "We Love America" sign incorporates Valentine's Day into the theme.

George Washington Wigs

Show pictures of George and other Presidents wearing wigs in a history lesson. One of the first political parties was named the Whigs. Have students make a wig. Cut 4" x 4" squares of white paper, roll them into circles, and glue the edges. Cut a gallon milk jug to form a helmet shape. Glue paper circles onto the helmet shape to make a wig. Glue the circles on each other when placing them on the headpiece.

Hatchets

Discuss with your students the famous "I cannot tell a lie" George Washington story.

by Jo Jo Cavalline and Jo Anne O'Donnell

Washington's Hat

Cut three 3" x 6" strips of black paper. Staple the strips together to form a triangular hat, called a tricorn.

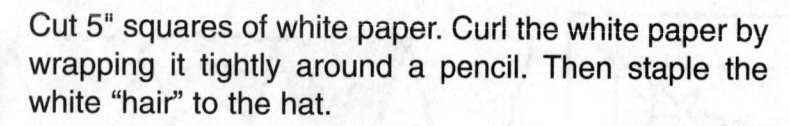

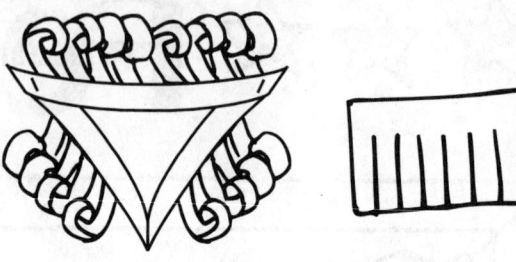

Cut 5" squares of white paper. Curl the white paper by wrapping it tightly around a pencil. Then staple the white "hair" to the hat.

Americana Hearts

Add these colorful hearts to your classroom. Each student needs an 11" x 14" piece of white paper. Cut a heart shape. Instruct children to draw a flag design in pencil on their heart. Then have them color in the design using red, white, and blue.

Music

Hang stars from the ceiling in your classroom. Write the title of a patriotic song on each one. Invite a different student each day to "wish upon a star." When they make their wish, they select a star. Sing the song on that star.

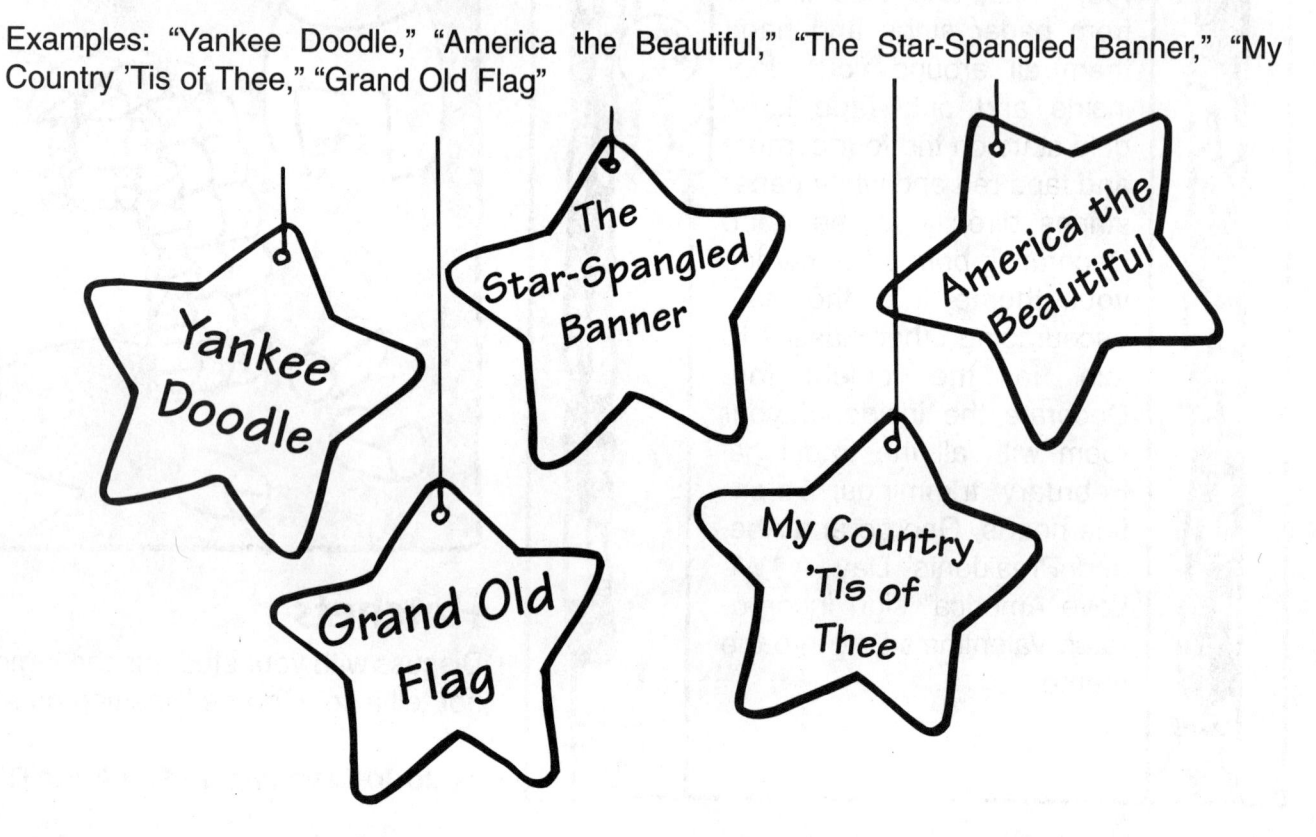

Examples: "Yankee Doodle," "America the Beautiful," "The Star-Spangled Banner," "My Country 'Tis of Thee," "Grand Old Flag"

February Snacks

1. Bring in cherry vanilla ice cream for a treat. This flavor is sometimes called "White House." Can you guess why?

2. Cut red finger gelatin into 4" squares. Make flags using gumdrops or beads for stars and whipped cream for stripes. Enjoy!

Guest Speakers

Invite speakers into your classroom from the Armed Forces. Call your local recruiting office for volunteers. Call your state representative or county commissioner's office for a list of speakers.

Ask a speech therapist or occupational therapist that is trained in sign language to visit your classroom. Teach your students to sign the Pledge of Allegiance.

Social Studies

Show pictures of Uncle Sam. His name comes from the initials *U.S.* and first became known from supply containers during the War of 1812. In 1917 he became the U.S. symbol for World War I. Posters show him saying, "I want *you* for U.S. Army." His image encouraged young men to enlist in the military to fight for their country. In 1997, it will be 165 years from the date when Uncle Sam was first caricatured in political cartoons featuring stars and stripes. He is still one of America's most recognized symbols. Hold a birthday party for Uncle Sam and recite the poem "Uncle Sam, I Am."

Patriotic Valentine Ideas

Make patriotic valentines to exchange. Use these examples, but encourage originality.

Uncle Sam, I Am

We all have the same Uncle,
His name is Uncle Sam.
He represents the U.S. of A.
Reminding me of who I am.

The red, white, and blue is symbolic,
Of loyalty, independence, and pride.
His finger is pointing to all Americans
To come and stand by his side.

He was born in 1917,
Recruiting volunteers for World War I.
His picture is still seen today,
We're the strongest nation under the sun.

I'll Flag You Down to Be My Valentine

Hey, Big Wig, B Mine

Red, White, and Blue, I'm Saluting You!

Hebruary Folidays

It was a typical Monday morning at the Wilfred Mumbly School.

"Good morning, children," chirped Ms. Pickett, the principal. "I hope you all had fun in the snow this weekend and are ready to get back to work! Billy Fenster has volunteered to read this week's birthday list, and then I have a special announcement before you return to class."

Mavis Beppo slid down in her seat and looked at the little holes in the ceiling tiles. This part never had anything to do with her. First of all, her birthday was in the summer. Secondly, she was always too scared to read the birthday list out loud in front of the whole school. *Just once,* she thought, *I'd like to hear my name up there.*

"And now . . . ," Ms. Pickett began as she walked back on stage, "I'd like to announce a poetry contest."

Mavis raised her head. *I'm a good poetry writer,* she thought.

"Anyone may enter," Ms. Pickett continued. "All you have to do is write a poem about February. The winner will get a box of chocolates and the winning poem will be read at the morning assembly on February 1st. You can get written details from your teacher. Poems can be handed in at the office any day this week. Happy writing!"

Mavis felt a rush of excitement as ideas popped into her head. *I could win those chocolates and get my name read.* She hurried back to her classroom and pulled out a piece of paper. All day long, whenever she had free time, she jotted down ideas for her poem. Valentine's Day. George Washington. Abraham Lincoln. Groundhog Day. *Holidays! That's it! I'll write about holidays!* She forgot to get the written details from her teacher.

By the time Mavis got home from school, she knew exactly what she was going to write. She wrote it once in pencil and then copied it in pen in her best handwriting. It was a long poem—20 lines, and it had everything she could think of about February. It would win for sure.

The next morning, Mavis hopped off the bus and ran toward the office.

"No running!" the bus driver yelled, so she walked really fast and slapped her poem on Ms. Pickett's desk.

On top of the filing cabinet was a huge, heart-shaped candy box with a puffy satin top. "Is that the prize?" she asked the secretary.

"I believe it is," came the answer over the typewriter.

Mavis could taste it already.

208   by Robin Schnell

At the end of school on Friday, Mavis's teacher stopped her as she was leaving the room. "Mavis, I have good news! You won the poetry contest! That gives you a whole weekend to practice saying your poem out loud before the assembly on the first."

"Say it out loud!" Mavis' face went white. "You mean I have to say it in front of the whole school?" She could feel her throat tying up in a little knot.

"Didn't you read the rules? You either have to say it yourself or your whole class can perform it with you, but then you have to share the candy."

Mavis took a copy of the rules from her teacher's desk and sat down to read them. "It says here, if the whole class does it, it has to be more than just reading it. How about if I make pictures for them to hold up?"

"I think that would be fine, but don't forget: it has to involve the whole class!"

Twenty kids, 20 lines, 20 pictures. What could go wrong?

Mavis drew and colored pictures all weekend, each illustrating a line of her poem. The lines were printed on the back and the cards were all stacked in order.

Before her class walked down to the gym, Mavis handed out the cards and explained that they should stand together in pairs and each read one line. Afterward, she'd share the candy with the whole class.

"Hooray!" they cheered, and ran down the hall to the gym. The only thing was, they didn't all stay in the right order when they went on stage. This is what they read:

The groundhog comes out of the ground.
Some said he should be king.

Washington was our first President.
He predicts the first of spring.

Abe Lincoln was a President, too.
He's furry, short, and fat.

The groundhog sleeps all winter long.
He wears a stovepipe hat.

A patriot was George Washington.
He flies in his bare bottom.

Cupid's not a soldier, though he carries a bow.
When the British came, he fought them.

The white-haired guy with bad false teeth
Set southern slaves all free.

The one in black with the beard and the hat
Chopped down a cherry tree.

We dance and play when it's Mardi Gras,
Though the date of it may vary.

There are lots of holidays
In the month of February.

The whole school whooped and hollered as Mavis shared her box of chocolates with her classmates. She never put her cards back in order, but maybe you can!

Holiday

Turkey Gobbler

I met a turkey gobbler
Just the other day.
I said to turkey gobbler,
"How are you today?"
   (Hands on hips, pretend to "talk" to turkey.)
He looked at me and said,
"Here's what I have to say—
Don't ask me such a question
When it's Thanksgiving Day!"
   (Look worried and shake head back and forth.)

Five Little Pilgrims

Five little pilgrims
Sat down to eat.
   (Show five fingers.)
The first one said,
   (Put up thumb.)
"What a wonderful treat."
The second one said,
   (Put up index finger.)
"Look at all this food!"
The third one said,
   (Put up middle finger.)
"It sure looks good."
The fourth one said,
   (Put up ring finger.)
"What's that I spy?"
The fifth one said,
   (Put up pinky finger.)
"That's pumpkin pie."
But before they ate the turkey or dressing
They all said a Thanksgiving blessing.
   (Clasp hands together and bow head.)

The Spinning Dreidel

Spin, little dreidel,
Spin, spin, spin.
Please, little dreidel,
Let me win!
   (Sit and spin around.)
Now, little dreidel,
My happy top,
Slow down, little dreidel,
It's time to stop.
   (Spin slowly, then "drop" to one side.)

by Judy Wolfman

Fingerplays

Snowflakes

Soft, white snowflakes
Fall through the air.
   (Wiggle fingers downward.)
They cover grass and roofs
And tall trees everywhere.
   (Spread arms out.)
Soft, white snowflakes
Do their very best
   (Wiggle fingers downward.)
To put a blanket on the ground
And let the flowers rest.
   (Spread arms out.)
But in the spring
When the sun comes to stay,
The soft, white snowflakes
Quickly run away.
   (Wiggle fingers and hide behind back.)

Santa Comes

Here is the chimney.
   (Make a fist, with thumb inside.)
Here is the top.
   (Lay other hand, palm down, over the fist.)
Take off the lid
   (Remove the hand.)
Out Santa will pop.
   (Pop out the thumb.)

Fingerplays

Jack Frost
To the tune of "Twinkle, Twinkle, Little Star"

Jack Frost dances in the night,
Painting window pictures bright.
But when morning time draws near,
Sly Jack Frost just disappears.
Jack Frost dances in the night,
Painting window pictures bright.

by Marie E. Cecchini

Icicles and Ice

Icicles hung from our roof
   (Hang fingers from one hand downward.)
And crept across the window.
But pretty soon, out came the sun
   (Make O with index finger and thumb of other hand.)
And melted every one.
   (Slowly bring fingers up into fist.)

by Judy Wolfman

My Snowman

I'll make a little snowball
   (Make a small circle with hands.)
Then make it big and round.
   (Make a large circle with hands.)
I'll roll it in the fallen snow—
   (Pretend to roll through snow.)
It never makes a sound!
   (Whisper these words.)
I'll give him a head and eyes,
   (Point to head and eyes.)
And a broom for him to hold.
   (Pretend to hold broom.)
Now a mouth, a nose, and scarf,
   (Point to each.)
So my snowman won't get cold!
   (Pretend to shiver.)

by Judy Wolfman

Falling Snow
To the tune of "Freré Jacques"

Snowflakes falling,
Snowflakes falling,
To the ground,
To the ground.
Now we can go skiing,
Now we can go sledding,
Down snow mounds,
Down snow mounds.

by Marie E. Cecchini

The Groundhog

Hey, little groundhog,
   (Bend over, hands cupped around mouth.)
It's time to get together.
Come out of your burrow
And check on the weather.
   (Make a loose fist with one hand, and wiggle index finger of other hand through the hole.)

& Sing-Alongs

I Love You

Guess what I made just for you—
(Hold hands behind back.)
From glitter and paper and lots of glue?
(Present "pretend" valentine.)
A special card on Valentine's Day
To say "I love you" in every way.
(Point to self and other.)

by Judy Wolfman

Little Snowman

To the tune of "I'm a Little Teapot"

I'm a little round man
    made of snow.
I'm standing tall
    while cold winds blow.

When the sun appears
    to warm the day,
Drip, drip, drip,
    I melt away.

by Marie E. Cecchini

Nine Little Snowmen

To the tune of "Ten Little Indians"

Down falls the snow, up go the snowmen,
Down falls the snow, up go the snowmen,
Down falls the snow, up go the snowmen
All made out of snow.

One little, two little, three little snowmen,
Four little, five little, six little snowmen,
Seven little, eight little, nine little snowmen
Standing in a row.

Out comes the sun, down go the snowmen,
Out comes the sun, down go the snowmen,
Out comes the sun, down go the snowmen
Melting all away.

Nine little, eight little, seven little snowmen,
Six little, five little, four little snowmen,
Three little, two little, one little snowman
Gone till another day.

by Sylvia Watson

Cooking with Kids

Welcome the season with some simple holiday treats.

Breakfast Soup

Ingredients
- 5 cups water
- 1 tsp. salt
- 2 cups oatmeal
- 3 ripe bananas
- 3/4 cup raisins
- milk

Boil the water with the salt. Add the oatmeal and cook for five minutes. Mash the bananas and add them to the oatmeal. Stir in the raisins. Serve warm, adding milk if desired.

Cinnamon Stix

Ingredients
- firm, dry bread slices
- 1/4 cup confectioners' sugar
- 2 T. brown sugar
- melted butter
- 1 tsp. cinnamon
- 1/4 tsp. nutmeg

Mix the confectioners' sugar, brown sugar, cinnamon and nutmeg together. Set aside. Cut the firm, dry bread slices into strips. Dip the bread strips into the melted butter, then roll them in the spice mixture. Place the bread sticks on a cookie sheet and bake at 375°F for about 5 minutes, or until toasted.

Candle Salad

Ingredients
- shredded lettuce
- pineapple slices
- bananas
- cherries
- toothpicks

Place shredded lettuce on plate. Lay a pineapple slice on the lettuce. Cut the banana in half and stand one half up, on top of the pineapple slice, over the hole. Attach a cherry to the top of the banana candle with a toothpick.

by Marie E. Cecchini

Either/Or Cookies

Ingredients

1/2 cup butter/margarine
3 cups oatmeal
1 cup honey
3 T. cocoa powder
3/4 cup powdered milk
1/2 tsp. salt
2 tsp. vanilla
1/2 cup peanut butter
1/2 cup raisins

Melt the butter in a saucepan over low heat. Add the oatmeal and stir well. Add the honey, cocoa powder, powdered milk, salt, vanilla, peanut butter and raisins. Use your hands to mix well. Batter will be stiff. Bake at 350°F, or refrigerate for about an hour, then eat.

Note: This batter also makes excellent molding material. However, be sure to flour both working surface and hands before creating any holiday shapes, as the dough is quite sticky.

Gumdrop Pops

Ingredients

gumdrop candies
milk
confectioners' sugar
toothpicks

Stick a toothpick into each gumdrop. Dip the gumdrops into milk, then sprinkle them with confectioners' sugar. Eat them as mini lollipops, or add a few to the top of a party cupcake.

Snow Toasties

Ingredients

bread slices
red jelly (strawberry or raspberry)
confectioners' sugar
holiday cookie cutters

Toast the bread slices. Use the cookie cutters to cut the toasted bread into holiday shapes. Place a spoonful of jelly on top of each shape; then sprinkle with confectioners' sugar to look like snow.

Snowy-Day Salad

Ingredients

lettuce leaves
pear halves
cottage cheese
raisins
cinnamon red-hot candies
black olives

Lay a lettuce leaf on a plate. Top with a pear half, flat side down. Cover the pear half with cottage cheese to resemble snow. Use raisins to give the snowperson eyes, buttons and a mouth. Add a cinnamon candy nose. For a top hat, slice a black olive in half, and arrange the halves perpendicular to each other above the head.

Clip Art for Winter Holidays

Celebrate Kwanzaa

Season's Greetings

Happy Hanukkah

Feliz Navidad

Happy New Year

Happy Holidays

Merry Christmas

Clip Art for Thanksgiving

217

TLC10110 Copyright © Teaching & Learning Company, Carthage, IL 62321-0010

Clip Art for Christmas

Clip Art for Christmas

219

Clip Art for Winter

Black History Month

The Ice Is Nice!

I ♥ Winter

220

TLC10110 Copyright © Teaching & Learning Company, Carthage, IL 62321-0010

Clip Art for Winter

It's Groundhog Day!

Happy Presidents' Day!

Happy New Year

Remember Dental Health

Bookmarks

"Snow" Doubt About It, I Love to Read!

Mush into a Good Book

Decorative Note

Borders

Note Pad

Winter Winners

You did a "Love"ly Job!

Fun-n-Frosty

Clip Art for Hanukkah

224

Clip Art for Kwanzaa

Self-Determination   Unity
Working Together   Faith
Cooperative Economics
Purpose
Creativity

Winter Newsletter

A Family Take-Home

Kids bored to the bone? Parental patience beginning to fray? If you answered *yes* to these questions, your household may be suffering from the dreaded winter doldrums (a.k.a. cabin fever). The perfect prescription for curing this seasonal ailment is involvement in productive activity—and the doctor is in. Below are some suggested activities you and your child can do at home to banish those midwinter blues.

Simple Science

The yearly celebration of Martin Luther King, Jr. Day encourages us all to learn to accept each other regardless of superficial differences. You and your child can experience something different, yet the same, in the plant kingdom with a simple seed experiment. You will need a mayonnaise jar, paper towels, soil, and seeds. For seeds, you may want to try popcorn, or save seeds from fruit you may have on hand such as apples or oranges. Fold a paper towel in half and set it inside the jar. Hold it against the glass as you fill the jar with soil. Gently slide the seeds in between the glass and the paper towel. Water the seeds and set the jar in a sunny window. Watch, wait, then observe the changes that take place. Different seeds germinate at different times, yet they all create root systems and stems. Seeds are different, yet the same.

On the Move

With the adornment of additional clothing, outdoor play in winter can still be enjoyable. For younger children, you can pull out the sandbox shovels and buckets. Their yard suddenly becomes a large "snowbox" in which they can build and create. Younger children might also enjoy playing follow-the-leader in your footprints as you walk, hop, or jump in a circular or zigzag pattern (remember to take smaller steps). Older children can build several snowpeople targets of different sizes, then practice precision pitching as they attempt to knock the hats off of the heads with snowballs. Everyone can shovel and load snow into wagons or onto sleds and transport it to another area where they can create snow sculptures. Older children, naturally, will sculpt in greater detail. Let the children make their sculptures more festive, in honor of Presidents' Day, by squirt-painting the white snow with red and blue. To make squirt paint, place water in a recycled mustard or dish detergent bottle, then add several drops of food color.

Mathworks

Recycle last year's calendar into a few number games to play with your child. First, you will need to cut the numbers apart—one or two months should do. Younger children can arrange the numbers in numerical order, or search for their house number, telephone number, age, date of birth, and so on. For older children, challenge them to arrange the numbers as if they were counting by 2s, or take turns creating math problems for each other. You can also place all of the numbers into a hat, have your child draw two or three, then add or subtract them.

The Reading Room

Laugh, learn, and take the edge off cabin fever by sharing a story or two. Check your school or public library for one or more of the following books:

Abe Lincoln's Hat by Martha Brenner, Random House, PreK-3.
Bunny Cakes by Rosemary Wells, Dial Books for Young Readers, PreK-2.
George Washington: First President of the United States by Carol Green, Children's Press, K-3.
Goodbye Old Year, Hello New Year by Frank Modell, Greenwillow Books, PreK-1.
Old Winter by Judith Benét Richardson, Orchard, K-3.
One Zillion Valentines by Frank Modell, Greenwillow Books, PreK-3.
St. Patrick's Day in the Morning by Eve Bunting, Houghton Mifflin, K-3.
What Is Martin Luther King, Jr., Day? by Jean Fritz, Putnam Publishing Group, PreK-3.
Will You Be My Valentine? by Steven Kroll, Holiday House, 1-3.

by Marie E. Cecchini

Creative Kitchen

'Tis the season to make hot cocoa. It will taste even better when you make your own mix. To make a personal cup of hot cocoa, place 1/3 c. powdered milk, 1 tsp. cocoa powder, and 1 tsp. sugar into a large cup. Stir in one cup of hot water. Add mini marshmallows and/or red cinnamon candies and stir to dissolve. If needed, add cold water or milk to cool cocoa.

Communication Station

Ring in the new calendar year by helping your child create a personal calendar for a family member or your home. Begin by placing a piece of typing paper over an old calendar page and tracing the lines; then help your child write in the names of the weekdays. Take this page to a copy machine and make 12 copies. Back at home, work with your child to write in the names of each month; then number the spaces accordingly. Page through the months again and have your child write in holidays, birthdays, and anniversaries. Staple the pages to the bottom half of a piece of construction paper. Your child can then cut up the old calendar pictures or use the fronts of greeting cards to create a collage design at the top.

Poetry in Motion

Your child will love making these secret valentine puzzle cards. First, draw and cut out a red or pink heart shape. Write the following rhyme on the heart:

> For Valentine's Day
> I've made you a game.
> Put the puzzle together
> And discover my name.

Then have your child write his or her name on a second sheet of paper and cut it into (not too many) puzzle pieces.

Lastly, children will need to place the heart and puzzle pieces into a clasp envelope. Then tell them to think of someone they can give this special valentine to.

From the Art Cart

Will the groundhog see its shadow or not? We'll know for sure on February 2nd. Either way, your child will love creating this groundhog puppet. You will need a paper cup, craft stick, brown paper, pencil, glue, scissors, and markers. For younger children, read the directions to them. Older children may read the directions themselves, but be available to help.

1. Color the craft stick brown.
2. Draw the head of a groundhog on brown paper. Cut it out.
3. Color a face on your groundhog.
4. Glue the head to the top of the craft stick.
5. Have an adult use the scissor to pierce a slit in the bottom of the cup.
6. Slide the bottom of the craft stick into the cup, through the slit, and out the bottom of the cup. By sliding the craft stick up and down, your child can make the groundhog pop up out of its "hole," then scurry back down.

Spring Song

When springtime's here,
How do I know?
The rain will fall,
The flowers will grow,
The sun will shine,
The cold will go,
But most of all
The wind will blow!

by Gloria Trabacca

Kid Space
School Yard Learning Adventures

Spring

Kid Space is a place of school yard beginnings. It is an ever-changing, fascinating place where children can connect with the natural world and learn all kinds of things. Kid Space is a safe place where kids can explore freely, embark on adventures and make learning discoveries all on their own. Make the most of the smells, the colors, the textures, the sounds, the excitement, the freedom and the peace and quiet.

Plant a Rainbow Garden

Kids won't hesitate at the chance to dig in the dirt and nurture some seeds.

You Need:
- garden plot
- garden tools: adult and kid sizes of shovels, hoes, rakes, trowels or spoons
- soil test kit
- fertilizer
- string
- garden markers
- flower seeds
- watering devices: hose or watering cans
- garden "attire" for practicality and effect: garden gloves, garden hat, rubber boots

What to Do:
1. Research and plan! Draw a rainbow-shaped garden plot with definite bands. Research a variety of colored flowering plants that will grow in your area in the same light and soil conditions. Choose hardy, fast-growing varieties of flowers. Find out all you can about the soil you will be planting in. Talk to local gardeners or the staff of a local nursery. Conduct your own soil tests or send a sample away to be tested.
2. Decide on the particular plants and color scheme for your "rainbow garden."
3. Purchase the seeds as part of a math lesson.
4. Start plants indoors if necessary.
5. Dig, dig, dig! Prepare the garden plot by digging, hoeing, raking, fertilizing and so on. You may want to draw a duty roster!
6. Plant the seeds or plants in your garden when the time is right.
7. Water, weed, feed and wait for the blooming of color.

Try This:
Take photographs of your rainbow garden and the young gardeners who made the garden bloom.

by Robynne Eagan

Kid Space
School Yard Learning Adventures

Discover Nature's Gardens

The plants that grow on the Earth (and in the sea) provide food, shelter and habitats for all living things. Plants create oxygen, purify the air and affect our weather. Nature's garden of living plants will grow, as it has been growing for billions of years, without your help.

Help your group to discover the wonder of nature's garden right on your own doorstep. Take a moment to appreciate the trees, wild grasses and flowers, sea plants or whatever growth you have access to.

How did the particular plants begin to grow in the particular location? How did the seeds get there and how were they able to grow without our help? Talk about the scattering of seeds through simple dropping or via the wind, animals and insects. Can you find some maple keys to demonstrate an intriguing dropping technique? Some plants produce runners, some new bulbs and some perennials just lie dormant until spring.

Nature's garden keeps us alive! Discuss the many wonderful things that plants provide for each and every one of us. Begin by discussing the air you breathe and the food you eat. Next look to the walls of your building and the floor you stand on. Don't overlook the clothing you wear, the heat source that warms you and the medicines that keep you well.

Garden Internet Connection

The Yuckiest Site on the Web–Worm World. What does Wendell the worm say to you? How about his cousins? Interviews are available by downloading wav files. Do you want to see live footage of a baby worm being hatched? It's here—in the multimedia section of worm world. It takes a little while to load. Be patient; it's worth it. http://www.nj.com/yucky/worm/

Take a photo tour of Moody Gardens at Galveston Island. What is the 10-story pyramid called? What's playing on the IMAX 3-D screen? http://www.moodygardens.com/moody.html

Cypress Garden—Find out what is in bloom at the world's most tropical showplace. What festivals occur during the spring and summer seasons? Interested in expert water skiing or gardening tips? http://www.florida.com/cypress-gardens/index.htm

Parents, too, will enjoy a somewhat virtual tour of the Ness Botanic Gardens. The colors of spring and summer are beautiful. Tour sites include the Jubilee Garden, Conservatory and Sorbus Lawn. http://www.connect.org.uk/merseyworld/ness-gardens/

Kid Space
School Yard Learning Adventures

Simple Spring Sensory Experiences

Share the wonder of nature! Encourage students to experience the wonder of spring using all their senses! This exercise will develop language, observation and analytical skills while teaching children about their five senses and the natural surroundings.

Spring Sights

Teach children to see things close up. What does mud really look like up close? Take a close look at buds, bark, leaves and raindrops. Encourage children to look at everything in a new way. Introduce new vocabulary with each experience. Scan the surroundings for a bigger picture. How is spring evident when you step back and take a look? How does the tree look? What about the school yard or the entire visible area?

The Sound of Spring

How does spring sound? Listen carefully for bird calls, mushy footsteps, dripping rain or gentle breezes. Close your eyes to enhance the experience.

Touch Spring

Feel spring in the rain, the mud, the gritty melting snow, wet puddles, the warming sun, fresh green sprouts and other tactile experiences that are present in your environment. What sensation does each child prefer about spring?

The Smell of Spring

Close your eyes again to sharpen your sense of smell. Spring has a smell all its own! Help your students express the smells they notice. Try to describe everything from fresh green growth to wet pavement. If you are lucky, you might find spring flowers, fresh mint or wild ginger to tantalize your sniffers! Some flowers produce a smell to attract insects that will assist the plant in the pollination process.

The Taste of Spring

Try to taste the air and then talk about the close relationship between the sense of smell and taste.

Gardening for the Senses

Use all of these senses as you plant your garden. How does the earth and compost look, smell and feel? What do the seeds look, smell and feel like? What changes will your senses notice once the seeds are planted in the earth?

Flower Garden Fun

Plant flowers in your garden and enjoy the blooms.
- Encourage children to monitor the growth process of various flowers.
- Measure the growth of flowers and chart the results on your daily calendar.
- Find and share stories and poems about flowers.
- Grow for color: Plant sweet peas, marigolds, nasturtiums or chrysanthemums.
- Grow for scent: Plant lavender, bergamot or roses that can be enjoyed year after year.

Kid Space
School Yard Learning Adventures

Make a Garden Journal

Use your garden as a learning adventure that grows into your science, language and creative arts curriculum areas.

You Need:
- spiral or three-ring notebook
- scissors
- paste
- writing and drawing instruments
- half of a brown paper bag

What to Do:
1. Cut a brown paper bag in half and remove the bottom piece.
2. Have children work the paper in their hands for many hours. They can crumple and flatten it, rub it with their fingers or against itself, fold and unfold it until the paper is soft and pliable. The paper can be worked at home and school over several days.
3. Cut the soft brown paper to cover the notebook.
4. Paste the brown paper over the notebook cover and then trim any remaining edges.
5. Decorate the covers of the garden journals with empty seed packages or copies of those used in your garden, and/or drawings of seeds, plants, gardens, vegetables or gardening tools.
6. Record daily entries in the journal to note the gardening process from planting to harvest. Children will develop keen skills of observation when there appears to be little happening in the garden! Encourage children to note colors, measurements, insect or feathered visitors, weather and sights and smells. Dated illustrations of the various stages of growth and a plant measurement record may be included.
7. The journal may be enhanced with a child's own tale of the planting of the garden—real or creatively embellished; printing or writing exercises using copies of poems or passages about gardens or plants; their own garden poetry; a list of things needed to make a healthy garden grow; garden theme math worksheets or problem-solving exercises; graphs, drawings or a collage of magazine cut-outs; and a report on a book about gardens, growing plants or a farm.

Caterpillar Fun

Celebrate spring with these fun-to-make caterpillars using inexpensive, easy-to-obtain materials. This project is a great way to introduce the life stages of a butterfly. The completed caterpillars make cute classroom decorations.

Materials:
Styrofoam™ "peanuts"—any size, shape or color (the more variety, the better)
12" pipe cleaners, one for each student
black construction paper
colored construction paper
markers or crayons
cellophane tape
scissors

Preparations:
Gather materials. Cut a 2" circle from colored construction paper for each student.

Demonstrate these steps for students to follow:

1. Bend over the end of a 12" pipe cleaner about 1/4" from the tip to keep Styrofoam™ peanuts from sliding off the end.

2. Thread Styrofoam™ peanuts onto the pipe cleaner one at a time until the pipe cleaner is nearly full. Stop about 3/4" from the end. This will be the caterpillar's body.

3. Draw a caterpillar face on the circle.

4. Cut "antennae" from black construction paper.

5. Tape antennae to the back of the caterpillar's face.

6. From the back, attach the face to the body with tape.

7. Bend the caterpillar's body into any wiggly shape you choose.

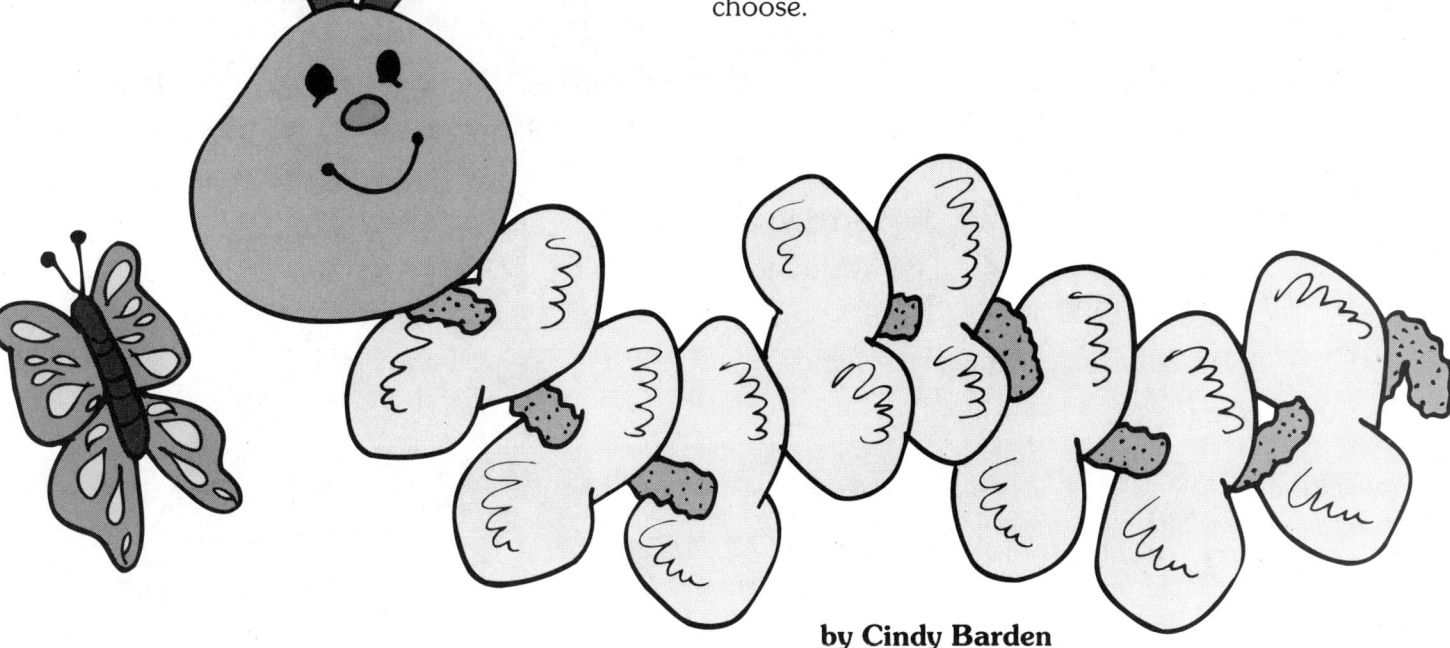

by Cindy Barden

Let the Wind Blow

Springtime brings with it a variety of weather: sun, rain and often wind. Wind cleans the air, brings clouds and rain, flies our kites and often makes children restless! Use these activities to focus that windy day energy and bring a breath of fresh air to your classroom.

Cory and the Wind

Read *Cory and the Wind* (pages 236 and 237). Discuss it with your students.

- Cory blew in the wind. What else blows in the wind?
- Cory felt the wind. What does the wind feel like? Can it feel different at different times?
- Can you see (smell/taste/hear) the wind?
- Can you make wind? How?

Related Reading
One Blowy Night by Nick Butterworth, Little, Brown & Co., 1992.
Winnie-the-Pooh and the Blustery Day by A.A. Milne.

by Gloria Trabacca

What Color Is the Wind?

Perhaps the wind has no color, but your students will enjoy using their own wind to make colorful kites!

Materials:
- prepared kite shapes or paper from which students may cut their own
- bowls
- tempera paint, thinned with extra water
- straws
- paint shirts

Place a variety of watered-down tempera paint in bowls on your covered work area. Spoon puddles of paint onto the kite shapes. Using straws, children may blow the paint around to create a design. If desired, add another color and repeat.

Kite Lotto

Kite Lotto is great as a small group center activity, or make enough for your entire class!

Materials:
- construction paper or tagboard
- gift wrap
- glue

Cut 9" x 6" gameboards out of construction paper or tagboard. Mark each one into six 3" x 3" squares. Using a pattern, cut kite shapes out of contrasting paper and gift wrap in matching pairs (e.g., for four gameboards, cut 24 kites and 24 matching kites for the draw pile). Laminate all gameboards and playing pieces. Have children take turns choosing from the draw pile. (For best results, put the pile in a small paper bag.) If the drawn card matches a kite on his gameboard, the student places it on the appropriate space. If the card is not a match, the card is returned to the draw pile.

Balloon Blow

This is your chance to blow away the competition!

Materials:
- 20-30 balloons in a variety of colors
- masking tape

Inflate balloons in advance. With masking tape, mark two lines on the floor, parallel to each other and six feet apart. Place five balloons halfway between the two lines. Standing behind one line, students take turns creating enough wind—using their breath or hand-held fans—to blow the balloons over the other line. Each turn lasts to the count of 10.

After each turn, the class counts how many balloons have crossed the opposite line. How many cross the line on the next turn? How many have crossed altogether now? Replenish balloons as needed.

For a simple exercise in graphing, prepare a blank chart, as well as balloon cut-outs. After each turn, count and graph how many balloons have crossed the line.

Wind Play

The wind is blowing through your room! Have your children become:

- a warm and gentle breeze
- an angry storm
- a kite-flying breeze
- a hurricane
- a tornado
- a cold winter wind
- a breeze strong enough to blow a wish star or dandelion fluff

Encourage your class to use sound as well as movement. Finishing with calmer breezes will help to prepare your class for quieter activities.

Cory and the Wind

Cory's long tail waved in the breeze. He watched the red part loop up and around the blue part of his tail. "I love to fly up here in the sky," he said to himself. On the beach below him, a boy and girl were throwing bread to some seagulls. A dirty gray bird dove down to snatch a piece before it hit the sand. Cory caught the wind and dove down too, swooping back up just before he touched the ground.

Soon the children finished their bread and the seagulls flew away. "Oh, I wish I could fly away like those birds!" Cory cried. "I don't want to stay on this string. I want to follow the wind!"

The string had been listening. "Ha! You can't get along without me! The wind would blow you far away. Every kite has to have a string." The string laughed at Cory.

Cory did not like to be told what to do, and he especially did not like to be laughed at. "What do you know anyway?" he said. "You aren't so smart, and you can't tell me what to do!" Cory tugged and twisted, climbing higher and higher in the sky. *I'm winning*, he thought, as he pulled away to the end of his string. *He'll be sorry he made fun of me!*

Just then, a gust of wind caught Cory. He felt it tug at his bright red body, straining against the string, until it snapped in two. "Hurray!" shouted Cory. "No more string. I'm free!" He soared higher and higher. The wind pushed him out over the ocean. Soon Cory had flown so far that he could hardly see the beach, but he didn't mind. There were many other things to see. Cory watched as a pod of whales swam underneath him. He saw the sun sparkle on the blue-green water. Some seabirds flew around Cory, then settled down on the water, poking their heads under to catch tiny silverfish. He watched as some purple and gray clouds blew toward him. The clouds were moving fast, and suddenly, just as the clouds reached Cory, the wind changed!

A flock of birds flew past, hurrying back to shore. "Fly home, little kite. The storm is coming!"

"I can't fly home!" he cried. "I'm not a bird. I am only a kite! A kite without a string." The wind blew angrily. Cory was tossed up and down, sideways and back up again. *Oooooh, I'm so dizzy*, he thought. *If only I had my string to hold onto.* "Please help me!" he shouted, as the last birds went by.

A big bird grabbed the blue bow on Cory's tail. "I'll help you." He flew quickly, but the storm was faster. Cold rain began to fall. Water ran off the bird's feathers, but Cory was soaked and shivering. The wind jerked him up and down in the bird's beak. Cory could feel the blue bow beginning to unravel. Frantically, he peered through the rain. He could see a small dark place on the water ahead. Was it land?

"Look!" Cory yelled above the wind. "What is that?" He turned to show the dark place to the bird. The bow came undone. "Help!" Cory's shout blew away on the wind, and Cory blew away, too. Down, down he flew, blowing in the wind. Down, down he blew, towards the dark spot in the water. Cory could see it more clearly now. *Well, it isn't land,* he thought, *but it's better than landing in the water!*

The little kite wriggled and jerked and spun, trying to reach the brown object before he fell completely. *Almost there, almost there, just a little more . . .* The rain began to fall harder, and Cory couldn't see where he was going. Cory closed his eyes as he felt an icy wave touch the tip of his tail. *Too late,* he thought. His tail floated out across the water, pulling him down. Suddenly Cory's eyes flew open. Something had grabbed him from behind.

Cory shook with fear, but then he heard a low voice. "Come here. I've got you now. Everything will be all right." The man turned Cory around and looked at him with kind brown eyes. "Well, you're a little wet, but you'll soon dry in the cabin." Ducking his head down through the doorway, the man took Cory inside and hung him gently near the heater. "How would you like to come home with me?" he asked. "My little boy has always wanted a kite like you."

"Oh, yes!" Cory cried. "I would like that very much!" He watched the man open a small drawer and search until he found a spool of string.

"Now hold still," he said. "We need to give you a string. No more sailing with the wind for you!"

"No more sailing with the wind for me!" Cory agreed happily. "I don't want to go wherever the wind goes anymore." He watched the man tie on his new string, happy to be safe once more.

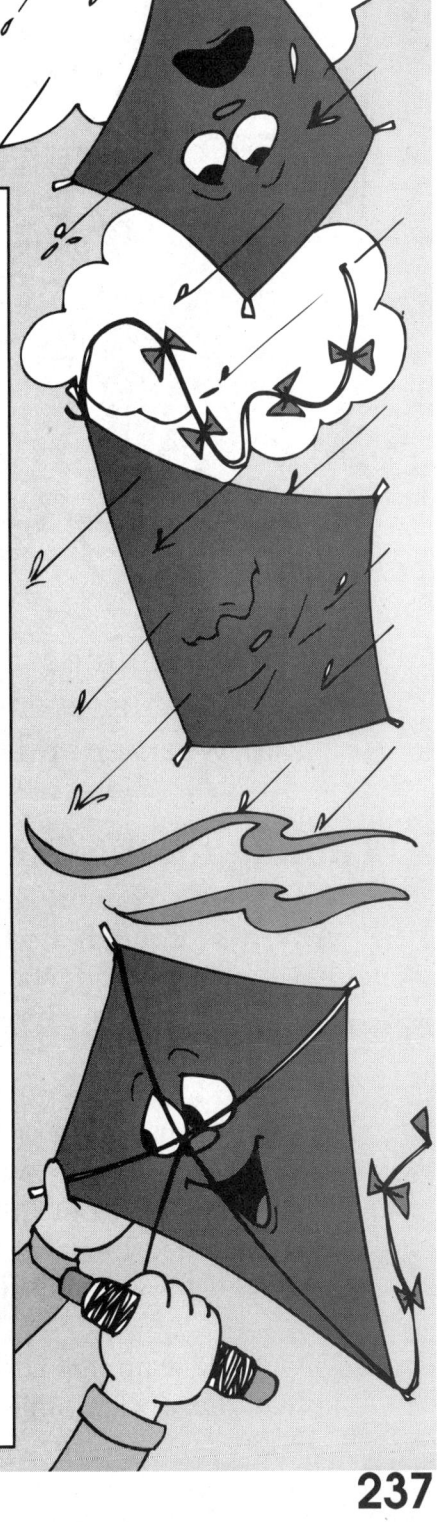

Come to the Spring Carnival

For fun and funds, there is nothing like a school carnival. Many schools rely on this spring event as the main school fund-raiser. Take advantage of the warmer weather and enthusiasm for an exciting and profitable spring fun fair.

Planning for the Carnival

1. Create a committed, creative team. Advertise through a school newsletter and have parents and staff personally invite good candidates. Spread the word and enthusiasm about your fair through media, flyers and word-of-mouth. Contact parents via school newsletter, word-of-mouth and direct calling to inform them of this significant event. Find out if families have skills, time, donated items or ideas to contribute. Share this information at your first meeting.

2. Divide the team into committees so you can spread the work around. You will need one or two team coordinators and committees for the following: games, special events, super raffle, food, prizes and donations, entertainment, advertising and other areas specific to your fair.

3. Arrange one meeting 8-12 months prior to the event and have committees meet separately. Committee coordinators can meet six months and three months before the carnival and then as frequently as necessary to coordinate the event, to assist one another and to ensure that work is not being duplicated.

by Robynne Eagan

Prizes and Donations

Many companies are happy to donate items to worthy causes—ask around! Large companies who produce items specifically related to school children will often donate if they receive a written request one year in advance.

Raffles and Large Prize Events

Here are some ideas of large prizes to be raffled off or given away. Sporting equipment, event tickets, autographed items from a local team, passes to ski slopes, pools, tennis courts, or skating rinks.

Gift certificates to restaurants, hair salons, theme parks or retail outlets. Food items from local grocery stores, ice cream shops, fruit stands or bakeries.

Factory donations of anything from toys and art supplies to auto parts and chocolate. Arts and crafts donated by local artists are always appreciated. Members of the school community, the local community, children's organizations or senior homes may be willing to donate hand-crafted items such as mittens, pencil holders, folk art, paintings, candles, clay work, picture frames, sewn items and so on.

Carnival Game Prizes

Purchase in large quantities to receive good discounts on the following:
- Large novelty or party supply stores offer small prizes of all kinds.
- Candy, gum, chips and cans of soda are always popular prizes.
- Pencils, markers, crayons, erasers and other useful art supplies make good prizes.
- Marbles, beads, collector cards, pogs and other trendy collectibles are desirable.
- You may be able to obtain free promotional materials from local businesses. Bookmarks, comic books, paperbacks or coloring books can be obtained inexpensively in large quantities.

Helpful Hints

- Keep meetings focused, informative and brief if you want return volunteers!
- Create a catchy name that will stick with your event-fun fair, carnival, spring fling or a creative name related specifically to your school.
- Make signs that will let everyone know that they are welcome.
- Think long-term. Although your profits may not be as great the first year—it will pay to make your fair an event worth attending. Provide good food, good entertainment and good prizes that will bring people back next year.
- Check local bylaws and liabilities regarding all events.

Popular Fund-Raising Ideas

Don't overlook the traditional forms of fund-raising—these are still around for good reason! Take advantage of the carnival crowds and enthusiasm to maximize your profits.

Bake Sale

Those fancy cupcakes and chocolate chip cookies are always popular! Price some items in the kids' range (5-25 cents) and others for a family crowd (50 cents–$2.00). You can include a limited selection of items in the $3.00–$5.00 range—cakes, loaves and fancy pies. Sponsor baking contests for students—the best decorated cupcake, cake or gingerbread man contest, the tastiest chocolate chip cookies, or the best lemon loaf. Entry items will be sold at the carnival and winning entrants will receive carnival tickets. Older students may put together a family recipe book to be sold at the back table. Staples or ring clasps can hold these together.

The Garden Center

Invite local garden enthusiasts to donate clippings, bulbs, bunches, seeds, seedlings and diggings from their gardens. Overgrowth from one's garden may be a wonder bloom for another's plot!

A teacher may initiate a potting project to start vegetables or flowers to be sold at the carnival. Prices will vary depending upon the donations received, but they will be a great bargain at any price for green thumbs and a wonderful boost to the beauty of your community.

The White Elephant Table

This sale benefits everyone. Treasures are traded while closets and garages are cleaned out!

The Diner

Run your carnival over the lunch or dinner hour and advertise the fine food ahead of time. Provide pizza, hot dogs, potato chips, cold drinks, coffee and other easy treats.

Face Painting

Provide face paints and some instructions to talented volunteers and start the lineup. You can charge between $1.00 and $3.00 for every face you paint.

Balloons

Balloons never go out of style. A helium tank, balloons and string will add to the atmosphere and provide another venue for profit—even at a nickel a piece!

Popcorn Wagon

Rent or borrow a popcorn wagon to be run by a trained volunteer.

Carnival Games

Game Tips: Sell tickets at 25 cents each or 5 for $1.00, and take 1-4 tickets for each activity or game. Clearly mark with tape or chalk where the lines should form for each event. Have participants return to the end of the line after each turn. Allow players the opportunity to move closer or to take extra turns if they need to.

Cake Walk

Materials:
- cakes
- walkway (marked with numbers 1-15)
- slips of paper marked 1-15 in a small bowl
- music

Directions:
1. Request cake donations. One class may choose to take on the responsibility of baking and decorating cakes for this event.
2. Choose a stretch of sidewalk, playground or hallway for this popular event. Mark the sections with numerals 1 to 15.
3. Allow 15 participants in each game and collect four tickets from each.
4. Have participants take their place on the walkway and wait for the music to begin.
5. Participants walk when the music plays and stop when the music stops.
6. When the music stops, a number is drawn from the bucket—the player on that numbered section wins a cake.
7. That player leaves the game and the remaining players keep walking when the music resumes. When the music stops again, another number is drawn. If no player is on the drawn number, another is taken from the bucket until a second player receives a cake.

Duck Pond

Materials:
- water table or trough
- hose or pump to keep the water moving
- ducks with markings on their undersides: half marked with a circle (small prize) five marked with a star (large prize) remainder marked with a diamond (medium prize)

Directions:
1. Children pay one ticket to play—then take one duck from the pond.
2. Give the child a prize that corresponds to the mark on the duck.
3. Allow the next child to take a duck.

Play Station

Materials:
- playground equipment, jumping mats, Hula Hoops™, scooter boards, sandbox or water table

Directions:
Students pay tickets to play in the area for a designated amount of time.

Fishing Pond

Materials:
- table or divider decorated to look like a pond
- "fishing rods" with clothespins on the ends
- prize packets to be clipped to the clothespins
- extra volunteers to hide "in the pond"

Directions:
1. Participants pay one ticket to fish. They toss their line over the table or divider "into the fish pond"— and wait for a tug.
2. Behind the scenes, volunteers clip a prize packet to the clothespin and then tug on the line when the prize is snagged.

Basketball Theme Toss

Materials:
- *decorated backboard with small basketball hoop
- stuffed or plastic characters to be thrown through the hoop

Directions:
1. Participants toss the characters through the hoop.
2. Prizes vary according to the number of "baskets" made.

* Consider the theme from a popular book or movie. Characters can often be obtained or borrowed. Give-away characters from fast food restaurants are usually in good supply.

Lollipop Tree

Materials:
- self-supporting board decorated and drilled with holes
- lollipops to stick in the holes

Directions:
1. Mark the bottom of a fourth of the lollipop sticks with a colored dot.
2. Players pull a lollipop from the tree. Those who pull a colored dot win a 50-cent piece and the lollipop; those who pull an unmarked lollipop keep the lollipop.

Other Games: Consider fun picnic-style races, water balloon tosses, obstacle courses, tricycle races, mazes, "The Wheel of Fortune" or marble shoot gameboards.

Ring Toss

Materials:
- full pop bottles or wooden pegs mounted to a board
- rings of plastic or rubber
- tossing line (marked with chalk, tape or rope)

Directions:
1. Each participant receives three rings.
2. Prizes will vary according to the number of rings that land on the bottles or pegs.

Special Events

Parents and extended family members, local businesses and parents' employers may be able to provide exciting events at little or no cost to the school. Look around! Let organizations know that their contributions will be acknowledged at the carnival and in the newspaper follow-up. You should provide volunteers to assist with these activities.

Horse, Pony or Wagon Rides

Anticipate long lineups if you are able to offer these exciting events.

Pitching Machine

Local sports park may donate one for the evening—or turn to the local police for a volunteer with a radar gun.

Dunk Tank

Principal, teachers and local personalities can take the hot seat. Collect tickets for each throw or one ticket for two or three throws.

Hot Air Balloon Rides

Some companies will provide these just for the free advertising. You can charge a fee of $3.00 to $6.00 for each person per ride. It's a great vantage point for photography!

Trampolines

Entertainment companies or area gymnastic clubs may provide a tramp and spotters to keep the activity safe.

Mini Electric Cars or Motorcycles

Set up a course and collect tickets for rides. This event is sure to be popular with little drivers! Monitor it carefully and provide ample volunteers.

Electronic Games

School computer equipment and borrowed equipment can provide a room full of electronic fun. Tickets can buy time on any of the games offered. When time runs out, players must return to the end of the line to play again.

Celebrity Signing

There has to be one—or at least a connection in your school community!

Tours of . . .

big rig, police car, fire truck, limousine . . .

Duck Races

Local fund-raising organizations may have duck racing troughs available, or you may find parents or community businesses willing to make a reusable one for you out of PVC pipe or metal troughs. You add the hose, water and plastic ducks.

Horseshoe Tournament

A local enthusiast is sure to enjoy setting up this event. Offer prizes and collect entry fees.

Silent Auction

Donated items can be displayed with bid boxes provided for each. Close the bidding one half hour before the carnival closes. Sort through the bids and present the goods to the highest bidder.

Bingo

Find yourself a good caller, a room full of tables, chips, cards and prizes. Charge a fee per game.

Card Tables

Is euchre or bridge popular in your area? Have an avid player set up a mini tournament on carnival night. Provide tables and a room. Collect player fees.

Talent Show

Allow students and local members of the community an opportunity to demonstrate their talents and entertain a crowd. Fiddle music, singers and other lively entries will be most successful. Do not expect to stage any full productions. Keep it light and fast moving. You will need to provide an indoor or outdoor stage.

Cycle or Running Race

Attract the athletic crowd by hosting a substantial cycle or footrace—for adults and children. Charge an entry fee and provide prizes.

Super Raffle

A super raffle offers many prizes in a children's and adults' draw. A successful super raffle needs many prizes, a supportive community and avid ticket sellers. The raffle committee will search the community for prize donations. Donation requests on school letterhead describing the event should be sent to area businesses and large "kid-oriented" companies six months to one year ahead of time. A school newsletter can request donations from parents of anything from handmade mitts and house-cleaning services to art, crafts or woodworking items. Parents can be asked to supply the names of companies or individuals who might be willing to donate and may approach their place of business on behalf of the school. This type of raffle allows local businesses an opportunity to advertise and contribute. Display the many prizes as they come in to raise the awareness and excitement for the raffle.

Tickets are sold by all members of the school and their families for 50 cents each or $1.00 for a book of three. Anyone who sells 10 books of tickets can be given a free book.

Have volunteers draw tickets and record winners throughout the carnival.

Passover סדר

Music
Teach students the song "Go Down, Moses."

When Israel was in Egypt land,
Let my people go.
Oppressed so hard they could not stand,
Let my people go.
Go down, Moses, way down in Egypt land.
Tell ol' Pharaoh to let my people go.

Passover is the Jewish Festival of Freedom and a spring holiday. It is a time to remember the journey of the Israelites out of slavery in Egypt and into freedom, as described in the book of Exodus in the Bible. The holiday lasts eight days. On the first two nights, Jews around the world celebrate in their homes with a special meal called a *seder*. The word *seder* means "order" in Hebrew, and during this meal special foods are eaten and rituals are followed in a certain order.

During Passover, Jews do not eat any leavened food. A leavened food is one that has risen. That means no breads, cakes or cookies made from flour are eaten. Instead, foods are made from matzoh meal without any leavening agents, such as yeast or baking powder. Matzoh meal is a special flour that is carefully watched to make sure that it does not rise. A flat bread called *matzoh* is made from this flour and is eaten throughout the eight days of Passover.

During the seder, Jews read from a book called the *haggadah,* which contains prayers and blessings and recounts the story of the Israelites' exodus from Egypt. Each participant in the seder is instructed to feel as though he or she was personally going out of slavery and into freedom. Matzoh and other special foods on the table remind people that the Israelites fled quickly.

A seder plate contains five separate items, each of which represents part of the story of the exodus. It has a lamb bone, which recalls the lambs' blood. There is a mixture of nuts and apples that looks like the mortar used by the slaves to make bricks. There is spicy horseradish, which reminds Jews that slavery is bitter. The seder plate also has green parsley to represent spring and an egg for new life. The parsley is dipped in salt water, which tastes like the tears of the slaves.

by Katy Z. Allen and Gabi Mezger

How Are You Free?

Challenge students to think of ways in which they are free and ways in which they are not free. It may help them to compare themselves to older or younger siblings. Have small groups of students work cooperatively to create lists. Then make a master list on the board. Ask students what it would feel like if they suddenly lost all their freedom. Afterward, have each student pick one way in which he or she is free and draw a picture to illustrate it. Create a bulletin board with the title "We Are Free."

The Drinking Gourd

Read the book *Follow the Drinking Gourd* by Jeannette Winter (Knopf, 1988), which tells about the escape of African Americans from slavery before the Civil War. Afterward, discuss what it means to be a slave. Ask the following questions: What do you think it was like to be a slave in Egypt? What do you think it was like to be a slave in the United States? If African Americans had a holiday to celebrate their freedom from slavery, what do you think it would be like?

Unleavened Bread

Purchase a box of matzoh in a supermarket or specialty market. Also bring to class a loaf of bread. Give students the opportunity to taste both. Explain that the bread has leavening, which means that it has risen and expanded from the original dough. This is what makes bread light. The matzoh has no leavening. Explain that during Passover, Jews remove all food containing leavening from their homes and eat only unleavened foods.

Seder Plate

On a paper plate, have the students draw and color the five items which belong on a seder plate.

First of April

When I woke up this morning,
Mom said, "There's no school.
Dad's won the lottery,
We're putting in a pool!
You sure need a haircut.
A Mohawk might look cool."
Then she spoiled it all
By yelling, "April Fool!"

by Timothy Tocher

April Showers

No lullaby compares to the peaceful tip-tap of gentle raindrops on the windowpane at bedtime. Invite your class to explore and enjoy the serenity of rain with the following activities.

My New Umbrella

I have a new umbrella
That's big and red and round,
To hold above my head
When rain comes plopping down.

The job of this umbrella
Is to keep me very dry.
So when I come home very wet,
My mom does not know why.

I tell her I don't really know
Why this happens to me.
The puddles that I step in
Only come up to my knees.

Umbrella Designs

Provide the children with paper, markers, scissors and umbrella pattern. Have them each cut out an umbrella and color the handle. Let them decorate their umbrella domes by gluing on bits of fabric, tissue paper or wallpaper.

Umbrella Fun

Share the above poem with your class. Discuss the purpose (job) of umbrellas. Have the children contribute ideas as to why the umbrella does not keep the child in the poem dry.

Umbrella Action

Supervise the children in rainy day balance beam activities. Help them walk across the balance beam forward, then sideways, while holding a child's umbrella in one hand. Also challenge them to try: (1) balancing beanbag "raindrops" in each hand; (2) holding a watering can in one hand and a bucket in the other; (3) holding their arms out to their sides; (4) extending their arms above their heads.

by Marie E. Cecchini

Measuring Rain

Use a wide-mouth jar to measure rainfall on several rainy days. Record the number of inches on a weather calendar for each successive day, emptying the jar in between. After several recordings, have the children review and compare the results. On which day did the most rain fall? The least?

Rainy Day Gear

Collect rainwear (slickers, hats, boots, umbrellas) to share with the children. Discuss the name and job of each article of clothing. Allow the children to make use of these for dramatic play. Umbrella play will need special supervision. Next, have the children dress in pretend rain clothes and take them on an imaginary walk in the rain. Invite them to open their pretend umbrellas, catch "raindrops" on their tongues, jump in imaginary puddles and so on.

Puddles

For Jumping: Use tape to create puddle formations on the floor. Have the children jump from puddle to puddle on one foot or two; have them jump into the puddles or over them. *For Tossing:* Make several paper puddles of various colors. Write numbers, letters or rainy day words on them, if you wish. Provide the children with beanbag "raindrops" and have individual students toss the beanbags into specific puddles (i.e. the blue one, puddle number two, puddle D and so on). Have older children pitch to any puddle, then read that rainy day word.

Rainy Days

Talk with the children about different kinds of rainy days. Introduce rainy day words like *sprinkle, drizzle, downpour* and *shower.* Discuss how rain comes down differently during each rainfall. Afterward, provide the class with colored water and paper towels or coffee filters. Have them use various utensils to make water drops on their paper towels. Encourage them to discuss the sizes and shapes of the drops from each utensil. Utensils might include different sizes of paintbrushes, spoons, fingers, toothpicks, drinking straws, pencils, toothbrushes and pipe cleaners.

Raindrops Mobile

Help the children cut cloud shapes from cardboard. Let them tape several yarn lengths at the bottom of their cloud shapes and a yarn loop at the top for hanging. Have them glue cotton onto both sides of their clouds. Provide them with a raindrop pattern, scissors, markers and scrap paper, and have them make raindrops. Let them tape one raindrop to each length of yarn.

Rain's Work
Talk with the children about how rain provides all living things with water. Have them collect pictures of plants and animals that need water to survive. Let them glue their pictures to a collage entitled "Rain's Work." Afterward, take the class outside and provide them with watering cans and water. Encourage them to act out the work of rain.

Center Raindrops
Prepare several umbrella shapes with numerals and tape each of these shapes to a container. Supply the children with raindrop manipulatives and have them count and drop the correct number of raindrops into each container. Patterns can be found on page 74.

Color Drops
Share the following poem with your class; then let them use droppers and tempera paints to make color drops on white paper and discover new colors.

Raindrop Sounds
Invite your class to play a listening game. You will need water, a dropper and an aluminum pie tin. Have the children close their eyes while you use the dropper to make "rain" on the pie tin. The children are to silently count the drops and tell you the correct number when the mini shower is over.

Sponge Clouds
After your rain cloud demonstration, share and discuss the following poem with your class. Then provide the children with natural sponges, which are more "cloud shaped," and allow them to make rain in a water table or tub.

Rainmaker
Have the children observe a rain-making demonstration. Boil water in a tea kettle or pot until a steam cloud forms. Hold a pie tin of ice chips in the steam cloud, and have the class watch for the formation of "raindrops." Help them conclude that warm air coming in contact with cool air forms water droplets.

Glitter Drops
Have the children draw and cut large raindrop shapes from white paper. Let them cover their raindrops with glue spots, then slightly spread the glue. Next, have them "rain" white or silver glitter over their pictures. If they wish to hang their raindrops, have them punch a hole at the top and thread it with yarn. A raindrop pattern can be found on page 314.

Peanut Butter Lovers' Day

Celebrated March 1

Literature

Incorporate books about peanut butter into the classroom. Add them to the classroom library or reading space and read them aloud for story time. Do not forget other areas of the classroom when introducing books. Place a book about peanut butter in the dramatic play area, at a clay or play dough activity, or with a cooking activity. Make a book tray that can be carried anywhere in the classroom. Include a book about peanut butter, peanut shells, empty peanut butter jars, and plastic knives on the tray. Try some of these books about peanut butter.

Make Me a Peanut Butter Sandwich and a Glass of Milk by Ken Robbins, Scholastic Inc., 1992.

Peanut Butter and Jelly by Nadine Westcott, Puffin Books, 1992.

Peanut Butter Rhino by Vincent Andriani.

Cooking

Cookie-Cutter Peanut Butter Sandwiches

Gather bread, peanut butter, plastic or butter knives, paper plates, and cookie cutters. Children can spread their own peanut butter and assemble a sandwich. Invite each child to choose a cookie cutter and press it firmly in the center of the sandwich. They may munch on the scraps and set the sandwich aside until everyone has had a turn. Write each child's name on their paper plate. Serve these sandwiches with milk. For more interest, make different breads available or use raisins to decorate the top of the cut sandwich.

Animal Zoo with Peanut Butter Glue

For a creative snack time, give each child a paper plate and an assortment of animal crackers and stick pretzels. Supply spoons and a bowl of peanut butter. Have children spoon and spread peanut butter on their plate and, use it as "glue" to hold together fences and cages created with pretzels. Then add animal crackers to create a zoo. Make edible "zoo" signs by spreading peanut butter on a large cracker and using pretzels and round cereals to make the letters. After making the zoo, children can have fun eating their creations.

Game

Tossing Peanuts with Shells

Arrange a variety of containers at different distances from the tossing line. Children toss peanuts with shells and try to get them into the containers.

by Carol Ann Bloom

Math
Peanut Guess and Count
Fill several clear jars, bottles, and vases with peanuts in shells. Vary the sizes of the containers and place a question mark on each. Fill some containers to the top and make others half or one-third full. Place a lid on each container. Invite children to guess how many peanuts are in each container. Smaller containers can be handled and shaken. Record estimates on a sheet of paper next to each child's name. At group time, spill peanuts out and count how many are in each jar. Check to see whose estimate is closest to the actual number of peanuts in each container. For more math fun, choose two distinctly different containers, such as a tall, thin one and a short, round one. Place the same number of peanuts in each and ask children, "Which has more?" Follow the same procedure.

Art
Peanut Butter Play Dough
Children can help mix a batch of this tasty play dough. Combine one cup peanut butter, one cup powdered milk, and three tablespoons honey. Provide rolling pins, cookie cutters, and foil-covered polystyrene food trays or egg cartons so children can re-create a bakery. Wash hands before this activity since the resulting cookies, cakes, and pies can be eaten for snack.

Language
One Food—Many Uses
This activity gives children an opportunity to orally share their ideas and experiences, as well as to see their verbalizations in print. Write the words *peanut butter* at the top of a piece of chart paper. Encourage children to share the many different ways they enjoy this food: peanut butter sandwiches, peanut butter and jelly, peanut butter cookies, peanut butter on celery, peanut butter candy, peanut butter and bananas, peanut butter ice cream, and so on. Prepare lists of other familiar foods and the many ways they can be prepared and eaten: eggs, potatoes, cheese, or apples.

Motor
Elephant Walk
Children assume the stance of an elephant: bend forward at the waist, spread legs slightly apart, lower head and hang arms toward the floor, clasping hands. Have the "elephants" walk with slow, heavy steps, swinging the arms side to side like an elephant lumbering through the jungle. Play slow background music or tap a steady, rhythmic beat to set the pace for an elephant walking. A trail of peanuts in shells can be placed on the floor for "elephants" to follow.

Music
Peanut Butter Cheer
Spell out the word *peanut butter* in a rhythmic cheer that begins:
"Give me a *P*." Children respond—"P!"
"Give me an *E*." Children respond—"E!"
"Give me an *A*." Children respond—"A!"
The cheer concludes:
"What's that spell?" Children respond—"Peanut butter!"
Continue cheering and spelling other words associated with peanut butter: *jelly, sandwich, jar, spread,* and so on.

Dr. Seuss Day

Background—Dr. Seuss' real name is Theodor Seuss Geisel. He was born March 2, 1904, and died September 24, 1991. He is known for his rhyming books and his magical nonsense words such as *triffula trees, schlopps, snuus,* and *zongs.*

Introduction—Have the students read *The Cat in the Hat, The Cat in the Hat Comes Back,* or *The 500 Hats of Bartholomew Cubbins.* Talk about the different hats students may have at home. Discuss various occupations some of their parents may have that require special hats such as nurse's cap, hard hat, fire hat, and so on. Designate March 2, or as close to that date as possible, as "Hat Day" on which students are asked to bring in a hat of their choice. In order to get away from always making graphs about their "favorites," we have some suggestions for graphing hats in a different way.

Graphing Directions—Have students wear or hold their hats. Briefly discuss the kinds of hats and make sure everyone knows the types of hats represented or the occupation the hat may represent. Let students brainstorm categories, like sports hats, job-related hats, silly hats, hats with designs on them, hats with words, and so on. Limit categories to three (or four for older children). Have students line up in rows according to the category which fits their hat. By doing this, the students are making a "real" graph. If there is a discrepancy about which row a child should be in, let that student give one reason why he or she chose that category. You may continue graphing other categories if the interest is there, or you might try doing the hat graph at the beginning and end of the day.

Extensions—Throw hats in the center of a circle on the floor or table. Randomly draw out students' names, one by one. Each child must pick a hat (other than his or her own) and match it to its owner.

More to Do—Do an author study on Dr. Seuss. Read Dr. Seuss books daily for a week or two. At the end of the study, have students draw a scene or character from their favorite Dr. Seuss book, labeled with the title. Make a wall graph by lining up the drawings in rows by title.

by Karen Reid and Joni Becker

Celebrate St. Patrick's Day

with an Old Irish Expression:

"There Are No Pockets in a Shroud!"

There's an old Irish expression:
"There are no pockets in a shroud"
which means you can't take them with you,
those things on Earth which made you proud!
But if you had one possession
you could take along with you,
which special one would you select—
something old or something new?

You might tell it in a story,
with a picture or a poem.
"If I could take one thing that's mine,
this is what I would take along!"
As you select what you like most,
you'll be setting forth your VALUES,
because you'll be revealing them
in the one treasure that you choose!

This poem will inspire a number of creative expressions (poems, stories, pictures), forcing students to make a choice of what they treasure most! These choices will reveal what the child values most and is an elementary way to introduce values.

The creative responses of the children, mounted on a large bulletin board or displayed in some other way, will be a composite picture of children's interests and might be titled "Our Values," an introductory way to show them early values!

Use the following discussion questions with your class:

1. How many children chose pets (living treasures)?
2. What toys did children select as most special to them?
3. Which items were given to them, and which ones did they make themselves?
4. How many of their choices have sentimental value, and how many have real value?
5. Are there differences in what the boys chose and what the girls picked?

by Peggy Meredith Cochard

Pinch, Paula, Pinch
A Do-It-Yourself St. Patrick's Day Story

by Mr. Fischer and _____
your name here

Paula Presley woke up late on March 17th. She woke up *so* late that she forgot she had already laid out her green outfit the night before! She went straight to her dresser and grabbed her favorite pink dress instead, since it was only one piece and would not take as long to put on as a pair of shorts and a shirt!

Okay, here is where you take over for a minute. Write down what Paula looks like. Is she skinny or short or blond or what? Tell about her in one good sentence. In the second sentence, write about what Paula's room looks like. Is it all pink, like her dress, or is it really messy? You might write something funny about how she trips over a pile of dirty clothes. Make it up yourself and write it down.

Paula Presley was so very late that even though she got into her pink dress quickly, she missed the bus. Luckily, her mom had time to drop her off at school on her way to work.

Now for your second job. Take three sentences this time, since it is a much bigger place you are telling us about, and describe what Paula's elementary school looks like. Is it two stories or one? How big is it? You can even give it a name if you want, because whatever you say the school looks like, that is what your readers will picture in their heads from now on!

Paula Presley was so very, very late that she did not even have time to notice that almost *everybody* in the whole entire school, even the principal, was wearing green! By the time she did notice, she was getting pinched by all the kids in her class!

"Pink, Paula?" they all asked her, in between pinches. "Who wears pink on St. Patrick's Day? Pinch Paula; pinch Paula . . ."

Okay, for your third job, tell how Paula feels as she's getting pinched. Does she get sad or mad? Does she cry or pinch back? Use two sentences to tell how Paula feels.

by Rusty Fischer

Ms. Richard, her third grade teacher, finally had to raise her voice, which she almost never did, and make the class stop pinching Paula.

All right, now describe Ms. Richard. Is she old or young? Pretty or scary? Sweet or mean?

By the time recess rolled around, Paula Presley had been pinched so many times that there were little bruises all up and down her arm. It looked like she had blue chicken pox! Ms. Richard held Paula back as the other kids rolled out the door like a tidal wave. Paula was glad. She knew they would all be waiting for her to be their big, pink "pinching bag" again!

Ms. Richard took a look at Paula's arms and asked if she was okay. Paula felt better now, so she nodded, and then Ms. Richard gave her something to stop everybody from pinching her. It was a _____!

Now fill in the blank above, telling what Ms. Richard gave Paula. Then take two more sentences to describe what Paula's teacher gave her. Of course it had to be something green to get everybody to stop pinching her, but what was it? A green scarf? A green hat? A frog to put in her pocket? Tell about it.

Paula Presley took the _____ from her teacher and flew out the door to find her friends. As soon as she got outside, kids started coming up to her, ready to pinch Paula, . . . but the _____ stopped them in their tracks.

Paula, safe from all the "St. Patrick's Pinchers," started looking around the crowded playground. Now it was her turn . . .

All right, for your last assignment, you get to finish the story. First, make sure you tell what the playground looks like, since that is where your story will end. What are all the kids doing? What are they playing on? Take two sentences to write about the playground, and then take four more to tell what Paula does at the end of the story. Now that she is safe, does she try and pinch other kids who are not wearing green? Does she get back at the kids who pinched her? Does she go off alone and wait for her friends to say they are sorry? These are just a few ideas, but you can make one up all on your own. Anything can happen, since you are finishing the story!

Directions: Read the story. Wherever you find italics type, follow the instructions and *do some creative writing of your own.* Use a separate sheet of paper.

Kid Space
School Yard Learning Adventures

St. Patrick's Day Green Hike

Hike for Green and celebrate this Irish holiday. Have students dress in something green and bring a green snack for sharing on this little hike.

On the hike, have students make a mental list of the green sights and smells they encounter along the way. Students are to keep these discoveries to themselves until the hikers meet for their green snacks.

Can you smell green? What about greenery? Use your imagination. How does green smell to you?

Are all greens the same? Of course not! How many shades of green do you think there are? How does the color green make you feel? What things does the color green make you think of? What do you think the color green could be a symbol for?

Potato Power

The potato crop has been very important to the people of Ireland for a long, long time. People often ate potatoes for breakfast, lunch, and dinner.

Although potatoes grow underground, they are not called a root vegetable, they are called a tuber. A tuber is a bulge in a plant's rhizome—another new word! A rhizome is an underground part of a plant's stem that is used to store extra food. A bulge on the plant's rhizome is called a tuber. The extra food and water needed by the plant is mostly water and starch, and that is precisely what a potato is made of.

Potato Bag Surprise

Have you ever reached into the potato bag and found a wrinkled brown thing with hairy white sprouts growing out of it? This unnerving-looking little surprise is a sprouting tuber.

The white growths are shoots—growing out of what is called the eye of the potato. A bud sends a shoot out of the eye of the potato. This sprout grows into a cluster that becomes the stem and leaves of the new potato plant. The hairy white strands at the bottom of the sprouts are the roots and rhizomes. The root hairs absorb water and food from the Earth to send up to the leaves. The rhizome swells and stores food when the plant is full grown. The rhizome becomes the tuber. The tuber of this plant is called the potato. It's the part of the plant that we eat. Potatoes grow in almost every country of the world.

by Robynne Eagan

The Middle Eastern New Year

The first day of spring marks the New Year's celebration in the Middle East. It is called *Noruz*, which means "new day." Noruz is celebrated by people of all religions in most of the Middle East. Some countries included are Morocco, Algeria, Tunisia, Libya, Egypt, Iraq, Iran, and Turkey. In Iran, Noruz is considered a national holiday which is the *Iranian New Year*. The celebrations go on for two weeks, ending on the thirteenth day after Noruz with another festive day called *Sizdar Bedar*. People usually picnic on this day.

The festive weeks are very family oriented. There is a great deal of traveling so families can be together. The children are entertained and amused by clowns. A traditional "fire-jumping" game takes place. Everyone jumps over a small bonfire. It is said that this fire burns away the sorrows of the old year. The phrase "May you live a hundred years" is said to all. What event do we celebrate where we wish people many more years? (a birthday)

The Middle Eastern people set up a *symbolic table* in their homes. Objects on the table include sprouted seeds, coins, sugar, vinegar, fruit, spices, flowers, a mirror, a candle, and a bowl of water with an uneven number of goldfish in it. The pastry *baklava* is served to all visitors *to make the New Year sweet*.

Bring a little of this Middle Eastern holiday to your classroom with a few of these activities.

Symbolic Table

Set up a table to display the objects discussed above. Give the children art paper and have them draw the objects.

by Tania K. Cowling

CLOWN PUPPET

Cut one large circle and four smaller ones from construction paper. Then cut two 6" and two 4" strips from construction paper. Fold the strips accordion-style. Glue the shorter pieces to the large circle for arms and the longer strips for legs. Affix the small circles to the strips for hands and feet. Attach a craft stick handle to the back of the large circle. Add facial features to look like a clown.

SPROUT SOME SEEDS

It is a custom in the Middle East to sprout seeds. Lentils and wheat seeds are placed in shallow bowls of water where they can sprout. Do this as a science activity. Observe how long it takes the seeds to sprout. Chart the progress on a colorful poster.

Be sure to change the water and rinse the seeds daily. Place them in a sunny spot so the sprouts turn green.

OVER THE FIRE

Place two or three small logs in the center of the classroom. Use construction paper, glitter, and other materials to create a bonfire.

Line up the children and have them jump over the bonfire one at a time. Chant "Happy New Year" and take turns jumping over again.

A SWEET SNACK

Baklava pastry can be purchased at most ethnic markets or bake a pan yourself. Recipes can be found in most cookbooks. Serve a sweet snack for a "sweet" year!

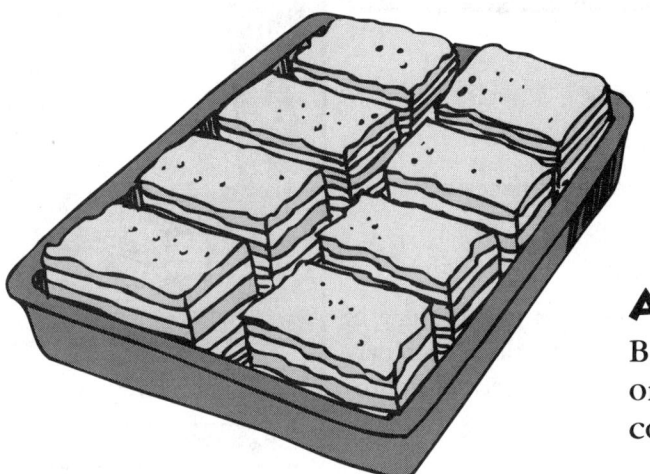

Purim

Haman

Queen Esther

King Ahasuerus

Mordecai

Purim is the happiest day in the Jewish calendar. Jews celebrate the story of Queen Esther. Children dress up, often as one of the characters in the story. They go to parties, carnivals, and the synagogue. Jews listen to the story of Queen Esther in the synagogue. They boo, stamp their feet, and shake noisemakers whenever Haman's name is mentioned. People give each other bags of cookies and sweets.

The story of Purim takes place in ancient Persia. King Ahasuerus marries the most beautiful woman in the land—Esther, a Jewish woman, the niece of Mordecai. Haman, the king's minister, plots to overthrow the Jews because he is jealous of Mordecai's influence. Esther risks her own life to expose Haman and saves her people. Tomie dePaola wrote and illustrated *Queen Esther*, published by Harper & Row. *Festival of Esther* (A Little Simon Book) is retold by Maida Silverman and illustrated by Carolyn Ewing.

Purim is fun! Dressing up! Making noise! Having a good time!

Stick Puppets

Tell the story of Purim with stick puppets.

Teacher Preparation: Have a puppet theater. If necessary, make one out of a large box.

Materials: craft sticks, paper, glue, crayons

Activity: Cut out figures of all the characters in the story of Purim. Color them and paste them to the craft sticks. Then perform the puppet play. Use a children's Purim book for an appropriate story line.

by Devorah Stone

Noisemakers

Every time Haman is mentioned during the reading of the story of Esther, everyone stamps their feet and makes noise. Graggers (Purim noisemakers) and other noisemakers are used.

Teacher Preparation
Put out materials and help put on lids if necessary.

Materials
plastic containers with lids such as yogurt containers and large plastic milk jugs, rice, pennies, small buttons, popcorn kernels

Activity
Have children put rice, pennies, small buttons, or popcorn kernels in plastic containers. Secure lid with tape. Shake and listen. Rice makes a different sound from pennies or popcorn kernels.

Helpful Hints
- Read the story of Queen Esther out loud and have the children use their noisemakers every time Haman is mentioned.

- The actual story is rather long for a classroom activity, so see if you can find a children's version from the library, a local synagogue, or on the internet.

- Listen to all the different sounds you can make using different containers and items.

Faces on Rice Crackers

Make the faces of King Ahasuerus, Queen Esther, and Haman on rice crackers.

Ingredients
- round rice crackers
- peanut butter
- soft avocados
- cream cheese
- long carrot strips
- sprouts
- cut-up peppers
- bananas
- sprouts
- cubed pineapple

Utensils
- plates
- dull plastic knives

Activity
Spread the peanut butter, soft avocado, or cream cheese on the round rice crackers. Then make faces by using the cut-up carrots, peppers, sprouts, and bananas. Cubed pineapple makes great crowns.

Pipe Cleaner Necklace and Bracelets

Teacher Preparation
Cut up Styrofoam™ egg cartons.

Materials
Styrofoam™ egg cartons, large beads, pieces of aluminum foil, rigatoni pasta, pipe cleaners

Activity
Children poke pipe cleaners through two sides of Styrofoam™ egg cartons. Instruct them to put beads or pasta on the pipe cleaners and wrap aluminum foil around them. They can make jewelry as well as headdresses, like crowns.

It's Spring; It's Easter

As Easter marks a new beginning, spring, too, signals new life and growth. Celebrate the holiday with activities that call on the skills of budding artists and authors.

It's spring.
Sunny skies and butterflies
Grasses grow and breezes blow.
Ducklings swim and bluebirds skim.
Flowers bloom and small bees zoom.
Young chicks peep and green frogs leap.
Church bells ring and children sing.
Bunnies hop and blossoms drop.
Butterflies and sunny skies.
It's Easter.

Activities

1. Copy and Illustrate one line of the poem.
2. Make an egg-shaped booklet. Copy one line from the poem on each page. Decorate the pages with drawings that remind you of spring and Easter. Cut the front and back covers from a wallpaper sample book. Add lines to enhance the pattern. Glue the egg shapes to colored construction paper. Cut the shapes out again leaving a thin margin of color. This will reinforce the covers and hide any writing on the back of the wallpaper sample.
3. Rewrite the poem replacing the nouns with pictures.
4. Prepare a choral reading of the verse.
5. Draw a picture of a spring scene. Use ideas from the poem.
6. Color Easter eggs. Before dying them, draw on the eggs with a white or other light-colored wax crayon. Ideas from the poem, such as rabbits, chicks, clouds, or flowers, may be used. Dip the egg in the dye and watch the design appear.

by Patricia O'Brien

Decorated Eggs

Conduct a paper egg decorating contest. The students may be awarded prizes for the most colorful egg; the best use of crayon, paint, or markers; the most beautiful or unusual egg; or the best use of a theme (rabbits, chicks, flowers, spring, etc.).

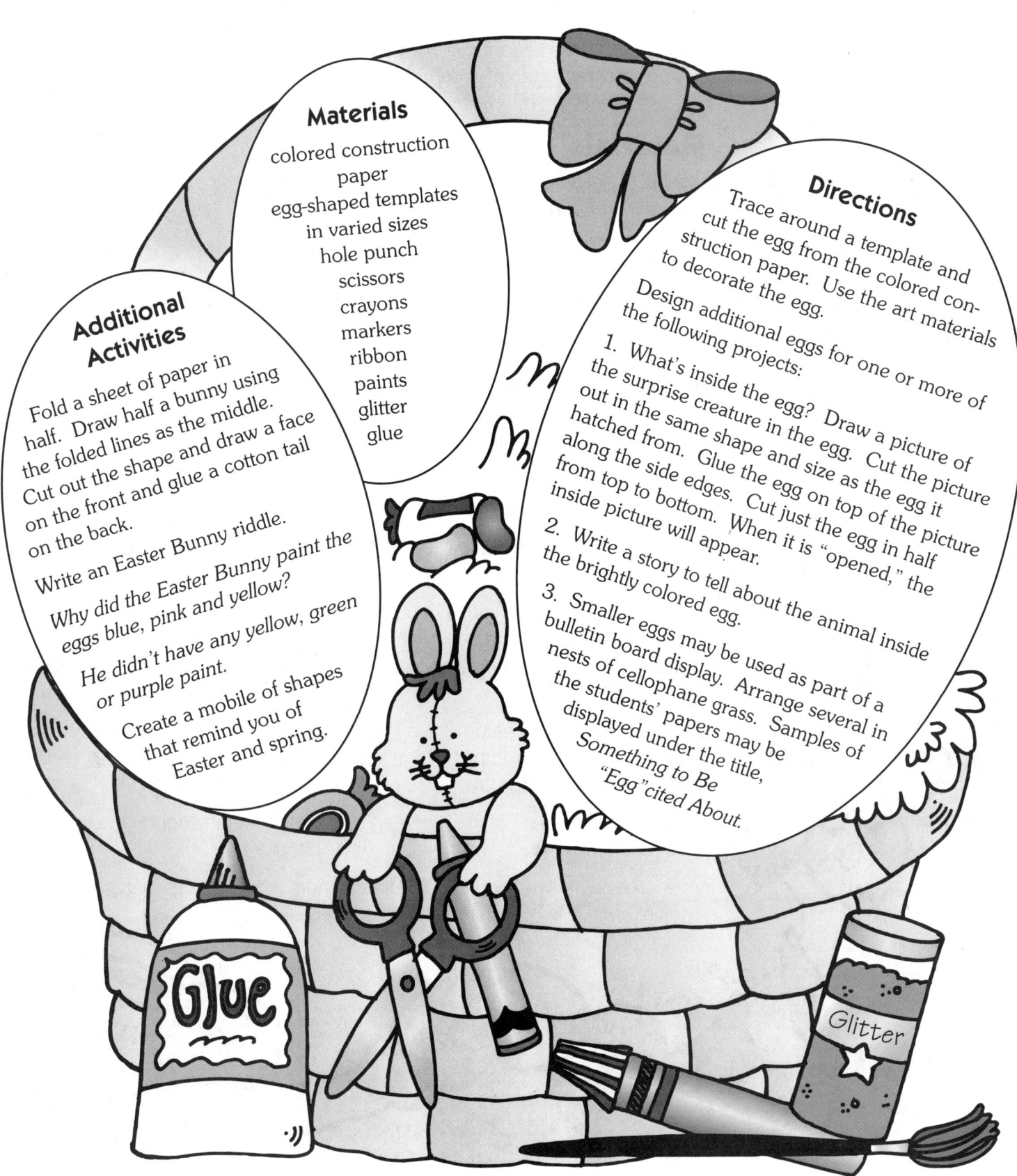

Materials

colored construction paper
egg-shaped templates in varied sizes
hole punch
scissors
crayons
markers
ribbon
paints
glitter
glue

Directions

Trace around a template and cut the egg from the colored construction paper. Use the art materials to decorate the egg. Design additional eggs for one or more of the following projects:

1. What's inside the egg? Draw a picture of the surprise creature in the egg. Cut the picture out in the same shape and size as the egg it hatched from. Glue the egg on top of the picture along the side edges. Cut just the egg in half from top to bottom. When it is "opened," the inside picture will appear.

2. Write a story to tell about the animal inside the brightly colored egg.

3. Smaller eggs may be used as part of a bulletin board display. Arrange several in nests of cellophane grass. Samples of the students' papers may be displayed under the title, Something to Be "Egg"cited About.

Additional Activities

Fold a sheet of paper in half. Draw half a bunny using the folded lines as the middle. Cut out the shape and draw a face on the front and glue a cotton tail on the back.

Write an Easter Bunny riddle. Why did the Easter Bunny paint the eggs blue, pink and yellow? He didn't have any yellow, green or purple paint.

Create a mobile of shapes that remind you of Easter and spring.

Easter Eggs Are

Kids love games, and hunting is a favorite, perhaps because it's so adaptable. It can be done individually or in groups, with objects partially or completely hidden, for a long or short period of time, all depending on the group doing the hunting. Take advantage of this to reinforce learning. Here are a few examples of hunts ranging from preschool to grade 3 level.

Materials

dozens of eggs cut from construction paper or old wallpaper books
dark marking pen
Easter baskets

Mark eggs with dots ranging from one to as many as children have learned to count up to. Youngest "finders" can identify the number indicated by the dots.

Write only as many numbers as there are children in the class. Let each child find one egg, then stand in a line in numerical order. A more difficult version: leave out some numbers (Ex. 0, 1, 3, 4, 7, 9, 11, etc.).

Number eggs from 1 to 50 (or higher). Finders put eggs in groups of even and odd numbers.

Mark some eggs with number dots, others with numerals. Have children match them.

Write on eggs numerals that are multiples of 2s, 5s, 10s and any other multiples children have learned. Finders separate them into groups accordingly. (Make sure there are enough duplicates so numbers like "6" could be in both the 2 and 3 piles.)

Write number sentences on one egg and the answer on another. Find matches. Or cut eggs in half (irregularly) with the sentence on one half and the answer on the other.

Mark eggs with letters of the alphabet. Let young finders identify the letter. Older ones might give a word that starts with that letter.

Mark some eggs with uppercase letters, others with lowercase letters. (Have many of each one.) Finders match them.

by Elaine Hansen Cleary

FOR HUNTING

For younger children, write a sight word on each egg. Finders read words.

Write a vowel sound on one egg (Ex. a) and a word using that sound on another (Ex. ate). This could be done on halves of eggs as well. Find the match. (This could be adaptable to a worksheet, directing children to color the egg with the correct sound.)

Write consonant blends on eggs. Finders think of (or use dictionaries to find) words using those blends.

For grades 1-2, write spelling words on eggs. Finders ask each other how to spell words they found, to give a meaning or to use in a sentence.

For grade 3, write spelling words leaving out one or two letters. (Ex. camp-ng, mo-nta-n). Write those letters on other eggs. (Ex. "u" or "i") Finders match as many of their own as they can, then work cooperatively with classmates to completion.

Write vocabulary words (from reading, science, social studies) on one egg, definition on another. Find and match by having one student read the word, whoever has the definition read it, or vice versa.

Have children make up four word sentences using subject, verb, object and modifier (Ex. Joe likes chocolate candy, or Seth found three salamanders.). Cut out four different colored eggs, writing one word on each egg. Teacher hides eggs. Children find one egg of each color, try to make a sentence. Sentences will not necessarily be the same as the original ones as they may find eggs written by different people (Ex. Seth likes chocolate salamanders.), but they will have fun using the subject-verb-modifier-object order.

Following the same format as above, make three eggs each, using phrases (Ex. The little dog-barked loudly-at the cat).

Write rhyming words on eggs. Teacher says a word; child with a rhyming word responds. Use words that have many possibilities (Ex. be, see, key, tree, me, etc.).

Note: Start preparing eggs well ahead of time. Take advantage of older students or parents to help with cutting and hiding.

Edible Easter Baskets

Graham Cracker Basket

An easy-to-make basket can be made by adapting the graham cracker "gingerbread house."

Materials

graham crackers broken into squares (5 for each child)
frosting "glue" (1 lb. powdered sugar, 3 egg whites, 1/2 tsp. cream of tartar)
cake frosting (white, pink, green or yellow)
small decorations (sprinkles, M&M's®, candy "flowers," jelly beans)
shoestring licorice cut in 6" lengths (1 piece for each child)

Directions

Lay one cracker square flat. Line the edges with frosting "glue." One square at a time, frost edges and fit them onto the base, forming a square box. Let dry until the next day! (Hint: If it is too difficult to get the sides to stand up, make it upside down, forming it over a greased or sprayed lunch milk carton. The carton can be removed easily once the "glue" has dried.)

One side at a time, frost the graham squares, decorating them with the sprinkles, etc. Put a ball of frosting "glue" at the top of two opposite sides and insert the shoestring licorice "handle." Let dry.

Fill baskets with *lightweight* candies such as marshmallow chicks, chocolate-covered pretzels, individually wrapped LifeSavers®.

Biscuit Dough Basket

Materials

biscuit dough (prepared or a box mix)
non-stick spray
shoestring licorice or ribbons (cut in 8" lengths)
regular size cupcake tins

Directions

Invert cupcake tins and spray with non-stick spray. Form dough over inverted cupcake tins. Bake at given heat. Before dough is cooled, poke two holes across from each other toward the top. When cooled, insert either licorice or ribbon for handles. Let cool completely before filling. Older children might cut the dough into strips and weave or crisscross them over the inverted cupcake forms.

Fill with small candies, miniature marshmallows, raisins or even trail mix.

Note: Prepared pie crust can also be used, if "baskets" are filled with pudding or pie filling.

by Elaine Hansen Cleary

Be Earth-Friendly Outdoors

Every Day Can Be Earth Day

When warmer months take us outdoors, there are many special ways to help our Earth. Many youth groups organize cleanup squads to pick up litter that has accumulated over the winter months around the neighborhood, school, parks and beaches. It's a good way to start an Earth-friendly season. (But be sure to wear protective gloves and watch out for sharp objects!)

At Parks and Campsites

- Trees are not only beautiful, they give us shade, supply oxygen, give shelter to birds and small animals and their roots help hold soil in place. Don't harm trees by carving into trunks, stripping bark or branches or driving nails into the trunks.

- Wildflowers are pretty for everyone to look at. Don't pick them! Leave them so they can reseed themselves and so others can enjoy this year and the next!

- If birds and small wild animals are about, don't feed them. This leads them to depend on people rather than using their own instinctive food-gathering skills.

- If you come across small holes for burrowing animals, don't plug them up. They're the way these animals get to their shelters.

- Camp fires for cooking or for warmth should be built only in prepared fire pits. Always be certain fires are completely out and no hot coals are left. It only takes one spark to spread a fire!

- Be especially careful with the plastic o-rings that hold soda cans together. Birds or animals get their heads caught in them and can choke or be unable to eat. Discard the o-rings properly. Cut a slit in each ring before you throw them away.

by Elaine Hansen Cleary

Earth Day Internet Connections

Decorative grocery sacks are a great way to get the community involved, and it's easy to do! Check it out at: **http://www.halcyon.com/arborhts/edshort.html**

You can do it! The environment is your business. Find out about pollution, the ozone layer and global warming. Shop wisely and get to know nature by making a bird feeder or a compost heap. Maybe you'll decide to visit an organic farm. You won't run out of Earth Day activities on this page: **http://www.cam.org/~cdsl_ps/Earth_Day/i-can-do.ht**

Around Home

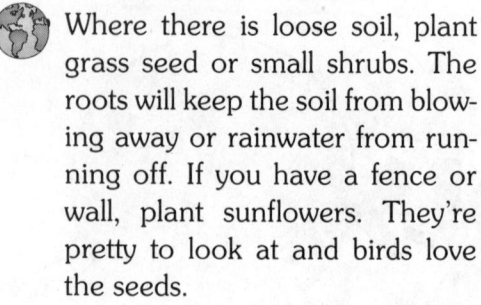

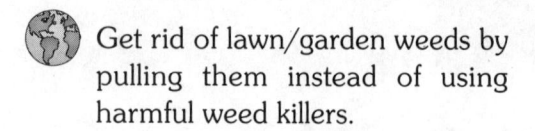

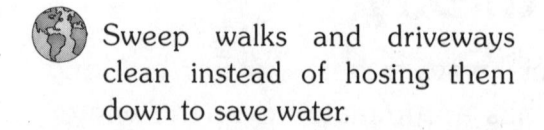

- Where there is loose soil, plant grass seed or small shrubs. The roots will keep the soil from blowing away or rainwater from running off. If you have a fence or wall, plant sunflowers. They're pretty to look at and birds love the seeds.

- Get rid of lawn/garden weeds by pulling them instead of using harmful weed killers.

- Sweep walks and driveways clean instead of hosing them down to save water.

- Never water the lawn on a windy day (the spray will blow away), nor in direct sunlight (the water will evaporate before it has a chance to sink into the soil).

- When in a swimming pool, don't waste water by splashing it out.

- Get drinks from a large container of water kept in the refrigerator rather than running the faucet until the tap water is cold.

- Be kind to birds and small animals by leaving a pan of water outside for them to drink.

- Whenever it's safe and possible, bike or walk to get around your neighborhood.

- When going to the playground, park or library with friends, be sure to car pool.

- Instead of turning up the air conditioner, cover sunny windows with shades or drapes.

- Open windows in the evening to let in cool air.

Picnic Time

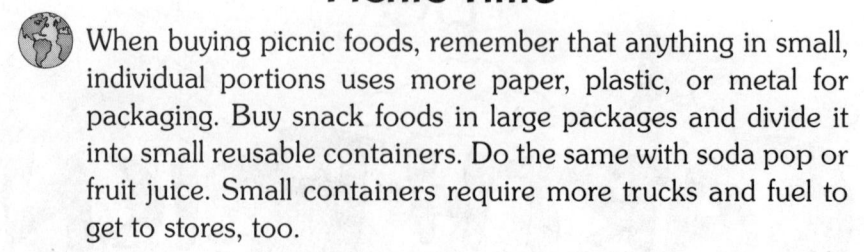

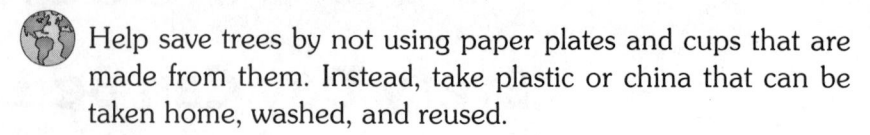

- When buying picnic foods, remember that anything in small, individual portions uses more paper, plastic, or metal for packaging. Buy snack foods in large packages and divide it into small reusable containers. Do the same with soda pop or fruit juice. Small containers require more trucks and fuel to get to stores, too.

- Store food in reusable containers rather than plastic wrap or aluminum foil. (If you must use foil, save it for recycling.)

- Help save trees by not using paper plates and cups that are made from them. Instead, take plastic or china that can be taken home, washed, and reused.

- Paper tablecovers, towels, and napkins waste paper, too. Use reusable cloth ones and carry damp washcloths for cleanup.

- Eating with your regular metal kitchen utensils is best, but if you do use plastic forks and spoons, be sure to reuse them as often as possible, then recycle when they are worn out.

Now for Cleanup

- Don't litter! Make sure garbage goes in trash barrels. If there are no recycling containers, take home any plastic, metal, or glass.

- If you cooked over a charcoal fire, make sure the fire is completely out before you leave.

What's Wrong Here?

Directions:
Explain to children that some people don't mean to hurt the Earth, but they are "Earth-careless." They do many harmful things just because they don't stop to think about the consequences of their actions. The Gooper family was like that. In the story (page 269) I'm going to read to you, the Goopers did many Earth-careless things when they went on a picnic. Listen carefully to see how many you can find. Hint: There are 12. *(For your convenience, they are in italics.)* Why was each harmful? What should they have done instead?

For very young children, stress the "wrong" parts with your voice and stop to name each one in turn, being sure to discuss what the Goopers SHOULD have done, as well as how they were careless.

Story: Picnic at Green Park

It was a beautiful day, so Mr. and Mrs. Gooper and their children Zena and Nobo decided to go to Green Park for a picnic.

Mother got the food ready and Zena sealed each item *in its own plastic bag*. Nobo put *small cans* of juice and soda in the cooler. Before long they were on their way. Father *turned on the air conditioner* in the car while Zena and Nobo *opened the windows* to let in the nice fresh air.

As soon as they reached the park, Zena spotted some pretty wildflowers and hurried to *pick a bouquet*. Nobo ran around looking for *insects to step on*. Father made the fire while Mother put a *paper cover on the picnic table* and set out *four paper plates, four paper cups and four paper napkins*. Then she put *a plastic knife, fork and spoon* at each place.

While they were eating, a squirrel climbed down a nearby tree. *Zena broke off a piece of her cookie and threw it to him. Nobo did the same with his potato chips.*

When they were finished, they put away the leftover food. Then *they dumped the soda cans and plastic eating utensils*, as well as the rest of the garbage, *into the trash can*. The plastic *o-rings from the soda cans blew away and landed near a clump of bushes*. "Time to go," said Father. "I'll *leave the coals in the fire pit to cool off.*"

"Didn't we have a lovely time!" exclaimed Mother.

"Let's do something to remember it by," said Zena. So they *carved their initials in the smoothest tree trunk* they could find.

Climbing into the car, Nobo unwrapped a stick of chewing gum and *dropped the wrapper on the ground*.

"Green Park is a lovely place to have a picnic!" said Mother, and they all agreed.

Suggestions for the Correct Things to Do

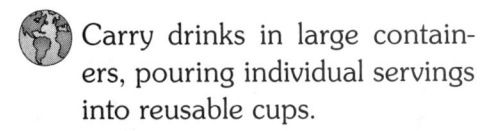

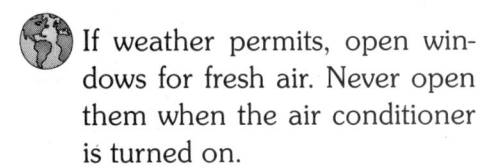

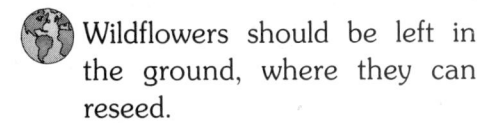

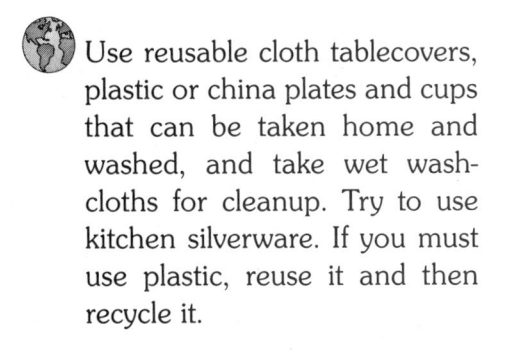

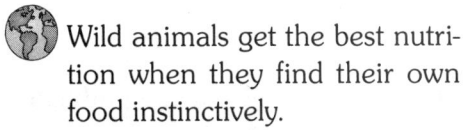

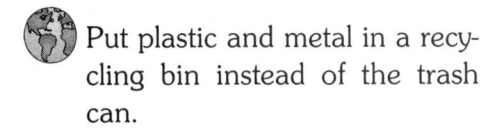

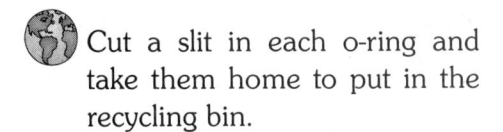

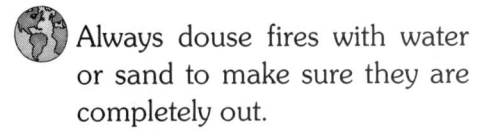

- Package food in reusable containers.
- Carry drinks in large containers, pouring individual servings into reusable cups.
- If weather permits, open windows for fresh air. Never open them when the air conditioner is turned on.
- Wildflowers should be left in the ground, where they can reseed.
- Let insects live to perform their own tasks in nature.
- Use reusable cloth tablecovers, plastic or china plates and cups that can be taken home and washed, and take wet washcloths for cleanup. Try to use kitchen silverware. If you must use plastic, reuse it and then recycle it.
- Wild animals get the best nutrition when they find their own food instinctively.
- Put plastic and metal in a recycling bin instead of the trash can.
- Cut a slit in each o-ring and take them home to put in the recycling bin.
- Always douse fires with water or sand to make sure they are completely out.
- Trees need their bark; leave it alone!
- Keep a litter bag in the car to hold papers you throw away.

Weather WISE

An Earth Day Look at the Weather

Earth Day is a good day to take a look at the weather—and how it is affected by the way we treat our natural environment. Pollution of the Earth, air and water is affecting our overall weather patterns and our planet in several ways.

Our life-style introduces pollutants into the air, soil and water; affects the delicate balance of gases in our atmosphere to such a degree that the world may be heating up a little every year; interferes with the water cycle; and uses up natural resources in our environment so quickly that many scientists believe that the animals, plants and their habitats may not last for another generation. These changes affect all of us, whether we live under the sea, in the treetops or in a house on Walnut Street.

What Can Be Done?

We can change our ways! Use Earth Day to help children recognize threats to the environment, to learn that they can make a difference and to celebrate the wind, rain and sunshine.

Children in the primary grades are usually very appreciative of the natural world and have a strong desire to protect it. Children should be made aware of the wonders of our natural environment and the dangers imposed upon it by our life-styles. Despite the seriousness of the plight of our natural world, be sure not to frighten children who are not yet desensitized.

Study Your Rainfall

How acid is your local rain?

Materials:
- acid test strips
- three clear glass containers
- tap water
- lemon
- juicer
- rainwater

What to Do:
1. Set one container outside in the rain until you have collected at least 1/4" of rainwater. Bring the rainwater inside and label the jar.
2. Squeeze juice from a lemon into one of the containers.
3. Fill one container with tap water.
4. Place the jars in a line. Dip the test strips into each container until liquid has been absorbed into the strips. Let the strips dry.
5. Note the color changes. The more pink the test strip becomes, the stronger the presence of acid in the particular liquid. Make a chart to record the color changes.

Weather Internet Connection

The "Weather Dude" is musical and knowledgeable. This site is designed for kids, parents and teachers, with all kinds of weather-related fun and information. Listen to songs to find out "What Makes Rain" and "The Circle of Our Four Seasons" (download audio wav files). Check in on stuff for kids, today's weather or learn about meteorology from A to Z. http://www.nwlink.com/~wxdude

by Robynne Eagan

Take a Look at City Weather

Our man-made environments affect the immediate weather our community experiences. Ask children to think about how the concrete jungles might interfere with the water cycle.

Where Have the Rain Clouds Gone?

Experiment with earth, wood and concrete. Which materials absorb water? Which do not? Most of the city buildings and surfaces do not absorb water. Where does the water go? These building materials do not absorb water, so the rains are drained away into underground drain pipes before the waters can evaporate and condense again into clouds. What effect might this have on plant life? The quantity of plant life is limited by the lack of growing space and the lack of rain. Fewer plants mean less water is returned to the air.

Feel the Heat

Because less of the sun's energy is used evaporating water, the streets, sidewalks and buildings are heated more intensely. Heat from these buildings and from vehicles in the city warm the air even further.

Wind Blocks

Place a fan in front of a cardboard barrier. Hold a pinwheel in front of the barrier and then behind it. What differences are noted? What effect might tall buildings have on the blowing wind?

How's the Rain?

Rain that falls in clean air is naturally somewhat acidic. Chemicals that pollute the air cause the rain or snow to contain more acid than usual. This rain is called acid rain. The acidity of rain is measured by its pH level. Pure rain has a pH level of 5.6. Acid rain is any rain with a pH level lower than 5.6.

Scientists believe the acid in rain is introduced into our environment through the burning of fossil fuels and the waste products of power stations. Look at car exhausts and factory smokestacks, for example. The polluting particles are very tiny and can travel very far before they fall onto our buildings and into our lakes in the form of acid rain. Have children record all of the places that they think they see pollutants being added to the air.

Children should be taught that despite the scary term, acid rain doesn't hurt us when it falls on us. Over time, acid rain does hurt our natural environment, which in the end harms us all. Acid rain poisons our water systems, kills lakes and rivers and the creatures who live in them, kills trees, affects crops and eats away at our human-made stonework structures.

Acid Rain

Make Your Own Acid Test Strips

The boiling process requires caution. It may be best to do this prior to class.

Materials:
- half of a red cabbage
- saucepan
- strainer
- glass bowl
- 4 cups of water
- stovetop burner
- white construction paper
- scissors

What to Do:
1. Boil half of a red cabbage in water.
2. Let it soak for several hours.
3. Cut the construction paper into 2" x 1/4" strips to make acid test strips.
4. Strain the cabbage juice through a strainer into a glass bowl.
5. Soak the strips of construction paper in the cabbage juice and then place them on a flat surface to dry.

Acid Rain and Plants

Materials:
- pumpkin seeds
- planting pots
- 1 cup vinegar
- sealed bottle or jug
- marker
- potting soil
- bottle of spring water
- 1 cup tap water
- bristol board

What to Do:
1. Plant pumpkin seeds in small pots.
2. Label half of the pots with **S** for spring water and the other half with **A** for acidic water.
3. Mix the tap water and vinegar together in a jug or bottle.
4. Water the plants labeled **S** with spring water and the plants labeled **A** with the acidic vinegar water, and place all plants in the same sunny location. Continue to water the plants with the designated solution when they are dry.
5. Make a chart for recording weekly observations. Leave space for illustrations and written descriptions.
6. Talk about the results of this study. How does it relate to your environment?

Holiday Sing-Alongs

by Mabel Duch

Maypole

This song is sung to the tune of "Are You Sleeping, Brother John?"

Under, over, under, over,
Round we prance,
Round we prance,
Weaving pretty ribbons,
Weaving pretty ribbons,
Maypole dance,
Maypole dance.

The Maypole dance is a May Day tradition in England.

From four to 12 children can participate in a Maypole dance at one time, but you must have an even number.

Materials

1. A strong, sturdy, firmly anchored pole from one and a half to two times the individual height of most of your children.
2. Strong "satin" ribbons in bright spring colors, 2 1/2" to 2 3/4" wide. (The ribbons should be about three times the height of the pole, and there should be one for each child.)
3. Paper or silk flowers to cover the base of the pole.
4. A wide, uncluttered area.

Construction

Alternating colors, fasten ribbons next to the top of pole with hammer and tacks or strong, wide strapping tape. Space them around the pole. If you like, fasten flowers over secured ends with rolls of narrow strapping tape. Fasten flowers at the base of the pole in the same way.

The Dance

Children should stand an equal distance from the pole, holding their ribbons up so they will be able to weave them. Ribbons should not trail on the ground. If any are too long, cut them.

Half of the children should be facing clockwise and half counterclockwise. They should weave in and out as they move around the circle. Decide which group is going to move in first. For example, the clockwise group could move in first. Each clockwise child would move in and under the ribbon of the first approaching child, then out and over the ribbon of the next one, alternating as he goes around the circle.

As they move around the pole, children may all march, skip or two-step, whatever you decide. They may sing the Maypole song or move to music. If they all move at the same speed, the dance will go smoothly. This may take a little practice, but the smoother the dance, the more the children will enjoy it.

Mother Goose Day

May 1st is the day set aside to honor Mother Goose and her rhymes. Mother Goose is a mythical character dearly loved by all who know her delightful fairy tales and jingles. Three countries claim to know who Mother Goose actually was. In England, they believe she was an old woman who sold flowers on the streets of Oxford. In France, she was believed to be Queen Bertha, patron of children. In the United States, people believe that Mother Goose was Elizabeth Vergoose, the mother-in-law of a Boston, Massachusetts, printer named Thomas Fleet.

The tales of Mother Goose were very old before they were ever written on paper. For many centuries, they were passed on from generation to generation by word of mouth. It was a Frenchman named Charles Perrault who put the rhymes in writing in 1696.

There are many collections of Mother Goose rhymes today, retold by various authors. The first collection of jingles was called *Mother Goose's Melody*, published by John Newbery of London in 1780. Several years later, it was reprinted and published in Worcester, Massachusetts.

Mother Goose Goes Electronic.
http://www.frontiernet.com/~kenc/mgoose.htm

Miss Muffet

Little Miss Muffet sat on a tuffet,
Eating her curds and whey.
There came a big spider,
Who sat down beside her
And frightened Miss Muffet away.

Spider Prints
Let the children thumbprint spider bodies onto white paper. Dip their thumbs into black poster paint and press on paper for a print. Stamp pads make a better print; however, ink is harder to wash off than tempera paint. Use markers to add spider legs and a face.

Spiderwebs
Punch holes all around the outside edge of a paper plate. Cut a length of colored yarn; wrap masking or cellophane tape tightly around one end to make a tip. Knot the end of the yarn and tape it on the back of the plate. Now, weave the yarn back and forth, in and out of these holes to produce a web.

by Tania K. Cowling

Old Mother Hubbard

Old Mother Hubbard went to the cupboard,
To give her poor dog a bone.
But when she got there,
The cupboard was bare,
And so the poor dog had none.

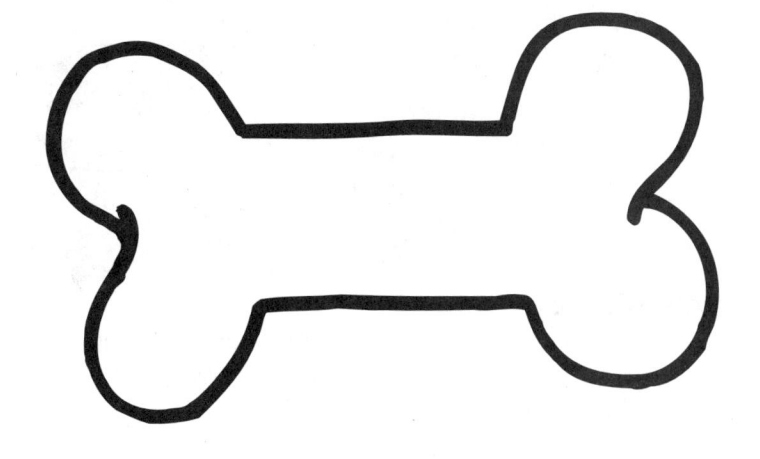

Dog Tag
Make dog tag necklaces for each child. Cut a large bone shape from poster board. Punch a hole at each corner on the top. Thread this with yarn to fit around the child's head. Have the children decorate their bones as desired with crayons, markers, stickers and so on. You could even glue on a real dog biscuit or two. The small dog biscuits come in multicolors and would be suitable for gluing on the necklace.

Doggie Bone Game
Take a store-bought dog biscuit and play this game (any replica of a bone will do). Seat the children in a circle, with the child who has been chosen as the "doggie" in the center with the bone in front of him. The "doggie" closes his eyes and one of the children from the circle sneaks up quietly and steals the bone. When the child is seated back in the circle, he hides the bone out of sight. The children all recite:

Doggie, doggie, where's your bone?
Someone took it from your home!

The doggie gets three chances to guess who has the bone. If he guesses correctly, the child who took the bone becomes the doggie.

Mary, Mary, Quite Contrary

Mary, Mary, quite contrary,
How does your garden grow?
With silver bells and cockle shells,
And pretty maids all in a row.

Mary's Garden
Plant flower seeds in soil using a Styrofoam™ cup for each child. Each student can plant, water and care for their own garden. Keep them on a windowsill and admire all the pretty flowers growing in a row.

Mary's Art Garden
Have the children draw a picture of a pretty maiden walking through her garden of flowers. Use crayons or markers to color the picture. For the flowers, use pieces of fancy wallpaper, wads of colorful tissue paper, flower photos cut from magazines and catalogs and so on. Glue these flowers in rows inside Mary's garden.

Jack

Jack be nimble; Jack be quick.
Jack jump over the candlestick.

Candlestick Game
Provide a real candle in a low candlestick. Place this on the floor. Have the children line up and march across the room, jumping over the candlestick as they recite this rhyme. Repeat the rhyme, each time substituting each child's name.

Candle Art
Take candles and rub them in design fashion across a piece of white paper. Next, take a dark tempera paint (slightly watered down) and brush it across the page. The wax will resist the paint and the design will show through.

Little Bo-Peep

Little Bo-Peep has lost her sheep,
And can't tell where to find them.
Leave them alone, and they'll come home,
And bring their tails behind them.

Fuzzy Sheep
Cut a sheep shape out of heavy paper or poster board. Draw facial features with markers. Have the children apply glue to the body surface and place cotton on top.

Yarn Painting
Clip a clothespin to a piece of yarn about 4" long. Dip the yarn into a flat container of poster paint. The child holds onto the clothespin and drags the yarn across the piece of paper, creating designs. Use different colors for dramatic paintings.

Hickory, Dickory, Dock

Hickory, dickory, dock,
The mouse ran up the clock.
The clock struck one,
The mouse ran down.
Hickory, dickory, dock.

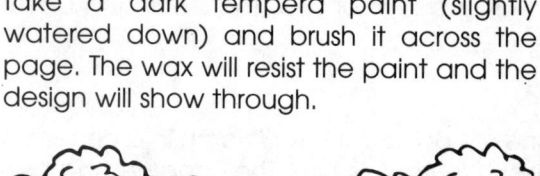

Hickory, Dickory, Dock Clock
Draw and cut out a clock face from cardboard or heavy paper. With the children, mark the numerals around the face of the clock. Make hands from cardboard and attach them to the center of the clock with a brass fastener. Now the children can move the hands of the clock and practice numeral recognition and telling time.

Mouse Puppet
Cut out a half circle from a sheet of gray paper for the mouse's body. Cut out two black circles and glue these onto the body for ears. Draw eyes and a nose with crayons or markers. Wrap a pipe cleaner around a crayon to curl it, then staple this on the back end of the mouse for a tail. Staple a craft stick to the bottom of the mouse to manipulate the puppet.

Cinco de Mayo

Puppet and Song

Materials:
- one pair of plain garden gloves
- cotton or stuffing
- yarn
- felt scraps
- fine-tipped permanent marker
- hot glue gun and glue

What to Do:
Prepare the teacher's glove puppet as the drawing shows and as indicated in the following instructions:

1. On the thumb of one glove (palm side), write *May 5* using the permanent marker.

2. On the other four fingers, draw faces on felt and glue one to each finger to make four friends. Yarn may be added for hair. Add a felt serape to the lower part of the finger for the boy. Add a flower to one of the girls' dresses.

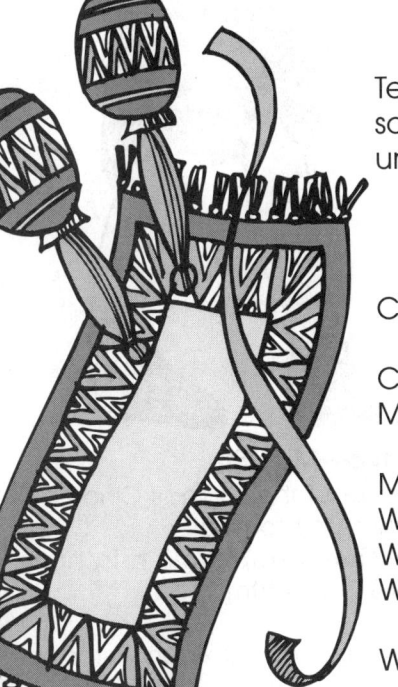

Teach the children the following song. Encourage them to echo you until they know it.

Cinco de Mayo
To the tune of "Frere Jacques"

Cinco de Mayo,
    (point to the palm)
Cinco de Mayo,
Means May 5th,
    (wiggle the thumb)
Means May 5th,
We will celebrate,
We will celebrate,
With our friends,
    (wiggle each finger)
With our friends.

*(Later substitute the word **amigos** for friends.)*

by Mary Ruth Moore

Matching Game

Preparations:
1. Obtain a paper pinata of any kind.
2. In an easily accessible spot in the pinata, cut a slit-like flap with a knife. The slit should be large enough to open and close to reveal sealable bags with game contents.
3. You will need three sealable bags–one for picture or replica of each object, one for the Spanish word card and one for the English word card. Prepare cards for the following words:

Object	Word Cards	
cat	gato	cat
dog	perro	dog
donkey	burro	donkey
May calendar	Mayo	May
five	cinco	five

Magnetic or plastic numbers from one to ten, two sets of word cards for each number in Spanish and English.

What to Do:
Using a pool foam log or a wrapping paper tube, students will hit the pinata until the bags fall out. When the bags fall, tell the students that now they have a matching game to play. Tell the students that they are going to learn some words in both Spanish and English. As the objects are removed one by one, you may tell the students the word for the object in Spanish; then they can retrieve the correct word in both Spanish and English. If your students are primarily Spanish speakers, tell them the word in English and find each matching word. Lay the objects and matching word cards on the floor so that all can see.

At other times, the pinata may hold objects for counting, words to become compound words, phonetic skill cards and so on. Virtually anything you would like to teach may go in the pinata.

Cinco de Mayo—May 5th
Find out more about the origin of Cinco de Mayo and other Spanish customs at:
http://128.123.31.49/vista/esl/m5_hstry.html
http://198.150.8.9/mex.html

All kinds of pictures on Mexican history can be found at:
http://gaia.ecs.csus.edu/~arellano/index.html

Mother's Day Tea

About a week before Mother's Day, the children design and take home an invitation for their moms to come and join us at our Mother's Day Tea, which we hold on the Friday before Mother's Day.

At the beginning of the week, we make pans of brownies, crispy rice cereal squares, butter tarts and a cake which the children bake and decorate. On Friday, the children, dressed in their best clothes, decorate the room with their artwork and fresh flowers. The moms join us for the last 60-90 minutes of class time. When they arrive, the children greet them and seat them on "big" chairs as opposed to our child-sized chairs. The children serve tea and coffee and invite the moms to help themselves to the treats set out on the tables.

About a half hour before dismissal time, the children gather on the floor in a circle. The moms are invited to join us on their chairs around the circle. We sing a song or two, then we usually read a story. *Are You My Mother?* by P.D. Eastman and *I Love You Forever* by Robert Munsch are two of their favorites.

The children finish the day by presenting their moms with a special card and picture that they have made for this special occasion and a fresh carnation.

The moms and children always have a great time; the children are usually on their best behavior. For some children, whose moms are not able to join us, they invite their grandma, aunt, godmother, baby-sitter or older sister. Most teachers are supportive of letting an older student out of class to represent "mom" for their younger sibling's special day. We have always had someone special come to our Mother's Day Tea for each child.

Please Join Us at Our Mother's Day Tea on

_____
Date

_____
Time

by Teresa E. Culpeper

Name _____

Gift Giving

Draw a line from each child on the left to the gift he or she chose to give on Mother's Day on the right. Use the clues to help you. Color the gifts.

1. Tanisha bought her mother a gift that was alive. It needs just sunlight and water.

2. Tony gave his mother something to wear. He wrapped it in a tiny box.

3. Maria made a gift for her mother. She baked it all by herself.

4. Marcus gave his mom a gift that came from a friend's pet.

5. Haley made her mother a gift. She let it dry and framed it before she wrapped it up.

6. Jamal and his sister found a good sale at a ladies' clothing store.

7. Betsy bought something her mother will carry a lot.

8. Bryce made something using an empty bottle and paints.

On the back, draw a picture of your mother. Think of something you might like to give her. Draw it in the picture.

280   by Ann Richmond Fisher   TLC10110 Copyright © Teaching & Learning Company, Carthage, IL 62321-0010

Father's Day

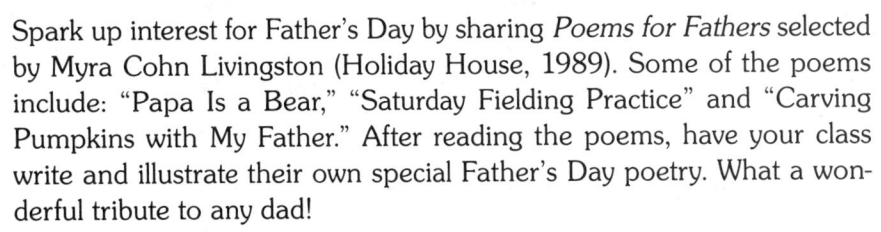

Spark up interest for Father's Day by sharing *Poems for Fathers* selected by Myra Cohn Livingston (Holiday House, 1989). Some of the poems include: "Papa Is a Bear," "Saturday Fielding Practice" and "Carving Pumpkins with My Father." After reading the poems, have your class write and illustrate their own special Father's Day poetry. What a wonderful tribute to any dad!

Delight your class with the humorous read-aloud favorite—*A Perfect Father's Day* by Eve Bunting (New York: Clarion Books, 1991). Come along and join the fun as a little girl named Susie takes her dad on a Father's Day outing to all of her favorite places. But who enjoys everything the most—Susie or her dad? After reading the book, ask your students to write a list of their favorite places to visit. Have them create a picture book entitled *Father's Day Fun,* telling about taking a dad, grandfather or special adult friend to some of the places on their list.

Here are more primary books perfect for Father's Day reading.

Gone Fishing

by Earlene Long; illustrated by Richard Brown
Houghton Mifflin Company, 1984

Join a father and his son on a fun-filled day of fishing. Dad is taking along his big fishing rod, while his son has a little one just the right size. What fish will they catch to take home to Mom?

Just Me and My Dad

by Mercer Mayer
Golden Books, 1977

Discover the hilarious ups and downs of a father and son camping trip. Even when a bear steals their dinner, they manage to find something else to eat. From pitching a tent to catching fish for dinner—these two campers experience the thrill of camping!

by Mary Ellen Switzer

Book Nook

Little Nino's Pizzeria
by Karen Barbour
Harcourt Brace Jovanovich Publishers, 1987

Tony is his father's best helper at Little Nino's Pizzeria, but suddenly everything changes. The restaurant becomes more elegant, and Tony seems to be in everyone's way. Tony is soon delighted when his father decides to reopen the pizzeria again with the perfect name—Little Tony's Pizzeria.

Papa, Please Get the Moon for Me
by Eric Carle
Picture Book Studio, 1986

When Monica asks her father for the moon, the dedicated dad decides to carry out her request. He climbs a long ladder to the moon and carries it down when the moon is small enough. This magical story is enhanced with the beautiful artwork of Eric Carle, and children will be delighted that some pages fold out into larger pictures.

King of the Playground
by Phyllis Reynolds Naylor; illustrated by Nola Langner Malone
Atheneum, Macmillan Publishing Company, 1991

When Kevin is bothered by a bully, who does he turn to? His father, of course! After talking the situation over with his wise father, Kevin is able to cope with the problem . . . even turning the bully into a new friend.

Owl Moon
by Jane Yolen; illustrated by John Schoenherr
Philomel Books, 1987

One winter night, a daughter and her father take a magical walk in the woods to see a great horned owl. The little girl learns two important lessons in owling—you must be quiet and very patient before you experience the joy of seeing this magnificent bird at night.

Father's Day Punch & Munch

For Father's Day, we hold a Punch & Munch Party. The children send invitations to their dads the week before. If their dad is unable to attend, they can invite their grandpa, uncle, godfather or older brother—whoever is available to represent "dad" on the special day. (It's amazing how many dads actually take time off and show up for their child's special party!)

The children greet their dads when they arrive and serve them punch and invite them to help themselves to the treats the children have prepared. For this occasion, we usually cut up fresh fruit and cheese and serve it with crackers and a sweet treat. Brownies are always a big hit!

Towards the end of the day, about a half hour before dismissal, we gather in our circle with the dads sitting on "big" chairs behind the children. We do some singing; some favorites are "Take Me Out to the Ball Game," "Daddy's Taking Us to the Zoo" and "Skinnamarink." Then we usually read a story. The children really like *Hop on Pop* by Dr. Seuss and *Pinocchio*. To finish off the day, the children give their dads a special card and a picture or gift they have made just for this occasion.

This day has always been a great success and a lot of fun for both the children and the dads. On occasion, we have even been known to set up our party outside and have circle time on the grass under a big tree. Dads are invited to join us, and most of them do so happily.

Sometimes you get discouraged
Because I am so small
And always leave my fingerprints
On furniture and walls.

But every day I'm growing—
I'll be grown up someday,
And all those tiny handprints
Will surely fade away.

So here's a final handprint
Just so you can recall
Exactly how my fingers looked
When I was very small.

---

by Teresa E. Culpeper

Gift Idea

Materials Needed:
plaster of Paris
small paper plates
gold spray paint
straws
newspaper
water

Directions:

Mix the plaster of Paris according to directions on the box. Pour enough into a paper plate to just fill it. Have children place an open hand gently but firmly into the plaster. Put a straw into the top of the plaster, just above the handprint so a ribbon can be tied through when the plater is dry.

Leave overnight to dry thoroughly. When dry, carefully remove from plate and place on open newspapers. Spray entirely with gold spray paint and leave to dry. Make sure you have a well-ventilated area to spray in. With supervision, the children can do this themselves.

When dry, tie a colored ribbon through the hole where the straw was. Glue the poem on this page on the back.

You Are Invited to Our
Father's Day Punch & Munch
on

_____
Date

_____
Time

Holiday Sing-Alongs

Flags

This song is sung to the tune of "Mary Had a Little Lamb." Replace the names in the song with the names of children in your class. Use different names each time the song is sung.

Johnny has a little flag,
Little flag, little flag.
Johnny has a little flag.
He carries it with pride.
Mary has a little flag,
Little flag, little flag.
Mary has a little flag,
And Jill has one beside.

We love our country's stars and stripes,*
Stars and stripes, stars and stripes.
We love our country's stars and stripes.
We're proud to hold it high.
We're marching with our country's flag,
Our country's flag, our country's flag.
We're marching with our country's flag.
See our colors fly!

*(Canadian children can substitute maple leaf for stars and stripes.)

Flag Making and Parade

This activity is appropriate for celebrating Memorial Day, Flag Day, the Fourth of July and Canada Day (July 1).

Materials

The flag pattern and 8 1/2" x 11" white paper; a 1/4" wooden dowel, about 24" long; red or blue plastic adhesive tape, 1 1/4" wide; cellophane tape or stapler; markers or crayons; paste or glue and scissors

Directions

Reproduce the flag pattern on white paper. Let the children color their flags with fine-tip, water-based markers. Canadian children can use broad-tip markers to fill in areas after defining outlines with fine marker.

Help children cut out their flags. They should follow these directions: 1) Cut along the top border all the way to the edge of the paper; 2) cut along the bottom border in the same way; 3) cut along the right border. DO NOT cut along the left border.

The white edge on the left side should be wrapped around the dowel and stapled or taped about 2 1/2" from one end.

Wrap the colored tape two or three times around the end of the dowel above the flag. Let it extend about 1/2" above the end. Flatten this extended piece so the flat side is on the same side as the flag. If the edges are rough, they can be trimmed.

Because the Canadian flag is symmetrical, children making this flag may color another flag, trim it all around, then paste or tape it to the back of the flag, with the design showing.

When the flags are finished, have the children parade around the school, singing the "Flags" song and holding their flags aloft.

Summer Safety Tips

As soon as summer arrives, a whole new series of children's activities starts . . . most of them outdoors and all of them with special ways to stay safe.

Holiday Events

Parades

- Stay back from the line of marchers . . . on a curb or behind markers.
- Some paraders throw candy out into the crowd. Don't dash out into the road for it; you might get injured. If you do get candy, make sure it's wrapped up, and let an adult check it for you.

Fireworks

- Many states have laws forbidding individual use of fireworks. Even if your state doesn't, it's safer to watch a public display, usually at a park or shopping center.
- Sparklers are favorites with children (and they're usually legal), but sparks will burn if they touch your skin. Also, don't throw used sparklers on the grass, sand or driveway; others may step on them and get bad burns. Instead, have a bucket of water nearby to put them in.
- If you do have sparklers, let an adult light them, and hold them well away from your face and clothing.

Picnics

- Keep food, especially salads and meat, in a cooler until you're ready to eat.
- Bring your own drinking water.
- Eat on a clean surface. (Bring your own table covering.)
- If a fire pit or outdoor grill is used, stay back from the flames and let an adult do the cooking.
- Food hot off the grill may be hot enough to burn your mouth; let it cool a little.
- If you're allergic to insect bites (especially bees), get medication from your doctor and always have it with you.
- If you are not allergic, keep ice available for bites and bumps.
- Have an adult check playground equipment before using it.
- Ask an adult to have a first-aid kit handy for minor scrapes.

Picnics at a Public Facility

- If there's playground equipment, ask an adult to make sure it is safe to use.
- If there's a wooded area with trails to walk on, always go with an adult, stay on marked paths and wear footwear.
- If you see wild animals, leave them alone!
- If you come across berry bushes, do not eat the berries.
- If there is a brook that looks clean, do not drink water from it.
- Make sure an adult is always supervising you.

by Elaine Hansen Cleary

Roller Blades and In-Line Skates

The same precautions of checking over equipment and choosing safe places to go apply to roller blades, too. An additional safety hint is to wear protective pads on wrists, elbows and knees.

Bicycles

Bikes that have been stored away for the winter need to be checked over carefully. Use this checklist for safe biking:

- BRAKES work properly and do not grab.
- STEERING is neither too loose nor too tight.
- TIRES have the proper amount of air.
- HANDLE GRIPS fit snugly and aren't too big around for the hands holding them.
- SEAT is fastened securely to the frame and adjusted for the height of the rider.
- PEDALS are the right size and the right distance for the feet to fit comfortably.
- CHAIN is not loose, and there is a protective shield over it.
- TRAINING WHEELS provide a proper balance.

If there is a bike shop in your neighborhood, it's a good place to get your bike checked and to purchase a helmet that fits properly.

No bike is fall-proof, so follow these rules for protection:

DOs:

Wear a helmet that is adjusted to fit the head without sliding around. Wear your helmet straight across your head, not tilted back. Choose a safe place to ride, like a bike path. Keep your hands on the handlebars. When you come to an intersection, get off your bike and walk it across. Remember that bikers must obey the same traffic rules as car drivers.

DON'Ts:

Do not wear loose-fitting pants, skirts or slacks that could get caught in the chain. Ride in driveways or on gravel or sand. Never go bike riding alone or give anyone else a ride on the back or handlebars of your bike. Do not ride at night.

Swimming

What's more fun than swimming and playing in the water? It's also potentially more dangerous than many other activities. Follow these swimming precautions for safe swimming at the lake or a pool.

DOs:

- LEARN TO SWIM! Take advantage of programs your community offers.
- Swim where there is a certified lifeguard on duty.
- Test the depth of the water by walking out until it is shoulder level.
- Get OUT of the water during a storm.
- Watch out for sharp objects or hot coals in the sand.

DON'Ts:

- Never swim alone. Always stay with a buddy and make sure an adult is supervising.
- Do not depend on inflatable tubes or rafts. They're not leak-proof or puncture-proof.
- Never try to save someone else by yourself. Throw a life-ring or yell for help.
- Do not run around the edges of the pool. You might slip and fall.
- No "horseplay" (pushing, dunking) or unnecessary screaming.

Name_____

The ABCs of Safety

Using alphabetical order for the first word of each sentence, make a list of safety rules. Use positive wording as much as possible. Older children will be able to generate their own words. Younger children should be given a word to start with. The words below will help you get started. Begin by asking, "What is something we should always do to be safe?" Any number of answers is possible.

Always   swim where there is a lifeguard on duty.
Be   sure to wear a helmet when riding your bike.
Cross _____
Do _____
Every _____
Form _____
Go _____
Have _____
Inspect _____
Jump _____
Keep _____
Leave _____
Make _____
Never _____
Open _____
Put _____
Quit _____
Remain _____
Save _____
Take _____
Use _____
Visit _____
Wear _____
X ray _____
Yell _____
Zoom _____

Summer Fun for Little Ones

Begin the summer experience right in the classroom
with some fresh, fun activities.

Tunnel Vision

Ants are one of the many insects we notice during the summer (especially at picnics). Give your children a peek inside the busy world of ants by having them help build an ant farm. To make a simple ant farm, remove the bottom section of an empty two-liter soda bottle, place a rock inside the bottle and cover the bottom opening with plastic wrap secured with tape. Place the bottle, bottom side down, on a sturdy tray by centering the tray over the inverted bottle, then carefully turning the two upright. Prepare a paper funnel to fit the neck of the bottle. Dig up soil and ants from an anthill and gently pour them through the funnel. Poke a small piece of dampened sponge through the opening, then sprinkle in a few food crumbs. Place a ball of cotton into the neck of the bottle and cover the opening with a piece of gauze secured with a rubber band. Cover the bottle with fabric, leaving it in the dark as if underground, but uncover it daily to replenish the food supply. After three or four days, ant tunnels and rooms should appear for your class to observe through the bottle.

Fun at the Beach

Supply the children with towels, straw hats, sunglasses, empty sunscreen bottles, buckets, shovels and bathing suits (large enough to fit over their clothing) for a pretend day at the beach. Specify a certain area as the beach. Toss several pillows next to the "beach" to act as the swimming area. Encourage your children to role-play a day at the beach, while taking the necessary precautions against harmful sun rays.

Beach Pictures

Experience some actual beach textures without ever leaving the classroom. Have your children paint pictures of the beach on pieces of cardboard using tempera paint mixed with a small amount of sand. When the paintings are dry, provide the students with glue and a variety of small shells. Let them glue real shells on their pretend beaches.

by Marie E. Cecchini

Beach Finds

As you talk about going to the beach, you may discuss or have pictures of some animals or plants we might expect to find in a beach habitat. Many children may even have a souvenir starfish or sand dollar. Invite everyone to make their own paper starfish or sand dollar by preparing cardboard patterns of each for the children to trace and cut from yellow or tan paper. Have them use small paintbrushes to cover their sea animals with glue, then let them sift sand over their creations. Use waxed paper under their glue work so the finished products will peel off easily when dry.

Camping

Another summer activity enjoyed by many families is camping. Help your class set up a pretend campground. Create a simple tent (perhaps a blanket over a table), roll up a few large towels to serve as sleeping bags, build a camp fire with rolled newspaper logs and make a few paper lanterns to provide light at night. Talk with the children about some of the things people do while camping, drawing from the experiences of any children who have been camping. Encourage them to "play camp" independently.

Creeping Crabs

Crabs are just one of the many fascinating creatures of the sea. They can walk in many directions with their 10 legs, sometimes making them appear almost comical, and their front legs end in claws, which they use when eating. Provide the children with small paper plates, markers, pipe cleaners, buttons, glue and tape for making individual crabs. Have them color the backs of two plates. Help them tape 10 pipe cleaner pieces to the inside of one plate (five on either side) for crab legs. Bend the tips of the front legs to resemble claws. Staple the plates together around the edges; then have the children glue two button eyes on their crabs.

Shells

Provide the children with a tray of various types of seashells for looking, touching and sorting. Encourage them to sort the shells by size, texture or color. Invite them to invent stories about some of the animals that once inhabited the shells. Tape-record their stories and have them draw story pictures to share with the class.

Fish Story

Share the counting poem on the right with your class. Make use of flannel board fish or stick puppet fish as you tell the story. Have the children act out the story by choosing five "fish children" at a time to play the parts, while the rest of the class recites the poem.

Paper Strip Fish

Cut 2" x 12" paper strips, one for each child. Provide the children with these strips and markers. Have them draw a fish face in the center of each strip and a fin at either side of the face. When their drawings are complete, bend each strip so the ends meet. Staple each fish about 2" in from the ends of the matched strips. Have the children open the ends of the strip up to the staple, forming a fish tail.

Fishing Poles

Let each of the children draw, color and cut out a paper fish. Have them include gills, fins, eyes and a mouth. Set these fish aside temporarily and take the class outdoors to search for small fishing pole sticks. When everyone has found an appropriate twig pole, help them tie a yarn length to each pole. Let them tape their fish to the opposite end of the yarn.

Five Fat Fish

Five fat fish were gliding by the shore.
Along came a net, and then there were four.
Four fat fish were diving in the sea.
Along came a bigger fish,
and then there were three.
Three fat fish swam the ocean blue.
One got stuck in seaweed,
and then there were two.
Two fat fish thought swimming was fun.
One nibbled on a little worm,
and then there was one.
One fat fish went swimming on home.
It was no fun swimming all alone.

Vacation Time

Discuss the word *vacation* with your students, and have them contribute ideas of why people take/need vacations. Have them name some fun and relaxing things to do on a vacation. Encourage them to bring in postcards or souvenirs of vacations they have taken to share with the class. Set up a vacation display area for independent viewing and discussion.

Picnic Time

During the summer, we can enjoy many activities outdoors, including picnics. Invite the children to help plan an outdoor picnic. Provide blanket room for everyone, and make use of items from your housekeeping corner for picnic setup. Have the children carry the picnic supplies in baskets, and let them bring their snacks outside for picnic food. Ask them to suggest games to play at the picnic.

Summer Beauty

When the summer sun shines, everything grows and blooms. Flowers are no exception. Provide the children with paper and markers and have them draw a picture of their favorite summer flower. After they complete their drawings, supply them with glue and real flower seeds. Have them glue flower seeds in the center portion of their blossoms.

Ice Cream Cones

Provide the children with brown triangle "cones." Have them draw lines on their cones with brown markers; then glue the cones to the bottom of a sheet of paper. Everyone has a favorite flavor, so supply several colors of paper, along with scissors, for the children to cut out scoops of ice cream. Let them glue their ice cream scoops at the top of their cones to complete their pictures.

Flavor Pops

Summer wouldn't be summer without flavor pops. The ones the children make will be pretend but will smell very real. Provide the children with white rectangular shapes resembling flavor pops, and prepare special paints for coloring them. Make use of several colors of tempera. To each paint color, add a few drops of cooking extract (peppermint, orange, vanilla, lemon and so on) to scent the paint. Let the children choose a "flavor" and paint their pops. When the pops dry, tape them to craft sticks.

Water Toss

For a new kind of water play, one you may want to take outdoors, you'll need a tub(s) full of water, several plastic containers and small plastic manipulatives or Ping-Pong™ balls. Have the children take turns tossing the small items into the floating containers as they splash into summer.

Sun Puppet

One thing we can't help but notice about summer is the big, yellow sun that sends down shining rays of heat. Have your class create sun stick puppets. First have the children color a paper plate yellow. Let them add a smiling face, if they desire. Next help them tape short, yellow crepe paper streamers to the back of their plates, forming rays of sunshine. Finally, staple each sun to a cardboard strip, making a sunny stick puppet.

Holiday

May Day

The first of May is a special day—
Around the Maypole we dance and play.
   (Dance around.)
We pick some lovely spring flowers
   (Pretend to pick.)
And are glad for April's showers!
   (Smile!)

My Mom

My mom is very kind and sweet.
   (On "my" point to self.)
She works and keeps our house real neat!
   (Pretend to clean.)
She cooks my food and irons my clothes.
   (Appropriate motions.)
When I need help, she always knows
   (Put hands on chest for "I" and hold palms
   up in front for "always.")
Exactly what is good and right.
   (Wag finger in emphasis on "exactly,"
   "good" and "right")
For Mom—a special kiss tonight!
   (Pucker up and throw a big kiss.)

May Flower

Here's a green leaf,
   (Show one hand.)
And here's a green leaf.
   (Show other hand.)
That, you see, makes two.
   (Put up two fingers.)
Here's a bud
   (Cup hands together.)
That makes a flower.
   (Show cupped hands.)
Watch it bloom for you!
   (Open cupped hands slowly.)

by Judy Wolfman

Fingerplays

My Dad

My dad is very big and strong.
   (Square off shoulders and flex muscles.)
He works hard all day long.
   (Pretend to do some kind of work.)
But he also likes to have some fun,
   (Pretend to do something that's fun.)
And he reads to me when day is done.
   (Pretend to hold a book.)
So to my dad I want to say,
"I love you every single day!"

Summer Sun

The summer sun gets out of bed
   (Extend arm horizontally.)
And climbs throughout the day.
   (Raise arm slowly.)
At noon it shines right overhead.
   (Hold arm straight up.)
At night it goes away.
   (Lower arm slowly and let it drop.)

The Beehive

I found a beehive!
   (Show fist.)
But where are the bees?
   (Pretend to look around the hive.)
They're hidden away where nobody sees.
   (Whisper this as you continue to look.)
Here they come—
Creeping out of their hive—
1, 2, 3, 4, 5.
   (Bring fingers out one at a time.)

The Firefly

When I look up into the sky,
   (Look up and point.)
I see a little light go by.
   (Wiggle two fingers.)
It is a little light with wings—
   (Continue to wiggle fingers.)
It's truly an amazing thing!
Just think—a little bug that's lit.
I wonder who thought of it?
   (Put finger to head and "think.")

Summer "Snack"tivities

Unusual, nutritious snacks can help promote healthy eating habits, stimulate creative thinking, improve manual dexterity and expand vocabulary usage (for example, *slice, dice, shred*). Sometimes playing with your food is a good idea!

Clowning Around

Ingredients:

- pita bread
- carrot shavings
- cherry tomatoes (whole and sliced)
- carrot slices
- wheat bread
- strawberries, chunked
- sandwich spreads (egg or tuna salad and so on)

Cut the pita bread open to form two circles. Cover one circle with sandwich spread and set it on a plate. Sprinkle carrot shaving hair at the top of the circle. Set two carrot slices into the sandwich spread for eyes. Add a cherry tomato nose and two cherry tomato slices for cheeks. Form a mouth with strawberry chunks. Cut a triangle shape from the wheat bread. Cover the triangle with a different sandwich spread. Set the triangle at the top of the head for a hat. Top the hat with a whole cherry tomato pom-pom.

Tempting Tents

Ingredients:

- ice cream cones
- raisins
- dry cereal shapes
- fresh fruit chunks
- peanut butter
- nuts
- sunflower seeds

Invert the ice cream cone and coat it with peanut butter. Decorate this tent with raisins, nuts, dry cereal shapes, sunflower seeds and fresh fruit chunks.

Spirit of America

Ingredients:

- graham crackers
- cream cheese
- blueberries
- strawberries, chunked

Spread cream cheese over the graham cracker to make the flag background. Cluster several blueberries in the upper left-hand corner of the graham cracker to form a rectangle shape. Set strawberry chunks in rows across the rest of the cracker to form the red stripes. Space the red rows apart, leaving a white row between each.

Tasty Turtle

Ingredients:

cottage cheese
green food coloring
green grapes
raisins
cheese slices

Tint the cottage cheese green with the food coloring. Place a mound of green cottage cheese onto the center of a plate for the turtle shell. Push a green grape slightly into the cottage cheese for a head. Add two raisins to each side of the cottage cheese mound as legs. Cut a small triangle from a cheese slice and add it to the back of the turtle for a tail.

The Cracker Family

Ingredients:

crackers, assorted shapes
carrot sticks
dry cereal shapes
raisins
peanut butter
cheese slice
sunflower seeds

Spread peanut butter on a round cracker and place it on a plate for a head. Choose a second cracker shape for the body and spread peanut butter on it. Use additional peanut butter as glue and add carrot stick arms and legs to the cracker body. Tear several small pieces from the cheese slice and place them at the top of the head for hair. Use dry cereal pieces, raisins, currants, sunflower seeds and so on to make a family and to decorate the bodies. Make a whole "Cracker Family."

Delightful Daisy

Ingredients:

sliced pineapple
celery stalk
apple slices
strawberries
lettuce leaf

Place one pineapple slice near the top of a plate. Set a whole strawberry in the center hole. Surround the pineapple with apple slice "petals." Slice the celery stalk lengthwise and place one piece below the pineapple for a flower stem. Tear pieces from a lettuce leaf and set them beside the celery stem for leaves.

Tic-Tac-Toe Lunch

Ingredients:

white bread
sandwich spread
 (peanut butter, egg or tuna salad)
wheat bread
cheese slices

Cut the bread slices into squares. Use these squares with your choice of spread to make mini sandwiches. Arrange the sandwiches on a tray in three rows of three, alternating bread colors. The layout should resemble a checkerboard. Cut the cheese slices into circles (for Os) and strips (for Xs) and place the Os and Xs on top of the sandwiches.

A Teddy Bear's Picnic

Everyone loves teddy bears, and teddy bears love everyone. Open your heart and imagination and have a ball. The students will love it and so will you!

Creative Writing

Have the students write a variety of poems, short stories and dramatic skits to be performed for the class at the picnic. They may start out with "Once upon a time . . ."

Acronyms are great ways to get started writing poems.

For short stories, some simple story starters are: "If I were a teddy bear . . . ," "If my teddy bear could . . . ," "My teddy and I . . . ."

Remember, let the students use their imaginations and get the creative juices flowing. They'll have a great time!

by Teresa E. Culpeper

Teddy's Cottage

Materials:
- large white art paper
- colored pencils, markers, rulers
- plasticine, bristol board, coffee stirrers, building manipulatives

On paper, have the students design and sketch a cottage for teddy. They should make both a front view from the outside, of the cottage, as well as a schematic layout of the inside. (This is a good time to put those math skills to work.) Don't forget to mark doors and windows.

Encourage interested students to design an actual model of the cottage using plasticine, wooden stirring sticks, bristol board or other building materials. These students are our future architects!

Edible Necklace

Ingredients:
- red shoestring licorice
- large size Gummi Bears

Give each child one piece of licorice and a dozen Gummi Bears. Push the end of the licorice through the middle (tummy) of the first bear. (Depending on how soft the candies are, you may need to make a small slit in it, using scissors or a knife.) Push the Gummi Bear along the licorice, leaving about an inch and a half at the opposite end. Continue threading the bears until they are all on the licorice. Tie the two ends of the licorice behind the child's neck. If the licorice will not fit the child as a necklace, tie it around the wrist for a bracelet. Either way, they can wear it, eat it and enjoy it!

Teddy Bear Fashions

Materials:
- large white art paper
- markers, pencils, crayons, pastels
- assorted fabric scraps
- scissors
- glue

On the paper, have the students design fashionable Ted's Wear for the following occasions: casual wear, beach wear, formal (party) wear, sleepwear, school wear and sportswear. Let students use the markers, crayons, pastels or colored pencils to complete the fashions.

Have interested students design the drawn outfits from actual pieces of fabric. Bring in a bear or two to serve as models.

Teddy's Tasty Dessert

Ingredients:
- 2 cups graham cracker crumbs
- 1/2 cup melted butter or margarine
- 1 can sweetened condensed milk
- maraschino cherries
- 1/4 cup granulated sugar
- 2 pkg. Dream Whip™
- 6 1/2 oz. can of pink lemonade*
- walnut or pecan slices

Mix the crumbs, sugar and melted butter together. In a 9" x 11" pan, press down 3/4 cup of the mixture. Whip the two packages of Dream Whip™ as directed. Add the condensed milk and lemonade. Whip until blended. Pour over the crumb mixture. Sprinkle with the remaining crumbs. Decorate with cherries and nuts. Cover with plastic wrap and freeze for several hours. (Overnight is best.) Cut to serve. (*You can substitute any frozen juice for the lemonade.)

Teddy Bearade

Ingredients:
- orange juice
- ginger ale
- ice cubes

Combine equal amounts of orange juice and ginger ale. Add some ice cubes and mix. This makes a great thirst-quenching drink.

Honey Bear Sandwiches

Ingredients:
- peanut butter
- banana slices
- honey graham crackers
- honey (optional)

Spread peanut butter on a graham cracker. Add a banana slice or two. Top with another cracker or leave it "open face." (For students who are allergic to peanut butter, spread the cracker with honey. For those students who are adventurous, add the honey along with the peanut butter and banana.)

Teddy's Crunch

Ingredients:
- miniature colored marshmallows
- peanuts (unsalted)
- honey
- seedless raisins
- coconut

In a large bowl, mix together all the ingredients except the honey. Drizzle the honey over the mixture and toss.

Watermelon Wishes

Welcome warm weather with a garden full of winning watermelon activities.

Measurement

For this hands-on math activity, you will need two whole watermelons, a weight scale and a cloth or paper tape measure. Invite the children to touch and attempt to lift each melon. Let them put their arms around each. Show them the scale, talk about weight measures and have them estimate the weight of each melon. Weigh each melon and compare the estimated weights with the actual weights. Next, show them the tape measure, talk about length measures and have them estimate the girth of each melon. Measure each melon and compare the estimated and actual results.

Comparison

For a tasty lesson in likenesses and differences, purchase a regular watermelon and a seedless one. Cut each into wedges. Have the children use all of their senses as they determine any similarities or differences between the two kinds. Do the watermelons look, feel, smell and taste the same? Do they sound the same when you take a bite or cut them with a knife? Can the children draw any conclusions? Which kind do they prefer and why? Save all seeds.

Estimation

Fill three different-sized containers with watermelon seeds. Ask the children to estimate the number of seeds in each container. Count the seeds in each and compare the estimated counts with the actual numbers. What can the children conclude about the relationship between container size and content amount?

Center Seeds

Cut several paper plates in half. Color the rims green and the inner portion red. Write a numeral on each of these watermelon slices. Provide the children with watermelon seeds. Have them read the numeral on each half-plate; then place the correct number of seeds on each watermelon slice.

by Marie E. Cecchini

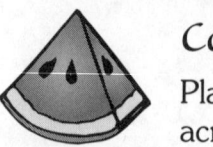

Counting Vine

Place a heavy strand of green yarn across your bulletin board to act as a watermelon vine. Prepare 11 green watermelon shapes, numbering them from zero to ten. Provide the children with clothespins and allow them to hang the paper watermelons on the vine in numerical order.

Fractions

Turn four paper plates into watermelon slices by coloring the rims green, the inner portions red and adding black seeds. Leave one plate whole and cut one in half. Cut the third plate into thirds and the remaining plate into fourths. Nest the plates and work with the children to demonstrate how the whole can be portioned into equal pieces.

Rolling Races

Have the children help design a special race course. Supply them with a large sheet of paper on which to map out the course. Use large red and/or green balls (or real watermelons, if you're brave) and let the children take turns rolling a ball/watermelon through the course. Use a stopwatch to time them. Compare the results.

Watermelon Art

Provide the class with paper plate halves, red and green paint and watermelon seeds. Let them paint the rims of their plates green and the inner portions red. Have them set watermelon seeds into the wet, red paint.

Watermelon Dough

Invite the class to help you make watermelon playdough. After it cools, place small amounts into plastic sandwich bags and tie with green ribbon for the children to take home.

2 c. flour   1 c. salt   2 c. water
2 T. cooking oil   4 T. cream of tartar
1 pkg. sugar-free watermelon-flavored gelatin

Place all of the ingredients into a saucepan. Stir constantly over medium heat until the mixture forms a ball. Remove from heat and cool.

Seed Jewelry

Necklace: Older children will enjoy using a needle threaded with dental floss to string watermelon seeds into a necklace.

Bracelet: For younger children, have them glue seeds to a paper strip. When the glue dries, punch one hole in either end of the strip, thread with yarn or ribbon and tie the ends together around the child's wrist.

Rind Painting

Dry several pieces of watermelon rind. Provide the children with paper and paints and invite them to create a stamped picture design using the dried rind. Encourage them to stamp with the sides, ends and outer curved portion. Do they notice any differences in the textures?

Seed Sounds

Let the children turn small paper plates, red and green tissue paper squares and watermelon seeds into rhythm shakers. Have them glue the tissue paper colors to the backs of the plates.

Remind them to glue green around the rim and red in the center. When dry, bend the plates in half (do not crease) and staple around the curve, leaving a small section open. Ask the children to drop a few seeds through the opening, then staple closed and shake, shake, shake!

Marking Your Page

Have the children make watermelon bookmarks to encourage them to read during their summer vacation. Supply paper strips, green markers and a green stamp pad. Have them draw green vines on their paper strips. Show them how to use their thumbs with the stamp pad to make thumbprint watermelons along their vines.

Watermelon Puzzle

Use markers to color a paper plate like a watermelon slice (green rim, red center, black seeds). Cut the plate into several puzzle pieces. Allow the children to use it during independent time. You may also want to let the students make individual puzzles to take home.

Planting

Provide the children with red paper strips and have them color a green border along the top and bottom. Let them color black seeds along the red section. Help them fit these strips around small yogurt containers with tape. Have them fill their containers with soil and plant watermelon seeds. When the seedlings sprout, let the children take them home to plant.

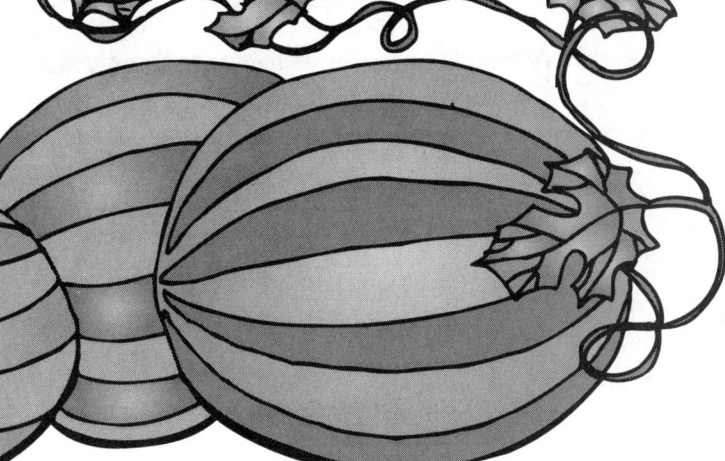

Letters

Program one long card with the word *watermelon* and 10 individual cards with the letters of the same word. Display the word card and have the children sort the letter cards, placing them in the proper sequence to spell the word correctly.

Number Words

Prepare two sets of cards, one set with a number word on each and the other with watermelon slice pictures to correspond with the number words. Encourage the children to match each word card with the card bearing the correct number of slices. Ask them to read the word cards.

Compound Words

Use the word *watermelon* to introduce compound words to your class. Demonstrate how two smaller words were put together to form a larger word. Note the meanings of each word. Ask for examples of other compound words. Write their contributions on chart paper and display the list for the children to review independently.

Watermelon Genie

Invite your children to "just suppose" a watermelon were a magic lamp. Have the class close their eyes and imagine what the Watermelon Genie would look like when it appeared after three rubs. What would they request from the genie? Supply them with paper and markers. Ask them to draw their vision of the genie. Have them write or dictate what they would wish for and why.

July

A Literature Unit Based on the Book *July*

by James Stevenson (Greenwillow, 1990)

Summer is the time for adventures. There are places to explore and extra time to wonder about the real and the imaginary. Long after summer is over, the memories remain. The following literature unit is designed to provide opportunities for students to study a story and make connections to their own lives. Follow-up activities provide curriculum-enriching ideas that focus on writing and organizational skills.

Summary:
When Grandpa was a boy, he and his brother spent the month of July with their grandparents near the beach. Fifty years later, he reminisces about their vacation and remembers the fun they had.

Questions:
The following questions review the story and require students to draw from their own experiences:

1. What was special about July?
2. How would you describe the boys' grandparents? How did they dress? What did they like to do? What were they like? Do they remind you of your grandparents in any way? How are they alike? How are they different?
3. Name some things the boys did for fun.
4. Have you ever played the same games or done the same things?
5. What other activities do you like to do during the summer?
6. There was a long list of things not to do. Which of the things are still forbidden these days? Are there any that people have reminded you not to do? Were there any you had never heard of before? If your parents made a list of things you should not do, what would be included?
7. Who did the boys steer clear of? Why were these people avoided?
8. What type of people do you try to avoid? Have you ever been pleasantly surprised when you got to know them better?
9. Why did the boy give up his idea of becoming a great tennis player?
10. What do you plan to do when you grow up? Do you change your mind often? Why?
11. What things did the children do at the beach? If you were there, what do you think you would have liked to do?
12. What two things did the boy want to do most? Did he get his wish? Explain what happened.

by Patricia O'Brien

Activities

The following suggestions provide ideas for thinking and writing experiences.

Writing Nonfiction

Below are ideas that may be used to present factual information.

1. Younger students may draw pictures to relate a vacation experience. Fold paper to make a booklet. Each page will feature one topic. Possible topics include:
   Where I went
   What I did
   What I liked the most
   What I wish I had done

   The children's drawings may be supplemented with their written or dictated responses.

2. Older students may either report on something they learned while they were away, or they may research something they wish to find out more about.

   Write an informative book based on what you discovered. While on vacation, questions may have come up about something you saw. For example, if an unusual animal was spotted, now is the time to learn more about what might have puzzled you.

   a. Write three to five questions for which you want to find answers.
      What does it look like?
      Where does it live?
      What does it eat?
      How does it defend itself?

   b. Read, watch videos and/or talk to an "expert" to find answers to your questions.

   c. Compile the information into a booklet. Each page of your report should answer one of the questions. Magazine pictures or drawings may be used to illustrate the information.

3. Draw a series of pictures showing the types of things you like doing during the summer. Write a caption to explain each picture.

4. Draw a picture of yourself doing your favorite summertime activity. Write or dictate the reason you enjoy doing this activity. Compile the pages into a class book of summer fun.

5. Keep a journal of a vacation adventure or a summer outing. Describe the events of the trip. Tell about people you met and the things you saw and did.

6. When people travel, they often send postcards to their relatives and friends to let them know they are thinking about them and having a good time. Use an unlined 4" x 6" or 5" x 8" index card to make a postcard. On one side, write a message to a real or imaginary person. Leave room for the address. On the other side, draw a picture of the place you visited.

Writing Fiction

James Stevenson wrote about a time he remembered. When authors write about their own experiences, their stories seem more real. Since Stevenson's stories are fiction, he can add things to make the events seem funnier or more exciting than they actually were.

1. Think of something you did one summer that you enjoyed. This would be a good idea for a story. Write about what you remember; then use your imagination to improve on what you recall.

2. Ask your parents or grandparents about a summer experience they remember when they were young. Pretend to be the person you interviewed and write about his or her summer memories as if they were your own. Use "I" and try to put yourself in his or her place.

Saving Keepsakes

Besides bringing home memories, we often collect things on an outing. Instead of putting them in a box and forgetting about them, encourage the children to create something with their "treasures."

1. Keep a scrapbook of pictures that remind you of your trip.

2. If photographs were taken, organize them in a photo album. Be sure to include information about when and where they were taken, who is in the picture, and what it is showing.

3. Small, interesting articles found outdoors may be hung from a branch to make a nature mobile. Use thread or fishing line to secure the items.

4. Divide a shallow box into smaller sections with strips of cardboard stapled to the sides. Sort and arrange your collection in the box. Tell someone about your collection and how you gathered it.

305

TLC10110 Copyright © Teaching & Learning Company, Carthage, IL 62321-0010

National Hot Dog Month

One of America's favorite foods is honored during the month of July. Here's a clue: what kind of dog has no bark, no bite, no tail and many names? Yes, it's the famous hot dog!

The Babylonians, ancient Romans, Egyptians and Greeks all had a form of sausage. It continued through the Middle Ages and traveled throughout Europe, where the sausage became famous in Frankfurt, Germany, in the 1850s. Legend claims that a butcher gave his sausage an elongated shape as a tribute to his pet dachshund and named it a "Dachshund Sausage." However, the name frankfurter became more popular since that was the town where it was created.

In 1883, a sausage peddler named Anton Feuchtwanger came to America. It was at the Chicago World's Fair where he sold his famous "red hots." This food was too hot to handle, so he passed out white gloves along with the food. This was not successful, so he then thought of the bun to encase the meat. Then in 1900, at a football game in New York City, a peddler walked around shouting "Get our dachshund sausage while they're red hot!" A famous cartoonist, Tad Dorgan, captured the scene in pictures; however, he couldn't spell the word *dachshund* so he substituted the term *hot dog* instead. From then on, it became a popular word and a fun food in the United States.

by Tania Kourempis-Cowling

Celebrate National Hot Dog Month in the classroom with these fun activities.

1. Make a hot dog booklet. Cut construction paper into the shape of a hot dog bun. Fasten several pages together with a brass fastener or stapler. On the first page, draw a picture of the frankfurter itself. The following pages could have pictures of the condiments used on this meat. Color a picture of mustard, ketchup, relish, onions, sauerkraut, chili and so on. A variation would be to find pictures of these condiments in magazines, cut them out and glue on the pages.

2. Make a stuffed hot dog out of recycled panty hose. Cut off the tops and feet and then stuff the hose with cotton or polyester filling. Tie the ends off to make a single hot dog, or section it off into 7" sections to form links. Paint a face and add wiggly eyes to make a funny-looking hot dog. Sing the wiener song.

3. Set up a hot dog snack table. Buy miniature links or cut hot dogs into bite-sized pieces. Pierce each with a toothpick and provide several sauces for dipping. Another favorite of children, as well as adults, is pigs-in-the-blanket. Preheat the oven to 375°F. Separate refrigerated crescent roll dough into triangles. Slit a hot dog lengthwise and fill with chunks of cheddar cheese. Place the hot dog along the short side of the triangle and roll it up in the dough. Bake for 12 to 18 minutes until golden brown.

4. Look for these books: *Hot Dog Cook Book* by William I. Kaufman (Doubleday, New York) and *Extraordinary Origins of Everyday Things* by Charles Panati (Harper & Row, New York).

TAKE-HOME

Sum Weighs Two Knot Forget Watt Eye Tot U

"Some ways to not forget what I taught you."

Who ever said spelling is important? They were right. (Being interested and understood is even more important.) As you end another school year, the same questions come to mind. Will the students retain a school year's worth of knowledge over the summer? There are no guarantees they will. Parents ask many times, "What can we do over the summer to help our children academically?" And to this, we reply, "Keep them thinking." Summer should be fun for children, and a time to explore. Here is a list of 20 ideas to send home with students on the last day of school.

1. Read road signs aloud.
2. Take a backyard field trip. Identify trees, rocks, bugs.
3. Plant a flower or vegetable garden.
4. Organize a neighborhood pet parade, and make signs for it.
5. Collect place mats from restaurants.
6. Take pictures of summer things—the pool, flowers—date them and put them into the sleeve of your winter coat.
7. Write a story about where your shoes walked today.
8. Go grocery shopping. Add up the bill. Count out the money.
9. Make birthday cards using magazine pictures.
10. Set up a lemonade stand—record prices and earnings.
11. Make a centerpiece for a picnic using things from nature.
12. Follow an ant. Videotape his trip—narrate it!
13. Collect rocks.
14. Make necklaces and rings from dandelions.
15. Listen to the birds. Are they conversing? Write what they're saying. Tape-record them.
16. Jump rope and count as high as you can. Or . . . name the states, your friends or words that being with a, b, c and so on.
17. Plan a scavenger hunt for your family or friends.
18. Have a yard sale—record earnings.
19. Keep a scrapbook to share.
20. Write lots of letters and postcards. Send one to me.
21. (Bonus) Find a four-leaf clover and wish for summer to last longer!

by Jo Jo Cavalline and Jo Anne O'Donnell

Happy Birthday, USA

July 4th is the birthday of the United States and the most important of all its national holidays. This holiday commemorates the adoption on July 4, 1776, of the final draft of the Declaration of Independence by the Continental Congress to proclaim America's freedom from British rule. Thomas Jefferson prepared the first draft of the Declaration of Independence and most of the writing is his, although various suggestions for changes were made and incorporated into the declaration both before and after it was presented to Congress. Finally on this day, John Hancock, president of Congress, signed the document. The document was then rewritten on parchment (animal skin) and 56 men supplied their signatures. Today, the parchment is displayed in the National Archives Building in Washington, D.C.

Every year, Independence Day (July 4th) is the legal holiday celebrated throughout the country with picnics, parades and fireworks displays after dark. Prepare your students for this holiday by making decorations and participating in numerous activities relating to this historic event. Don't forget the symbols of the United States independence including the flag, the Liberty Bell and the Statue of Liberty.

by Tania K. Cowling

Books to Read

The Fourth of July by Mary Kay Phelan. Nonfiction book about the origin of the Declaration of Independence and its signers. Harper, 1966.

Fourth of July by Charles P. Graves. Descriptions of the many patriotic symbols associated with this day. Garrard, 1963.

Fourth of July by Barbara M. Joosse. Fiction story of a little boy handling his responsibilities at home and marching in a parade. Knopf, 1985.

Henry's Fourth of July by Holly Keller. Henry is an opossum looking forward to his first Fourth of July celebration. Greenwillow, 1985.

Firecrackers

Cover rolls of wrapped candy with crepe paper. Tie at each end with yarn; then fringe the paper. Glue on paper stars and stripes.

Rocket Rolls

Tape four craft sticks to a roll of candy so the candy will stand up. Wrap the roll and the top part of the sticks with red construction paper. Paint the remaining part of the sticks with black paint. Make a rocket top by cutting a circle the size of a half dollar from white paper, slitting it and rolling it into a cone. Glue this on top of the roll of candy to make a rocket.

Patriotic Refreshments

Serve some red, white and blue snacks to the children for added fun. Make pinwheel sandwiches with peanut butter and strawberry jelly. Cut the edges from a slice of bread. Flatten the bread slightly with a rolling pin. Spread the filling and carefully form each slice into a roll. Cut the roll into bite-sized pieces. Serve red fruit punch with "blueberry bombs" (ice cubes). Place several fresh or frozen blueberries into each section of an ice cube tray. Freeze and serve these with the punch. Make star-shaped gelatin using molds and red or blue-flavored gelatin. Add a little whipped cream for a white topping.

Burst of Colors

Group eight plastic straws and tie them together at the center. Arrange the straws so they will stand up. Press large colored gumdrop candies onto the top of each straw.

Nickel Race

On one side of the nickel you will find Thomas Jefferson, the third President of the United States, and his home, Monticello, on the other side. To play this game, you will need three nickels and a piece of masking tape placed on a tabletop for a finish line. Each player lines up the three nickels at the end of the table. The first nickel is heads up and the other two nickels are tails up. The object of this game is to race the three nickels all together to the finish line. You may use only one finger on the last nickel to push all three forward. Keep trying because it isn't easy!

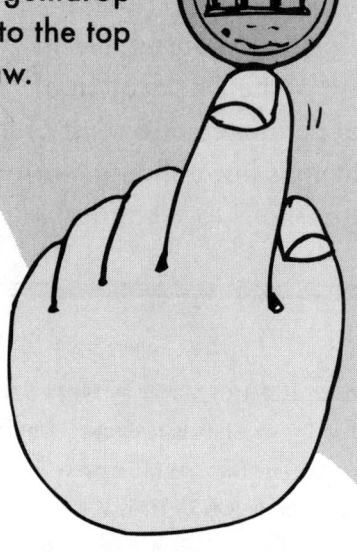

Independence Flyers

Make a paper plate flyer to use during your classroom parade and for outdoor play. Staple strips of crepe paper or ribbon to one edge of a paper plate. Punch two holes and tie a ribbon hanger to the opposite side of the plate. Now that the construction part is done, decorate the plate itself with patriotic pictures and designs, using all kinds of art materials. Hold the independence flyer while marching around and watch the streamers blow in the wind.

Decorations

For a patriotic atmosphere, decorate with lots of red, white and blue. Have the children write messages with markers on balloons before they are inflated. Let them wish the USA a happy birthday with a catchy saying written on each balloon. Inflate the balloons and hang them around the classroom, along with crepe paper and ribbon streamers. Cut out silver stars from heavy gauge aluminum foil and attach these to the streamers. Make construction paper replicas of the flag, the Liberty Bell and the Statue of Liberty to decorate the room.

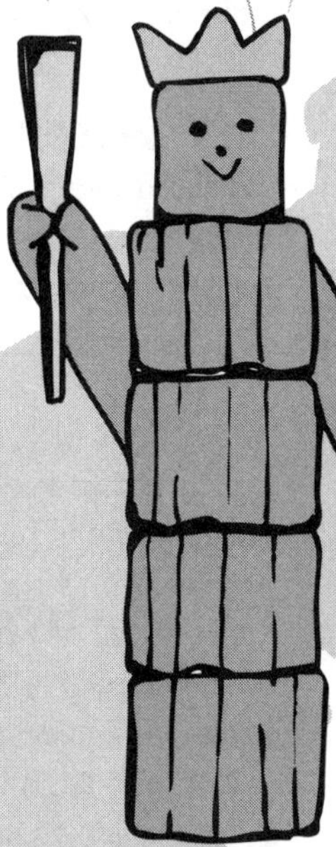

Statue of Liberty

This statue is made of caramel candies "glued" together by moistening each with water. Stack four caramels for the body. Cut half of a caramel for the head. For arms, cut a caramel in half and shape each piece into an arm (one holding a torch). Cut a crown from another candy caramel. Moisten these with water and sculpt this statue.

Sorting and Counting Game

Give the children a box containing red, white and blue poker chips. Let them sort the chips by color and then count them.

Flip the Beanbag Game

Make a patriotic beanbag from a piece of red and blue felt. Fill it with dried beans. Divide the children into a red team and a blue team. Teams stand at opposite sides of the room. The number of players on each team should be equal. Someone flips the beanbag in the air. If it lands with the red side up, the red team must all laugh out loud, while the blue team must be quiet and keep a straight face. Anyone on the blue team that fails to do so is out. Throw the bag again. If it turns up blue, then the blue team laughs and cheers, while the red team must be silent. Continue flipping the beanbag until all players on one team are out. The children must pay attention as one false laugh could take them off the team. This is a great game for observation and attention.

A Family Take-Home

Summer newsletter

Is your child bored after just a few weeks of summer vacation? Are you concerned that recently learned math and language skills will be forgotten? Well, there's no need to worry because you (yes, you!) can engage your child in at-home activities that will help to relieve the boredom and maintain learned skills. A suggested list of such activities follows.

Vacation Lingo

During the summer school break, many families plan vacations. Use your child's anticipation of upcoming events as an opportunity to maintain language skills. Obtain pamphlets and brochures, and discuss places you'd like to visit and what you expect to see and do while you are there. During your stay, purchase a few postcards. Encourage younger children to dictate a few lines to send to special friends and relatives. Let them add a small drawing and help them to sign their names. Older children may write their own messages or copy one you have written from their dictation. Take this opportunity to illustrate postal format with regard to placement of stamps, address and return address. Upon your return, make use of your pamphlets, brochures, vacation photos, etc., to assist your child in creating a souvenir/memory collage of the trip.

Water Tricks

A favorite vacation spot for many families is near water, salt or fresh. You and your child can have some fun experimenting with both fresh and salt water right in your own kitchen. First, fill two bowls with water. Have your child count and add four or five tablespoons of salt to one bowl of water; then stir until the salt is dissolved. Salt water is heavier than fresh water, and therefore, will support heavier objects than fresh water. Demonstrate this to your child by using two fresh, raw eggs. Gently place one egg in each bowl. Note that the egg floats in the salt water only. Suggest that your child collect some other household items (i.e. a pasta shape, paper clip, pencil, crayon, seashell, button, guest soap) to set into each bowl and discover which, if either, bowl they will float in. Provide paper and glue for younger children to make two collages, one for fresh water and one for salt water.

Super Simple Snacks

Snack activities are suitable for all ages. Activities such as these enhance vocabulary development and sequential order, as well as encourage children to make use of measurement. **"Cone"wich:** Have your child assist you in making egg, tuna or chicken salad. Let your child scoop some of this sandwich salad into an ice cream cone for a delicious, nutritious treat. For an Independence Day treat, try making three separate bowls of sandwich spread. Add food coloring to the mayonnaise to make one bowl red and one bowl blue, leaving the third bowl white.

Sunny Sherbet Shake: With your child's help, measure 1 cup of vanilla yogurt, 1 cup of orange sherbet and 1 cup of sliced peaches into a blender. Blend, then pour into a plastic container. Let your child count and add three or four ice cubes. Seal the container tightly with its lid and have your child shake the drink. While the drink chills for a few minutes, let your child color an American flag on a small piece of paper. Tape this flag near the top of a drinking straw. Now, pour the shake into a favorite glass or mug, add the straw, sip and enjoy.

by Marie E. Cecchini

Sound-Off 1, 2

Work with your child to construct a Fourth of July wind chime. First you will need to cut the center out of a white plastic lid to form a ring. Let your child wrap this ring with red and blue pipe cleaners. Next, help your child count and tie small objects such as bells, buttons or seashells to several strands of red, white and blue yarn. The first strand should contain two items, the second three items, the third four items, etc. Make use of a specific color pattern for the yarn, such as red, white, blue, white, etc. The number of strands you need will depend upon the size of your ring, so you might want to choose a smaller ring for younger children and a larger ring for older children. Older children can also tabulate and count out the exact number of bells, shells, etc., they will need to complete the project. To finish, help your child tie four strands of equal length yarn to the ring, separating it into quarters. Then let them tie the ends of these four strands together to form a loop for hanging. Now, hang and wait for a summer breeze.

Cleaning Up

A toy tag sale can be a great new avenue of excitement. Together you can sort out toys that are never used or have been outgrown. Guide your child through pricing the items. Let your child write out price tags and make posters to advertise the sale. Role-play "buyer/seller" with older children to help them learn how to count out change. Talk with younger children about monetary names and values. On the day of the sale, be on hand to assist your young entrepreneur with setup and cleanup. Younger salespeople will also need assistance giving change. At the end of the day, box up any leftover toys and donate them to a local day care or charity. Help your child total the profits. Encourage your child to spend only some of the earnings for a special purchase and to save the rest.

Beach Ball Fun

Share some beach ball fun with your child right in your own backyard. First, act out the rhyme with an imaginary ball, then try it with a real one.

My Beach Ball

Blow up a beach ball,
Large or small,
   (blow)
And round as round can be.
   (hold arms in a circle)
Then toss that ball,
   (toss ball in the air)
And watch it fall.
   (move head to watch ball fall)
Now bounce it one, two, three.
   (bounce ball three times)

Once younger children have mastered bouncing and catching, challenge them to see how many bounces and/or catches they can achieve in a row. Older children can try "trick" throwing such as overhand, underhand or behind the back. Also, let them try bouncing the ball under one leg. Challenge their math skills by having them bounce answers to simple addition or subtraction facts.

Animal Cracker Art

Enjoy some 3-D fun with your child by creating animal cracker scenes. Let your child use markers to create a background scene on sturdy paper or cardboard. Suggestions might include a forest, jungle, zoo or pet shop. When the drawing is complete, help your child glue animal crackers to several places on the picture. Be prepared to listen as your child's storyboard comes to life with the addition of the animals. Younger children will enjoy telling their stories on tape so they can listen and enjoy several times. Encourage them to share their stories with their friends and other household members. Encourage older children to put their stories down on paper; then help them add their picture to the front as a book cover.

Book Possibilities

Books are for pleasure as well as learning. Share the joy with your child. Stories of family fun and relationships:

Cohen, Ron. *My Dad's Baseball.* Lothrop, 1994. (K-3)
Davis, Maggie S. *Something Magic.* Simon & Schuster, 1991. (K-3)
Kastner, Jill. *Snake Hunt.* Four Winds, 1993. (K-3)
Oppenheim, Shulamith Levey. *Waiting for Noah.* HarperCollins, 1990. (PreK-2)
Rochelle, Belinda. *When Jo Louis Won the Title.* Houghton, 1994. (K-2)
Zolotow, Charlotte. *This Quiet Lady.* Greenwillow, 1992. (K-3)

Clip Art for Spring & Summer

314

Happy Mother's Day!

Clip Art for Spring & Summer

Spring Is Here!

Clip Art for St. Patrick's Day

317

Clip Art for Earth Day

Clip Art for Easter

Hippity-Hop!!!

To:
From:

Happy Easter

319

TLC10110 Copyright © Teaching & Learning Company, Carthage, IL 62321-0010

Books Are "Bee"utiful!

A Huge **Hooray** for
_____,
who did super at
_____!

Way to Go!